ECHOES OF EMPIRE

*An Accidental Historian's Journey
through the Post-Ottoman World*

JAMES S. KESSLER

ISBN: 978-1-4834-4482-6 (sc)
ISBN: 978-1-4834-4481-9 (e)

Because of the dynamic nature of the Internet, any web addresses or links contained in
this book may have changed since publication and may no longer be valid. The views
expressed in this work are solely those of the author and do not necessarily reflect the
views of the publisher, and the publisher hereby disclaims any responsibility for them.

Lulu Publishing Services rev. date: 03/02/2016

For Steven and Shirley Kessler, who made it all possible.

And when I heard a description of the seven climes and the four corners of the earth, I longed to travel with all my heart and soul. So I became utterly wretched, a vagabond crying out, 'Might I roam the world?'

- Evliya Çelebi, *The Seyhatnâme*

CONTENTS

MAPS AND PHOTOGRAPHS

NOTE ON SPELLING

Considering the scope of territory covered in this text, it should not come as a surprise that I encountered a great number of languages during my journeys. Even during the Ottoman period, when Ottoman Turkish was the "official" language of the empire (at least for the elites), most people continued to use a different "mother tongue" within their specific linguistic communities. On the streets of Istanbul, as the imperial capital, one would have heard dozens of languages: Turkish, Greek, Armenian, Arabic, Kurdish, and various Slavic languages, among others.

This poses a challenge when trying to write about the empire and its successor states. By necessity, I have been inconsistent in my approach to spelling the names of people and places in order to focus on clarity. In general, however, if a language uses a Latin-based script—such as modern Turkish or Croatian—I have used the standard spellings, unless the word is known commonly in the English-speaking world in a different form (a simple example: Istanbul versus İstanbul). If the language uses another script, such as Cyrillic or Arabic, I have tried to strike a balance between formal transliteration and readability. And again, if the word is commonly known, I have gone with the most common English spelling (example: Cairo versus al-Qāhira in Arabic or Kahire in Turkish).

PREFACE: CAUSING A *KALABALIK*

I wasn't sure I had heard correctly. Had the Swede said "kalabalık" amidst the sing-song of his Swedish conversation? It couldn't be. The tongue-tripping *Kalabalık* is one of my favorite Turkish words, meaning either a "crowd" or "crowded"—or better, a "throng" or "thronged." Why would a Swede be using a Turkish word in the middle of a Swedish sentence?

Well, it's a funny thing: kalabalık, or kalabalik as the Swedes spell it, is a Swedish word adopted from the Turkish, meaning essentially a "ruckus" or "tumult" (not hard to see the relation to the original). But the question remains: why was the word adopted?

It all begins with the *Kalabaliken i Bender*, the Skirmish at Bender...

***

I first encountered the story of the Kalabalik, or fragments of it at least, in 2013 while preparing to visit the odd, Soviet holdover of Transnistria, an unrecognized breakaway state from Moldova.

Although the focus of my travels in Moldova had been on its Ottoman past, I had decided to visit Transnistria (or, more formally, the Transdniestr Republic) more out of curiosity about its quirky present. But as I was reading about the place, a nugget of information caught my attention: the Transnistrian town of Bender had been an Ottoman outpost and a Swedish king, Charles XII, had lived in exile there as a "guest" of the Ottoman sultan, Ahmet III (r. 1703-1730). In Turkish, due to his stipend from the sultan, Charles became known as Demirbaş Şarl.[1] Near the end of his stay in Bender, a crowd (note: kalabalık) of disgruntled locals—upset by the rising debts being accrued by the Swedes—attacked the Swedish settlement. The Sultan's elite military guard, the Janissaries, sided with the

---

[1]   Literally, this means "Ironhead" Charles, but *demirbaş* here refers to the fixed amount of money allotted by the Ottoman treasury to support the king's stay in Bender. Thus it is a sort of royal stipend.

Ottoman subjects and put Demirbaş Şarl under house arrest, eventually moving him to Istanbul where he became more of a P.O.W. than exulted guest.

Both the Ottomanist and world history teacher in me had been intrigued by the outlines of this story. How did a Swedish king and his entourage end up guests, and then prisoners, in the Ottoman Empire?

Sweden, and really Scandinavia in general, gets short shrift in most standard history narratives, even in texts that focus on Europe. The northern reaches of Europe have come to be seen as peripheral not only geographically, but also historically. One always reads about Germany, France, Italy, Spain, and Britain in their European contexts, as well as about their global—often colonial—exploits. But about the only mention of Scandinavia will be something along the lines of: that's where the Vikings came from. And then Scandinavia all but disappears until the twentieth century, especially post-World War II, when countries such as Norway and Sweden became known as economic powerhouses and leaders in global peace initiatives (e.g., serving as the Nobel Prize headquarters). Yet the story of Demirbaş Şarl shows just how much is missing in the standard historical narrative.

While wandering in Sweden in the summer of 2014, I tried to learn more about this strangely romantic figure. First, I read up on the Great Northern War (1700-1721) that pitted the young king (he was only fifteen years old when he was crowned in 1697) against a powerful alliance of Denmark-Norway, Saxony-Poland-Lithuania, and Russia[2] at a time when Sweden was seen as a major imperial power. This war, usually mentioned in passing (if at all) in textbooks, was not a simple skirmish (kalabalik!), but involved much of Europe at the time—even drawing in the Ottoman Empire, as two of the major antagonists bordered it to the north. Indeed, it marked a major realignment of the political powers of Eurasia. Russia, under Peter the Great, would become more of a force with which to be reckoned; actually, some see this as the true beginning of the Russian Empire. Even famous Saint Petersburg was founded in the midst of the war, on the site of a Swedish town called Nyenskans.

---

[2] You read correctly: Norway-Denmark was under one king, as was Saxony-Poland-Lithuania. European history is rife with these kinds of configurations.

Ironically, it is perhaps due to this often-overlooked war that Sweden became marginalized in history narratives. Before the war, Sweden was ascendant, controlling large swaths of territory around the Baltic Sea and a few overseas colonies.[3] Even at the beginning of the conflict, the anti-Swedish alliance was surprised to discover that the Swedish king was so far from easy pickings, as he turned out to be a shrewd and powerful military leader. But when Charles XII lost against Peter the Great's forces at the Battle of Poltava (1709)—which forced him into Ottoman exile—Sweden's political future began to be less certain. And with Charles' death in 1718 (under mysterious circumstances), that future was sealed. Sweden's importance ebbed (at least in the eyes of historians) and its empire shrank. Had Demirbaş Şarl won the Great Northern War, perhaps the story would be different.

But I want to get back to Charles XII as Demirbaş Şarl, the Ottoman exile. Why did he end up in Bender? In the early stages of the Great Northern War, the Swedish king was remarkably successful, despite his youth. First he defeated Norway-Denmark, ruled by his cousin Frederick IV, which forced the Norwegian-Danish ruler to sign a peace treaty. He also had early successes against the Russians in the eastern Baltic region and managed to depose the Polish ruler and put his own puppet king on the throne. However, it seems Charles got cocky. He aimed for Moscow, and his luck changed. He ended up being defeated at the Battle of Poltava in what is now Ukraine, as mentioned above—and then fled with about a thousand of his men to the closest non-Russian ally he could find, the bordering empire of the Ottomans.

At first the Ottomans welcomed the Swedes, as they were enemies of the Russians, who were growing rivals to their own imperial ambitions in the Black Sea and Caucasus. But, in the end, Demirbaş Şarl's constant scheming to avenge his losses and his soldiers' profligate habits soured local support, which caused the Kalabalik to erupt in 1713. After the ruckus, the Swedish king would spend about a year in Istanbul as a glorified "prisoner" of the Sultan Ahmet III, during which he apparently studied Ottoman naval engineering and tactics. When he returned to Sweden,

---

[3]   There was even a New Sweden (Nya Sverige) in North America, a colony on the Delaware River from 1638-1655 (so before Charles XII's reign), a little tidbit of American history I never learned in high school.

he even commissioned two battle ships that he christened with Turkish names: *Jarramas* (*yaramaz*=naughty) and *Jilderim* (*yıldırım* = thunder). Strangely, these names also were used for later Swedish ships—so the surprising Ottoman-Swedish connection didn't quite die with the death of Demirbaş Şarl in 1718!

***

Of course, while in Stockholm, I tried to locate Charles XII's grave. Like most of the Swedish royals, he is entombed in the Church of Riddarholmen, situated on a small island just off of Gamla Stan (Old Town). I crossed the short bridge and immediately confronted the out-sized, red brick bell tower of the church; it loomed large over the rest of the low-slung buildings crowded on the island. However, my investigation was quickly thwarted—when I approached the entrance, I discovered the church was closed for rehearsals of an upcoming play. But my disappointment turned to delight when I saw what the play was called: *Carolus Rex* (i.e., King Carl... or Charles). How fitting that the final resting place of Demirbaş Şarl/Charles XII would be the venue for a theatrical production about his crazy life! I am sure the Kalabalik of Bender was in it.

Once an Ottomanist, always an Ottomanist. Even in Sweden.

Map 1: The Ottoman World Today

"CLOSED FOR RESTORATION": AN INTRODUCTION

"Closed for restoration."

At least that's what the sign said on the door of the Tourbet al-Bey, the Tomb of the Beys. I thought I would have to content myself with wandering around the outside of the structure, looking up at its bright green, fish-scale tiled domes. But out of nowhere an elderly, but quite sprightly, man appeared with a key and motioned me to the door. I wasn't sure this was legit, but I wasn't going to pass up the opportunity to peek inside the final resting spot of the Ottoman *beys*[4] who had ruled Tunisia on behalf of the Ottoman sultans.

Although the main entrance passage and several of the interior courtyards were piled with rubble or pitted with excavations, the burial chambers were largely intact. Just dark and dusty; lonely. Appropriate, somehow, for an almost forgotten—yet perhaps the most important— corner of Ottoman Tunis.

In a mixture of French, Arabic, and rudimentary English, my guide led me through the rooms that were devoted to the beys' wives and concubines, those for the male members of the family, and lastly to the chamber holding the cenotaphs of the beys and pashas themselves.

I almost expected to see ghosts sliding between the graves.

---

[4]   "Bey" is a Turkish/Ottoman title that roughly means "lord," with an original meaning closer to "chieftain." It was also used as a general honorific, but in the case of Tunisia it was a significant title (essentially Bey versus bey, although the Arabic script does not indicate capital letters). Throughout this book, you will encounter various Ottoman titles that took on different meanings depending on place and time. Another particularly common one is *paşa* or pasha (which is the form I will use from this point onward).

The Beys' Tomb, Tunis

I was well aware that I was further west in the Ottoman world than I had traveled thus far. Only reclusive Algeria is more western.

And now this distant North African outpost of the Ottoman Empire, Tunisia, was my home.

What better vantage point from which to reflect on my life and travels as an accidental historian of the Ottoman Empire!

***

In many ways, *Echoes of Empire* has been a long time in the making, representing what now amounts to half my life, a period that has been spent studying, traveling, and even working in the former Ottoman lands. Although I know that as a twenty-year-old undergraduate boarding a plane to spend a year abroad in Jordan and Egypt—the first time I had left the United States other than Canada—that I had no idea that initial leap into the Middle East was the beginning of a life-long journey. A journey that will not end with the publication of this book.

That first experience in the region, during which I continued my studies in Arabic and Islamic history at the American University of Cairo, solidified a growing interest in Middle Eastern history in general and with Ottoman history in particular. In the years to come, I would undertake a Ph.D. in the field and travel ever more broadly. Even when I decided to leave the formal academic career track and began teaching secondary school world history, the Ottoman world kept drawing me back. Indeed, I have been teaching at international schools for the past few years in Sudan and now Tunisia: both, as chance would have it, former Ottoman lands.

Since 2007 or so, I have been writing about my travels on various blog platforms, generally fusing tales of my personal experience with ruminations on history, politics, and culture. Perhaps it is the teacher in me, but my blog entries became not only a means to balance deeply personal impressions and memories of all I had seen and done with my intellectual passions—but, also, a means to share my reflections with a wide audience. A chance to "teach" beyond my classroom.

For a number of years, my travel writings were intermittent, subject to the school year calendar and its defined breaks—spring and summer, in particular. And, not surprisingly, my writings on the Middle East were somewhat less frequent. However, after I moved to Khartoum in 2010, both my travels and my writing expanded. At that time, I was living in one of the remotest corners of the Ottoman Empire, and the rest of the realm was within easy striking distance. I was able to return to Egypt and to explore little-known outposts of the Ottoman world in Africa, including

Djibouti and parts of Ethiopia. I also visited the countries of the Persian Gulf, from Kuwait to Oman. Still, it was not quite enough.

After completing my contract in Sudan in spring 2012, I decided to fulfill a dream of taking a sabbatical year and using that time to focus on travel and writing. Of course, one of my top priorities was to explore even more of the Ottoman world—this time the fascinating arch from the Balkans over to the Caucasus.

And though I didn't know it at the beginning, *Echoes of Empire: An Accidental Historian's Journeys through the Post-Ottoman World* was on its way to being born.

***

I should probably start off by stating what this book is not.

Although it does cover perhaps the broadest geographic range of the Ottoman realm found in any one book, it is far, far from comprehensive. There are some major gaps in my travels, some partly due to political instability—Iraq, Yemen, Somalia—some due to difficulties in acquiring a visa—Eritrea, Russia, Iran. Others are due to the simple fact that I haven't yet had a chance to visit (notably Algeria). Hopefully, in future editions I will be able to add materials as I continue to explore.

Still, depending on how you define what constitutes former Ottoman territory (an issue I will get back to shortly), I have managed to visit at least thirty-five of approximately forty-five present-day countries that were carved out of the empire. Not too shabby, if I say so myself.

Also, obviously, each territory discussed could warrant at least a book length treatment, if not a library full of books. By necessity, my treatment will be limited by own experience in and of each country or region discussed.

What else is *Echoes of Empire* not?

It is not a scholarly tome. Although what you will read is clearly informed by my training as an Ottoman historian and does address academic topics—history, historiography, nationalism, etc.—I intended from the start to make *Echoes* accessible to a broad, curious audience, not just to a small circle of academic specialists. In that vein, I've avoided in-text citations and the like (but I do use footnotes—I'm a historian, after all!). For those interested in digging deeper into any of the topics I discuss, please check out the "Further Reading" section at the end of the book.

It is not a textbook. Although *Echoes* is also informed by my career as a secondary school teacher, it is not designed specifically to be used in the classroom. This is not to say I don't want people to learn from *Echoes*, or even that it couldn't or shouldn't be read in a classroom setting. Teachers could use the book as a supplementary piece to more standard history or cultural studies textbooks, but should note that, for public schools, it does not align with most U.S. state standards.

It is not a travel guide. Although *Echoes* is first and foremost about my travels in the Ottoman world, you will not—generally!—find suggestions for what hotel or hostel at which to stay or what restaurants at which to eat. There are no listed museum opening times and admission prices. No suggested itineraries. However, perhaps the book will inspire others to visit parts of the former Ottoman world I have explored, especially areas less frequented by tourists. Perhaps it will enrich the understanding of those who are traveling in the places covered in the book.

So what *is* it?

Echoes of Empire is a hybrid that brings together my personal travel experience with observations filtered through both my training and passion for Ottoman history and my work as a world history teacher who tries to show connections across time and space. It is a literary chimera, or better a jackalope—a mix of memoir, travelogue, and history.

In addition, *Echoes* is more of a series of discrete, though often interlinked, articles than a straightforward narrative. And it doesn't follow a straightforward chronology. Many parts first saw light as blog entries, especially on *Beyond the Boundary Stones*, but also on *A Khawaja in Khartoum, Dispatches from Planet Qart-hadast*, and on my personal page on Travelblog.org. Other portions were written specifically for this book, either as prefatory material or to fill in the gaps of my earlier experiences in the Ottoman world.

I should also note that what I have written reflects personal opinion, which is sometimes—probably often—at odds with the way locals might perceive their history and culture to be. While I do my best to present multiple perspectives, especially on the more contentious issues, I know that my own biases as an American-born historian of the Ottoman Empire and as a secondary school teacher of world history will shine through. Of course, any factual errors that might appear are fully my responsibility.

***

So this book focuses on the Ottoman world.[5] But what do I mean by "Ottoman"? What gets to count as part of the former Ottoman Empire? Indeed, the label "empire" is itself problematic. Did the Ottomans even consider their state an "empire" in the way we think of the term now? This actually has been the source of some contention in the academic world!

For my purposes, I am not going to get too embroiled in the debate. I will be using very broad definitions of both Ottoman and empire in order to embrace the full, amorphous spread of the Ottoman realm. It expanded and contracted, amoeba-like, over its centuries of existence. Some areas were even physically separated from the core of the state, islands of Ottoman-ness scattered across Afro-Eurasia. The means of administration of the various components of the empire also differed both in place and over time. Some areas were fully bound to the center; others were essentially tributary states that had a fair degree of autonomy. Some places were under Ottoman control for many centuries (such as Anatolia, the Balkans, and the Arab lands), others for only a brief period (like the city of Oranto in Italy, for just one year). Sometimes an area was gained by the Ottoman Empire, then lost, and then reabsorbed, as we will see especially when discussing the frontiers of the empire.

For my purposes, I count any territory that was, even if only briefly and tenuously, considered by the Ottoman sultans to be within their jurisdiction as fair game for my explorations and comparisons.

The reader will also notice that a major preoccupation of my travels in the Ottoman lands is how the Ottoman past is reflected—or, better yet, "echoed"—in the present. Actually, this is perhaps the central theme that binds my disparate writings together. In some cases, most notably in the Balkans and parts of the Caucasus, the Ottoman past is felt very closely and is often used as a tool to bolster nationalist sentiments (usually in a oppositional sense, as in "We overcame hundreds of years of Ottoman—or

---

5   With the occasional historical or cultural digression outside the Ottoman framework, as is the wont of a world history teacher.

'Turkish'—oppression to gain our national freedom") and to justify current political actions. Sometimes, groups or individuals romanticize the Ottoman past, viewing it as a time of greater stability, greater tolerance, greater glory. In other places, the memory is less visceral but, almost subconsciously, a major part of the present-day culture. In still others, the Ottoman period is essentially forgotten. But I think that even then there are important lessons to be learned. Why might that era not be considered important now? Sometimes silences speak volumes.

Echoes of Empire is organized in broadly geographic and roughly chronological order (in terms of absorption into the empire). Rather than starting with Turkey, as some might expect, I have instead chosen to situate it in the center of the book, in large part to symbolize its geographic centrality in the former empire as well as its importance as the Ottoman heartland. But I also hope that by starting with the Ottoman "periphery" I can de-emphasize the "Turkish" dimension of the Ottoman world, as at its peak it was a truly multiethnic, multilingual, multi-confessional entity containing a veritable kaleidoscope of peoples. Ottoman Turkish might have been the imperial language, but this didn't mean the so-called Turks were a majority (and, as we will see, the term "Turk" is problematic during most of the Ottoman era).

The first major section focuses on the "European" territories, starting with what might be considered the outermost edge of Ottoman "Europe"— Hungary up to the "Gates of Vienna"—and then quickly moving on to the Balkans, as this territory was one of the first to be conquered outside of Anatolia. The chapters will then follow an arc around the Black Sea to the Caucasus. Most of this material is built on the articles I wrote during my sabbatical travels in 2012-2013.

This will bring us to Turkey, thereby completing a circle of sorts around the Black Sea. I first visited Turkey during my study abroad year in Cairo in 1993-94, then studied there for a summer in 1997, and next lived in Istanbul from 1998-2000. I have visited a number of times since, including as recently as spring of 2014 in the midst of the political controversies surrounding Recep Tayyip Erdoğan and his leadership of the Justice and Development Party (known by its Turkish acronym, A.K.P.). Thus, Turkey and I have had a relationship of twenty-plus years.

Following the section on Turkey, the book will turn to the region south of Turkey, the core of the so-called "Middle East"—here understood to be primarily the predominantly Arab lands carved from the Ottoman empire, but obviously including the state of Israel and parts of Iran (although I have not yet had the opportunity to venture into Iran, only to stare across its border with Turkey).

The rest of the book will focus on "Africa" (a surprisingly contentious name, as we also will see)—including in this case Egypt and the rest of North Africa, as well as the often forgotten Ottoman lands that dribbled down the Red Sea coast to the Horn of Africa (Sudan, Ethiopia, Djibouti, and others), and wrapping up where this chapter begins: in Tunisia.

Finally, in the "non-conclusion," I attempt to make some sense of the disparate stories I have encountered and recounted and what they might mean for the incredible array of countries and territories that once were part of the Ottoman Empire. What is the Ottoman legacy today? What can be learned from the echoes of empire that still reverberate in the post-Ottoman world?

PART I

The Western Balkans and the Habsburg Frontier

Map 2: The Western Balkans

It was a scene out of Dr. Zhivago. As the scowling Greek conductor motioned me off the train, sometime in the middle of the freezing January night, somewhere on the Greek-Turkish border. All I could see was dark forest, high banks of snow, and a small, lonely customs house. Was I to be left in this no man's land? Without even a proper coat to keep me warm? My heart sank.

But I followed the man into the harsh lights of the hut, where a Turkish border agent, smiling, informed me that I just needed to get a visa, a new regulation. I handed over twenty-five dollars, and with much relief reboarded the train to continue my journey to Istanbul—a city about which, at that point, I had only dreamed.

***

I came to Ottoman studies in a very roundabout manner. When I began my undergraduate studies, I was planning on pursuing a degree in biology. I had been seen by many of my peers as a science geek in high school; I had even worked in a molecular biology lab at Ball State University and won a spot at the International Science Fair my senior year.

However, due to a random placement in a freshman-writing seminar in Near Eastern Studies when I started at Cornell, I decided to take my humanities electives in that department. In the spring semester, I signed up for a course on al-Andalus, or Islamic Spain, mostly out of curiosity. Spain had been under Muslim rule? How had I not known that? Why had no one ever taught me that? Under the dynamic tutelage of Dr. Ross Brann, an expert in the Hispano-Arabic and Hispano-Hebrew poetry of al-Andalus, I fell in love with the history and culture of this fascinating period. Thus, to the surprise of friends and family, I began to drift away from biology into the study of Islamic history.

As I started tackling Arabic, and quickly fell in love with its script and even its complex grammar, I took a leap and decided to declare a major in Near Eastern Studies. As a new major, I was assigned an advisor in the department; I was lucky to get Dr. Leslie Peirce, an Ottoman historian perhaps best known for her work on the imperial harem and the power wielded by certain women in the Ottoman family. Wanting to get to know her better, I signed up for her survey course on Ottoman history, another topic about which I knew little.

Dr. Pierce would gather her students around the large, wooden table in her classroom, and not only teach but tell stories. She guided us through the development of the Ottoman state, from its origins as just one of a number of tiny *beyliks* (territories controlled by a bey) under the leadership of Osman—who, supposedly, had a dream that one day his family would rule much of the known world[6]—through the point of empire's assumed apogee under the reign of Sultan Süleyman the Magnificent, and on to its dismemberment at the end of World War I. She introduced us to a vast array of historical characters and events, covering nearly six hundred years of Ottoman history, and did so with a remarkable, quiet passion.

I was, to put it mildly, enraptured.

I am often asked: Why the Ottoman Empire? Honestly, it is hard to pinpoint what it is about this particular empire, among so many other fascinating empires, that struck a chord. It just did. Of course, professors like Dr. Brann and Dr. Peirce brought their fields of study alive when I was sitting in their classes, but the sense of emotional connection is much harder to explain. It may take a lifetime to figure out the attraction. But whatever the case, my obsession with all things Ottoman was sparked in Dr. Peirce's Ottoman history survey, and so I was compelled to add Turkish to the list of languages I needed to learn. And I've never looked back.

In order to continue my training in Islamic history, I spent my junior year in Jordan and Egypt, mostly intending to focus on building my Arabic skills. During that time, however, I found that I was consistently drawn to the Ottoman heritage of these countries, and frequently poked around mosques and palaces and tombs that evoked the period of Ottoman rule.

Then, during my winter break, I made the fateful decision to fly to Greece and make my way back to Cairo by land on my own. At that point, I was young and inexperienced as a traveler, and I was at the beginning of my training as a historian, Ottoman or otherwise. I just thought it seemed like a fun idea. However, that journey, including the snowy stop in the middle of nowhere between Greece and Turkey that I described at the beginning of this chapter, would prove to be the first steps in a lifelong

---

6   This origin myth of the Ottomans is told at the beginning of Caroline Finkel's highly readable *Osman's Dream*, one of the few histories of the empire intended for a lay public.

quest to explore the full extent of the Ottoman world and in honing my skills as a traveler, historian, and writer.

When I landed in Athens, all I knew were the stories of ancient Greece and Greek mythology. I knew vaguely at that point that it had been part of the Ottoman Empire after the conquest of the Byzantines (thanks to Dr. Peirce's survey course), but I knew nothing of the important role played by Greek-speakers in the empire and the tumult of nineteenth-century Greek nationalism that set off a chain reaction of nationalist separatist movements across the Ottoman Balkans. I didn't know that the Parthenon had been used as a mosque at one point. I didn't know the "father" of modern Turkey, Mustafa Kemal Atatürk, was a native of Salonica, now Greek Thessaloniki. I didn't know much. Instead, I examined the obvious—the ancient ruins and modern cityscape—and then hopped on a train to Istanbul.

It is only now, with decades of experience under my belt, that I look back at the first solo trip with a mix of pride in my twenty-year-old greenhorn self for setting forth and depending on my own wiles to make it back to Egypt, horror in my twenty-year-old greenhorn self for setting forth and depending on my own wiles, and regret that my younger self was so uninformed. Yet the regret is mild. I might not have been able to fully appreciate Greece and its connection to the Ottoman past compared to my time in Egypt, but as I continued on to Turkey and then through Syria and Jordan, my sense of interconnection grew. It would establish a foundation for all my future travels.

So, in a way, I would not have appreciated my more recent trips in the rest of the western Balkans and on the Habsburg-Ottoman frontier—the focus of the following section—as fully had it not been for that brief trip to Greece so many years ago. The first chapter, looking at Hungary and Austria, stems from a trip I made in 2009, while the subsequent chapters on Serbia, Bosnia and Herzegovina, Croatia, Montenegro, Albania, Macedonia, and Kosovo are based primarily on my experiences traveling through the Balkan region in 2012.

KNOCKING AT THE GATES OF THE CITY OF THE GOLDEN APPLE: HUNGARY AND AUSTRIA

The dome arched above, punctuated by small bulbs of glass that allowed in a tepid light. Steam—or maybe it was my general blindness without glasses—enveloped the space in a thin haze. *Drip. Drip.* The echoes of condensation hitting the stone floor rang against the walls.

I could have been hanging out in a *hamam* (Turkish bath) in Istanbul. But I wasn't.

Up a steep, cobbled road, I found a tidy rose garden on a hill that overlooked a wide river. Within the garden, a grey octagonal tomb sat neatly, its crescent and star glinting in the hot morning sun. I peeked through the iron-gated window and saw the cenotaph enshrouded in a green cloth with gilded Arabic lettering embroidered on its edges.

I could have been visiting a Sufi's tomb in Istanbul. But I wasn't.

Instead, I was in Buda(pest).

There's not much that remains of Ottoman Buda, at least not much that is visible. There are still a number of "Turkish" baths, but only a couple—the Király, which I went to, being one of them—that still retain part of the original Ottoman structure. And then there is the lonely tomb of Gül Baba, who was apparently a companion of Sultan Süleyman the Magnificent and a Bektashi (or Bektaşi) Sufi. The tomb is still a pilgrimage site for Bektashi mystics.

But there's more that remains of the city's Ottoman past than just these isolated remnants. Budapest, like most cities with so many centuries of history, has both the physical memory of its different historical periods (evidenced by its amazing variety of architecture) and the less tangible historical memory that is used to define and interpret the city (which is most apparent in descriptions at museums and tourist spots, but also sometimes less formally). I was only in Hungary a short while, but I could quickly tell that history had a particular importance to Hungarians. And much of it revolved around the word "occupation."

The Ottoman period, which lasted for 150 years (give or take), is almost always referred to as the "Turkish Occupation" (or, in the National History Museum, as the "Ottoman Occupation"). This phrase makes it very clear that many Hungarians consider this an unfortunate blip in Hungarian history, a time when the Magyar people lost their independence to an alien people. It also tries to distance Hungarians from any influence the "Turks" might have had on them and their culture. The Ottomans were occupiers, oppressors: that's all.

Interestingly, while Habsburg domination, which came shortly after that of the Ottomans[7], was obviously not appreciated by all, it seems to have been accepted begrudgingly. The Dual Monarchy Period, when Franz Joseph reframed the Habsburg's empire as the Austro-Hungarian Empire, is perhaps even more widely accepted, as it served as a recognition of Hungarian difference (and elevated Hungarians essentially to an equal status with the German-speaking Austrians).

My rough-and-ready interpretation of why the Ottoman era is always cast as an occupation is that the Ottomans (invariably referred to as "Turks") were Muslim, and so were not "European"; the Habsburgs were Christian, and so were "European." And the Hungarians see themselves as firmly in the European sphere.

Oddly, though, they also seem very proud of their unique origins and decidedly non-Indo-European language. They are descendents of pagan horsemen who galloped off the Asian steppes, not unlike the Turks. This ancient history is chronicled pretty closely at the National History Museum. And, perhaps more importantly, it is glorified in the nineteenth-century nationalist extravaganza that is Heroes' Square, built for the 1896 Magyar Millennium celebration (i.e., the one thousandth anniversary of the arrival of the Magyar horsemen). Ancient Magyar kings and heroes, including Árpad and St. Stephen—and some scary looking horses with antler-armor!—look down elegant Andrássy Avenue, with its Gucci and

---

[7]   The Treaty of Karlowitz in 1699 ended Ottoman rule; the signing of the Szatmár Accord in 1711 recognized Habsburg authority over Hungary.

Louis Vuitton outlets. More recent heroes, such as Lajos Kossuth[8], also appear in the pantheon. Perhaps not surprisingly, the square is hugely symbolic for Hungarians. It is even where Imre Nagy's reburial ceremony was conducted in June 1989.[9]

Somehow, though, despite celebrating their pagan-warrior days, Hungarian historiography tends to focus on the Magyars' "Western" heritage after the adoption of Christianity. Perhaps the Ottoman period, then, cuts too close to the bone. It is fine to glorify the romantically noble, warrior origins of the early Magyar nomads, but it's also important to recognize that they have progressed and become fully European—even if their language is decidedly of the steppes.

So my experience of Budapest's Ottoman past ended up—other than my time spent walking around the lonely Bektashi tomb and soaking in the Turkish baths—being more in its absence.

But not so when I traveled to the town of Eger, about eighty-five miles northeast of Budapest.

***

The year was 1552. A great Ottoman army, ten thousand men strong, descends upon the Hungarian town of Eger, besieging its castle. It should have been easy pickings, but the brave townspeople—despite being vastly outnumbered—held back the marauding horde for a month, eventually defeating the Turks. However, the Ottomans weren't finished yet; they came back forty-four years later to avenge their earlier defeat by the citizens of Eger.

At least, that's the basic story that is told about Eger. But the turn-of-the-century writer Géza Gárdonyi embellished the story even more

---

[8]   Lajos Kossuth was a major leader during the Magyar nationalist uprisings in 1848 (one of the many liberal revolutions that swept through Europe at that time). Although Hungary ultimately didn't gain independence then, the stage was set for the establishment of the Dual Monarchy in 1867 that officially turned the Austrian Empire into Austria-Hungary (or the Austro-Hungarian Empire).

[9]   A more recent Hungarian national hero, Imre Nagy was a communist who briefly served as president of Hungary in 1956, when the country tried to go its separate way from the U.S.S.R. When Moscow clamped down on the straying Hungarian communists, Nagy was executed and cast as a traitor. But in the waning days of Soviet control in the 1980s, Nagy was rehabilitated as a Hungarian hero.

in his 1901 novel *Eclipse of the Crescent Moon* (subtle, that one!). In his fictionalized version of the first siege of Eger, he has the women of the town pouring hot soup onto the Turks from the castle ramparts. Although this part of the story seems to have been Gárdonyi's own invention, it is now portrayed in a relief carving at the entrance to Eger Castle, and the novel is required reading in school. In this case, fiction trumps reality.

It is perhaps not too surprising, considering this small city's dramatic history, that the Ottoman dimension is much more visible here than in most other parts of Hungary. There are several statues commemorating the bravery of the Magyars as they fended off the invaders. There are exhibits at the restored castle detailing the battles. And there is one lonely minaret left standing in a little square, a strangely delicate—even vulnerable—thing without a mosque to give it purpose.

The Minaret of Eger

It was largely to seek out that minaret that I finally tore myself away from Budapest and made the day-trip to Eger. In some ways, as so often is the case, the journey ended up being as much a part of the experience as the destination.

Although I had been told there were frequent, almost hourly, trains and that it would take two hours, the reality was that the Eger-bound trains left only about every two hours and took closer to three hours (it was a *gyors*, meaning "fast", train—but it seemed to make every local stop).

The almost-empty train rattled across a landscape of grasslands, patchy forest, sunflower fields, and worn-around-the-edges villages. Most of the train stops were simple outposts that had seen better days, some of which were in the middle of nowhere. Sometimes, only a lone passenger or two would board or disembark. Where were they going? Storm clouds kept threatening on the horizon.

Eger, the end of the line, was a cheerful exception to the other train stations. Small, but well kept. And the town, too, seemed prosperous, perhaps because it is a destination both for foreign and local tourists (there was even, oddly, a Citibank branch).

I spent the day visiting the historical monuments and trying to understand the narrative of Magyar resistance to Ottoman ("Turkish") oppression that pervaded the stories told by the informational plaques at the sites and in the items available in the tourist-trap souvenir shops. There was almost joy apparent in their telling the tale of the "Terrible Turk."

All in all, the trip to Eger[10] gave me at least a cursory glance at the Hungary that exists outside of Budapest, one that is rather different from the bustling capital. And, yes, I got to make my pilgrimage to the lonely minaret, climbing to its narrow summit to see how much remained of Eger's Ottoman past in the jumble of its streets and buildings. From my airy perch, a cool breeze tussling my hair, I could see that that the answer was: very little.

---

[10]   I should also note that Eger is known for its wine production. Just outside of town, in a place evocatively called the Valley of the Beautiful Women, you can hop from one wine cellar to the next to try the local tipple, all while listening to Roma music. It was a nice way to unwind from a day of Ottoman touring.

However, it was about time to move on, to venture to the city that marks the deepest point at which the Ottomans penetrated Western Europe, making Christendom quake with fear. Or so the story goes.

***

The Ottomans made two attempts to capture "the city of the golden apple," as they often called Vienna, but to the relief of Christendom both sieges were unsuccessful. The first one was in 1529, under the command of Süleyman the Magnificent (who died shortly afterwards while he was still on campaign in the Hungarian plains[11]); this siege was not so significant in the grand scheme of things, but it did heat up the Habsburg-Ottoman rivalry that would last for centuries. The second siege in 1683 was really the most important, at least from the perspective of the Viennese (and much of the rest of Western Europe). The Habsburg victory was more decisive, and not only in terms of defending the city; it also began the long process of pushing the Ottomans out of much of the Balkan territories that they had possessed since the fifteenth and sixteenth centuries.

It can be argued that Vienna became what it did because of those two sieges. After the first siege, the Habsburgs decided to make sure Vienna's defenses were strong in case of future attacks. They had a strong wall built around the city, essentially along the route that is now marked by the Ringstrasse (Ring Road) as it circumscribes the Innere Stadt (Inner City). Then, after their victory in 1683 (and subsequent victories to come in battles in the Balkans), the Habsburgs went on something of a building spree, populating the city with opulent baroque, rococo, and (later) neo-classical buildings, many of which still stand today. What better way to show how powerful you are (or want to be seen as) than by creating a cityscape of impressive architecture? Vienna's imperial profile seems a strong assertion of not simply Habsburg power but also of European/

---

[11] There have been serious attempts to locate the burial site of Sultan Süleyman's heart, which was supposedly left in the Hungarian town of Szigetvár while his body was transported back to Istanbul. This seems to be part of a growing rapprochement between Hungary and Turkey, and thus a softening of Hungarian views on their Ottoman past. See the *National Geographic* article on the subject: http://news.nationalgeographic.com/news/2014/06/140620-ottoman-empire-suleyman-hungary-turkey-sultans-heart/

Christian defiance, set as it was on frontier of the Habsburg and Ottoman worlds.[12]

***

Defeating the Ottomans in a series of key battles does make one cocky, it would seem. Prince Eugene of Savoy, the Paris-born Habsburg military hero, first participated in the Siege of 1683 and then went on to lead a number of crucial campaigns against the Ottoman Empire. His capture of Belgrade in 1718 ended a long stretch of conflict, but left the Ottomans with a fraction of their Balkan territories. When Prince Eugene returned to Vienna, he built up a complex of baroque palaces and gardens—the Belvedere—in honor of his own exploits; this complex almost outshone those of the Habsburg royalty who resided in the Hofburg. Who can blame him, though: what victorious prince doesn't need an upper and a lower palace? The Habsburgs weren't so pleased with the prince's uppityness, but they couldn't really do anything considering it was under his masterful guidance that the Austrian Empire was now ascendant in the Ottoman-Habsburg rivalry. When the prince died, Empress Maria Theresia quickly snatched up the property for the royal family. The last Habsburg occupant was Archduke Franz Ferdinand—and we know what happened to him.

There's not much in the Belvedere complex to show that Eugene of Savoy was the great vanquisher of the "Turks." However, that absence is rectified at the nearby Heeresgeschichtliches Museum (Museum of Military History), a touchingly old-fashioned affair that traces Austrian military endeavors from the Thirty-Years War through World War II. For me, the focal points of the museum were the displays on the Ottoman Campaigns (and the display on the assassination of Franz Ferdinand, complete with the car in which he and his wife were shot and the bloodstained uniform he was wearing!). There are several key pieces of booty taken from the Austrians' Ottoman opponents, including a number of standards and,

---

12 And how could I forget the coffee? What would Vienna be without its coffeehouses? But where do you think that tradition originally came from? These iconic Viennese institutions would not have existed were it not for the Habsburg-Ottoman rivalry, as the Habsburg subjects discovered the joys of coffee and the coffeehouse culture from the Ottomans (a "fad" that took hold in the empire in the early sixteenth century).

most impressively, an entire imperial war tent. There are also prominent displays of Prince Eugene's personal effects and several large portraits (I am not sure the powdered wig suited him).

As for the Archduke's assassination in Sarajevo in 1914 and the "Great War" that followed: ironically, these events would lead to the former imperial rivals becoming allies—unfortunately for them, on the losing side. After World War I, there would be neither a Habsburg nor an Ottoman empire.

FRONTLINE: SERBIA

The enormous, rambling fortress of Smederevo stretches along the banks of the Danube about twenty-eight miles from Belgrade; it was built in the early fifteenth century on the orders of the Serbian Despot, Đurađ Branković.

During this era, the Serbians, having already suffered great defeats—including at the Battle of Kosovo in 1389, an event to which we will return—had managed to carve out a tenuous independence between the rival powers of the then-independent Hungarian Kingdom, the Venetian Republic, and the expanding Ottoman Empire. The Serbian Despot decided to throw in his lot with the Hungarians, choosing vassalage to another Christian state rather than domination by the Muslim Ottomans. But becoming essentially a buffer state had its disadvantages, as early Serbia was now on the front line of regional—and, more menacingly, imperial—conflict.

Smederevo saw a series of sieges and battles between the medieval Serbian state and the Ottomans from the 1430s to 1459, at which point Ottoman forces finally captured the fortress and absorbed most of the central Serbian lands. What little that remained of the Serbians' fragile independence came to an end when the Ottomans took control of Belgrade in 1521. Serbian lands would remain under Ottoman authority for more than four hundred years, until 1877.

Smederevo Fortress

Today, Smederevo is a forlorn spot. While it is supposedly being considered for UNESCO World Heritage status, at present the once-mighty stronghold is a dilapidated structure—a state not helped by the serious damage inflicted upon it during World War II—that is marred with graffiti and trash. The day I visited in the late summer of 2012, almost no one was wandering the vast, scruffy park inside the walls or visiting the slightly better preserved castle itself. It struck me as odd that a monument of both such grand size and such grand importance to Serbian history would be so derelict. Of course, in part, the problem is money, as it is expensive to restore and maintain such historical sites.

However, I found myself wondering if the neglect stemmed less from monetary concerns and more from a Serbian sense of national loss. After all, why preserve what is now a symbol of Ottoman domination, a reminder of when the early Serbian state ceased to be? The silence at Smederevo said much.

***

The Balkans[13], a motley collection of countries occupying an area that roughly corresponds to the lands south of Hungary, down through Greece, constitute a rather small corner of the world. Yet the region has played an astoundingly disproportionate role in many key events in world history. Countless empires have fought over this strategic peninsula, with its kaleidoscopic array of ethnic groups, languages, and religions, each power leaving its own flavor to the Balkan soup. It possesses such a complicated history (and present) that it almost makes my head hurt trying to put all the pieces together. Which is precisely why I decided to travel across the Balkans in 2012-2013.

Serbia, being on what became the Habsburg-Ottoman frontier and serving as a source of much resistance to imperial rule (on both sides of the border), felt like a good starting point to begin my explorations of the region. And Belgrade seemed like a good starting point to begin my explorations of Serbia.

***

"They used to hold Beer Fest in Kalemegdan, until a guy fell into the zoo and got eaten by a bear... Oh, and here is the Roman well; a tourist fell in and died..."

I had been told that Serbia was quite safe these days, but apparently wandering around the sprawling citadel complex of Kalemedgan in Belgrade—the first of the Serbian fortresses I was to explore—was not for the faint-hearted. If I was to believe these stories my friend Dusica, a former colleague from Khartoum, was telling me, this was a treacherous place indeed. People seemed to fall from its glowering heights on a regular basis. But I persevered and braved these "dangers" at Kalemedgan as I began to explore Belgrade's Ottoman-Habsburg frontier past.

Belgrade—Serbia's dynamic, energetic capital—at first glance offers few outright Ottoman sights to see. Most of its physical fabric is a crazy weave of elegant *fin de siècle* Habsburg architecture and grim Yugoslav

---

[13] I should note that the term "Balkan" is a construction that is relatively new in historical terms, only applied to the region and its people from the late nineteenth century onwards. Actually, it simply referred to one small mountain chain, but somehow it came to encompass a much broader territory.

socialist edifices. But dig a little deeper, and you can find a few reminders that Belgrade was once an Ottoman *paşalık* (domain of a pasha) that practically overlooked the southernmost edge of the Habsburg Empire.

Actually, the Belgrade neighborhood of Zemun, once a separate town, belonged to the Habsburgs who had absorbed the Hungarian Kingdom. Inside the city's citadel, there are flourishes left of the Ottoman enhancements that were added to the originally Serbian structure— including the Stamboul Gate, the remains of a Turkish bath, a now-dry fountain, and a rebuilt tomb for a certain Damat Ali Pasha. Tucked in the old city, not far from the citadel, there is also a small mosque and a decaying, apparently all but forgotten, tomb of a Sufi saint.

There would probably be more; however, with a certain zealous, nationalist ferocity, most of the Ottoman structures have been "erased" from Belgrade. But, as I quickly discovered, the Serbs couldn't erase Ottoman influence entirely.

I was pleasantly surprised that between the vestiges of my high school Russian and my somewhat stronger Turkish abilities, I was able to recognize a remarkable number of words in Serbian.[14] A simple example of the Serbian-Turkish vocabulary exchange is *višnje* (Serbian) and *vişne* (Turkish) for sour cherry. There's also something very familiar about the central role that *kafanas* (loosely, coffeehouses) play as places to socialize over coffee or something stronger (*rakija* or *rakı*), often with lively musical accompaniment. There is a familiarity, too, in the intense hospitality that visitors are shown. Indeed, I was struck by how generous the Serbians were, and how patient many of them could be with my fumbling attempts to communicate with just a handful of words and phrases in Serbian. They seemed genuinely delighted that I was making any effort at all to speak their language. People I didn't know paid for food and drinks because I

---

[14] "Serbian" as a distinct language really doesn't exist—despite what many Serbians might say—as it is essentially the same as the languages spoken in Croatia (Croatian), Bosnia (Bosnian), and even Montenegro (of course, Montenegrin!). The old distinction that Serbian was written in Cyrillic script, while Croatian was written in Latin, doesn't hold much water these days either. Both the Cyrillic and Latin scripts are used in Serbia, and it appears the Latin version is starting to win out in some areas. But when referring to the language spoken by Serbians, one must say they are speaking Serbian. Not Serbo-Croato-Bosno-Montenegrin!

was a guest. It was almost embarrassingly touching, and was similar to how I felt in my years living in Turkey.

Yet even more than frontier Belgrade, the old administrative towns of southern Serbia, the next stops in my journey, were to provide the clearest indication of Serbia's Ottoman past.

***

When I arrived in Niš, I stumbled off my bus and into a hectic market and thought: *I'm now somewhere in the Middle East.* Although my initial impression was challenged when I started exploring other parts of town, overall, the sense that I was in a place more comfortable with its Ottoman past remained.

At the heart of the city is an imposing ruin of a citadel, now largely given over to a large park that was also going to serve as the venue for a jazz festival the weekend I arrived: called with great Serbian humor, "Nishville." Unlike Kalemegdan in Belgrade, this fortress more clearly exhibited its Ottoman heritage. Most prominently, the main gate—the Istanbul Gate—retains its Turkish inscriptions. And just inside the entrance, a refurbished bathhouse had been converted to a restaurant, appropriately called Hamam (although—blasphemously—they served pork!).

Hamam, Now "Hamam"

But Niš is infamous for a darker episode of its Ottoman past, an event that occurred in the waning days of imperial control of the Serbian lands. In 1809, a Serbian rebellion led to the Battle of Čegar. Realizing that defeat was imminent, one of the Serbian leaders, the Duke of Resava, led a suicide mission during which he and his followers blew up the Ottoman gunpowder magazines—and in the process killed not only himself and four thousand of his men, but also ten thousand Ottoman soldiers.

In fury, the Ottoman commander redoubled his efforts and defeated the Serbs—and then, as a gory warning against further rebellion, he ordered that the resisters be beheaded and scalped. The scalps were stuffed and sent to Istanbul, while the skulls—all 952 of them—were embedded into a ghastly construction that is now called the Tower of Skulls. Only fifty-eight skulls remain in the structure, as families over the years tried to "collect" their loved ones from the wall. But the tower—and the memory of what it represents—continues to stand.

This horrific event—and memorial—backfired on the Ottoman commander. Instead of cowing the Serbian resistance, it became a powerful symbol that fed into the newly emerging nationalism and enflamed both the Serbs and other Balkan groups. It became an easy reference to underscore the stereotype of "Turkish"[15] cruelty and oppression (despite the fact that it was an unusual event), and it incited further insurrections.

Within a couple generations, Serbia would be lost to the Ottomans.

The Tower of Skulls has now become a major part of the Serbian national mythology, one that glorifies Serbian resolve, even in moments of defeat. However, such a narrative makes it difficult to examine historical moments such as the Battle of Čegar in all their murky complexity.

Staring into the empty sockets of one of the remaining skulls, I wondered how this man or boy would tell his own story if given the

---

[15] It is very common for Europeans—and others—to refer to the Ottomans as "Turks." However, this is not quite accurate. Due to the extreme heterogeneity of the Ottoman elite, who were drawn more from the people of conquered territories than from the Turkic groups who came to Anatolia from Central Asia, it is almost impossible to define "Ottoman" on ethnic terms. Indeed, often the ones fighting for independence in the Balkan region were essentially fighting other men who also had origins in the Balkans. For example, a Turkish-speaking Muslim Ottoman officer might trace his heritage to a Serbian-speaking Orthodox Christian family.

opportunity. Would he be surprised or bemused to find that his remains are now a nationalist monument? Would he be honored?

***

From Niš, I headed west into the *Balkan* Balkans, the actual mountain range, to Novi Pazar. I was dropped off unceremoniously at the edge of a shuttered market area on the side of the "highway." I had, I realized, arrived at the start of *Eid al-Fitr* the celebration at the end of Ramadan. Every shop was closed.

The city is the heart of a largely Muslim corner of a staunchly Orthodox Serbia, so everything was closed for the holiday. As I shouldered my backpack and went in search of the UFO-shaped Hotel Vrbak, I knew immediately that I was in a very different part of Serbia from what I had seen during the previous few days, even compared to Niš. Some questionable pieces of socialist-futurist architecture were interspersed with Ottoman-era mosques, a collapsing hamam, and a number of whitewashed wooden homes with red tiled roofs. I could have been in an Anatolian village deep inside Turkey (except, of course, for the socialist bits). But I was in Serbia, somewhere near the border with Kosovo, in the area that was the flashpoint for much of the conflict that has riven the Balkans since the earliest days of Ottoman presence in the region (and continues to cause trouble between Serbia and its neighbors).

Here, obviously, the Ottoman past was very present.

Although there were not many specific sites to see in Novi Pazar, its atmosphere made me very nostalgic for my days in Turkey. I sat in one of the numerous cafes that ring the main square, sipping strong cups of Turkish coffee and watching dapperly dressed older men smoke cigarettes and gossip the day away. The call to prayer echoed across the town. Shops that sold dried fruits and nuts dotted the market area.

At night, the center of Novi Pazar was thronged with post-Ramadan revelers who were licking ice cream cones and walking arm in arm. Women, some in *hijab* and others in micro-minis, navigated the crowds. Children raced around the main square with their Eid toys. The joy was palpable.

***

Today, Serbia has an image problem, and it knows it. I tried to visit without any preconceived ideas of what I would experience, but it was hard not to harbor some lingering notions of Serbian violence. This is, of course, the land associated with Slobodan Milošević[16] and which is often, but not always correctly, seen as the instigator of—and the worst promulgator of—conflict in the region. When Yugoslavia fell apart in the early nineties, Serbian officials were intent on holding on to what territory they could. Even now, many Serbians simmer over the independence of Kosovo, failing to accept the loss of a territory they see as an integral part of Serbian territory.

Yet, as my Serbian friend Dusica noted, people on all sides of the many Balkan conflicts committed atrocities, and on all sides the common people suffered. As always, the story was and is much muddier than is often presented.

Thankfully, after traveling in Serbia and experiencing the extreme hospitality of the Serbians, I managed to overcome any negative associations I might have had with this complicated place and people... but it was time to move on. After saying my good-bye to Serbia and my new Serbian friends, I hopped on the slow train to Sarajevo—the next stop in my Balkan tour.

---

[16] Slobodan Milošević was the infamous President of Serbia (1989-1997) and President of the Federal Republic of Yugoslavia (1997-2000) who was charged by the International Criminal Tribunal for the former Yugoslavia with war crimes that were committed during the wars that erupted during the breakup of Yugoslavia (though he died of a heart attack while awaiting trial). We will return to his role in the Balkans in the Kosovo chapter.

THE HEART OF THE BALKANS: BOSNIA-HERZEGOVINA

Sarajevo is indeed an extraordinary city. As soon as I stepped out of my sauna of a train from Belgrade (note to self: never take a ten-hour-long train ride during a heat wave in a train without air-conditioning *or* functioning windows), I felt it—and Sarajevo's train station is in a rather ugly part of town! I knew in the first few minutes, looking up to the green hills that frame the city and across the bustle of humanity in front of the train station, that I was going to extend my stay.

In the grand scheme of things, Sarajevo is not large. The total population is less than 500,000, and the historical core of the city—where most tourists spend their time—could be crossed in about fifteen to twenty minutes on foot (assuming one is not stopping to see the sights or drink a coffee). But this city packs a wallop well beyond its physical size or smallish population, particularly for those, like me, who have a passion for history.

Its name sounds almost mythical when you hear it: Sarajevo. Beautiful, mysterious, important. As both a student of Ottoman history and a world history teacher, the name of this city had come up again and again in my studies and lessons. I couldn't not go and see it with my own eyes. This is, of course, the city where the Ottoman and Habsburg empires vied for control of the Balkans; where Gavrilo Princip shot the Archduke Franz Ferdinand, which set off the chain of events that led to World War I; where German and Partisan forces fought during World War II; where the 1984 winter Olympics were held; and where the horrendous 1992-1995 siege unfolded.

All that history still echoes in Sarajevo, and yet Sarajevans also seem to take great pride in the city's present and future.

Sarajevo's Magic

***

"Let's have dinner in Istanbul, and dessert in Vienna…."

The heart of Sarajevo, the core that makes my historian's heart sing, is the largely pedestrian thoroughfare of Ferhadija Street. I started in Pigeon Square, the main nodal point for Ottoman Sarajevo, the area of town called Baščaršija; Ferhadija stretches from the square through the main market area, passing some of the most important monuments of the Ottoman era, many from the time of Gazi Husrev Bey's governorship (the second Ottoman governor of Bosnia): his elegant mosque, a medrese (school), a bezistan (covered market), a couple hans (inns), etc. Other structures from his time are just a block or two away, such as the large hamam (bath house) that now serves as the Bosnian Cultural Center. More coffeehouses and Bosnian restaurants—all of which serve up excellent *burek* and *ćevapi*—than I can count are packed into the side streets.

Then, within a few minutes of walking amidst "Istanbul," I entered "Vienna." Ferhadija suddenly transforms into a street lined with late nineteenth- and early-twentieth century Habsburg buildings, a clear stamp of the imperial rule that was newly imposed in Austro-Hungary during the years just before World War I. A little further on, past the pedestrianized zone, Habsburg starts to give way to stark, even grim, Tito-ist Yugoslav architecture. Basically, Ferhadija is Sarajevo (and Bosnia) in a nutshell.

Despite its many permutations, Sarajevo's origins are wholly Ottoman. The first half of its name, *saraj*, is the Serbo-Croatian spelling of the Turkish-Persian word, *saray*, which means "palace." The second half is more contested. The prevailing theory is that it is also Turkish—from *ova*, or field around the palace. This would mean the original form was Sarayovası. Others think it is simply the more Slavic ending *-evo* that one finds in names such as Smederevo (see the previous chapter on Serbia).

Whatever the case, the town—at first known as Bosna-Saray—was founded by the Ottomans in the mid-fifteenth century shortly after they conquered this part of Bosnia.[17] It quickly developed into the largest and one of the most important cities in the Balkans—a prize that many began to covet. It also became one of the most cosmopolitan urban centers in the region, with important Catholic, Orthodox, and Jewish communities that were largely integrated with the Muslim population. This remains a hallmark of Sarajevan society—although, sadly, now minus the Jewish population that was decimated in World War II.

For reasons that remain unclear, Bosnia and Herzegovina[18] was one of the few regions in the Balkans where there was large-scale conversion to Islam, which resulted in a significant local Muslim population. The process was gradual—not the forced mass conversion that some Christian Balkan nationalists often claim—but it happened, unlike in neighboring Serbia. Perhaps because of its stronger Muslim heritage, I got the sense that Bosnians (at least Bosniaks, as Bosnian Muslims are often called) and Sarajevans especially are much more accepting, even celebratory, of their Ottoman past than most Balkan peoples. For this reason, I was able to be

---

17 There were settlements in the valley, and possibly an earlier town called Vrhbosna, but its exact location is unknown and it was no longer extant by the time the Ottomans arrived.

18 The use of the double name to describe the country stems at least as far back as the merger of two Ottoman *eyalets,* a type of administrative unit, in 1853 (though the eyalets were linked before this, too).

more open about my "Ottomania" in Sarajevo than I was in other former Ottoman territories in the Balkans.

As I wandered the narrow streets of Baščaršija, trying to decide where to stop for my next round of Bosnian coffee or to indulge in some rich Bosnian concoction of meat and *kajmak*, there were moments I almost forgot that I was not in Istanbul. And although "Vienna" was just a few minutes walk down Ferhadija, I felt like I was a world away from the Europe that most people imagine as "European"—a distinction that made little sense in the Ottoman era.

***

While in Sarajevo, I stayed in a guesthouse that was essentially right next door to Markale Market. Nowadays, the market is just that, a place where vendors hawk piles of beautiful looking fruits—luscious figs and plums were in season—and colorful vegetables. But it was also the site of not one, but two, terrible massacres during the Bosnian War. The last one, in August 1995, served as the "final straw" that pushed N.A.T.O. to step in to end the conflict. I got chills when, as I walked through the War Museum, I came across a photo of a man, torn apart by shelling, who was draped over the market's street side railing—a spot I walked by every day during my stay in Sarajevo.

There were other such moments, such as when I climbed up to the Jewish cemetery with my friend Sara (a one-time resident of the city and an avid Bosnia-phile). Set high in the hills that rise sharply above Sarajevo, the cemetery offers a lovely, panoramic view. But then I remembered oh, this was one of the spots from which snipers fired upon the city. Some of Sara's friends actually lived in the direct line of fire from the position where we were standing: they spent several years of their childhood being shot at by unseen fighters who hid behind Jewish gravestones.

But what I came to find fascinating was that, despite the dark tragedy of the war, Bosnians in general—and Sarajevans in particular—are some of the most remarkably warm and upbeat people I've encountered. They haven't forgotten the traumas of the siege—actually, they often make darkly humorous jokes about the time!—but they have not let it dampen their enthusiasm for their beloved city and its rebirth.

Two of the most enthusiastic Sarajevans I met were Adnan and Samir, the brothers who ran the guesthouse near Markale. They went out of their way to show off the city and its surroundings to me (and pretty much every guest who I saw come and go). For instance, one day Adnan went above and beyond the service that one would expect when he drove a few of us to the Igman and Bjelašnica mountains, where the Olympic skiing competitions took place. It was an excursion that underlined what an unusual travel destination Bosnia can be once you get away from the old center of Sarajevo.

On the way to Igman, we passed in and out of the "entity" of the Republika Srpska (or Serbian Republic—not to be confused with the independent Republic of Serbia), one of the strangest political demarcations in the Balkans.[19] As Adnan drove past the "Welcome to the Republika Srpska!" sign, I half expected to be stopped and asked to show my passport. Instead, we zipped through the "entity" with little sign of having crossed a distinct territory, other than an increase in the use of Cyrillic script on signage and the different uniforms on the police. Without even noticing the point of reentry, we were soon back in the Federation of Bosnia and Herzegovina (not to be confused with the full country of Bosnia and Herzegovina, of course).

As we climbed into the beautiful mountains, we saw signs that warned us of minefields: *Be careful where you hike!* We also stopped at the bombed-out carcass of an Olympic-era hotel, another chilling monument to the destruction of the war—one with gorgeous mountain views. Further up, we came to the isolated wooden mosque that had been built by Muslim soldiers who hid in the forest during the conflict; I almost stumbled into it before I saw it, lost as it is among the trees. Several men were praying within its rough timber walls. The Olympic ski slopes were ghostly in their summer barrenness.

---

[19] The Dayton Accords of 1995, which ended the Bosnian War, divided Bosnia and Herzegovina into two "entities": the Republika Srpska (the Serbian Republic) and the Federation of the Bosnia and Herzegovina (which is predominately Croat and Muslim Bosniak). I will discuss this bizarre political arrangement in more depth later in the chapter.

It was all a fascinating mix of stunning beauty and stunning tragedy.

***

While I knew in theory that Bosnia and Herzegovina has had one of the worst post-war political experiences of any of the former Yugoslav republics, somehow it took seeing the country with my own eyes and hearing the stories of its citizens to really get just how messed up things there truly are.

Although Sarajevo is famous for many historical moments, for the most part the name Sarajevo only became a household word when it was transformed into the epicenter of the horrible conflict that ripped Bosnia and Herzegovina apart in the early and mid nineties, when the former Yugoslavia convulsed in violence. From 1992 to 1995, Bosnian Serb forces besieged the city—nestled as it is in a deep, narrow valley that allowed chillingly perfect sight lines for the snipers. The siege inflicted unimaginable destruction, both physical and psychological, on Sarajevo and its proud people.

Since the signing of the 1995 Dayton Accords (or, more formally, the General Framework Agreement for Peace in Bosnia and Herzegovina), which brought an end to one of the bloodiest conflicts to erupt in the early days of Yugoslavia's dissolution, the country has had some measure of peace. But at what cost?

Bosnia and Herzegovina, with its already strange double name, actually has had a quite long history as a distinct political unit, from the medieval Bosnian kingdom to its incorporation into the Ottoman Empire as a *sancak* and then *eyalet*[20] (even, almost uniquely, keeping its former pre-Ottoman name). Its separate identity, to various degrees, was maintained even when it was absorbed into the Austro-Hungarian Empire and later when it became part of the relatively short-lived Kingdom of Serbs, Croats, and Slovenes—and, of course, within Yugoslavia.[21] Bosnians take a certain pride in this long history.

No other Balkan country better represents the illogicality of applying the concept of "ethnicity" or "nation" to any group within the region's

---

[20] *Sancak* and *eyalet* are terms for various Ottoman administrative units.
[21] Only during World War II did it lose its historical boundaries.

ethnic and religious soup. As I mentioned previously in regards to Sarajevo, Bosnia had one of the largest populations of Muslim converts in the Balkans. Although these Muslims differed in religion from their neighbors, they shared a common South Slavic language and a common heritage of ethnic heterogeneity that stemmed from crisscrossing trade routes and the shifting of empires. Most Bosnians simply identified themselves by religion: Catholic, Orthodox, Muslim. It was only towards the end of the nineteenth century, due to growing pressure from nationalist Croats and Serbs outside of Bosnia, that Bosnian Catholics really started to call themselves Croats and Orthodox Christians Serbs.[22] The Muslims were often (and sometimes still are) claimed to be "Islamized" Croats or Serbs, only becoming defined as a separate "nation" well after the establishment of Yugoslavia. Such ethno-religious labels are seen now as ancient and inviolate, but were extremely fluid until hard-liners demanded "clarity."

However, in Bosnia and Herzegovina, which has long had the most heterogeneous mix of Catholics, Orthodox, and Muslims in the region, the lines were often blurred by mixed marriages and simple lack of adherence to religious practices. This was especially the case in cities such as cosmopolitan Sarajevo, where the communities lived side by side.

Most outside observers of the various Balkan wars in the 1990s accepted the line that the conflict was fueled by "ancient hatreds," but when I listened to the stories of some of the Sarajevans who suffered during the siege, I was struck by how often solidarity actually crossed "ethnic" lines, at least in the city. Although many Bosnian Serbs were roused to fight against the supposed threat of both Croats and Muslims that would come if Bosnia gained independence from Yugoslavia, many Sarajevan Serbs advocated and fought for independence, standing with the city's Croats and Muslims. These Serbs, of course, were cast as traitors by Serbian nationalists. In other parts of Bosnia, Croat and Muslim forces were allies—though as seen in the horror of Mostar, nationalist provocations (again, generally from outside Bosnia) eventually drove the former partners apart and into bloody conflict (see below).

---

22   Before the twentieth century, many rural folk in the Balkans, particularly those following Orthodox Christianity, called themselves "Greek"—not because they considered themselves as having Greek origins but because they followed the "Greek" (Orthodox) Church.

The current tragedy is that the Dayton Accord perpetuates and solidifies these Balkan national and ethnic myths, trying to establish peace by making the country ethnically "fair." The state of Bosnia and Herzegovina was divided into the two "entities," the Federation of Bosnia and Herzegovina, which is mostly Croat and Muslim, and the Republika Srpska. There are also three presidents—one Croat, one Serb, one Muslim—who rotate as head president. One result of these changes is that voters now have to decide who they are ("Well, dad is a Croat, mom is a Muslim… So that makes me a…?"). Another consequence is that those who fall outside all three of the categories are not eligible for political office (sorry Jews, sorry Roma).

Whenever intrastate political territories and political representation have been defined based on religion and/or ethnicity, the strategy generally has backfired horribly. Lebanon, anyone? Yet, that was precisely the strategy decided upon in Ohio. Such identity politics are made all the more ridiculous by the fact that Bosnian "ethnicities" are simply religious identifications, as I have already mentioned.

So the war might be over, but resentments linger and are exacerbated. As a result, the political system spins its wheels, going nowhere. The peace is tenuous at best.

Fortunately, Sarajevo has by now very much risen from the ashes of the war that occurred in the nineties. Much of the city has been rebuilt and renovated, and its streets are bustling with restaurants, cafés, and shops. Tourists are thronging back. But there are still plenty of reminders of the war—bullet holes still riddle some walls; mortar cavities gape in the sidewalks and some buildings; and cemeteries are overflowing with graves inscribed with the years 1992, 1993, 1994, 1995. The siege is not forgotten—far from it—but there is a general sense that Sarajevans are moving on, taking great joy in their beloved city's rebirth.

الْمَوْتُ شَرَابٌ كُلُّ نَاسٍ شَارِبُه

Smrt je piće koje će svako kušati

"Death is a wine we shall all imbibe."

As I was to see, other parts of Bosnia and Herzegovina are, for now, more troubled. Let's hope the rest of the country soon follows Sarajevo's example.

***

As soon as we pulled away from the hostel, the Serbian turbo-folk started blaring from prominently placed speakers—repeating a phrase that sounded very much like "a cup of tea!"—and the van started hopping up and down and jigging to the side, tossing the fifteen tour group members around like dice in a jar. There was a look of vague terror in everyone's eyes. What had we gotten ourselves into? And for *twelve* hours? I had thoughts of tossing myself out the door every time the van started to slow down.

Welcome to the wild ride that is Bata's tour of Mostar and Herzegovina!

When I booked a dorm bed at a hostel in Mostar, I knew that they ran a popular tour of the surrounding area. There were hints that it was unusual ("Did you meet Bata? He's, well, energetic..."), but how different could it really be from the standard circuit of historical and natural sights?

I handed over my fifty-five Bosnian marks and naively expected to sit back and relax for the day.

But as soon as the door to the hostel burst open, accompanied by the sound of a very loud bicycle horn and an equally raucous "GOOD MORNING!", I knew we were in trouble.

Energetic? Understatement of the year!

Bata herded our bewildered group of backpackers (a word Bata loved to cluck as often as he could: "Backpackers! Backpackers!") out to his van—which he referred to as his "girlfriend." And then he did his absolute best to scare people out of joining the trip during his pre-tour "pep talk."

"Backpackers, the van registration states 8+1—I made it 8+12!"

"Backpackers, there's no air conditioning!"

"Backpackers, you will be horrified by the music when I translate the lyrics!"

All this shouted at the top of his lungs.

Everyone laughed nervously, unsure just how much of a joke it all was. But no one backed out.

And, oddly, in the end, I was happy I braved the insanity!

***

It quickly became apparent that Bata's unorthodox approach to guiding a group of foreigners was a deliberate attempt to unsettle us, to make us think about what was really insane: all that Mostar and Bosnia and Herzegovina had suffered during the war in the nineties and continues to experience (while throwing in a little fun and dark humor, too).

With that goal in mind, the first part of the tour—the Mostar bit—did not concentrate on the famous Old Town and the iconic Stari Most (Old Bridge—which we will get back to shortly).

"Backpackers! You can see that on your own!"

Rather, Bata drove us through areas few tourists visit. He showed us the rapid development of the "Croatian" side of town, with its fancy coffee shops and gleaming shopping malls (six built in one year, and a seventh that was a repurposed school).

He showed us the new Croat university center, with its high-tech buildings, and contrasted it to the university center on the "Bosnian" side of the city, which shares grounds with a refugee camp and a military installation and has a "gate" that is knocked out of a former military wall.

He pointed out the football stadium that had once been the home of the local Mostar club, but which now is "leased" to a Croatian team.

He showed us the renovated buildings along the former front line that stand eerily vacant since they are just façades—they have no electrical wiring or running water.

He showed us the resurrected Austro-Hungarian birthday cake of a school—all stripes of varying shades of orange—which is the only school in the city where Croats and Bosniaks study in the same building (although not in the same classrooms).

If we had not noticed before the tour, we were made to see how divided the city remains since the war ended. A division—Croat versus Bosniak, Catholic versus Muslim—that had not been so sharp before the conflict.

After we left Mostar, we embarked on a grand sweep of Herzegovinian territory.

The reason the country is, and has long been, Bosnia *and* Herzegovina is that Herzegovina once had been ruled by a self-proclaimed "Herceg" (from the German word *herzog* for "duke"), Stjepan Vukčić Kosača, during the period when the medieval Bosnian kingdom was weakening and before the Ottomans took control. The name stuck, and ever since Herzegovina has been an integral, if distinct, part of Bosnia. Bata pointed out the duke's castle high on a hill, near the town of Blagaj, which would be our last stop of the day.

Our first stop outside of Mostar was the Catholic pilgrimage boomtown of Međugorje, which was the site of a supposed Virgin Mary appearance in 1981. During the Yugoslav era, the pilgrimage "industry" was suppressed, but in the years since the end of the Bosnian War the area has convulsed in development (fueled by millions of pilgrim and expat dollars). The town's streets were lined with souvenir shops selling every imaginable Mary related trinket: T-shirts, mugs, candles, buttons, clocks, even snow globes. I am not sure I have ever seen such a brazen mix of religiosity and commercialism; it sort of turned my stomach.

I have to admit I was happy to say farewell to Međugorje and head to something far more holy in my eyes: the natural wonder of the Kravice ("Backpackers, midget cows!") Waterfalls.

Much of Herzegovina is an arid, Mediterranean landscape, quite different from the more temperate clime of Sarajevo, which is just two hours away. The land is stony and covered in either hardscrabble shrub or vineyards. So it is quite spectacular to find, in such a dry world, waterfalls gushing *out* of limestone cliffs into clear, blue pools of refreshingly cool water. After a long harangue about what to do and not to do, Bata left us to our own devices for a couple of hours at one of these pools. Giddily, we clambered up slippery rocks into the splash pools and caves that were hidden behind the cascades. It was like a natural water park, made just for us to cool off after a hot van ride with crazy Bata.

After a typically meat-centric Bosnian lunch—would you like some meat with your meat?—Bata bundled us back into his "girlfriend," and off we went again in an eardrum-bursting blast of turbo-folk. We weren't sure where he was taking us as we sped down extremely narrow, but still two-way, roads twisting through the hills. We still didn't know when he finally pulled up to the remains of a grey fortress wall. We followed him sheepishly through the main gate—"Backpackers! How can it be a main gate when it is the *only* gate?!"—and down an ancient cobblestone road.

There it was: a picture-perfect panorama of Počitelj, an Ottoman-era fortress town built of stone in a natural amphitheater. Although it had lost much of its strategic importance after Bosnia and Herzegovina came under Habsburg control in 1878 (before the formal annexation in 1908) and was largely destroyed during the war in the 1990s—as it had had a predominantly Muslim population—Počitelj has largely been rebuilt in a semblance of its former glory. Still, there is a ghostliness to its rejuvenation; many of the homes remain empty, as few families were comfortable returning after the destruction.

We did, however, get to enjoy some Bosnian hospitality at one of the homes that is still in use. We were offered bowls of fresh fruits—figs, plums, grapes, peaches—that had been picked from the little orchards in the town, glasses of syrups—mint, elderflower, pomegranate—and cups of Bosnian coffee. I think that this stop was a highlight for everyone on the tour.

Although night had set, we were not yet finished. Bata, forcing us to jump into the van as it rolled by Počitelj's "main" gate, had other plans.

With his now-expected maniacal pace, we zipped down the hill and on to Blagaj, the town we had spotted in the distance earlier in the tour.

He parked just below the duke's castle, which was lost in the darkness high above us, and guided us to a floodlit Ottoman building that was tucked beneath an imposing, outward-slanting cliff. This is a famous *tekija* (or *tekke*: Sufi center), originally founded by the Bektashis (see the chapter on Hungary). For Bata, this was also the spiritual beginning of Bosnia, as he claimed that the tekija is built on the site of an earlier Bogomil religious retreat. The Bogomils—a mysterious, vaguely Christian group, which some Bosnians see as their precursors—emerged in the tenth century and practiced their unique faith from Bulgaria to Bosnia. The Bogomils' fusion of beliefs—Christian and neo-Manichaean, among others—is sometimes used as an argument for the essential unity of present-day Bosnians, regardless of whether they are Catholic, Orthodox, or Muslim.[23]

That quiet moment spent sitting in the silent stillness across the river from the Ottoman tekke made the turbo (folk)-charged tour more than worth it.

"Backpackers, here we go!"

***

Stari Most (simply "Old Bridge") often makes the top-ten lists of most famous bridges in the world. And, indeed, there is something about this elegant stone arch that is mesmerizing, compelling one to examine it from every possible angle to get just the right photograph of its poetic reach across the Neretva River. Thousands of day-trippers from the Croatian coast come to do just that, and then perhaps wander through the twisting, atmospheric streets of Mostar's[24] old town for an hour or so. If they are lucky, one of the town divers will climb to the highest point of the bridge and plunge eighty feet into the icy, blue-green waters churning below. It is all too easy to forget that there is a very dark story behind the current bridge.

---

[23] The truth is that no one really knows much about the Bogomils and their beliefs, other than that Byzantines considered them heretics. They faded into obscurity after the Ottoman conquests in the Balkans, and they have become, since then, a conveniently obscure ancestral group—one to which it is easy to ascribe whatever belief system one would like.

[24] Mostar means "Bridge Keeper" (*most* = bridge, *ar* = keeper/guard).

You see, the Stari Most as it stands today is not very "stari." The original sixteenth-century bridge, built on the order of the Ottoman sultan, Süleyman the Magnificent, was demolished in 1993 by Bosnian Croat forces during the Bosnian War. They were completing what the Serbian army had already started: blasting apart all the bridges connecting the two halves of Mostar.[25]

This heartwrenching act of destruction was intended to be a symbolic cutting of ties between the Bosniak and Croat populations. But it failed on all fronts. First, the division of the city had never been absolute. As with other urban centers in Bosnia and Herzegovina, Catholics, Muslims, and Orthodox had lived together on both sides of the city. Only during the war were the ethnic lines hardened. On a more strategic front, the river didn't become the border or frontline that the Croat forces had intended. Actually, the frontline settled further to the east.

I didn't have to go very far from the rejuvenated tourist area around Stari Most to see how scarred Mostar remains. Actually, the war damage is more visible, more visceral than what I saw in Sarajevo.

A particularly unsettling symbol of the war rises high above the "Croatian" sector: the concrete skeleton of what had been intended to be a large bank office, but which came to be used as a snipers' "nest." Although such a landmark would likely be fenced off in the United States, this building is not. I was free to roam amid the rubble, over broken glass and even the occasional shell casing. I reached the top by climbing a metal fire-escape ladder, where I got a 360-degree view of Mostar and the surrounding mountains.

It would have been beautiful—if I hadn't realized that people had been shot from just this point. I got the same shivers I experienced when I stood in the Jewish cemetery in Sarajevo and looked out over the city.

Back at the bridge, I watched the tourists snap their photos and cheer on the divers. Many of them probably didn't give much thought to the fact that the original bridge had ceased to be about twenty years ago and

---

[25]   On the subject of historic Ottoman bridges in the Balkans, I highly recommend Nobel Prize-winning Ivan Andrić's unusual novel, *Bridge on the Drina*. Serving as the central character of the novel, the bridge is a real Ottoman structure built on the order of the famous Grand Vezir, Sokullu Mehmet Pasha (or in Serbo-Croat, Mehmed-Paša Sokolović) in the town of Višegrad in eastern Bosnia.

was only resurrected at the turn of the new century (it officially reopened in 2004). For these tourists, it is simply a picturesque Ottoman bridge, an engineering marvel of an earlier age.

But I think that, for the people of Mostar, it is a sign of resilience. As Bata put it: "This bridge will be *older* than the original—it will last more than 500 years!"

Somehow, I believed him.

SARAJEVO REDUX

I had to come back. According to local lore, if you drink from the fountain outside the Gazi Husrev Bey Mosque in Sarajevo's Baščaršija—and I had drunk deeply—you will return. It was destiny.

(Although finding a cheap flight from Istanbul also helped.)

You probably have already guessed from much of what I wrote at the beginning of this chapter on Bosnia and Herzegovina that I had developed a particular affinity for Sarajevo when I first visited. So, it should not be too surprising that once I returned to the Ottoman world after a winter hiatus spent in warmer Southeast Asia, I felt the call to revisit the city. Thus, before I set forth on my grand circuit around the Black Sea, I decided to fly back to Sarajevo in order to explore its fascinatingly complex story even more and to venture further afield in Bosnia and Herzegovina.

***

Sarajevo in Snow

I didn't have to play the tourist during this second visit to Sarajevo. I had already poked into most of its fascinating nooks and crannies the last time I was in town, so this time I mostly just revisited the spots that I wanted to see again and meandered from one coffeehouse to the next (and from one eating establishment to the next!). Also, as winter had lingered in the region, I had the pleasure of seeing the city beautifully laced with fresh white snow, which provided an incentive to re-photograph this most photogenic of cities.

I did, however, get to experience a few new things, thanks to my friends Adnan and Samir.

When they took me to the wine bar, Vinarija Topić, I noticed that pretty much everyone in the room—young, old, male, female—was singing heartily along with the group of musicians who were weaving through the crowd, performing old regional favorites. Every now and then, Adnan or Samir would lean over to inform me: "This one is from Slavonia" or "That one is from the Dalmatian coast." Everyone seemed to not only know all the words but also to have an imprinted musical map of all the traditional songs. I found myself marveling at this collective cultural memory and uninhibited participation. There really is nothing like it in the U.S., and it made my heart swell with joy.

Samir also drove me up Trebević, a small mountain that looms above the city. It that was the site of the 1984 Olympic bobsled and luge runs; now, these structures stand eerily derelict, crumbling and covered in graffiti and broken glass, the forest gradually reclaiming the concrete and steel. The mountain was also a front line during the war in the nineties, so there are many abandoned, bullet-ridden houses and former restaurants to add to the spookiness of the area. Nevertheless, when I looked down from Trebević, I couldn't deny that the view of the valley that cradles Sarajevo is one of the most beautiful vistas I've seen so far.

Back down in Sarajevo, as I wandered in the hillside neighborhood just behind the Markale Market, I passed a grandmotherly woman who was toddling along with some grocery bags; she struck me as familiar.

Where had I seen her before?

Had we met?

Then it dawned on me: a few days earlier I had watched a video recording of this woman as she related her horrific story as a survivor of genocide at the Srebrenica memorial exhibition. All of her male family members—husband, sons, and others—had been killed in the summer of 1995.

I was reminded once more of the powerful and present immediacy of the conflicts that had ripped the former Yugoslavia apart.

When I was previously in Sarajevo, I made an effort to explore all the layers of history that this city has to offer, not just the more recent story of siege and war, which is the focus of many of the tourists who are now venturing to Bosnia and Herzegovina. Actually, what initially drew me to the city was its Ottoman past and my desire to learn more about its transition to Habsburg rule. But I couldn't ignore the Bosnian War and the siege of Sarajevo: the signs were all around me—not simply in the buildings still pockmarked with bullet and mortar holes, but in the stories of the people who make this city their home. The gregarious, life-loving Sarajevans I met had almost all been through the conflict or, at the very least, had family members and friends who suffered through the many horrors of that time.

However, there was one dramatic story that I didn't delve into fully on that first trip: the genocide in Srebrenica that occurred in July 1995. In part, this was due to the fact that the massacre had not taken place in Sarajevo, and the city had been my main focus back in August. But perhaps it also had something to do with an unconscious avoidance of yet another tale of sickening brutality.

I began my education on Srebrenica at the exhibition next to Sarajevo's Catholic cathedral. I entered an elevator with the phrase "You are my witness" emblazoned in three languages—Bosnian/Serbo-Croatian, Turkish, and English—on the mirrored interior. When I exited the elevator, the first thing I saw was a wall covered in thousands of names, those of the victims. A recording of a thudding, beating heart echoed through the exhibition. In the main hall, large black-and-white photos chronicled the present realities of the genocide survivors and the process of identifying the victims. There were also consoles where I could watch video recordings from the Cinema for Peace project, which aims to collect the oral histories of 10,000 survivors. One of these recordings was of the woman I passed by chance in the streets a few days later.

The exhibition was a powerful memorial to the Srebrenica genocide, but somehow it wasn't enough for me to look at photos and watch videos. I needed to see the place where the events unfolded—I needed to go to Srebrenica itself.

Skender, a lanky, curly-haired Bosnian guy who was only eight years old when the war started—young enough to remember everything, too young to really understand the nature of war, as he explained—led our small group up to the gate of the memorial in Potočari, the village near Srebrenica that was the center of the drama. The rows of white tombstones, representing only a fraction of the total number of victims, spread across a level field and up a gentle slope just across from the former Dutch U.N. base.

As it turned out, we had arrived on a day when a memorial service was to be held, so a number of mothers and wives of the victims—who were almost all men and boys—were praying at the graves.[26] A large stone at the entrance displayed the figure 8372—the latest estimate of the number who died.

Srebrenica Memorial

---

[26] The graves are only for those victims for whom approximately seventy percent of the remains have been identified. There is a center in Tuzla for DNA analysis of the bodies, which were often jumbled in mass graves. In many cases only a bone or two of a victim has been positively identified, but according to tradition the family can't perform a burial ceremony until at least seventy percent of the body is found. Many families still wait for the opportunity to put their loved ones to rest.

So what had happened in July 1995 in this corner of Bosnia and Herzegovina, a two-and-half hour drive from Sarajevo, not far from the Serbian border? Unfortunately, despite the fact that events unfolded nearly two decades ago, much remains a mystery. Here are the broad brushstrokes:

When the war in Bosnia broke out in 1992 and the Bosnian Serb army began to occupy large swaths of territory, Srebrenica and other towns in the surrounding area—most of which had a majority Muslim population—were surrounded, and thereby cut off from regions that were held by the national army. As the Serb forces advanced, reducing the size of the enclave, thousands of refugees poured into the small town of Srebrenica, which led to severe overcrowding and food shortages. Similar to the situation in Sarajevo, everyone was living under siege conditions.

In April 1993, after assessing the deteriorating situation, the U.N. declared Srebrenica a "safe area" and established a U.N. Protection Force (UNPROFOR) base in town, first with Canadian troops, then Dutch. Under the agreement, the enclave was declared a demilitarized zone, so those living in the area were required to give up their weapons. The Serbs were also supposed to withdraw heavy weapons. However, this resolution was more often ignored than honored. As a result, the humanitarian crisis deepened.

By early 1995, few supply convoys were getting through and the Bosnian Serb army was building up forces in the area. Many civilians died of hunger. In early July, the Serbs went on the offensive and began to capture more and more of the "safe area." On the tenth, the army entered Srebrenica; the U.N. forces fired warning shots, but, consistent with their brief, did not fire directly at the advancing forces. The next day General Ratko Mladić—who wasn't arrested until 2011, after having lived in hiding for over a decade—marched triumphantly into Srebrenica, claiming it for the Republika Srpska.

This is when a dire situation started to become a catastrophe.

Fearing for their lives, nearly 25,000 Bosnian Muslims made their way to the Potočari U.N. compound. Many of the men and boys, suspecting that they were not going to be protected by the Dutch forces, fled into the surrounding mountains with the hope of reaching the relative safety of Tuzla. Most of them would not survive.

Those who arrived at the gates of the U.N. compound assumed they would be allowed to enter; however, despite the large size of the compound, a decision was made to only admit five thousand or so refugees inside, mainly women with babies. Twenty thousand were left outside the gates.

It was then that—in full view of the Dutch officers—Serb forces began to separate the men and boys who remained in Potočari, claiming they were interrogating them for war crimes. Almost all of these men were executed and dumped into mass graves in the area. A similar fate awaited any of the men who were caught during their march over the mountains. The U.N. forces did little or nothing. The question of why they failed to respond remains unanswered.

In the end, it is estimated that over eight thousand men and boys were killed in various corners of the U.N. safe zone in an unabashed program of "ethnic cleansing" by the Bosnian Serbs. The exact number of victims remains uncertain, as mass graves and solitary bodies are still being discovered.

The general conflict in Bosnia and Herzegovina did not come to an end until later in 1995, when U.N. forces—finally spurred by events such as the second Markale Market massacre in Sarajevo (which occurred a month after the Srebrenica genocide)—started to attack Bosnian Serb positions. Eventually, a peace treaty was signed in the fall of 1995 in Dayton, Ohio. I've already written a little about the misguided peace of the Dayton Peace Agreement and its impact on the current political situation, so I won't delve into that too deeply here. However, one of the outcomes of that agreement was the establishment of two "entities" in the country—the Federation of Bosnia and Herzegovina, which is predominantly Muslim and Croat, and the Republika Srpska, which is overwhelming Serb.

Bizarrely, despite all the atrocities that were recorded in the U.N. safe zone, Srebrenica and the surrounding towns became part of the Republika Srpska.

Somehow, even before I set foot in Potočari and Srebrenica, I could tell we were arriving in a place where dark feelings still fester. The evidence of the war was as clear in the bombed out villages as it had been in war-ravaged Mostar.

I was astounded to learn that, despite the magnitude of the atrocities in 1995 and the continuing hostilities in the area, some survivors are actually returning and trying to reestablish themselves in their old homes. Our tour group even had the privilege of sitting down to a home-cooked meal prepared by one such family, the Efendićs. They warmly welcomed us into their home, a neatly restored two-story house sandwiched between two others, both of which remained quite damaged from the war. They seemed to be prospering, despite the overall weak economic situation in the region. I had to agree with our guide, Skender, that such people are heroes of a sort. I don't think I could have come back if I had suffered such trials.

The trip back to Sarajevo was mostly silent. I think the six of us who had taken part in the Srebrenica tour were a bit shell-shocked from what we had seen and experienced.

Still, the determination of the returnees who are carving a niche for themselves in this troubled part of Bosnia and Herzegovina gives me some hope in the indomitable human spirit. As do the women and men who are brave enough to tell their stories, such as the grandmother I saw in Sarajevo.

People, I am finding as I visit the far-flung corners of this world, are remarkably resilient.

***

When I returned to Sarajevo, I visited the old cinema, Kino Bosna. The tables and chairs, all fully occupied, crowded every available open space; people even lounged with their drinks in the stadium seating. I squeezed into the last available spot, tucked up on the former stage. A musical trio—a guy with an accordion, another with something like a ukulele, and a singer —wove in and out of the crowd, performing merry songs that I could not understand, but for which the audience, young and old, clearly knew every word.

A small group of twenty-something guys sitting next to me offered rounds of rakija and asked me where I was from between bouts of laughing and belting out the latest song and crying over a friend's imminent departure to Italy. One guy leaned towards me, waving his arm to indicate the cheerful chaos, and said: "Sarajevo is the best city! No matter where you go, you always come back!"

Indeed. There is so much about Sarajevo, and its past, to excite my historian's imagination. In the end, though, it will be the Sarajevans and their *joie de vivre* that will draw me back again and again—with or without a drink from the Gazi Husrev Bey fountain!

THE BLEEDING EDGE: CROATIA

Modern Croatia is an oddly shaped country, a sharp boomerang that frames Bosnia and Herzegovina (and that, except for a few miles of coastline, all but cuts its neighbor off from the sea). To travel from many parts of its northern wing to the southernmost point of its coastal wing, the fastest path would be to cut through Bosnian territory, but buses and the limited train service of the region tend to make the tortured long route around the arch of Croatia. This odd political formation bespeaks its near-constant history as a frontier land, including the time when it served as the bleeding edge of the Habsburg and Ottoman Empires.

Although I first dipped into Croatia in 2007 for a long weekend excursion in the Istrian peninsula while visiting friends in Slovenia, I didn't really get a good sense of the country then.[27] During my Western Balkans trip in 2012, I had a chance to explore more fully; I visited both wings of the boomerang, with stops along the gorgeous Dalmatian Coast—most prominently Split and Dubrovnik—and, towards the end, the north— Zagreb and its environs.[28] Due to time constraints, I wasn't able to visit the eastern tip of the boomerang, the region known as Slavonia: this was a real shame, as it was the part of Croatia tied most firmly to the Ottoman world. But I had to save that for another trip.

Still, my journey from Split to Dubrovnik helped me better understand the often tortured Habsburg-Ottoman frontier that emerged along the Dalmatian coast after Venetian power began to wane, and it would help me better understand Montenegro's position in the battle for control of the Adriatic coast of the Balkans.

---

[27] I did, however, quickly fall for Istria's raw beauty and its lovely Venetian-era hilltop towns. And its truffles.

[28] Zagreb was never within the Ottoman domain, despite its close proximity to Slavonia. It is very much an Austro-Hungarian city, which was once commonly known in German as *Agram*.

Split is perhaps most famous as the home of Roman Emperor Diocletian's palace, a building so sprawling that over time the city emerged *within* its walls. When I wandered the narrow, atmospheric streets of the old town, I was actually in the palace—although this fact is almost completely obscured by centuries of architectural accretions. From the Byzantine era onward, it became a prominent port city, sometimes enjoying a "free state" status as various powers—Hungarian and Venetian, for example—vied for control of the region and its trade routes. However, it was brought firmly into Venetian hands by 1420, and remained so until Napoleon came onto the scene in 1797.

During much of those nearly four hundred years of Venetian rule, Split served as an important trading point with the Ottomans, who by the fifteenth century controlled much of the Balkan interior (essentially, much of the land just outside of Split; even today, the Bosnian border is a short drive away), as well as good chunks of the Adriatic coast south of Split (as we will see with Dubrovnik in just a moment). Even when Split was absorbed into the Austrian Empire after its brief stint under the French, the Ottoman Empire would be its closest neighbor until the beginning of the twentieth century. So in some respects, Split was a perfect starting point for me to think about the political fault lines that cross through the region.

However, I truly entered Ottoman Croatia when I arrived in Dubrovnik.

Today, Dubrovnik is Croatia's tourist darling, a sparkling gem of a walled city that situated on the impossibly beautiful Adriatic coast; it is a favorite stop for the cruise ships that disgorge thousands of gawking tourists. While it deserves the attention it gets, I have to admit I was a little turned off by how much it had been scrubbed clean into a nearly Disney-esque version of its historical self. The tourist hordes—and the countless souvenir shops and tourist-oriented restaurants—didn't help.

But I'd come with a purpose…and a strategy.

There is one thing that I've noticed in my years of traipsing around the globe: tourists tend to be late risers. So, I woke early on my first full day in the walled city and meandered its stone cobbled streets all by myself. The worn marble felt cool and slippery under my feet; the shadows slanted sharply across the shuttered shops and restaurants. The only sounds came from church bells. Only the occasional well-groomed, well-fed street cat was there to keep me company.

Then, as soon as the ticket office opened, I climbed to the ramparts of Dubrovnik's famous defensive wall—which is completely preserved—and circumnavigated its irregular oval. It was easy, then, to see the city's attraction in the gorgeous tumble of its red roofs, the spires of its stunning churches, and the blue-blue of the Adriatic lapping at its gates. I savored the view before the scene was marred by a crush of foreign visitors.

From my vantage on the wall, there was little to indicate that Dubrovnik had once been an odd little vassal state of the Ottomans. It looked more like the Venetian towns lining the rest of the coast. Nevertheless, as the Republic of Ragusa, it had been a rival to—not a part of—Venice.

Dubrovnik first became an Ottoman tributary state in 1458, just a few years after Sultan Mehmet the Conqueror captured Istanbul. A few decades later, it was absorbed as a protectorate (which came with an increased demand for tribute), becoming the gateway for Ottoman trade in the Adriatic Sea[29], but Ragusa/Dubrovnik continued to operate as an essentially independent state—which explains the near absence of any physical markers of Ottoman rule, even though it was a part of the empire, at least in name, until the beginning of the nineteenth century.

By the time I tore myself away from the lovely vista of city and sea and descended to the polished streets below, the tourist mobs had arrived, jarring me from my Ottoman reveries. I have to admit I was ready to escape the crowds sooner rather than later, and hopped on a bus that was heading to my next Balkan destination: Montenegro. There, in jewellike Kotor, I was to get a sense of what Dubrovnik must have been like before it became a tourist trap.

---

[29] Ragusa was a particularly important point of trade between Florence and the Ottoman Empire. Goods were transported overland between Ragusa and Istanbul via the important trading towns of Bosnasaray/Sarajevo (Bosnia), Novi Pazar (Serbia), Skopje (Macedonia), Plovdiv (Bulgaria), and Edirne and Istanbul (Turkey)—all of which have or will be discussed in this book. Goods then crossed the Adriatic between Ragusa and the Italian peninsula.

THE BLACK MOUNTAIN: MONTENEGRO

THEY rose to where their sovereign eagle sails,
They kept their faith, their freedom, on the height,
Chaste, frugal, savage, arm'd by day and night
Against the Turk; whose inroad nowhere scales
Their headlong passes, but his footstep fails,
And red with blood the Crescent reels from fight
Before their dauntless hundreds, in prone flight
By thousands down the crags and thro' the vales.
O smallest among peoples! rough rock-throne
Of Freedom! warriors beating back the swarm
Of Turkish Islam for five hundred years,
Great Tsernogora! never since thine own
Black ridges drew the cloud and brake the storm
Has breathed a race of mightier mountaineers.

      - Alfred Lord Tennyson, *Montenegro* (1877)

Slavko waved his still-lit cigarette in a sweeping gesture that encompassed the entire 360-degree panorama, while also stabbing the air for emphasis at particular points on the horizon.

"There is Njegoš's village, where he was born; there is Cetinje, the old royal capital; there is Lake Skader with Albania on the other side; there is the sea and the Bay of Kotor; over there, past the smoke from the wildfires, that's where Durmitor is—Bosnia and Serbia are only 50 kilometers further. From here, Njegoš could see everything he ruled; we can see 70 percent of the whole country."

The mausoleum of the famous Montenegrin bishop/prince/poet Petar II Petrović-Njegoš—a stolid, vaguely fascistic monument that was built between the world wars—rests at the top of the second-highest peak[30] of Mount Lovćen. This is the mountain that the Venetians called Monte Negro—the Black Mountain—the name by which this tiny country is now known.[31]

From this vantage, as Slavko pointed out, I was able to soak in a view that encompasses Montenegro almost in its entirety. Although small and young in terms of its modern incarnation (the country declared independence from Serbia in 2006; in the Balkans, only Kosovo is "younger"), this patch of sea-fronting mountains exemplifies the convoluted and tumultuous history of the whole region. And, as I stood on top of Lovćen, I realized just how little I knew about it. This was to be a major theme of my Balkan travels!

***

Before we reached the summit of Lovćen, we made a quick coffee stop at a modest roadside stand that had perhaps the most spectacular view of the stunning Bay of Kotor in all of Montenegro. As I sipped my very large Turkish coffee from a paper cup, I stared in wonder at the cloverleaf folds of this complicated "fjord" surrounded by sharply peaked mountains, with tiny fortified towns ringing the shoreline. It looked like a 3-D map; it couldn't be real. Even the gigantic cruise ships plying the inlets looked like toy boats from this view. I could see why this bay was such highly prized territory for seafaring peoples.

Coastal Montenegro, and especially the Bay of Kotor, came under Venetian control in the late fourteenth century. Although Venice was one of the greatest of the seaborne trading empires, it was soon struggling with another Mediterranean power, the Ottoman Empire, which was

---

[30] The second highest because apparently Njegoš hoped there would be a greater Montenegrin leader than himself who would claim that spot. Instead, there's now a TV transmission tower in that location.

[31] I find it curious that it is the Italian version of the name that has stuck. In the South Slavic language of the region—which, as I have noted in a previous entry, can be called Serbian, Croatian, Bosnian, or Montenegrin, depending on which country you are in—"black mountain" is Crna Gora. Perhaps the three consonants in a row scare people, although it's by no means the worst example: consider Trieste in Slavic: Trst.

a growing presence in the Balkans at the time. For a while the bay was divided between Venetian and Ottoman authority, with major scuffles for control of strategic towns and forts, but ultimately the Venetian Republic became the dominant power on the coast—at which point it named the area Albania Veneta.

The mountainous interior of Montenegro, however, was brought firmly into the Ottoman realm, attached in various forms to other Balkan *sancaks* (and once, from 1514-1528, was briefly defined as its own). At least in theory, Montenegro remained part of the Ottoman Empire until 1878, when the Ottomans lost the Russo-Turkish War of 1877-78 and had to sign the Treaty of San Stefano.

This is, by the way, the conflict that so inspired Lord Tennyson to pen his poem, *Montenegro.*

The Slavic "tribes" in the deepest mountains, though, fought fiercely against both Venice and Istanbul from the earliest days of imperial rule. They often rallied around bishops of the Orthodox Church, who then became something of a political power in the mountains (which led to the establishment of the dynasty that produced Njegoš). In the end, the Ottoman authorities took the pragmatic route and just let the rebellious mountain people be, and instead concentrated on consolidating control over the more manageable bits—like valley towns.

That continued until the nineteenth century, when nationalism-fueled revolt took hold of the Balkans as a whole, complete with Russian-supported uprisings. (The Balkans, you might remember, were where a pesky little conflict now known as World War I got its start—due in large part to said nationalist revolts and imperial interference.)

The nineteenth century also brought an intensification of the fighting between the Habsburgs—who had incorporated the Bay of Kotor into their Dalmatian holdings after the collapse of Napoleon's empire in 1815[32]—and the Ottomans. Now the Habsburg-Ottoman frontier extended well down the Adriatic coast. Everyone wanted the strategic Bay of Kotor, it seems.

---

[32] Venice lost the Bay of Kotor in 1797, at which point it was absorbed into the Habsburg realm. It would experience several decades of political tug-of-war between the Habsburg Empire, France, and Russia, before resettling into full Habsburg control.

Over the centuries of conflict with the many political giants that vied for power in the Adriatic Sea and Balkan Peninsula, the Montenegrins forged a distinct identity that even Tennyson romanticized. This sense of difference from the rest of the Slavs in the Balkans, despite their common language and adherence to Orthodox Christianity (the Montenegrins were similar in this way to the Serbs), is just as powerful today. Indeed, my guide, Slavko, was fond of telling me how brave and strong Montenegrin men were: "My uncle, he is strong like bear!"

And yet, it was only with the 1878 Treaty of Berlin[33] that a fully independent Montenegrin state began to emerge, first as a principality, then as a kingdom. But, as with so much of the history in this area, that moment of independence was to be relatively short-lived—the tumult of the twentieth century was just around the corner. Montenegro would soon enough find itself amalgamated into a political entity that would eventually be called Yugoslavia.

***

Before I had crossed the border from Croatia—a hair-pulling experience that took nearly two hours, even though my bus was second in line to cross[34]—I had known of Montenegro's reputation as a thorn in the side of the Ottomans (and the Venetians), and seeing the landscape made it all so clear how that could be. Even when simply circling the Bay of Kotor, I was agape at the drama of mountain and sea. The steep rock face rises swiftly from the pristine, blue waters of the bay; the coastal towns cling to the brief boundary between the two realms.

---

[33] The Treaty of Berlin, a revision of the Treaty of San Stefano that had been signed earlier in the same year, recognized the independence of Serbia, Romania, and Montenegro, and also granted autonomy to Bulgaria. It was essentially the death knell for the Ottoman presence in the Balkans.

[34] As there isn't much love lost between the former Yugoslav republics, I suspect that some border officials deliberately make the crossings more painful than need be. In this case, a Croatian official boarded the bus, collected all our passports in order. But when he returned, he plopped the whole pile in the lap of a poor woman in the front, who then had to match each passport to the correct passenger. By the time, everyone had his or her passport back, we had reached the Montenegrin post—where the chaotic process repeated itself.

However, it wasn't till I had climbed to the top of Mount Lovćen and stood in the shadow of the mausoleum of Njegoš that I truly understood just what a natural fortress this area is. Montenegro offered suitable refuge for a fiercely independent people trying to fend off pesky empires.

AS IF IT WERE YESTERDAY: ALBANIA

"They took my land in the center of the city. I had to go into the mountains to protect my religion.... Is it right that we suffer?"

It took several rounds of such statements before it began to sink in: F.[35] was not talking specifically about himself, or even about the present. He was describing events—or rather, a certain interpretation of those events— from nearly five centuries earlier. But for him the trauma was as vivid and painful as if it had happened to him personally.

Perhaps because I come from the U.S., where many Americans consider the past to be a dead thing, even pointless to examine, I have long been fascinated by how deeply felt history can be in other parts of the world. This seems particularly true in large swaths of former Ottoman territory, where people discuss the "Turkish occupation" as if it had occurred yesterday— and there are few places where the emotion over historical events, often in the distant past, is as passionate as in the Balkans.

F. was a clear case in point. He happens to belong to the Catholic minority in Albania, which makes up only about 10 percent of the country's population. I didn't know of his Catholic heritage until he began expounding on the plight of his people towards the end of a leisurely dinner. We, his audience, were a small group (an American, an Australian, and a German), relaxing and eating under an expanse of grape arbor in the guesthouse garden. In his view, the Turks (and then the Albanian converts to Islam) forced the Catholics—the true Albanians, according to F.—off their land, leading them to live in poverty high in the mountains. He says that their descendants still persecute Christians and receive all the advantages in Albania. And, moreover, he believes that today's Muslim

---

[35] I will not give his full name, as F. is well known in his community and is otherwise—like every Albanian I've had the pleasure of meeting—hospitable to a fault. We just happened to disagree dramatically on the topic of Islam!

Albanians should be held responsible for the actions of their forebears five hundred years ago.

At first, much of what he said regarding his view of Ottoman rule was the familiar rhetoric of many non-Muslim communities in the Balkans. I listened respectfully, occasionally trying to point out that most of us at the table had a hard time understanding how you could hold someone responsible for a supposed wrong they didn't commit. However, at one point F. turned to me and said: "But you should understand! It is like 9/11! You see what they [Muslims] are really like!"

I had to speak up then.

The timing of this conversation made it particularly important to me that I try to convey to F. that I saw no connection whatsoever between a one-time act of terrorism and a historical process that had unfolded over centuries. It had not been long since unrest in the Muslim world over a movie that was commonly viewed as an affront to Islam, *Innocence of Muslims*, had led to such tragedies as the death of the U.S. ambassador to Libya, the burning of the German embassy in Khartoum (where I used to live), and the attack on the school in Tunisia (where I was moving the following year). But I wanted him to know that I couldn't view all Muslims as bad people—"backstabbers" as he called them—because a few individuals had done horrible things.

Unfortunately, F. seemed startled, even hurt, that I couldn't see the "obvious" similarities between the actions of Muslims in Albania five hundred years ago and of al-Qaeda more recently. We went round and round in circles, but each time I tried to explain my position, F. would retreat with a snappish: "You don't understand. Tourists come for one, two days, they don't understand. Americans, Western Europeans, you favor the Muslims! But wait, just wait, 9/11, it will happen again! Then you will understand!"

Matthias, the poor German guy who was caught in the middle of the crossfire tried—after making his own effort to explain how glad he was that people living in areas of Europe that had once been conquered by Nazi Germany didn't hold him personally responsible for that occupation—to broker a peace. But in the end, all we could do was call an end to the conversation. As we retreated to our respective rooms, Matthias whispered to me: "Now I think I understand the Albanian blood feuds...."

I was left rattled, but as I prepared myself for bed, I began to realize just how illuminating the frustrating "debate" had been. I came to the Balkans in large part to develop a better understanding of its über-complicated past and present; here was a perfect example of just how hard it was going to be to achieve that understanding—and yet it energized me to dig even deeper.

How is that F. and others like him can feel so strongly about a period of time of which they have no living memory? I may never know, but I will continue to try.

Anyway, such was my introduction to Albania!

***

I crossed into Albania from Ulcinj, a heavily Albanian town in Montenegro. The location of my crossing was illustrative of the blurred ethno-linguistic lines that fail to match the current, rigid national borders. Still, once the bus pulled into Shkodra (or Skhodër), I knew immediately I had entered a much different part of the Balkans than what I had traveled through so far. This was a wilder and woollier frontier that showed very visible signs of its many decades as a closed-off country; I also knew immediately that I was going to relish my travels in Albania.

Even after the conversation I detailed above, which occurred shortly after I settled into Shkodra, my draw to Albania was not shaken. As I progressed through the country, visiting quirky Tirana, the capital; beautiful Berat, a museum-piece of Ottoman architecture; beguiling Gjirokastra (or Gjirokastër); and other little towns and villages, I found myself constantly inspired and intrigued. One can't say that Albania is ever boring!

***

"Meet me in front of the pyramid."

"The what?"

"The pyramid. Everyone knows it."

I still wasn't sure I had heard my host correctly. A pyramid? In Tirana? I knew that one errant Bosnian archaeologist claimed to have identified the oldest pyramids in the world in Bosnia, but I had not heard of an Albanian pyramid.

Nevertheless, when I arrived in Tirana, stumbled out of a *furgon* (minibus) from Shkodra, and walked into the center, I knew exactly what my new friend had meant.

Just across the Lana River (which, unfortunately, is more of an open sewage drain), right on the major thoroughfare of Boulavard Dëshmorët e Kombit and in the midst of some of the glitziest new development in the city, rose the decaying carcass of a building from Albania's final days of communism. The "pyramid" is a socialist fantasy of sloping concrete and glass that was intended to be a museum for the infamous dictator Enver Hoxha, designed by his daughter and son-in-law shortly after his death. It had only a few years to serve its original purpose before one of the most repressive communist regimes in the world collapsed in the early 1990s, part of the chain reaction that swept Eastern Europe and then the former U.S.S.R. in the heady years between 1989 and 1992. While it apparently served as a nightclub and conference center in various incarnations in the post-communist era, it now is empty and derelict, slowly falling apart, accruing layers of anti-Hoxha graffiti. No one seems to know what to do with it now. But I think the "pyramid" serves as an eloquent memorial to both the bitter memory of the fifty years of isolation and oppression that the Albanians suffered under Enver Hoxha and to the rapid transformation that Albania has witnessed in the past twenty years.

I found it interesting just how many other travelers I encountered on my trip who were also on some sort of grand Balkan tour (even if few had an Ottoman-themed bent!), their itineraries encompassing a large number of the countries in the region. With these Balkan journeys, there seem to be two main directions of travel: clockwise or, as I was doing, counterclockwise. This meant that I often would intersect with people who had been where I was going, which allowed for a foretaste of what was ahead. Those travelers who had already been in Albania when I was still making my way through Montenegro seemed to fall into two major camps: the ones who disliked the country terribly ("Don't go there! It's a waste of time! The food is awful! Nothing works! Bypass Tirana completely!") and the ones who thought it was one of the best places they had ever visited ("The people are super friendly and hospitable! It's beautiful! It's an adventure! Fascinating!")

I took this as something of a challenge. What would I think of Albania?

As many of my friends know, places that are closed or difficult to enter hold a special appeal to me. Until the early 1990s, Albania was about as closed as they come, a North Korea in Europe. Enver Hoxha (1908-1985) was so paranoid that he had mushroom-shaped bunkers built all over the country—many of which are still around—and tried to keep all Albanians in and everyone else out. A half-century of such a life is bound to have an impact, and so it wasn't a surprise that Albania's opening to the outside world was a painful process.

This was captured vividly in the wonderful 1994 film *Lamerica*, in which two Italian con artists come into the newly "free" country and try to make a quick buck in the chaos of the early experiments with capitalism. When I watched the film in college, I wasn't turned off by its rather grim (albeit sympathetic) portrayal of the country and its desperately poor people; instead, I became even more anxious to visit. I went so far as to contemplate applying for a Fulbright grant to Albania before I headed to grad school, but the horrible economic crisis in 1996, which stemmed from a series of collapsing pyramid schemes (how fitting!), curtailed that plan. But I never stopped wanting to see this anomalous Balkan country.

Now that I was on my tour of former Ottoman territories, I was finally able to set eyes on Albania and to begin to make my own judgments on what it was like. And what a different place it turned out to be compared to the stark, grey images from *Lamerica*!

Whether they found it a difficult place to travel in/around or not (I was pleasantly surprised at how easy it was—but then again, I had just spent two years traveling in Africa![36]), I really didn't understand those who complained that Albania was boring or a "waste of time." I found it utterly, endlessly fascinating.

And, by the way, the food was fantastic.

Consider the capital, Tirana. While I had heard that it had been spiffed up in recent years—with former socialist block housing getting bright, whimsical coats of colorful paint and new developments popping up left and right—I wasn't prepared for just how sophisticated, even cosmopolitan, it is now. Still, there was just enough evidence of the former

---

[36] Admittedly, the public transport "system" can be a challenge, and the roads, away from the shiny new highways, are pretty rough-and-tumble. But everyone is keen to help you get where you need to be.

Tirana to give even a newcomer such as myself a clear understanding of how profound the transformation had been over the previous twenty years—most notably, the Pyramid.

But the towns that were really to capture my imagination and heart—Berat and Gjirokastra—were still to come in my Albanian journey.

***

As always, I did things a little backwards.

I should have read Ismail Kadare's *Broken April* before going to Shkodra, and then waited to read a *Chronicle in Stone* until just before coming to Gjirokastra. Instead, I finished *Chronicle in Stone* while in Shkodra and didn't pick up *Broken April* until Berat. I read *The Siege* before I even got to Albania, so that doesn't count.

Ismail Kadare, probably Albania's best-known writer and a frequent contender for the Nobel Prize in Literature[37], has produced a body of work that digs deeply into the Albanian soul and explores its often tortured past and present. I will admit that when I first read *The Siege*, set in the early days of the Ottoman conquest, I was not convinced that he deserved all the attention he had gotten. Although I knew the book was supposed to be a thinly veiled critique of the repressive communist regime under which he lived, I had a hard time getting past his very Orientalist depiction of the Ottomans who were besieging the unnamed, fictional Albanian city in the novel. Kadare seemed far more obsessed with the sexual predilections and perversions of his characters than with making a political statement. But that might just have been me.

However, I am glad I gave Kadare a second chance once I knew that I was going to visit Albania. I picked up *Chronicle in Stone*, and almost from the first line—"It was a strange city, and seemed to have been cast up in the valley one winter's night like some prehistoric creature that was now clawing its way up the mountainside."—I knew that I was going to enjoy the novel. *Chronicle in Stone* is set in the author's hometown of Gjirokastra, and takes place mostly during World War II. This was a time when many different forces occupied the city; two of particular note were Italy and Greece, between which control was volleyed back and forth, back

---

[37]   He did win the inaugural Man Booker International Prize in 2009.

and forth. His loving descriptions of the city and its quirky inhabitants captured my attention and solidified my plans to include Gjirokastra in my Albanian itinerary. Here's an evocative example:

> *It was a slanted city, set at a sharper angle than perhaps any other city on earth, and it defied the laws of architecture and city planning. The top of one house might graze the foundation of another, and it was surely the only place in the world where if you slipped and fell in the street, you might well land on the roof of a house—a peculiarity known most intimately to drunks.*

The Slanted City: Gjirokastra

Since I was reading *Chronicle in Stone* as I entered Albania and as I was exploring the northern city of Shkodra, I wasn't to know just how accurate Kadare's description of Gjirokastra truly was until almost the end of my journey through the country.

Shkodra is the *de facto* capital of the Gheg-speakers, one of the two main dialect groupings in Albania—the Ghegs dominate in the north and the Tosks dominate in the south. The Ghegs are especially identified with what might be the most (in)famous dimension of the Albanians' already unique culture: the blood feud. It sounds like a practice from the deepest depths of history, a practice rooted in an ancient code of honor and conduct. This code is called the Kanun, and it regulates almost every aspect of life. The Kanun's sway was, and is, especially strong in the mountains—which are called, appropriately, the Accursed—and high plateau of northern Albania, not far from Shkodra. As with the mountainous interior of Montenegro, the successive empires and occupation forces that have held sway in the region found it difficult to control this wild corner of the country. As a result, it is not surprising that the old traditions, including the terrifying cycle of vengeance that can be set off in a blood feud, remained strongest here.

I had heard about the Albanian blood feuds before I came to the country, but I had imagined it was a concept that was fading from the culture as Albanians become more integrated into the "modern" world. As it turns out, I was badly mistaken.

Indeed, just two weeks before I arrived in Skhodra, there was a double honor killing of two young men in a village just thirty minutes away. F., the guesthouse proprietor, informed me that there actually had been a resurgence in the practice since the fall of communism, especially in the north: "Albanians in the south, they are softer, they don't do these things as much." I found it difficult to square this deadly sense of honor with the obvious warmth and extreme hospitality of the Albanians I was meeting. How could they be so kind and giving with complete strangers and yet often be bound to kill each other over wrongs that had been committed sometimes generations earlier?

Bread and blood: two very different sides of the Albanian coin. Both these dimensions of Albanian culture, though, are expressed in the Kanun.

Obviously, I wanted to learn more about the blood feud after hearing all this in Shkodra. A fellow traveler who was wrapping up his time in Albania recommended that I pick up another of Kadare's novels, *Broken April*, to get a better understanding of the intricacies of the Albanian code of honor. Luckily, after crossing paths with Scott and Vanessa, an Australian couple that I had met in Sarajevo and that had just finished reading the novel, I was able to get my hands on an English translation of the book.

In *Broken April*, readers are introduced to the musing of Gjorg, a young man who has been charged with avenging the murder of his brother, part of a seventy-year-old conflict between his family and another, a feud that had already consumed forty-four lives:

> *He tried to call to mind families that were not involved in the blood feud, and he found no special signs of happiness in them. It even seemed to him that, sheltered from that danger, they hardly knew the value of life, and were the more unhappy for that. Whereas clans that were in the blood feud lived in a different order of days and seasons, accompanied as it were by an inner tremor; the people were more handsome, and the young men were in favor with the women.*

Kadare, uses Gjorg's story and his reactions to the forces of the blood feud to explain the power of this tradition. Without glorifying it, he manages to unearth the chilling logic of the system and how it involves protecting the honor not only of the living but also of their ancestors. Even as a complete outsider—and pacifist!—I was able to see why it would be so hard for some families to break from the cycle, even today.

For their sake, however, I hope the Albanians will be able to set aside the blood feud and concentrate instead on burnishing their reputations as some of the world's most gracious hosts.

By the time I reached Gjirokastra, I was about halfway through *Broken April*; I was immersed in the now-distant northern Albanian landscapes it describes and the period in which it is set, the fleeting years of the Kingdom of Albania between the world wars. Yet I was, at the time, wandering the cobbled streets of Gjirokastra, Kadare's "slanted city." I experienced both a geographic and temporal dissonance, I think.

When I was in Shkodra, I could only imagine Gjirokastra's staircase stack of houses based on the images found within the pages of *Chronicles of Stone*, but once I got there I saw fully what Kadare meant about slipping and falling onto a roof. This city, the birthplace of both Ismail Kadare and of the ruthless Enver Hoxha, was even lovelier—and more sloping!—than I had pictured. The city's gentle rhythms seemed a universe away from the pointed violence of the northern blood feuds about which I was reading.

Perhaps it's a good thing that I tackled the two novels in the order I did. By reading *Chronicle in Stone* before visiting Gjirokastra, I was better able to conjure the city as it was during Kadare's childhood and to appreciate all that still remains from that period. Oddly, however, the writer's own house is essentially an unmarked, empty shell; it is crying out to be restored. And, because I read *Broken April* after spending time in Shkodra, I wasn't influenced to see death around every corner.

Whatever the case, these two novels enriched my stay in Albania immeasurably. I am glad I gave Kadare a second—and third—chance.

***

Not since Bosnia and Herzegovina were the Ottoman "ghosts" I had sought as vividly solid as those that I experienced in Albania. In some ways, this is not so surprising, considering that Albania, like Bosnia, is one of the rare Balkan states to have a significant local Muslim population (in Albania, it is a solid majority) and was under Ottoman rule for nearly five hundred years. Yet this is also the country that was ruled by Enver Hoxha, one of the twentieth century's most notorious dictators, who ruled Albania with a choking grip from 1944-1985. During those forty-one years, Hoxha not only did his best to isolate Albania from much of the world (with the interesting exception of developing an alliance with China, rather than the U.S.S.R.), he also managed to unleash considerable destruction on the cultural heritage of his country. He went so far as to ban religion outright, something not even the other communist regimes in Eastern Europe were bold enough to do. So it was a welcome surprise to see just how much of Albania's Ottoman past is still extant, not only in the physical remains of some of the best preserved Ottoman towns I have seen (even compared to those in Turkey), but also in the stories that Albanians tell of their history.

As with the rest of the Balkans, the Ottoman history of Albania is complex. The Ottomans first began to acquire territory in what is now southern Albania as early as 1385, and were firmly ensconced by 1415. Gjirokastra was made the capital of the *sancak* of Albania just a few years later. But it wasn't all smooth sailing for the Ottomans in the fifteenth century.

I didn't have to spend much time in Albania before I saw images of and heard stories (many, many stories) about the Albanians' favorite historical figure, a man who has been turned into something of a national demi-god: George Kastrioti—oddly, also known by the very Ottoman name and title, Skanderbeg (from Iskender Bey). Born into a prominent Albanian landowning family who had become Ottoman vassals, Kastrioti was sent to the Ottoman capital as a royal "hostage" where he trained to become an Ottoman official, converting to Islam in the process. He was even appointed to be the governor of the *sancak* of Dibra (a territory that included parts of what is now Macedonia as well as parts of Albania), and fought for the Ottoman Empire for nearly twenty years. All this is largely glossed over in the current nationalist narrative, however.

What matters most to Albanian nationalists is what Skanderbeg did from 1443 until his death in 1468—the period when he not only renounced his Ottoman ties but also actively fought against the empire. From his capital in Kruja, in the mountains just outside of modern Tirana, Skanderbeg led a number of successful campaigns that drove the Ottomans out of much of northern Albania. He even withstood three direct sieges (which was possibly the fodder for Ismail Kadare's novel *The Siege*). Although the Ottomans were able to reassert their authority over all of Albania following his death, at which point they ruled relatively uninterruptedly until 1912, Albanians now look to this ex-Ottoman as a symbol of Albanian resistance to non-Albanian leadership—no matter who the leaders might be. F., the guy with whom I tussled on the Muslim-Christian relations issue, actually said something along the lines of: "The E.U. should appreciate Albania more. Skanderbeg saved Europe from Islam!" So, according to this logic, even though Albania eventually "succumbed," it at least provided a bulwark against the further spread of the dreaded Ottoman Muslims!

Today, in Kruja, in the remains of Skanderbeg's castle, there is a not-so-subtle museum devoted to the man. When I entered the building I was confronted by a twice life-size relief sculpture of the warrior, surrounded by his fellow "freedom" fighters. A replica of his helmet and sword hold a place of special honor in the museum's collection: the real deals are held somewhere in Vienna, much to the Albanians' collective chagrin.

Elsewhere, Skanderbeg's name is used to label roads, squares, and various Albanian products (Skanderbeg rakija, anyone?). Even a gas station chain uses his name—but in the unfortunate variant, Kastrati.

***

In almost every town I visited in Albania—not just Kruja—there is a fortress of some sort. Which certainly says something about Balkan history right from the start.

Many of these castles/forts pre-date the Ottomans, as many are of Byzantine origin, but the Ottomans claimed these fortifications as they solidified their hold over Albania and made them their own. More interestingly, at least for me, the fortresses became the central points of new (or at least revitalized) towns with very Ottoman forms. The two best preserved of these Ottoman-era Albanian fortress-towns are Berat and Gjirokastra, both of which are postcard-beautiful examples of the genre (though both are surrounded by the not-so-beautiful socialist constructions of the Hoxha-era).

Gjirokastra was saved from destruction during the reign of Enver Hoxha, largely due to the fact that it was his hometown. But why Berat was spared remains a mystery to me. I am extremely thankful that it happened, but when so much else was destroyed, how did its tumble of stone-and-timber homes survive? Why was it designated a "cultural monument" and other towns not? No one seems able to explain it.

I was especially happy to see that the interior treasures of many of Berat's buildings were also preserved. Actually, the city was full of wonderful surprises behind what were often fairly plain doors. On my first evening, I was wandering aimlessly around the Kalasa neighborhood within the Berat castle walls—one of the few such neighborhoods that is still a lived-in space, not just a museum—and stumbled on the Onufri Museum.

I vaguely remembered having read about a museum of Byzantine icons in Berat, but had not planned on visiting it just then. But since I was there, why not?

When I entered the museum, I found that it was actually an old Byzantine church—and in the main worship hall there was one of the most beautiful Orthodox iconostases I had ever laid eyes on. I hardly knew where to look first, as the iconography was so dense and rich in detail, set in a luminescent paneling of dark wood and gilt. Eventually, my gaze settled on Saint George, golden haloed and red caped, spearing an unlucky soul. I thought: we of Protestant background sure have missed out on the church décor front!

But I think my favorite such Berati surprise was the unassuming Helveti Sufi tekke at the base of the fortress hill. When I looked through its windows, all I could see were plain white walls. However, a man with a key appeared out of nowhere and ushered me inside, then pointed upwards. My mouth dropped open.

The ceiling was a masterpiece of interlocking wood paneling, richly and intricately painted. So too was the gorgeous upper gallery, ringed with the ninety-nine names of God. It was one of the loveliest examples of interior artistry that I had seen in any religious building—and I would never have known it was there had it not been for a bit of luck.

At that moment, as I stared upward, I could have left Albania and been happy. I figured I had seen the best of what the country had to offer on the Ottoman front. But I am glad I pushed on.

***

I really didn't think I could top Berat, but after a very bumpy, extremely cramped four-hour bus trip through central Albania, I laid eyes on Gjirokastra and fell instantly in love. Before getting out of the bus, I had already decided I'd stay at least an extra day than I had planned.

Described beautifully in Kadare's *Chronicle in Stone*, as I've already explained in some detail, Gjirokastra is stunningly situated on the steep slopes, ridges, and valleys just beneath one of the largest castle-fortresses in the Balkans. The houses, an interesting mix of traditional Ottoman mingled with local flavor, are practically stacked one on top of the other due to the steep terrain. The whole complex looks over an expansive valley and sharply rising line of mountains. Even Berat didn't quite have this natural-and-architectural "total package" beauty (though it, too, was pretty darn amazing!).

While Gjirokastra doesn't possess as many specific historical and cultural sites as its Ottoman sister, Berat, it manages to convey a greater sense of a living and breathing Ottoman town. It most definitely is not a museum. Even the guesthouse where I stayed has been in the owner's family since Ottoman times. This small city proved a fitting endpoint to my travels in Albania.

Next stop: Macedonia.

THE MACEDONIAN
QUESTION: MACEDONIA

There was still a bit of a morning chill as I sat down at the café. A few other men were already huddled over small cups of coffee or tulip-shaped glasses of tea. A delivery boy shuttled back and forth from the shop to his bike, deftly balancing a hanging tray in one hand, steering with the other, as he delivered hot beverages to the surrounding neighborhood. I ordered a *türk kahvesi* from the waiter. It was just like my usual spot back "home" in Ortaköy in Istanbul.

Except I was not in Istanbul. I was in Ohrid, Macedonia.

***

During my travels in 2012, it had been easy for me to see the impact of the Ottoman Empire on the western Balkans. There were the obvious physical remains—the mosques (some derelict, others very much still in use), the hamams (often turned into restaurants, art galleries, etc.), the hans/caravansarays (turned into restaurants and souvenir shops), even whole towns (Berat and Gjirokastra, among others)—as well as the less tangible, though still obvious, influences on the kaleidoscope of Balkan cultures. Not least of all on the types and names of all the delicious foods I encountered!

But I don't think I'd felt the presence of the Ottoman era as acutely as I did when I arrived in Macedonia. Which, I must say, came as something of a surprise to me.

It took me a few days to figure out why Macedonia's Ottoman-ness felt so, well, Ottoman. I think a large part was the simple fact that modern Turkey seemed closer than anywhere else that I had been in the Balkans—this was due not only to the geography of the area (I had been just as close to when I had been in southern Serbia), but also to the presence of a substantial Turkish minority in the country. For example, I regularly heard

Turkish on the streets of Ohrid and Skopje, and I was able to dust off my own language skills when I ordered at restaurants or asked directions. When I was in Skopje, I was even approached once and asked a question in Turkish: the man had assumed that I was a Turk, too! Moreover, Turkish businesses and products (Halkbank, Ülker, Mado) were more prominent in these locations than anywhere else I had traveled in the region.

However, I realized quickly that the Ottoman connection went deeper than the occasional sense that I had been transported to present-day Turkey.

Turkey is Close

One of the things that initially drew me to the Ottoman Empire was its great diversity—ethnic, linguistic, cultural, religious. With the emergence of nationalism in the nineteenth century and the dissolution of the empire into a gaggle of separate nation-states (often accompanied by population transfers), that diversity all but disappeared. I often say that I wish I could have experienced Istanbul before World War I, when the city still had significant communities of Greeks, Armenians, Jews, various Slavs, and many others. Actually, the city had been less than fifty percent Muslim at the time, and there were dozens of languages heard on its streets. Nowadays, there are only vestiges of that earlier cosmopolitanism.

Obviously, in a region as mixed as the Balkans, it was particularly tough to draw national borders without including many people who didn't identify with the new national paradigms. Even tiny Montenegro has a large Albanian minority, as well as people who claim Serb and Bosnian identities (as opposed to Montenegrin). Macedonia has the same issue; not all people who reside in Macedonia fit the nationalist model of "Macedonian"—but defining who gets to be Macedonian is an even more slippery affair than determining the already fluid identities of other Balkan groups, especially the Slavs (see below). I think that this complexity stems from the fact that Macedonia is smack-dab in the center of the Balkan cultural mash-up—and is therefore more like what the Ottoman Empire used to be like.

Even in Skopje, the national capital with its current nationalism-fueled, monumentalist-building extravaganza, I heard Macedonian, Albanian, and Turkish spoken in the cafés; I also saw signs in two or three of those languages posted throughout the city. It's a polyglot society that is surely somewhat reminiscent of the old Ottoman Skopje.

Of course, the physical reminders of Ottoman rule in Skopje are also numerous and intriguing: the remains of Ottoman markets and travelers' inn (a testament to Macedonia's central position in the trade routes in the Balkans); the hamams; and some beautiful, unusual mosques, such as the Sultan Murad Mosque—one of the largest in the Balkans—and the Yahya (or Jahja) Pasha Mosque, which is topped with a pyramid-shaped roof rather than the more typical Ottoman dome. When I turned my back on the sometimes bizarre structures being erected in the town center,

I could almost imagine Ottoman Skopje while I wandered through the older parts of town.

***

Other than Ohrid and Skopje, the Ottoman bookends to my time in Macedonia, I had a bit of an Ottoman surprise in the middle of my trip: Bitola.

I ended up in Bitola almost by accident. On the recommendation of Vanessa and Scott, the Australian couple I first met in Sarajevo, I had decided to add a stay of a few nights in a special guesthouse in the village of Dihovo, at the edge of Pelister National Park. However, due to my own calendar-challenged timing, I had made a reservation at the guesthouse for the wrong month. When I showed up at their door, they were surprised to see me—and in the end they only had a room to offer me for one night. A little bummed, I decided I would spend a night down in nearby Bitola, just to get a feel for another Macedonian town. I'd heard it was nice.

Somehow, I had never registered the fact that Bitola was the former Manastır, which had been one of the most important cities in the Ottoman territories of the southern Balkans, particularly in the nineteenth and early-twentieth centuries. Indeed, it had been known as the "city of consuls," since a number of diplomatic missions had maintained consulates here, and it was where Atatürk, the founder of modern Turkey, had finished his formal schooling. It should have been a must on my Ottoman itinerary. However, my sense of where the old Manastır was situated had been fuzzy at best. That is, until I began walking the streets of Bitola and saw the vestiges of its Ottoman past—including Mustafa Kemal's military high school. I thought to myself: "Ah, so *that*'s where I am!"

I could have easily breezed through Bitola on my way from Ohrid to Skopje and missed this lovely and important Ottoman-era city. It was a "ghost" with a new name.

My experiences in Macedonia taught me to be extra vigilant in my search for the echoes of the Ottoman Empire in today's Balkans. They proved that some of the region's "ghosts" are often very much alive... and that others are often hiding behind (or within?) other historical phantoms.

***

Macedonia is at once both world famous—or, more accurately, infamous—for its bitter row with Greece over its use of the name "Macedonia" and all but forgotten due to the dramatic history and political drama of the rest of the Balkans. I contend that this combined infamy and obscurity sums up Macedonia's position geographically, historically, politically, and culturally in the region.

First, there is the matter of the name. As I have already noted frequently, history is felt with an often intense immediacy in the Balkans. Something as simple as a name can become a fierce rallying point for one group of nationalists—or, more often than not, multiple groups. "Macedonia" is perhaps the most notorious example in the Balkans.

In its broadest geographic sense, "Macedonia" applies to the area that roughly corresponds to today's independent Macedonia; the northern part of Greece (also called Macedonia); and parts of Bulgaria, Albania, and Kosovo. The name first gained currency as the name of a small kingdom that wielded real power under the leadership of Philip II (r. 359-336 BCE)—the father of Alexander of the Great. You might have heard of him. Of course, this was a political entity that existed thousands of years ago and that has no significant connection to any of the states that now occupy the region. But because ancient Macedonia produced one of the most famous historical figures of all time, the name has taken on a symbolic weight that is far out of proportion to its workaday five syllables.

When Yugoslavia began to disintegrate in the early nineties and Macedonia became an independent state—something it achieved peacefully, unlike almost all of its fellow Yugoslav republics—it was immediately attacked by Greece for its "illegitimate" use of the name Macedonia. Greece claimed that the term was historically and rightfully Greek, since Alexander was not only a product of Greek culture but had also Hellenized much of the known ancient world during his powerful if brief reign. For most Greeks, Alexander is Greek. Full stop. And thus the name Macedonia, too, is properly Greek. It was, therefore, impossible for a group of Slavic speakers to be real Macedonians.

Of course, all this ignores the fact that ancient Macedonia wasn't—at least not at first—technically part of the "Greek" world of squabbling city-states, which included most famously the great rivals, Athens and Sparta. In fact, Philip II took advantage of the political strife in the Hellenic realm to conquer most of the city-states and incorporate them into his kingdom. He did admire Greek culture and learning, however, and cultivated these in his court. He even managed to hire the services of Aristotle to tutor his precocious son.

Thus, when Alexander succeeded his father, he was not the master of "Greece" (which didn't really exist as a separate state, and definitely not as a nation) but of a hybrid Greco-Macedonian kingdom. The massive empire he created continued that process of hybridization, in which Greco-Macedonian culture blended with that of the other areas that Alexander now ruled. There was not a simple imposition of Greek mores on, say, Egypt, where the Greco-Macedonian rulers actually adopted the role of pharaoh and even had themselves mummified when they died (although using Greek-style portraiture to identify their mummies). So, at most one can say Alexander was Hellenic; he was not Greek in the modern national sense.

Still, this didn't stop Greece from demanding that Macedonia change its name. As a compromise, Macedonia had to officially call itself— bizarrely—the Former Yugoslav Republic of Macedonia (FYROM). Now, though, as Macedonia has gained greater confidence as an independent state in the international community, it is asserting its right to call itself simply the Republic of Macedonia.

But who were the ancient Macedonians, then, if they weren't exactly "Greek"? That's a tough question. It is perhaps easiest to say it was anyone who happened to live within the fluctuating borders of the Kingdom of Macedonia in the middle of what is now called the Balkans. As is the case today, the Balkans of old were a crossroads that brought a bewildering array of peoples, each of whom left their mark (and often their language). Slavic speakers probably entered the region in the sixth century C.E., but they would have intermingled over time with speakers of ancient Greek, Illyrian, Romance, and so forth. Sometimes, conceding that such mixing occurred, nationalists will lay claim to a group that now speak a different language as being co-nationals who were led linguistically astray. For example, some Greeks might claim that Macedonians are really just Slavicized Greeks (not unlike the religious appropriation that occurs in Bosnia, where Bosniaks are often considered Islamized Serbs or Croats). Macedonians are even claimed by other Slavic groups, especially Bulgarians, who claim them as "little" Bulgarians.

Perhaps because of all these attempts to usurp their identity, Macedonians today are now actively asserting themselves as a distinct people, a distinct nation. Hardcore Macedonian nationalists make claim to the glory days Alexander the Great. They have even erected a not-so-subtle statue of their national hero in the center of Skopje, much to the fury of Greek nationalists. Perhaps it's a bit of overcompensation, but I suppose it is an understandable reaction to all the fuss over who gets to claim "Macedonia" and who gets to be a "Macedonian."

What is less understandable for me is why Macedonia is so often forgotten outside the debacle of the name debate.

Macedonia is the underappreciated crossroads of the southern Balkan region, and is often seen by travelers as a nothing more than a country through which to transit to other countries—with possible stopovers in Skopje and Ohrid, made for no other reason than to be able to say that they had been in Macedonia. Even during the Yugoslav era, it was the poorest republic in the federation: Croatia, Slovenia, and Serbia—even Bosnia—were far more industrialized, while Macedonia remained largely an agricultural backwater. When it gained independence, there were none of the landgrab attempts that occurred in other parts of the former Yugoslavia. Actually, Macedonia's transition to independence was perhaps the most peaceful of any of the republics.

This is likely part of the reason why some visitors seem less interested in visiting Macedonia than some of its neighbors; it might be seen as too "easy," even boring. Bosnia, for example, has a certain edge due its recent war. Albania retains a reputation as an "unexplored," almost lawless territory. But Macedonia? Isn't that the place that Greece doesn't like?

I think this sense of Macedonia being somehow a "second class," or less exciting, Balkan destination inadvertently seeped into my subconscious, influencing my opinion of the country before I arrived. It was the country to which I gave the least thought in terms of planning my Balkan tour.

Yet once I crossed the border, I realized just how wrong I had been.

First of all, Macedonia is remarkably beautiful. It is perhaps only because it shares the Balkan neighborhood with countries like Montenegro and Albania, which are famed for their dramatic mountain-scapes, that its own mountain and forest scenery get short shrift in tourist guides. But my hike on Mount Pelister had me ohhing and ahhing the whole way; it was perhaps the most bucolic, serene excursion into nature I had made since I arrived in the Balkans.

Macedonia also has plenty of historical sights to keep one busy, sights that are not just limited to the many Byzantine churches and monasteries of Ohrid. I, of course, was particularly taken with the Ottoman wonders of Bitola and Skopje.

But even more importantly, Macedonia's relatively peaceful transition to independence belies the fact that it was at the very heart of the upheaval that wracked the region starting in the late nineteenth century, then continuing with Balkan Wars in the early twentieth century. Macedonia was an important—maybe even the most important—nodal point in the region during the waning years of Ottoman rule and the rise of Balkan nationalisms. It was even the site of the first semi-successful uprising against the Ottomans, the so-called Ilinden Uprising of 1903, which took place near Bitola. After World War I, the territory was divvied up between Serbia, Bulgaria, and Greece—everyone wanted a piece of the Macedonian pie.

Yet all of its fascinating history seems to have been forgotten by the world outside the Balkans. The "Macedonian Question" that so consumed the Balkans and the Great Powers at the turn of the twentieth century, a mere hundred years ago, is now mostly a local concern.

I definitely think that Macedonia deserves far more attention than it gets: it clearly represents the crazy complexity of Balkan history, politics, and culture. It was there that the Turkish, the Greek, the Slavic, and the Albanian realms overlapped (and still do!), and it was there—or at least around there—that the questions of national identity in the Balkans were most fiercely argued.

THE BATTLE OF, AND FOR, KOSOVO

The bus dropped me off at the side of the new highway, about six miles north of Pristina, somewhere in the middle of nowhere. There was no town, just me and miles of rolling plain. But just over a slight rise in the flatness, I could see the top of a grim, dark tower: my destination.

I trudged up the dirt road to the gate of the Gazimestan Memorial, where two bored police guards stirred to life upon seeing a lone American approaching. With warm smiles they asked for my passport and wrote down my details. For what purpose, I wasn't really sure. Then they waved me into the memorial grounds.

After scratching my head over the meaning of the Serbian inscription adorning the tower[38], I climbed the twisting staircase inside and emerged into the bright autumn sun. I looked out over the plain, which was mostly given to agricultural purposes, and two enormous power stations billowing white smoke. A faint line of mountains ringed the horizon, obscured a bit in the morning haze. It wasn't the most dramatic scene I'd ever seen, but I still got serious chills.

Because on that plain, now dominated by cows and power plants, the Battle of Kosovo had unfolded.

***

---

[38] I discovered later that the inscription is the so-called "Kosovo Curse," supposedly uttered by Prince Lazar (though apparently it's actually from a 1845 nationalist adaptation of the original):
> Whoever is a Serb and of Serb birth
> And of Serb blood and heritage
> And comes not to the Battle of Kosovo,
> May he never have the progeny his heart desires!
> Neither son nor daughter,
> May nothing grow that his hand sows!
> Neither dark wine nor white wheat.
> And let him be cursed from all ages to all ages!

The keenest of my readers may have noticed that during my western Balkans tour I circled the tiny, newborn country of Kosovo. When I started planning my trip, I didn't really think of Kosovo in special terms; it was simply going to be part of my itinerary because it was one of the former Ottoman territories in the western Balkans. But it wasn't long before I realized that Kosovo was going to be absolutely central to my plans, for many reasons.

Most practically, I had to be careful about when I visited Kosovo in relation to Serbia, which doesn't recognize Kosovo's independence. You can't enter Serbia from Kosovo if you have crossed the Kosovo border from another country, as Serbia will consider you as having entered its territory illegally. And it can be problematic if you try to visit Serbia later if you already have a Kosovo stamp in your passport.

So, I had to visit Serbia before going to Kosovo. But when was I going to slot Kosovo in? Between Montenegro and Albania or Macedonia? Between Albania and Macedonia? Or, as I ultimately decided, near the end of my trip, just before I circled back to Trieste?[39]

As I wrestled with the sequence, it became ever clearer that Kosovo was the key to the whole trip. My interests in the Ottoman Empire and contemporary nationalism (as well as the intersection of these two) all come together in this tiny enclave in the middle of the Balkans.

Kosovo certainly has an impact on all of its neighbors far out of proportion to its size.

***

The year 1389 has a special significance in the Balkans, but most especially to the Serbs. In this year, a battle occurred on the high plain of Kosovo. This battle pitted the army of the newly emerging Ottoman Empire, which was under the leadership of Sultan Murad I,[40] against

---

[39] Trieste—the former Austro-Hungarian port that is now a sidelined Italian city all but surrounded by Slovenia—was my starting and ending point for my travels in the western Balkans. It was certainly an appropriately frontier city from which to reflect on the Ottoman world that begins just at its doorstep.

[40] Murad I was really the first true Ottoman sultan: he expanded his family's holdings across Anatolia and into the Balkans and established a genuine empire. He was only the third Ottoman ruler, coming after Osman I (who gave his name

the combined forces of various Serbian and other Balkan principalities/ kingdoms, which were headed by Prince Lazar Hrebeljanović.

While there are few reliable sources regarding the Battle of Kosovo, what is known is that both sides lost a considerable percentage of their forces as well as both of their leaders. In a normal world, this would have been considered at best a draw. But many Serbians now, interestingly, cast the battle as a defeat—*and* as a key component of their national mythology.

I have to admit that I found it strange that Serbians would grant their supposed loss at the Battle of Kosovo such importance. But over the course of my travels, I began to get a sense of the reasons why. It's not so much about who won or lost, but more about how the Serbs fought and where—the place they see as the cradle of their civilization. The battle is now presented as the example *par excellence* of Serbian bravery in the face of the arriving Turkish-Muslim "hordes." They were decimated in their attempt to save the Balkans from the growing Ottoman Empire, but gave the powerful new force a run for its money.

Ultimately—despite Sultan Murad I's own death at the hand of a Serbian warrior, Miloš Obilić, and the heavy losses his army suffered at the Battle of Kosovo—Ottoman expansion into the Balkans continued. Even before they had captured the crown jewel of the former Byzantine world, mighty Constantinople, in 1453, the Ottomans were well established in the area that now includes most of what is modern Serbia, Kosovo, Albania, Bosnia and Herzegovina, Macedonia, Greece, Bulgaria, and Romania— essentially, most of the Balkans.

Thus, for the Serbs (and others), the Battle of Kosovo began the nationalist narrative of five-hundred-plus years of "Turkish" oppression. And the reverberations of the Serbs' defeat are felt with remarkable strength in the much more recent political turmoil that bedevils present-day Kosovo—a sort of battle *for* Kosovo, if you will.

1389 might have been more than six hundred years ago, but I would never have known it when I spoke to the people in Serbia or (even more obviously) Kosovo. The Battle of Kosovo is central to the debate over the legitimacy of Kosovo's declaration of independence from Serbia, and in

---

to the dynasty) and Orhan I. The first two rulers were beys—though both are now referred to as sultans.

many respects the story of the battle was what fueled the political forces that led to the dissolution of Yugoslavia as a whole.

On June 28, 1989, in commemoration of the six-hundredth anniversary of the Battle of Kosovo, Slobadan Milošević gave an infamous speech at the base of the Gazimestan memorial. In that speech, he drew comparisons between current political and economic issues in Yugoslavia (and, in particular, in Kosovo) and the Battle of Kosovo. The speech's backdrop was the growing conflict between the Albanian majority—who had been the majority in Kosovo since at least the nineteenth century, but who became even more so during the twentieth—and the Serbs—who felt increasingly besieged by the growing Albanian population in what they still considered their land.

Because of its contentious ethnic make-up, Kosovo had been granted some degree of autonomy within the federal structure for much of the Yugoslav era, but it was never designated a full republic and remained connected to Serbia. In the 1980s, Kosovar Albanian nationalists began to agitate for greater self-governance (and even independence), while Serbs wanted greater ties to Serbia. Tensions rose, and conflict between Albanians and Serbs became increasingly heated and violent.

By 1989, Milošević, who was by then president of Yugoslavia, pushed through an amendment to the Yugoslav constitution that stripped Kosovo of most of its previous autonomy, which enflamed the anger of Kosovar Albanians. A couple of months later, he delivered his Gazimestan speech. The stage was set for the nationalism-fueled conflicts that began to rip Yugoslavia asunder just a few years later.

Interestingly, Kosovo, the Yugoslav territory where Yugoslavia's breakup symbolically got its start, was the last to achieve independence; it was recognized only in 2008. Only South Sudan (also of the Ottoman realm) is younger in the family of generally recognized states. Serbia, of course, refuses to accept the "secession."

***

But at what cost did Kosovo's independence come?

The same day that I had visited Gazimestan, I hopped on a bus to head to Mitrovica, a large, important town in northern Kosovo—and the center of the continuing standoff between Serbia and Kosovo.

Shortly after I arrived, I walked up to the bridge that crosses the Ibar River. It was almost empty, except for a lone, stray dog that was wandering aimlessly across the pavement. This bridge, blocked by a pile of rubble to prevent vehicular traffic, marks the boundary between the Serbian enclave to the north and the Albanian majority in the south. Serbian flags flutter densely on the northern side. U.N. and armored police vehicles guard the "border," maintaining an uneasy truce.

In Pristina, Kosovo's lively capital, one can easily forget the recent war (except for the very noticeable absence of Serbs). But in Mitrovica the war really hasn't finished. I could feel the tension in the air. Where once Albanians and Serbs had lived together, they now live in separate quarters and under different political jurisdictions. They watch each other warily across the Ibar, each convinced that they are in the right.

Before I retreated from the bridge, I noticed some graffiti spray-painted onto the aluminum siding of one the Serbian guard posts. I couldn't help noticing the number, traced in vivid red: 1389.

***

There are two burial spots/tombs situated at the edge of the territory where the Battle of Kosovo took place, both within walking distance from Gazimestan. The one that is closest to the memorial, looking lonely in the barren landscape, is the recently renovated Bayraktar Tomb, the resting spot of Sultan Murad I's fallen flag bearer. A bit further away, a half-hour hike along the new highway, the Sultan's own tomb-complex rises from the plain (although it is partially hidden by new construction).

Tomb of the Flag Bearer of Sultan Murad I

This tomb, recently renovated with help from Turkey, represents something of a counterbalance to the Serbian nationalist version of the Battle of Kosovo story.

A family called the Türbedars (the very name a reference to their profession), originally from distant Bukhara, has guarded the tomb since it was built shortly after the battle. Today, the complex that they maintain is a leafy refuge that memorializes Murad I. Here, he is presented not as the murderous villain out to destroy the Serbs and to conquer the "civilized" Christian world, but rather as the important Ottoman leader who made the Ottoman state into an empire. Here he is, a leader cut down in his prime—what more would he have been able to accomplish had he not been "murdered" by a Serb opportunist? It's a very different narrative of the Battle of Kosovo.

But as my guide—who was not, alas, a Türbedar—said, history in the Balkans is never really just history.

"History, it is policy."

PART II

The Eastern Balkans
and the Black Sea

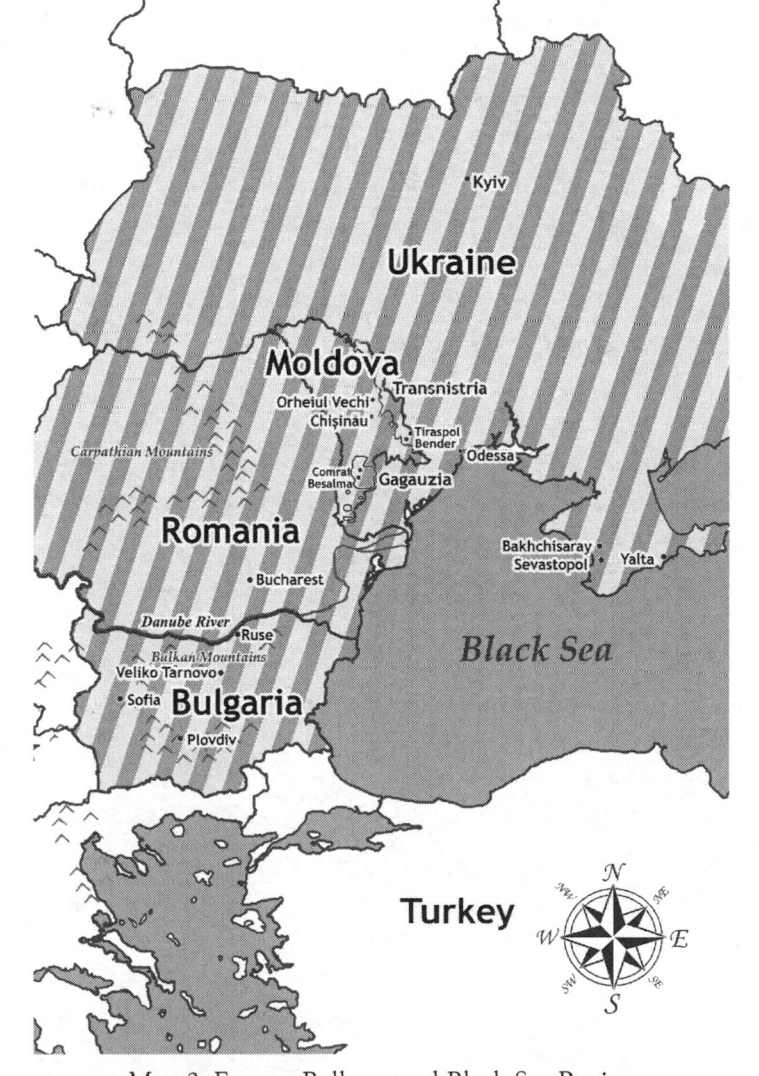

Map 3: Eastern Balkans and Black Sea Region

During my senior year at Cornell, 1995-1996, I took a course on the International Relations of the Former Soviet Union; this was a fascinating opportunity considering the U.S.S.R had only dissolved a few years previously. For my final research paper, I decided to focus on the smallest, least known of the former republics, Moldova, a country that few people (even now) could find on the map. Despite—or more likely because of—its relative obscurity, I found myself intrigued by this young country that managed to combine my interests in both Soviet and Ottoman history. That it was riven by not one, but two separatist movements just added to the allure.

I finally got to visit Moldova in 2013—and was able to dip into both of its separatist territories: the wonderfully named Gagauzia (which has achieved a certain peace with Moldova proper by agreeing to autonomy without full independence) and the Trans-Dneistr Republic, also known more simply as Transnistria (which remains officially at war with Moldova, although there has been no real fighting since the mid-nineties, and people routinely travel between the two territories). You also will remember that I passed through the old Ottoman town of Bender in Transnistria—the temporary home to a certain Swedish king I discussed in the preface to this book.

My visit to Moldova was part of a broader sweep around the Black Sea, a trip that started in Istanbul—all Ottoman roads lead to it, of course—and progressed by land through Bulgaria, Romania, Moldova, and Ukraine. Although I continued to Georgia (which required that I fly across Russia, due to the near impossibility of securing a transit visa and its closed borders with Georgia), I will wait to describe that portion of the journey until the Caucasus section.

Although these countries share proximity to the Black Sea as well as a past that is connected to the trade and cultural links that crisscrossed its waters and fed into the Mediterranean to the south, they are remarkably different from one another. There are the obvious linguistic differences— some are Slavic-speaking, such Bulgaria and Ukraine, while others are Romance-speaking, like Romania and Moldova. All are predominantly Orthodox Christian, but follow national churches.[41]

---

[41] Despite many decades of Soviet rule, when religion was officially discouraged, the various Orthodox churches have seen a resurgence in the years since independence and are closely linked with national identity, as I shall illustrate.

There are also major differences in how the various peoples think and talk about the Ottoman past. In part, this is indicative of how their specific territories were ruled by the Ottomans. In Bulgaria, the memory of Ottoman "occupation" is still vivid, and anti-"Turkish" sentiments are a major element of Bulgarian nationalism. In Romania and Moldova, there is little that remains to remind anyone that they were part of a set of Ottoman vassal states, although you might hear in passing that the origins of the original Dracula, Vlad the Impaler, were Ottoman.[42] On the other hand, in Ukraine, or at least in Crimea, there is a great sense of pride in the period of the Crimean Khanate, an ally and then part of the Ottoman Empire. The Crimean Tatars, deported by Stalin in 1944, were returning and rebuilding their cultural heritage in places like Bakhchisaray.

When I visited the Black Sea region in the spring of 2013, I had no inkling of what was going to unfold in Ukraine a year later. I watched the news in utter shock as Crimea, the focal point of my Ukrainian travels, took center stage in a political drama that pitted Ukraine and Russia against each other in a conflict straight out of the Cold War era. Russian-speaking Crimeans (likely with a little nudging from Moscow) declared independence, and then promptly turned around and asked to be united with Russia. Pro-Russian Separatists in other corners of Ukraine followed suit, resulting in what amounts to a civil war. The crisis is still not resolved. There were even calls from Transnistria to be absorbed by Russia, but its diminutive voice has been lost in the hubbub of the Ukrainian situation.

Much of what follows is based on the period when I was visiting, and so does not reflect on the current political situation

---

[42] Vlad III, or the Impaler (Țepeș in Romanian), was a prince from Wallachia, one of the Romanian territories that became vassals to the Ottomans. Vlad's father, Vlad II Dracul, in order to prove his loyalty to the Sultan, sent Vlad Junior and his brother, Radu cel Frumos, as royal "hostages" to the Ottoman court in 1442. This was not unlike the Albanian leader Skanderbeg's boyhood experience. Although both Vlad and his brother received a thorough Ottoman education, only Radu cel Frumos converted to Islam and entered Ottoman service. Vlad III returned to Wallachia after his father's death and became the new *voivoda*, initially with Ottoman support. But soon, and again like Skanderbeg, Vlad III turned against the Ottomans, fighting a series of wars and skirmishes with his former overlords. However, he was defeated by Ottoman forces—led by his brother Radu no less—in 1462. The family drama is stunning.

BACK TO THE BALKANS: BULGARIA

The approach to the city was not promising. A couple hours earlier I had wrangled with a xenophobic border agent who was deeply suspicious of all the visas and stamps in my passport—sorry, I like to travel! I then had passed one desolate, dilapidated village after another, all backdropped by a gray, rainy day. As the bus entered the city's outer limits, things didn't appear much better; at least not at first. I watched hulking, mostly abandoned communist-era factories and rows of depressing block housing slip by before I disembarked at the edge of the bus station.

But then, after a short taxi ride, I found myself standing in the middle of a stone-cobbled street, surrounded by lovely Ottoman-style homes that were painted in bright colors. Out of one of these—a mustard yellow, timber-framed structure—a woman emerged and said: "Welcome, James!"

I knew then that I was going to fall hard for Plovdiv and its many-layered history.

***

Plovdiv, the second largest city in Bulgaria, is one of the oldest continuously inhabited cities in Europe, with roots that reach back at least to ancient Thrace in the fourth century B.C.E. At that time, there was a fortified settlement called Eumolpias built on the crest of one of the three hills that now form the core of historical Plovdiv. The jumbled ruins of that Thracian town, just a two-minute walk from my "home," the Old Plovdiv Guesthouse, served as an atmospheric perch from which to scan almost the entirety of the present city, with remnants of its many incarnations still clearly visible in the urban sprawl.

The Thracian settlement was later conquered by Philip of Macedon—father of Alexander the Great—who expanded the city he named Philippopolis (this was perhaps an example for Alexander, who would go on to found quite a few Alexandrias). Next came the Romans, followed by their Byzantine successors. In the 1200s and early 1300s, the city switched hands frequently between the Byzantines and a series of Bulgarian leaders who ruled independent kingdoms in the area. However, by 1364 it had been conquered by the Ottomans, who renamed the city Filibe. It would remain Ottoman territory until 1885, seven years after the western part of present-day Bulgaria had already gained independence from the empire. Therefore, Plovdiv—one of the major cultural and political centers of the Bulgarian nationalist movement that is often referred to as the Bulgarian Revival—lost its chance at becoming the capital (Sofia, further west, took on that mantle).

The post-Ottoman years would prove to be a tumultuous period for the newborn (or reborn, depending on your view) Bulgaria; this period included a long stretch as an Eastern Bloc country under the firm tutelage of the U.S.S.R. until 1989. It also hasn't been smooth sailing since the fall of communism, even after Bulgaria became a member of the European Union in 2007. Plovdiv, an important city in the country, has weathered the political and economic crises of the twentieth and twenty-first centuries better than other towns. Yet, just a short drive away, one can find dying villages that are inhabited mostly by aging pensioners.

Each empire, each state, each ideology has left its mark on Plovdiv. It thus belongs to that class of city that I've come to realize is particularly appealing to me—cities that wear their history heavily but openly, all the layers visible, if not always easily juxtaposed.

***

The Museum of the Bulgarian Revival, also a short walk from my guesthouse, occupies one of the loveliest of the Bulgarian Revival mansions that are scattered through Plovdiv's Old Town. It was originally built for a rich merchant with the intriguing name, Georgi Kendindenoglu. While the focus of most of the museum's exhibits is on the Bulgarian struggle for independence from the Ottoman Empire, a small room on the ground floor is devoted to the earlier Ottoman periods, I think intended to set the stage for the national "revival" that was to come in the mid- to late-nineteenth century. Yet, just as the hybrid name of the original owner and the very structure of the house illustrate, the two components of the museum make for a fascinating, if perplexing, marriage.

The language of the national revival, with its appeal to romantic nationalism and the heroism of freedom fighters who aimed to liberate Bulgaria after five centuries of Ottoman Muslim rule[43], seemed to be, if not contradicted, at least complicated by the exhibits. The various displays glorified the city's supposedly peaceful cosmopolitanism during much of the Ottoman era, when the town was a rich center of trade that was inhabited not only by Bulgarian speakers, but also by Greeks, Armenians, Sephardic Jews, Roma, and (of course) Turkish-speaking Muslims. This part of the museum also drew attention to the assistance that various Ottoman sultans had given over the course of the nineteenth century toward the promotion of a distinct Bulgarian identity, most notably by allowing the establishment of Bulgarian language schools and creating a separate Bulgarian Orthodox Church with its own exarch—something the Greek Orthodox Patriachate resisted vehemently.[44] It might be said, even, that the very conditions that allowed for the emergence of a modern Bulgarian nationalist movement were, in part, due to the changing Ottoman system in which the Bulgarians lived and which the nationalists hoped to overthrow.

This is not to say the Bulgarian nationalists didn't have rightful grievances against the Ottoman state, but—as is so often the case with nationalisms in general, and those in the Balkans in particular—more recent issues were (and are) often cast in ancient terms. As the museum itself clearly showed, there was a time when the diverse peoples of Plovdiv managed to coexist and even thrive. The mansions of the wealthy Bulgarian, Greek, and Armenian merchants were built on an Ottoman model and then shaped to the emerging "Western" tastes of the nineteenth century—the same process that was reshaping Istanbul's architectural aesthetic in the same period. Nevertheless, the vision of the Bulgarian Revival ideologues required that cities like Plovdiv become more Bulgarian

---

[43] There were a series of Bulgarian kingdoms and empires in the region beginning shortly after the Slavic migrations that reshaped the ethnic and linguistic map of the Balkans in the 600-700s, some of which were quite powerful. It was to these past Bulgarian glories that the Bulgarian nationalists of the late Ottoman era looked.

[44] One of the first "new" Bulgarian Orthodox churches was established in Istanbul in 1849, very near the Greek Orthodox patriarchate. The original wooden structure was replaced by the famous cast iron Church of St. Stephen in 1898.

and less cosmopolitan. There needed to be a distinct other—and the Ottoman Turks, as the ones who had conquered the Balkans centuries earlier, became the obvious target.[45]

Ottoman Revival

Before I arrived in Plovdiv, I read somewhere that there used to be fifty mosques in the city. Considering the size of the pre-communist city, I had a hard time believing that figure. Indeed, today there are only two: the Dzhumaya (Arabic: *juma*) or Ulu Mosque, a grand three-domed mosque of the early Ottoman period that still functions as a mosque, and the unmarked, unused Imaret Mosque. However, once I saw a photo of turn-of-the-century Plovdiv, I understood that fifty might not have been an exaggeration. Where today there are row upon row of dreary socialist apartment blocks, there used to be a red-tiled community of

---

[45]   The Greek Orthodox clergy were in same ways the first target, as they were seen as trying to suppress the ancient Bulgarian church, which had been recognized as an autocephalous church in the tenth century—the oldest in the Slavic world. But the Ottoman rulers were cast as the ones who had allowed for Greek dominance in the first place.

Ottoman-style buildings, complete with a forest of minarets. It's rather gut-wrenching to think just how much of the city was wiped "clean" in the twentieth century. Luckily, the mansions in the old town remain, perhaps protected by the geography of the craggy peaks of the hill on which they rest, as well as the two previously mentioned mosques and one hamam (which is now a temporary art exhibition space).

As I have said of places like Istanbul, I wish I could have known Plovdiv during its earlier, more diverse, days. Plovdiv today is beautiful (with the exception of its grim suburbs) and full of warm, welcoming people. Yet as I walked the steep, cobbled streets admiring the Bulgarian Revival homes in the Old Town—homes once occupied by families of Bulgarian, Greek, and Armenian heritage—I found myself longing to experience its earlier Ottoman incarnation

***

I sometimes had to be slightly circumspect about my academic background as an Ottomanist while traveling in the Balkans. Not that I expected to be attacked or anything, but—as I have indicated many times—there are people in the Balkans, old and young, who often have very strong opinions about the Ottomans (or, as they frequently and somewhat erroneously call them, "Turks") and the era of Ottoman rule in the region. Indeed, over the course of my journey, I was subject to a number of fascinating harangues about the centuries of oppression inflicted on one nationality or another (see the chapter on Albania for a particularly captivating example).

So, as you might imagine, it was quite refreshing to meet a Bulgarian with a more tempered perspective—a guy named Velin, who served as my guide and driver to see the Bachkovo Monastery and Asenovgrad Fortress, as well as the Rhodope Mountains that serve as a backdrop to both sites. When he found out that I studied Ottoman history, he took a keen interest in finding out my perspective, as well as in explaining to me what he knew. Right off, he dismissed the strident tones of many nationalists who still talk of five hundred years of the "Turkish yoke": "It's normal for a strong empire to assert its authority. The Bulgarian empire was strong once, too. It stretched between the Black Sea, the Aegean, and the Adriatic. It dominated the people in the territories it conquered. Then Ottomans came along and they were stronger and took over. It's normal." Indeed.

Sometimes I feel like I come across as an Ottoman apologist, which is really not my intent. I just want people to examine the events that they discuss in all their complexity. Rarely are political and cultural conflicts—especially in a place as dizzyingly complicated as the Balkans—clear-cut. There are rarely "good guys" and "bad guys." Situations change constantly over time and place. People had, and have, remarkably fluid identities.

Even the Bulgarian identity, which might at first seem a bit easier to define than the muddle of former Yugoslav nationalities (Serbs, Croats, Bosnian Muslims, Montenegrins, etc.), is not so straightforward. For example, there are many Bulgarians who see Slavic Macedonians as part of the Bulgarian nation (and hence Macedonia as a part of "Greater Bulgaria"), even as many current Macedonians vehemently promote a separate identity. The earlier historical construction of the Bulgarian identity, however, is even more intriguing in my eyes.

Considering the importance given in the national narrative to the Bulgarian national struggle —or its "revival"—against the Ottoman "Turks," it is a little surprising to learn that the earliest use of the term "Bulgar" was first applied to a nomadic Turkic[46] group in Central Asia, much like the group that would give rise to the Ottomans; there was even a Bulgar khanate on the Volga River—hence the name, Bulgar. It appears that a group of these Bulgars migrated from the steppes north of the Black Sea into the Balkans in the late 600s C.E., defeating the Byzantines with the aid of Slavs who had already settled in the area. They soon established the first Bulgarian empire in the Balkans, which lasted from 681-1018.

The conquering Turkic Bulgars soon became slavicized, absorbed into the much larger Slavic-speaking population. The language that emerged during that time is now known as Old Bulgarian.[47] So, if this general

---

[46]   In order to distinguish the language and culture of Turkey from the broader linguistic and ethno-cultural realm of Central Asia, common practice is to use "Turkish" when referring to the language of Turkey and "Turkic" for related languages.

[47]   I should also note that the Bulgarians adopted Christianity in 864 under the Khan/Tsar Boris, accepting the Orthodox form of the Byzantine Empire—their sometime ally but more-often-than-not enemy. But they also were, as already noted, one of the first Slavic groups to establish an autonomous church, complete with their own patriarch. Reasserting their early independence from

sketch of the origin of present-day Bulgarians is accurate, they are really of mixed Turkic and Slavic heritage—not unlike many of the Turks in Turkey today, who due to the interminglings of the Ottoman era share little in common, at least appearance-wise, with the Turkic groups of Central Asia. So, really, Bulgarians and Turks are more alike than they are different.

With all this as background to my travels in Bulgaria, it was fascinating for me to observe how the past was represented in each of the spots I visited. Plovdiv was a good starting point, but each town I explored offered a new angle on the Ottoman-Bulgarian story.

After Plovdiv, I moved on to Veliko Tarnovo, a beautiful town that is situated on a dramatic, snaking curve of the Yatra River. This was an early capital of the Bulgarian Empire and has, off and on, served as an important political center for Bulgarians up to the present day. Not surprisingly, then, there are a fair number of important historical sites and monuments in Veliko Tarnovo that are dedicated to the Bulgarian nation. I wandered the impressive ramparts of the Tsarevets Fortress, a huge complex in which the Bulgarian royalty resided from 1185 to 1393, the year the Ottomans fully defeated the Bulgarian tsars. Just below the stronghold, by the river, there is the highly reconstructed Church of the Forty Martyrs, which served as the venue for Tsar Ferdinand's proclamation of full independence of Bulgaria from the Ottoman Empire in 1908.[48] One of the more recent monuments, an outsized communist-era monstrosity called the Asen's Dynasty Monument, glorifies, not so subtly, the second Bulgarian Empire that emerged after the Asen family defeated the Byzantine Empire in

---

the Greek-dominated Greek Orthodox patriarchate became a major rallying point for early Bulgarian nationalists.

[48] If you have paid attention to the dates in this chapter on Bulgaria, you might have noticed that there were several independence dates. This is due to the messy history of the Balkan conflicts and wars in the late nineteenth and early twentieth centuries, pre-World War I. In 1878, the region was divided into two parts, one a Bulgarian principality with its capital in Veliko Tarnovo (nominally under Ottoman suzerainty) and the other called Eastern Rumelia (including the city of Plovdiv), which remained an Ottoman province. Macedonia, which had been promised to Bulgaria in an earlier version of the treaty, also remained in Ottoman hands. Seeking "union" with Eastern Rumelia (and Macedonia), the newly independent Bulgaria fought in a series of wars that eventually led to the proclamation of a Bulgarian kingdom in 1908, when Eastern Rumelia was joined to the Bulgarian principality.

1186. Nearby is the Mother Bulgaria Monument that focuses on the later struggle with the Ottomans. Ironically, the "eternal" flame at the base of this monument, a flame that is supposed to burn in remembrance of all those who died fighting the Ottomans for Bulgarian freedom, was extinguished the day I visited. Symbolic?

My last stop in Bulgaria was Ruse, a city that is situated on the banks of the Danube just across from my next destination, Romania. Ruse, in outward form, is quite different from the Bulgarian towns I visited in the central and southern parts of the country. Although its architectural heritage is suffering a similar kind of neglect in these cash-strapped times, that architectural heritage is more inspired by Vienna than by Istanbul—even though the city was never under Habsburg rule.

It was, however, one of the most important trading points between the Austro-Hungarian and Ottoman Empires; after all, it was the major Ottoman port on the Danube River. Perhaps due to its regular contact with the "West," Ruse—called Ruschuk when it was under the Ottomans—became a major center for the Bulgarian Revival movement. When Bulgaria began to gain independence from the Ottoman state, the aesthetic model for developing the city turned even more markedly to the Habsburg capital.

Today, there are very few material remains from the Ottoman period—some discarded tombstones and one forlorn mosque next to a Muslim school (that bears half an Ottoman inscription above its main door). I found this near total silence about the town's important role as an Ottoman trading port to be rather deafening.

***

I hadn't been sure what I was going to make of Bulgaria before I arrived. I had dealt with echoes of its history while in the western Balkans, especially in Macedonia, when I traveled there in the late summer and early fall of 2012. I had also read about its important role in the Balkan Wars before the final breakup of the Ottoman Empire after World War I. Friends who had already visited gave it mixed reviews—loving it or hating it, with little feeling in between (not unlike Albania). And yet, the country was all but a blank for me before I arrived in Plovdiv. I left with a little more understanding, I hope, of its dramatic history—and with a keen desire to return. I might even come out as an Ottomanist more fully next time!

ONCE BITTEN: ROMANIA

As was true for the start of my trip to Bulgaria, my arrival in Romania was far from auspicious. The van from Ruse in Bulgaria had just arrived at the Romanian side of the border and the driver was asked to stop for some document checks. I decided to get out and stretch my legs a bit while we waited, then spied a currency exchange booth just a few meters away. I figured I might as well get some Romanian *lei* now while the border bureaucrats did their bureaucrating.

However, as soon as I stepped up to the window, I noticed that four or five not-so-friendly looking dogs had encircled me—and one, completely unprovoked, growled menacingly and took a lunge at my knee, snapping its sharp teeth. Thankfully, it didn't puncture my pants, and a loud yell was enough to get the pack to back off. Still, I was rattled. I had heard about the Romanian problem with wild dogs. But, really, I'm attacked three minutes after arriving? Welcome to Romania!

All of my negative feelings regarding the country, however, melted away almost as soon as I arrived in Bucharest. I came to the city with few expectations, as I considered it more of a rest stop on my way to Moldova[49], a place to get some errands done and not much more. My preconceptions—those dangerous things that I try so hard to fight against—had been colored by my studies of the Cold War, the Ceausescu era, and the 1989 revolutions[50], as well as by many a traveler's report that portrayed the city

---

[49]   Originally, I was planning on spending more time in Romania, but as a result of staying in Istanbul a bit longer than originally planned and making a return trip to Sarajevo, I lost some days on my Black Sea tour. I decided to postpone Romania until a future date, when I would be able to visit it properly. Now, having gotten a taste, I'm all the more excited to do so. At the very least, I need to return and trace the crazy story of Vlad the Impaler's Ottoman past.

[50]   In 2009, I had the pleasure of participating in a National Endowment for the Humanities (N.E.H.) summer seminar on the history and philosophy of the peaceful revolutions of 1989. While Romania's revolution was far from peaceful, it was included in our examination as a counterpoint to what unfolded in places

as, in a word, grim. Even guidebooks tend to be dismissive of the city, going so far as to suggest alternative entries to the country so that one will have a better first impression of Romania.

Thus, I was more than pleasantly surprised to find that, at least in its present form, Bucharest is a remarkably vibrant city with great character, and even beauty. Gone are the days of little or no electricity and food (during which Nicolae Ceausescu's wife, Elena, flew to Paris to get her hair done). Yes, there are the very visible reminders of one of the world's worst dictatorial regimes; the most visible of these is the jaw-droppingly gargantuan People's House or, as it is called now, the Palace of the Parliament, the second-largest administrative building in the world. Ceausescu ordered this marble monstrosity built after being "inspired" by the architectural "wonders" of Pyongyang and Beijing during a visit to North Korea and China in the early 1980s. Of the nearly nine thousand buildings in Bucharest, nearly 1/3 were destroyed to make way for the Palace, the Bulevardul Unirii (Unification Boulevard), and the surrounding complex of government and apartment buildings. He didn't live to see his hubristic dream completed, though; the white elephant was only finished in 1994, five years after Ceausescu was swept from power and executed. The building is mind-blowing—in all respects.

Yet what remains of the earlier Bucharest is truly lovely and is fast being renovated. Indeed, the city is full of amazing French Belle Époque and Neo-Romanian architecture, which reminded me of what an elegant city it had been in the nineteenth and early twentieth centuries. This had been, like it is today, a cultured urban center in the midst of an otherwise quite rural, agrarian country.

Sadly, Bucharest's Ottoman heritage seems to have been largely erased, even before Ceausescu's destructive edict. However, despite its important status as a political and economic center for the Ottoman vassal state of Wallachia (which included the presence of Ottoman officials), Bucharest apparently never possessed the trappings of a more typical Ottoman town or city: most notably, there were no mosques, hamams, or bazaars. So, even before the broad destruction wrought on the city by Ceausescu, there were

---

like Poland, East Germany, and Czechoslovakia. Most likely, this was due to the fact that there was a clear bad guy in Romania's case—Nicolae Ceausescu—whereas the government in, say, East Germany was largely faceless.

few outright classical Ottoman structures. The Ottoman past in Bucharest is thus barely a whisper. Actually, the only mention of the Ottomans I heard in Romania were the tales of Vlad the Impaler's ("Dracula's") valiant efforts to keep the empire at bay.

***

I was bitten by a dog—not Dracula—when I entered Romania; by the time I left, I had been "bitten" by an unexpected admiration for Bucharest and a desire to explore the wider country in depth. Once bitten, not twice shy.

MOLDOVA, MOREOVER

I was only one of three passengers on the creaking Soviet era train that chugged overnight from Bucharest to Chişinău. The surly conductor, possibly also Soviet era, seemed put out that she had to keep an eye on the random American traveler, though she spent most of her time smoking between the carriages anyway.

Somehow the emptiness was unsettling, so my sleep was fitful at best. As I lay in my bunk, rocking side to side with the uneven rhythm of the train, I found myself questioning this endeavor: why was I going to a place no one seemed to want to visit? A place that, according to one recent pop survey, was one of the unhappiest countries in the world? Why in the heck was I going to Moldova?

Yet I also knew I had been surprised by Bucharest. Perhaps Moldova would exceed expectations, as well.

I must have finally fallen asleep properly, because I was startled awake by a pounding at my compartment door. A smiling—smiling?—uniformed border guard asked for my passport and, without fuss, stamped my entry into Moldova. I had just entered the first of the former Soviet republics that I would visit during my Black Sea circuit.[51] As I looked out the window, I saw a sunny day and lovely, rolling farmland. Yes, just maybe, I was glad I had made the effort.

Modern Moldova corresponds roughly to a region once called Bessarabia, which in turn was a part of the Principality of Moldavia[52] (from which the current name is derived, obviously), one of the Romanian

---

[51] Moldova was, at that point, only the second former Soviet republic I had visited, despite my long time interest in the U.S.S.R. and my high school study of Russian. I had the opportunity to work with teachers at a school in Serdar, Turkmenistan for two weeks in 2008. Perhaps it's a little odd that the first ex-Soviet country I visited should be the most difficult to enter!

[52] Moldavia and Wallachia, the other Romanian principality, united in the mid-nineteenth century, which would form the basis of what now constitutes Romania.

vassal states within the Ottoman Empire. The region was separated from "Romania" after the Russo-Ottoman War of 1806-12 when, by agreement in the Treaty of Bucharest, the eastern portion of Moldavia, or Bessarabia, was ceded to the Russian Empire. With the emergence of the Soviet Union in the early twentieth century, Moldova was transformed into a Soviet Republic—the smallest and perhaps most neglected one.

So, as I stumbled groggily out of my train and began to walk through Chişinău towards my hostel—which was, I kid you not, behind a shopping center called MALLdova—I found myself in a quintessential frontier land. Ottoman, Romanian, Russian, Soviet. Moldova, at the very least, was going to be interesting.

I didn't expect to find many physical remains of the Ottoman period; I knew that, like Bucharest and much of present-day Romania, Ottoman rule in much of the territory north of the Danube had been largely hands-off. As long as the Romanian leaders paid their tribute, they were pretty much left alone. In the end, though, I was to get a stronger sense of the Ottoman ghosts and echoes in Moldova than in Romania.

There were the statues memorializing the heroism of Ştefan cel Mare, prince of Moldavia between 1457 and 1504, who is idolized for his fights against the Ottomans to maintain the independence of his principality.

There are also some scanty remains of the Bessarbian frontier conflicts between the "Turks" and the locals, such as the stone outlines of a fortress in Orheiul Vechi (Old Orhei), a complex of archaeological sites and working Orthodox monasteries about thirty-seven miles north-east of Chişinău.

Perhaps the memory was more vivid in Moldova than in Romania because it had changed hands so many times. It is hard to know.

In addition to ferreting out Moldova's Ottoman heritage, I also visited the two breakaway regions that had piqued my interest when I was preparing my research paper on then newly independent Moldova, all those years ago at Cornell. That both had Ottoman connections was a wonderful bonus.

"Back in the U.S.S.R.!": Transnistria

I walked up to the window and handed over my immigration card and passport. The man behind the window, who wore a drab green military uniform that sported epaulettes with the red and green stripes of his country's flag, scowled at the sight of my documents and asked, in gruff Russian, what my destination was. After conferring with the officer next to him, he got up and walked into a back room—with my passport.

My heart sank. All the stories I had heard about this border crossing flooded into my head. Were they going to try and extort a big bribe before giving my passport back? Would they keep it, leaving me stranded?

But a few minutes later, the guy reemerged and handed back my passport and the departure card. He jabbed a finger at a message that had been scrawled in English at the bottom: "Go 21:00." The message was clear: leave before 9 p.m. But I was being allowed in, *sans* bribe!

I had just entered one of the strangest political entities of the twenty-first century: the breakaway Trans-Dneistr Republic, a last, tiny holdout of the U.S.S.R. that had been carved out of the former Moldavian Soviet Socialist Republic.

***

While my primary motivation for choosing to travel in and around the Balkans, the Black Sea region, and the Caucasus was a desire to see a large swath of the former Ottoman world, these travels overlapped to varying degrees with some of my other major interests—particularly the Soviet period and the revolutions of 1989 that led to the fall of communism in the Eastern Bloc countries and eventually to the collapse of the U.S.S.R. itself in 1991.

Moldova, while not on many people's holiday itineraries, was always a definite on my list of countries to visit during my sabbatical year, as it brings together all of those interests. These interests are long-lived; during my time as an undergrad, I examined the viability of Moldova as an independent state for the final project of an international relations course.

Already one of the smallest of the former Soviet republics, at independence it had to deal with two separatist movements: the Russians of the narrow Transnistrian region and the Gagauz in southern Moldova. There was also serious speculation that the Romanian-speakers of Moldova would seek unification with Romania. At first glance, it seemed unlikely that the country would survive as a separate political entity.

Yet today, more than two decades after its declaration of independence, Moldova is alive and (mostly) kicking. The possibility of union with Romania was quickly abandoned—in large part because Romania, already one of the poorest countries in Europe at the time, didn't want an even poorer addition to its territory!—and the two separatist movements eventually, in a fashion, resolved themselves. The Gagauz nationalists accepted a degree of autonomy within Moldova rather than full independence for Gagauzia, or Gagauz Yeri. The Trans-Dniestr Republic (T.D.R.), or Transnistria, after a brief but deadly civil war in 1992, reached an uneasy truce with the Moldovan government—it's officially a "frozen conflict"—and still operates as a separate state (although unrecognized by the international community) under the longtime leadership of President Igor Smirnov. I had to see both of these territories during my short visit to Moldova.

First up was Transnistria. If you look at a map of this non-country, you might notice a slight resemblance to Chile in miniature. It is only a little more than sixteen hundred square miles that basically consist of a narrow strip of land along the banks of the Dniester River (hence the country's name), sandwiched between Ukraine and the rest of Moldova. The capital, Tiraspol, is only forty-three miles away from its political rival, Chișinău, so it makes for an easy day trip.

Easy, that is, in terms of travel time.

Until fairly recently, Transnistrian border crossings were notorious for intimidation and bribe shakedowns. However, my pre-travel homework seemed to indicate that this kind of activity had largely cooled down, so I decided to take the risk and venture into this political anomaly. From Chișinău's Central Bus Station, I caught one of the regular minibuses to Tiraspol.[53] Those of us who were not from the republic had to fill out a two-part immigration arrival/departure card, which we then presented when we arrived at the very official-looking border. Other than my brief

---

[53] Oddly, despite the "frozen conflict" there is a remarkable amount of travel back and forth between Moldova and its breakaway republic; I even saw Transnistrian license plates on the cars that were driving around Chișinău.

moment of panic when the border officer took my passport into the back room, the process went remarkably smoothly. No shakedown for me.[54]

Once in Tiraspol, I was able to breathe a little more easily—and I could begin to fully appreciate just what a surreal place it was to which I had traveled. Transnistria is a frozen sliver of the former U.S.S.R., a place where Soviet communism and the adulation of Lenin still beats strongly. Along the main drag of 25 October Street, I was able to find the towering House of Soviets, complete with a fiery-looking bust of Lenin situated prominently in front. The police and army officers wear old-style Soviet uniforms. The currency—yes, the T.D.R prints is own money—is called the ruble. I noticed, too, that all the signs were in Russian only (unlike bilingual Chişinău).

Last Holdout of the U.S.S.R.: Transnistria's House of Soviets

---

[54] I did hear, however, from Ian—with whom I would later visit Gagauzia (see next section)—that when he entered from the Ukraine side he had been pulled aside and questioned intensively by two glowering officers—but he, too, was eventually allowed in without having to cough up any money.

There is not much specifically to see in Tiraspol, but as I wandered the streets I was left wondering where—and, more importantly, when—I was. Most of the people with whom I interacted were pleasant enough (except for one old woman from whom I asked directions; all she said was a huffy *"Chto?"*—"What?"—before stomping away), but I did get the sense that they were a little surprised to see a tourist poking about. From such a short visit, it is impossible for me to know what the general Transnistrian feels about their miniscule, unrecognized country and its lingering tensions with Moldova. Still, I got the sense that they are fiercely proud of their pseudo-independence. This doesn't leave me much hope for a future reconciliation between the Trans-Dneistr Republic and Moldova.

As ominous-looking rain clouds started to darken the sky, I decided to jump on the next minibus back to Chişinău. We crossed the slow-moving Dneister River and, after a brief stop at the "border" near Bender, the erstwhile home of Demirbaş Şarl (see preface), we found ourselves back in fully recognized Moldova.

And back to 2013.

Through the Looking Glass: Gagauzia

The wild boar emerging from the plaster tree really made the exhibit, I thought. Yes, right out of the tree...

Ian and I were at the Museum of Local History in Comrat, and were being followed room to room by a grandmotherly woman who only spoke Russian and who seemed baffled that two Americans kept trying to use Turkish with her. Most of the exhibits were about the history and culture of this odd little Turkic enclave in southern Moldova, though confusingly— considering that we were in the capital of the autonomous region—most of the exhibits were only labeled in Russian.[55]

But the room with the stuffed boars, including an apparent tree-boar, needed no written explanation. Our "guide" beamed proudly as she turned on the lights to reveal the show-stealers of the museum.

---

[55] Sadly, my high school Russian seems to have all but atrophied. I can remember some words and phrases, but I can't seem to string a sentence together anymore. I had hoped it would revive a bit faster than it did.

Somehow it all seemed perfectly normal in this surreal land known as Gagauzia.

***

Moldova, as I have mentioned, is not a big place. From Chişinău you can reach even the furthest reaches of the country in about three hours by public transport. So, like the Trans-Dneistr Republic, you can visit the main sights of Gagauzia in a day trip. However, this is another corner of Moldova that seems not to get many tourists (not that Moldova in general is a major tourist magnet!). It's really more of a place for specialty tastes—especially those with a keen interest in Turkic history and languages.

Bizarrely, it just so happened that while staying in the hostel in Chişinău—which was almost empty due to the fact that this was the low season—I met another American Turcophile, Ian, who also planned on making the trip to the Gagauz lands. What were the chances? We decided to go together.

The border crossing into Gagauzia turned out to be a lot easier than the Transnistrian one, as there wasn't an actual checkpoint. The only way we knew we had entered Gagauzia—or, as it is more formally known, Gagauz Yeri—was the large sign welcoming us to the autonomous region and the large Gagauz flag fluttering in the wind. When we arrived at the bus station in Comrat, the tiny capital of the self-governing territory, it didn't at first look much different from other Moldovan towns. But then we heard it: Gagauz, the Turkic language of this interesting ethnic group who resides in southern Moldova, the world's only predominantly Christian Turkic group.

***

As the U.S.S.R. was dissolving during the chaotic days of 1991, Gagauz nationalists declared independence from the Moldavian Soviet Socialist Republic; this declaration came a full month earlier than that of their Trans-Dneistrian counterparts. They were fearful of what might happen to their small ethnic group—which numbered approximately 250,000 total, with less than 150,000 living in Gagauzia itself—when a

Romanian-dominated Moldovan government came to power.[56] However, unlike the Transnistrian conflict, an agreement was eventually reached in 1994 with the Chişinău government that established a "national-territorial autonomous unit" for the Gagauz. While this unit consists of several non-contiguous territories, the various parts that make up Gagauzia are all found in the southwestern corner of Moldova. Within the autonomous area, Gagauz Turkic is an official language (along with Romanian/Moldovan and Russian) and the Gagauz people fly their own flag (but alongside the Moldovan one).

These distinctions may not seem like a lot, but somehow the place feels different from the rest of Moldova.

Perhaps due to the decentralized nature of the territory and the fundamentally rural/village-based society, the "national" sights are scattered around Gagauzia, rather than concentrated in the tiny capital of Comrat. And so, strangely enough, the National Museum—as opposed to the local history museum that was previously mentioned—is located in the village of Beşalma, about twelve miles from Comrat. Ian and I figured that the museum should be our starting point in order to get the lay of the land in Gagauzia. But how were we to get there?

When we pulled into the Comrat bus station and heard the first strains of Gagauz, we discovered that there was a bus leaving for Beşalma at noon from a different part of town. It was 11:55.

We jumped in a taxi and arrived just in time to catch a rickety, full-sized bus—our first surprise, as most of the buses in Moldova are minibuses—that was packed to the brim with mostly *babushka*-types carrying large satchels of produce that had been procured at the morning market. There were no seats left, so Ian and I stood, crammed in the aisle. As the bus jolted forward and began its snail-paced trip to the "suburbs," I was happy to realize how much I could understand of the conversations

---

56   The origin of the Gagauz is quite obscure, with many different theories floating around. Some believe they are turkified Bulgarians (but, as I mentioned in the chapter on Bulgaria, it is highly likely that the early Bulgarians were slavicized Turkic-speakers!), while others believe they are descendants of nomads from the steppes. Whatever the case, there is little record of the group before they moved from Bulgaria to southern Bessarbia (now Moldova) in the early nineteenth century, in the wake of growing conflicts between the Ottomans and Russians.

that were being held around me. Gagauz turned out not to be so different from Turkey-Turkish. Every now and then one of the babushkas, almost as wide as they were tall, would push her way past me, practically shoving me into the lap of one of the other women; at first I assumed this meant they were planning on disembarking, but this didn't always seem to be the case. They would push to the front. And wait.

As we approached Beşalma, one of the women—a near caricature of a babushka, apple-faced and dressed in a bright floral dress and matching headscarf—struck up a conversation, delighted to hear that I could speak and understand Turkish. "You are going to museum, yes? I will show you where to get off." The bus pulled into town and stopped, yet hardly anyone moved. "Next stop, past the *cami*."

Had I heard right?

The mosque?

The bus started again, and then promptly stopped again maybe a hundred feet later, just past the Orthodox church. "Here is museum!" It was just as far as from this stop as from the first stop, but Ian and I wiggled our way out of the bus into the bizarrely expansive and spookily empty town square. When we looked back, we saw that none of the women had gotten off the bus. Wasn't this the last stop?

We never figured out what to make of that bus ride or its strange passengers.

The strangeness continued when we stepped into the National Museum. When we knocked, a young woman appeared from a side office, clearly startled to see guests. She began speaking to us in Russian; we tried Turkish. She spoke in Russian; we tried Turkish again. Finally, we realized that though she was working at the Gagauz National Museum, she didn't speak Gagauz—and she seemed not to be able to fathom that we weren't comfortable in Russian.[57] For the rest of our time in the museum, she chattered away rapid-fire in the language. Luckily, she was joined by two other women who did know the local language and with whom we could communicate more easily. But all three followed us very closely as we went from room to room, explaining the obvious to us at each point.

"This is a pitchfork," pointing at a pitchfork.

---

[57]   Even the national Gagauz University in Comrat uses Russian as the language of instruction. The attempt to keep Gagauz Turkic alive might not ultimately succeed.

"This is a Gagauz painting," pointing at a painting.

Ian and I began to suspect that they were never going to let us leave the museum, that perhaps they would keep us for their next exhibit: "Here are two Americans who actually came to visit our museum!"

Before leaving this Twilight Zone of a village, we stopped to grab a few snacks at the local grocery shop—a large but mostly empty affair near where the bus had dropped us off. A few locals were hanging out and wanted to know what strange creatures had descended on their town. One gentleman, when he heard we were Americans, asked us if we were *yankis*. Ian and I were both puzzled at first. The guy repeated the word a couple times before it finally dawned on me: "Ah! Yankees! Yes, yes, we are Yankees."

***

Back in "cosmopolitan" Comrat, things were slightly less strange. But only slightly. We enjoyed seeing the signs in Turkish and Gagauz ("Hoş Geldiniz!"); the Atatürk Kütüphanesi (Atatürk Library); the prominent Lenin statue in front of the government building; the Gagauz National University, with its bizarre collection of statues in front (Suleiman Demirel? Nursultan Nazarbayev?[58]); and the canary yellow Orthodox church. Gluttons for punishment, we also ventured into a second museum—the local history museum where we were confronted by ferocious tree-boars.

Although at times it felt like we had walked through the proverbial looking glass, I thoroughly enjoyed our day spent immersed in this little Turkic bubble. It felt like it had been the right way to wrap up my time in the frontier land of Moldova, before I moved on to a city that shared a similar history of between-ness: Odessa.

---

[58] Demirel was president of Turkey from 1993-2000; Nazarbayev has been president of Kazakhstan since 1991.

BORDERLAND: UKRAINE

I am not sure why there are two plates of late-Ottoman epigraphy, dated 1921, on the side of the Vorontsov Palace, tucked under the eave of a secondary entrance. The new paint job makes them a little difficult to decipher, but they are there, on a building that was purposely built as the home of the local governor of what was then a very young city.

This small remnant of Ottoman text was an intriguing reminder that this relatively modest palace marked the site where the Russians took over a little-known corner of the Ottoman Empire and established one of the most (in)famous ports the world has known. Odessa—even the name rings of mystery.

***

When I crossed the Danube into Romania, I entered a different kind of former Ottoman territory. Like many empires, the Ottoman state governed its vast holdings using a variety of methods: some direct, others not so much. Much of the Balkan Peninsula became thoroughly integrated into the empire and remained so for centuries, but north of the Danube, Ottoman control generally took the form of imposed vassalage. Among these Ottoman vassal states were the principalities of Transylvania, Wallachia, and Moldavia/Bessarabia[59]—which collectively corresponded roughly to present-day Romania, Moldova, and a bit of Ukraine—and, on the northern shores of the Black Sea, the Crimean Khanate, which was ruled by a Tatar descendent of the Golden Horde. In exchange for Ottoman protection, the princes and khans paid tribute to the Ottoman sultans. These territories served as important buffer states between the Ottoman heartlands and the Habsburg and Russian empires.

---

[59]   The Black Sea coast of what is now Romania and part of southern Ukraine was, however, more directly administrated by the Ottoman Empire as the province of Silistra. This included the territory that is now the Odessa *oblast*.

Although I didn't really have a chance to deeply explore the Ottoman period in Romania, there is not much physical evidence of Ottoman suzerainty in the region, anyway. Indeed, there are far fewer reminders of Ottoman rule north of the Danube than there are in either Bulgaria or the western Balkans.

So, when I arrived in Odessa, the most important port on the western shores of the Black Sea and currently a Ukrainian possession, I didn't expect to feel any more Ottoman-ness than I had in Romania or Moldova. Nevertheless, the Ottoman frontier came more alive for me here than in Bucharest or Chișinău.

Odessa is actually a rather young city; it was founded in 1794, several years after the capital of that great upstart, the United States of America, was established.

There was an earlier, smallish Tatar settlement where Odessa now sits, a nowhere place called Hajibey that was incorporated into the Ottoman realm in 1529 and where a tiny Ottoman fort—rather grandiosely called Yeni Dünya (the New World)—was established. However, the settlement was taken by the Russians in a non-battle during the Russo-Ottoman War in 1792, one of the many conflicts between the Ottomans and Russians in the late-eighteenth and early-nineteenth centuries as the Russian empire began to push further and further south, thereby coming into increased contact and conflict with its southern rival. After the "capture" of Hajibey, Catherine the Great decreed that a city should be built at this lonely place, a cliff top situated at the boundary between the grassy steppes and the expansive sea.

As the engineers and architects were given essentially a blank slate with which to work, the new city was designed according to the then-prevalent Enlightenment ideas of rationality. The core of the city today is very much a grid that is built around wide, tree-lined avenues interspersed with green parks. Most of its historic buildings are stately examples of nineteenth-century European designs. Nothing remains of the little Muslim village or the small Ottoman fort that once stood here.

However, the very founding of Odessa occurred due to the friction that resulted from the Russian and Ottoman rivalry for control of the Black Sea. Moreover, as a free port at the southern edge of the Russian empire and for many decades the main trading hub between the Black

Sea and Mediterranean, it was a cosmopolitan city caught between the Ottoman, Russian, and even Western European worlds, populated by a kaleidoscope of ethnic, national, and religious groups. These factors help to explain why the city became the birthplace for a number of revolutionary and nationalist movements that would challenge Tsarist rule in Russia and further erode the Ottoman presence in Europe, including significantly the secret Greek nationalist society, *Filiki Eteria*. This organization would help instigate the first successful "national" uprising against the Ottomans, carving out an independent Greece in the southern Balkans. Thus, even though it is a city built in post-Ottoman time and territory, Odessa, for much of its young history, was inextricably linked with the Ottoman realm, both shaped by and helping to shape that empire.

Today, Odessa is no longer the important port that it once was[60], nor is it any longer a major site of political and cultural ferment. It has also lost much of the great diversity that defined its first century of existence. Now, its population is predominantly Ukrainian identified, though predominantly Russian speaking (a legacy of its foundation as a "Russian" city).

Still, Odessa is one of those cities, like Plovdiv in Bulgaria, where the ghostly memories of an earlier diversity and an earlier greatness still linger vividly both in its physical remains and in its ineffable—put palpable—sense of nostalgic loss. I thus was able to feel the Odessa of the nineteenth century within its present form; I could imagine the comings and goings of its port as I stood at the top of the city's famous Potemkin Stairs, facing out to the churning of the Black Sea that had once been a battleground between Russia, the Ottoman Empire, and the rising powers of Western Europe. Again, I wish I could have known it then.[61]

---

[60] However, it is now one of the most important cruise ship stops on the Black Sea—as I got to experience firsthand when I saw a horde of German tourists ascend the Potemkin Stairs from the docks.

[61] My wanderings in Odessa were brought particularly alive by the wonderful book *Odessa: Genius and Death in a City of Dreams* by Charles King. I recommend it highly to anyone interested in Odessa (or the history of the Black Sea world in general).

My time in Odessa would prove, however, to be merely a warm-up for Crimea, which was perhaps the part of my Black Sea tour I had anticipated most.

***

My native land abandoned long,
I sought this realm of love and song.
Through Bakchesarai's palace wandered,
Upon its vanished greatness pondered…
- Alexander Pushkin (From "The Fountain of
Bakhchisarai"[62])

I had hardly set down my bag when Shevkiye, a small but proud grandmotherly sort, dressed in a long, dark coat and a floral headscarf, motioned me to a seat in her kitchen. She sat primly on her own seat, hands folded in lap. With great seriousness, she said: "Welcome to Bakhchisaray. I am happy you have come to see our home and to learn something of the Crimean Tatar people…."

As she began to tell her family's personal story of exile and return, I knew that I had found something different than a typical guesthouse; this was going to be more than a place to sleep and have breakfast. This was going to be an immersion in Tatar history and culture.

Which is exactly why I had come to this little town with a big history in central Crimea.

Crimea is one of those places that have experienced more history than it should be able to handle. While not a very large territory, this almost-island in the north of the Black Sea has attracted the attention of peoples and empires with its salubrious weather, dramatic beauty, and strategic location from at least as far back as the days of the ancient Scythians and Greeks. Since then, the peninsula has been settled, occupied, fought over, and conquered by a truly dizzying array of characters.[63] There were marauding Goths and Huns; there were the states of Kievan Rus' and the

---

[62] For the full text in English, visit http://www.online-literature.com/ alexander-pushkin/2799/.

[63] It reminds me of the Levantine coast, actually—see the chapter on Lebanon.

glittering empire of Byzantium; there were various groups of Mongols and Turks, including the Golden Horde and later the Crimean Khanate and the Ottoman Empire; there were trading communities of Venetians and Genovese. The Russian Empire laid claim in the late-eighteenth century, when German-speaking farmers were brought to cultivate the land—then came the U.S.S.R. in the twentieth century, followed by German occupation during World War II. After the collapse of the U.S.S.R., Crimea became part of independent Ukraine; however, it had a special status as an autonomous republic. And in 2014, Russia acquired the territory by rather dubious means. Crimea's Mongol and Turkic past, not surprisingly, were its major draw for me, although I was also attracted by its Russian/Slavic and Soviet borderland status. So many of my historical interests wrapped into one neat package!

Above all, I came to Crimea to learn more about the Crimean Khanate, one of the Ottoman Empire's most important vassal states, and about the post-Ottoman experience of the khanate's people: the Crimean Tatars. The khanate first emerged in 1441 as one of the states formed by the gradual disintegration of the much larger Golden Horde, itself originally just one piece of the world's largest contiguous land empire: the Mongol Empire. The first Crimean khan was Hacı Giray, who proclaimed the Crimean cave city that is now called Chufut Kale (see below) as his first capital before moving on to Bakhchisaray, just a few kilometers away—the town that is now most associated with the khanate and the Tatars. His tomb rises proudly at the edge of this city called the "Garden Palace."

The Khanate became an Ottoman protectorate and vassal almost immediately after Hacı Giray's death, as the empire intervened in what became a contentious succession rivalry. However, the relationship that developed between the Ottoman Empire and the Crimean Khanate was quite different than that between the Empire and the Romanian vassal states. Although the Ottoman sultan had the right to veto the choice of khan, the Empire and the Khanate essentially acted more as allies than as master and subject. The Ottomans generally administered the Crimean coast, but for the most part allowed the khans to do their own thing in the interior and in the grassy steppes to the north.

To begin my Tatar education, I decided to start in the logical place, the spot where Hacı Giray proclaimed his khanate, the aforementioned Chufut Kale—the path to which began practically at my guesthouse's front door.

The cave city of Chufut Kale is carved into the top of a steeply sided, narrow plateau. From the edges, I was able to see far into the valleys that define this ancient outpost, as well as view the entire geographical drama of central Crimea, complete with its other jagged plateaus and deep valleys that spread in all directions. A stone street that leads from the eastern defense wall sports a pair of ruts that are over a foot deep in places, carved by centuries of rolling wear. The ruins themselves—often modest from the outside, but cavernous and multi-roomed inside—look as if they were abandoned a thousand years ago; I was startled to find that this had been a living community until the 1870s, the center of one of Crimea's most fascinating and mysterious communities: the Turkic-speaking Karaites.[64]

However, the Karaites weren't the first residents. Chufut Kale bore witness to much of the comings and goings of Crimea's never-dull history and housed some of the region's most important historical characters, including of course the first Crimean Tatar khan. It was a well-protected spot, easy to defend, which allowed Hacı Giray to solidify his authority. Once he had done so, he turned his eye to the valleys below to establish a new capital that would be worthy of his ambitions and a place he could call his own. Chufut Kale had too much of a past already.

Thus was Bakhchisaray born, a city that was immortalized by Pushkin in his famous poem.

---

[64] Karaism, in general, is a pre-Talmudic form of Judaism that accepts only the Tanakh (Old Testament) as valid, although there are now adherents who claim that it is a distinct religion. The origin of the Karaites of Crimea is hotly debated. Some believe they are descendents of the Khazars, a Turkic-speaking group that converted to Judaism and established a Jewish state in Central Asia; others claim that they were simply turkified (due to being in contact with the Tatars) when they migrated to Crimea. Just below Chufut Kale there is a ghostly Karaite cemetery, half hidden in a grove of old oak trees. The Karaites believed that this was a sacred space.

Palace of Bakhchisaray

***

When I was in high school, I had the opportunity to spend my last two years at the Indiana Academy for Science, Mathematics, and Humanities, a residential program for gifted and talented students. One of the things that excited me most about this opportunity was a chance to choose a language that was not offered at most public schools. Besides the more typical Spanish, French, and German, one could take Chinese, Japanese, and Russian, among others. I am not sure why I gravitated towards Russian, but I think even my sixteen-year-old self could somehow sense the lovely literary pathos of that language—even though I had never read any Russian literature at that point! Through our wonderful Russian teacher, Ms. Hobar, I learned to decipher the Cyrillic script and began to tackle Russian's incredibly complex grammar ("Please, not verbs of motion! No!"). However, I think I most appreciated how she made Russian culture and literature come alive. Indeed, I am quite sure none of her students will ever forget her descriptions of the great poet Alexander Pushkin—or rather "Puuuush-kin" (said with your eyes closed and lips heavily puckered).

Even though I sadly let my Russian language skills atrophy as I moved in a different linguistic direction and began studying Arabic and Turkish, I retained my love for the classic Russian writers, Pushkin among them.

The fact that Pushkin wrote a poem set in fabled Bakhchisaray provides a unique literary lens through which to examine the area: a Russian Orientalist perspective on the Crimean Khanate. The timing of Pushkin's visit adds further intrigue to his perspective, as the Khanate had only been conquered by Catherine II a few decades before the dashing poet wandered through the crumbling palace, where he heard the romantic tale of the harem that inspired him to write his famous poem—a poem that was later even transformed into a ballet.

I waited to visit what remains of old Bakhchisaray until my second day in the area. I knew that much had gone to ruin (or had even been destroyed) after the Russians took control of the Crimea in the late eighteenth century—and even more had vanished after the horrific deportation ordered by Stalin in 1944, an act that essentially emptied Crimea of Tatars and sent them to far-flung corners of the U.S.S.R. such as Uzbekistan. For different reasons, the Russian and Soviet leaders viewed the Tatars—Turkic-speaking Muslims—with deep suspicion. Catherine II saw them as allies of her great enemy, the Ottomans; Stalin, in his growing paranoia, suspected the Tatars of sympathizing with the Germans during World War II. Surprisingly, the Khans' Palace, the most famous building in Bakhchisaray, survived all the historical drama—perhaps due to its fame, which, at least in part, can be attributed to Pushkin's poem.

Inside the main palace building, there is a courtyard with several fountains. One, tucked in the far right corner, has a bust of Pushkin next to it. This is the Fountain of Tears that the poet immortalized—although it is not in its original spot. Rather, it supposedly stood in the gardens next to the tomb of a beautiful Polish girl with whom (if the tale is to be believed) Qırım Giray Khan fell in love. When she died, the khan was so grieved he ordered a fountain built that would weep continually for her, just as he wept. This is the story Pushkin heard that he transformed into this romantic poem:

> *Not yet has time's rude hand effaced,*
> *Still do the gurgling waters pour*
> *Their streams dispensing sadness round,*

As mothers weep for sons no more,
In never-ending sorrows drowned.
In morn fair maids, (and twilight late,)
Roam where this monument appears,
And pitying poor Maria's fate
Entitle it the FOUNT OF TEARS!

How much is true and how much is fantasy is difficult to discern. However, I think the weeping fountain and the nostalgic poem serve as powerful symbols for the Crimean Tatars and all they have lost. And, like the marble fountain and the palace, the Tatars have survived the past two centuries with remarkable resilience.

Although there are not nearly as many Tatars in Crimea today as there were prior to 1944, many families have returned and are trying to reclaim their past and build a solid present and future. Although much was destroyed or left in disrepair after the deportations, the Tatars who have returned are restoring and rebuilding Bakhchisaray with remarkable energy. Even the palace, which has survived, seems to be in the process of re-restoration, as much of the Soviet era "restoration" was quite shoddy. There are also Tatar restaurants and Tatar cafés strewn throughout the length of the town. And Tatar families, like that of my host Shevkiye, have opened their homes as guesthouses to introduce tourists to not only the surrounding tourist sights, but also to Tatar culture. It is something of a Tatar renaissance.

Yes, I could sense a lingering sadness in Bakhchisaray for what was lost and can never be regained, just as in Pushkin's version of the Tatar khan's tragic love story. However, more powerfully I could sense hope and joy, just as Pushkin does in the conclusion of his poem:

The bard shall wind thy rocky ways
Filled with fond sympathies, shall view
Tauride's [Crimea's] bright skies and waves of blue
With greedy and enraptured gaze.
Enchanting region! full of life
Thy hills, thy woods, thy leaping streams,
Ambered and rubied vines, all rife

With pleasure, spot of fairy dreams!
Valleys of verdure, fruits, and flowers,
Cool waterfalls and fragrant bowers!
All serve the traveller's heart to fill
With joy as he in hour of morn
By his accustomed steed is borne
In safety o'er dell, rock, and hill,
Whilst the rich herbage, bent with dews,
Sparkles and rustles on the ground,
As he his venturous path pursues
Where AYOUDAHGA'S crags surround!

***

Initially, I had included Kyiv—or, more familiarly, Kiev[65]—on my sabbatical itinerary, mostly for utilitarian purposes. Yes, getting to the city after my visits to Odessa and Crimea would be a slight detour on my

---

[65] During my short time in Ukraine, I was able to get a flavor of the interesting language politics in the country. The official language of the country is, of course, Ukrainian; however, from its days in the U.S.S.R. (and even earlier during the Russian Empire), the closely related Russian is still widely spoken. In some places, such as Odessa, Russian is spoken more than Ukrainian, even though a majority of the people identify as Ukrainian. This is largely due to the fact that Russians founded the city, and Russian was the lingua franca for its extremely diverse community. In Crimea, Russian also holds sway—but for quite different reasons. Most importantly, there remains a large Russian community that is still loyal to Russia (this is especially true in Sevastopol, which still serves as the base for the Russian navy due to a special agreement between Ukraine and Russia). Yet in both Odessa and Crimea signage is usually in Ukrainian, not Russian. In Kyiv, the country's capital, I was not surprised to find that Ukrainian was much more widely used, but even here Russian is common and seems to be accepted as a language of exchange almost everywhere. Apparently, however, there are places in Ukraine, especially in the west (which I didn't have the opportunity to see) where speaking Russian is deeply frowned upon. As a sensitive tourist, trying to at least use pleasantries in the native language, all this makes for a cultural minefield. How should I even say "Hello" or "Thank you"?

Ottoman trajectory around the Black Sea. However, I couldn't continue by land to Georgia, as I would have liked: Russia still maintains its crazy, Soviet-esque visa regulations, which makes getting a transit visa extremely difficult and extremely expensive. An even greater obstacle is the rather cool relationship between Georgia and Russia—you know, a recent pesky little war and occupied territories, that's all. As a result, land crossings between the two countries are not recommended. Thus, if I were going to follow my clockwise path from Turkey to Georgia, I would have to either fly or go by ferry—and, currently, the Black Sea ferry services are rather erratic and expensive. Kyiv, as the capital of and largest city in Ukraine, was the most convenient place from which to find a cheap flight to Tbilisi. So, Kyiv it was.

Still, I was more than happy to make such a detour, as Kyiv figures prominently at the intersection of many of my other historical interests: the Khazars, Vikings, Mongols, the rise of Russia, and the emergence of the U.S.S.R., to name just a few. Once a part of the Turkic-Jewish Khazar state, it was captured in the ninth century by the slavicized Varangian Rus' (Viking) dynasty, which is considered to be the first "Russian" royal family. Under the Rus', Kyiv became a major center of eastern Slavic culture and, when the rulers adopted Christianity, a major center of Eastern Orthodoxy and a rival to Constantinople. Essentially, Kyiv is considered the birthplace of both Russian and Ukrainian culture.

In 1237, the city was attacked and destroyed during the Mongol invasions, an event that turned the Slavic princes further north in Novgorod and Moscow into Mongol vassals. Kyiv was later absorbed by yet another political power, the Polish-Lithuanian Commonwealth. In 1667, Kyiv was once again brought under the control of the Russian Tsars as they began to consolidate power and create the beginnings of a true Russian empire. Then, of course, came the U.S.S.R.... As a world history teacher, how could I not but be fascinated by all that historical drama?

Kyiv is one of those cities that many people know about, but can't quite place. The name strikes a bell, if for anything its association with a certain famous chicken dish. It's somewhere... Over there... But that's about as far as it goes.

After spending a long weekend in Kyiv, during which I sought out historical ghosts (such as paying homage to the grave of Yaroslav the Wise[66] at St. Sophia Cathedral) and visited friends from Khartoum (when you travel as much as I do, you meet many other similarly minded travelers— my world has grown quite small!), I couldn't help but be baffled by this touristic indifference. The city is truly gorgeous, set as it is among rolling hills that are covered in woods and parkland. Its beauty is increased by its location on the banks of the wide Dneiper River and by the fact that it is filled with architectural gems from several centuries and a surfeit of golden onion-domed churches and monasteries. There is also a lively restaurant and café scene (which I, of course, just had to check out).

The fact that I had arrived on the nicest weekend of the year, according to my friends, probably helped win me over to the charms of Kyiv. The weather was stunning: warm and clear, almost summery. Everyone was out and about in the streets. All the trees were fast en-cloaking themselves in greenery. Flowers were beginning to bloom.

On my last night, I went with my friends on a short sunset river cruise. We slipped past many of the major sights of the Kiev: the candle-shaped Famine Memorial, dedicated to the millions who died in Stalin's planned famines; the Lavra complex, with its multitude of golden-domed churches and cave monasteries; the gargantuan Motherland Monument, a stainless steel statue of Soviet strength built in honor of those who died in the Great Patriotic War (World War II); and the wonderfully tacky hydropark, with hundreds of sweaty, beefcake men working out on antiquated metal equipment or simply lounging on the beach. As the sun sank, it dipped behind a towering white cloud, creating a magical show of light and color to frame the scene. A perfect ending to my visit to the city where Russia and Ukraine got their starts.

---

[66] Yaroslav the Wise was the ruler who codified early Russian law and under whom Kievan Rus' reached its "golden age."

PART III

Tackling the Caucasus

Map 4: The Caucasus

The Caucasus is a relatively small territory; it is sandwiched between the Black Sea and Caspian Sea on the west and east, respectively, and straddles both the slopes of the Greater and Lesser Caucasus Mountain Ranges—the mountain systems that lend their collective name to the region. Although the region constitutes at most 150,000 square miles (the actual dimensions are a little fuzzy, as it depends on what is included in one's definition of the region), about the same size as the state of Montana, the Caucasus is one of the most diverse regions on earth.

On the southern side of the Caucasus, there are the three independent states of Georgia, Armenia, and Azerbaijan, all former Soviet Republics. In the northern Caucasus, there is a patchwork of seven Russian republics, many with tongue-twisting names: the Republic of Adygea, Karachay-Cherkessia, Kabardino-Balkaria, North Ossetia-Alania, Ingushetia, Chechnya, and the Republic of Dagestan (none of which, sadly, I have been able to visit so far, due to strict visa regulations). Within these Caucasian political entities, on both sides of the mountains, there is a dizzying array of languages spoken and religions practiced. For example, in tiny Dagestan alone there are more than thirty distinct languages and hundreds of dialects!

None of this is too surprising, I suppose, when one considers just how isolated many of the valleys in the Caucasus Mountains are. These are, to put it mildly, serious mountains. Mount Elbrus, the highest peak, is more than 18,500 feet high. Furthermore, the region has been a cultural and political crossroads almost since the beginning of complex human society; it has also been a much sought-after prize by almost every empire that rose and fell anywhere in the vicinity.

Of particular interest to me, the Caucasus region was the intersection point of the Ottoman Empire, Safavid (later Qajar) Persia[67], and the Russian Empire—and, in fact, remains an intersection point for the nation-state successor states of modern Turkey, Iran, and Russia (and, of course, the

---

[67]   The Safavid Dynasty reigned from 1502 to 1736, and was followed by the relatively brief era when Iran was ruled by the Afghan leader, Nader Shah (1736-1747). Then came the Zand Dynasty, which ruled from 1750 to 1794, before being replaced by the Qajars, who controlled Persia until 1925. Generally, the Safavids and Qajars played the biggest role in the struggle between the Ottomans and the Persians for control of the Caucasus.

U.S.S.R.). At times, the area was divided into many independent states that were ruled by Armenian, Georgian, Turkic, and Iranian dynasties, with various degrees of independence from and dependence on the neighboring empires. Sometimes those imperial neighbors conquered and absorbed portions of the territory. Sometimes the boundaries fluctuated wildly between one empire and another. The result is an incredibly convoluted history, one that makes even that of the Balkans seem relatively easy to grasp.

My connection to the region began with an early interest in Azerbaijan that stemmed from my undergraduate honors thesis on the development of Azeri nationalism in both Iranian and Soviet Azerbaijans.[68] Actually, in many respects, my research into Azeri history served as a gateway to Ottoman studies, as it kindled my interest in the Turkic world in general. In turn, as I delved deeper into both Azeri and Ottoman history, my interest in Armenia grew, in large part due to a desire to understand more clearly both the catastrophic events of 1915[69] and the more recent tensions over Nagorno-Karabakh. Georgia, however, remained something of a mystery until my visit in 2013, despite its tantalizingly proximity during my years living in Turkey.

Despite my greater background knowledge of Azerbaijan and Armenia, Georgia became my "home base" in the Caucasus, due largely to its current openness to the outside world and extremely strong relations with the U.S., and it quickly worked its magic on me. As I came and went from my visits to Armenia and Azerbaijan, I reveled in the legendary hospitality of the Georgians and the stunning landscapes with which this little country is so blessed. And I learned a little history along the way, too.

---

[68] The name "Azerbaijan" applies both to the independent Republic of Azerbaijan (a former Soviet republic) and its neighbor to the south, the northwest region of Iran. Iran has a large population of Azeri-Turkic speakers, constituting up to 16 percent of Iran's population according to the CIA World Factbook.

[69] I will discuss the importance of this year in Armenian history in the chapter on Armenia.

STAR TREK MEETS SILK ROAD: GEORGIA

As my taxi from the airport crested a hill just above the city center, I got a glimpse of one of the strangest cityscapes I've ever seen. In the midst of the Georgian and Armenian churches topped with conical roofs that looked very much like gnome hats and the crumbling mansions with enormous wooden balconies, there was the presidential palace with its egg-shaped glass dome, the mushroom-roofed Public Services Building, the undulating Bridge of Peace, and a metallic double squash or tilted vase-shaped building that I think is intended to be a theater someday. A zipping set of space-age gondolas crossed the scene, heading up to the glowering remains of the Nariqala Fortress. I couldn't tell if I was in the eighteenth or the twenty-fourth century—or both simultaneously.

However, I knew for certain I had arrived in Tbilisi.

Star Trek Meets Silk Road

Once I pulled up to my guesthouse in the Old Town, I realized that things were going to be even more complicated "on the ground." The building and immediate neighborhood didn't exactly look promising. Atmospheric, yes; livable, no. The door was made of decaying wood panels; it had probably once been painted a vibrant red, but the color was now mostly peeled away. The glass window above the door was broken. The staircase inside was slightly askew. However, once I reached the guesthouse quarters on the second floor, all was bright and cheery, clean and modern. I was to find that a number of places in the yet-to-be-renovated parts of Tbilisi's Old Town were like this: dilapidated on the exterior, well kept on the interior.

Tbilisi, it would seem, likes to keep you guessing.

***

Even if I knew little about the country, I had been looking forward to visiting Georgia for a long time. When I was living in Turkey during the late nineties, it was temptingly close, though at the time the border crossing was not as simple as it is today. There were stories of a local warlord controlling the region of Adjara[70] and of corrupt border officials fleecing travelers who came in from Turkey. However, there were also the stories of Georgian hospitality and the country's great food and wine. What I knew of the region's history also more than intrigued me, as the Caucasus region was (and is) a collision point of numerous cultures and empires, as I have pointed out. Surely this would have left its mark on Georgia: I wanted to see for myself.

The Georgians—predominantly Christian members of an ancient church[71] who speak a complex, consonant ridden language that is written in a gorgeous, curvy alphabet—were part of a world that saw the comings and

---

[70]   Adjara is an autonomous republic within Georgia, a holdover from the Soviet era. Until 2004, President Aslan Abashidze controlled the region with an authoritarian grip; he even had his own militia. After he lost political support from Russia, though, he left Georgia. Since then, Adjara has become more integrated into Georgia.

[71]   One of the early Georgian kingdoms was known as Kartli (or Iveria/Iberia), which was centered in Mtskheta. When the king and queen converted to Christianity in the fourth century (due to the supposed miracles of St. Nino),

goings of Persians, Byzantines, Arabs, Seljuk Turks, Mongols, Ottomans, and Russians. They lived—and live—next to Armenians, Azeris, and members of the countless ethno-linguistic groups that occupy the soaring mountaintops and plunging valleys of the Caucasus range. At times, there were powerful Georgian kingdoms that extended even into Anatolia; occasionally, these kingdoms were absorbed into the political power of the day.

But the closest I had gotten to Georgia prior to 2013 was when I visited the ruins of a remote Georgian church that was situated in the hills outside of Erzurum in far-eastern Turkey during the spring of 2000 (an experience which I will come back to in the chapter on Turkey).

More than a decade later, I finally got to explore this country about which so many travelers rave. Tbilisi, as my Georgian entry point, proved to be a heady mix of cultures, fascinating history, and fast-paced development. Really, it is where Star Trek meets the Silk Road!

Modern Georgia, like its neighbors Armenia and Azerbaijan, might have ancient antecedents, but its current form is quite new. The general area was consolidated as "Georgia" during the nineteenth century when the Russian Empire extended its influence into the Caucasus, and the current borders were defined during the Soviet era in the early- to mid-twentieth century. Independence didn't come until 1991.

So what was Georgia before the Russians, and then Soviets, entered the picture? Like everything else in the Caucasus, that's complicated.

The "Golden Age" of Georgian history is often considered to be the eleventh and twelfth centuries, when a weakening of both Byzantine and Seljuk influence in the Caucasus allowed a unified Georgian state to emerge for the first time. At the peak of its political influence, under King David IV the Builder (r. 1089-1125), this Georgian kingdom controlled most of the territory between the Caspian and Black Seas. However, the appearance of the Mongols in 1236 marked the beginning of a precarious time for the Georgian state, as it came under repeated attack from wave after wave of Central Asian forces. By 1446, in the face of repeated raids from

---

Kartli became only the second kingdom to adopt the new faith—just a couple decades after Armenia had.

the Turcoman Akkoyunlu and Karakoyunlu ("White Sheep" and "Black Sheep") Confederations[72], the last unified Georgian kingdom collapsed.

In the centuries that followed, several small Georgian kingdoms emerged, all of which were dependent for their survival on the protection of the larger imperial powers who vied for influence in the Caucasus. Starting in 1501, when the Safavid Empire was established under the charismatic leadership of Shah Ismail, these Georgian statelets would be caught in an Ottoman-Safavid tug-of-war that lasted for centuries. Even after a treaty— known as the Peace of Amasya—was signed in 1555, dividing the Georgian kingdoms into two spheres of influence (Imereti for the Ottomans and Kartli-Kakheti for the Safavids), the two empires would fight for control of the region, sometimes extending their reach at the expense of the other (as when the Ottomans took control of Kartli-Kakheti between 1732 and 1735). Still, in a very rough sense, one can say that western "Georgia" was more closely tied to the Ottomans and eastern "Georgia" to the Safavids and subsequent dynasties who ruled in Persia.[73]

The political winds began to shift, though, as the eighteenth century drew to a close. Erekle II, king of Kartli-Kakheti (r. 1762-1798), not happy to be under the thumb of the Persian state (which was then under the control of the short-lived Zand dynasty), looked northward to the growing Russian Empire as a possible alternative protector—one that was Christian to boot. Interestingly, Erekle II, perhaps hedging his bets, also maintained diplomatic relations with the Ottomans, even during the Russo-Ottoman War of 1787. In the end, however, Russia was not yet interested enough in the southern Caucasus to offer much help, and with the Russians and Ottomans preoccupied with their own imperial rivalry, Kartli-Kakheti (western "Georgia") was left exposed.

The newest political force in Persia, the Qajar leader Agha Mohmmad Khan, deposed the last Zand Shah in 1794 and pushed his forces into

---

[72]   The term "Turcoman" or Turkmen is of unclear origin, but generally refers to specific Turkic groups that are now found in Turkmenistan and in Iraq and Syria who are descendents of the Turcoman tribes who controlled large swaths of Persia/Iran after the collapse of Seljuk authority in the region.

[73]   It's interesting to note that the Safavid dynasty was actually of Turkic origin, like the Ottomans. Over time, however, the Safavids adopted Persian as their court and literary language. Similarly, the Qajars, who came to power in the late-eighteenth century, were Turkic speakers who had become "Persianized."

the Caucasus, going so far as to burn the city of Tiflis (now Tbilisi) to the ground in 1795—an event that left a lasting mark on the city's urban landscape; although modern Tbilisi is a wild mix of centuries, as I've mentioned, the oldest structures date from after the devastation of 1795. This act, of course, did not endear the Georgians to the Qajars and thus pushed many leaders to look again to Russia as a benefactor and protector.

As the Russian Empire spread south to the Black Sea and Caucasus, coming into increasing conflict with the Ottomans and now Qajars, the Georgian kingdoms came to be of more interest to the Tsars. Starting with the absorption of Kartli-Kakheti in 1801 (albeit with much protest from the Georgian nobility!), Russia began to annex more and more of the Georgian-led lands and other parts of the Caucasus. The Kingdom of Imereti, the Ottoman vassal, was taken in 1810; other Ottoman territories like Batumi and Abkhazia[74], which are now part of modern Georgia, were firmly under Russian authority by 1878.

There was a dramatic, if brief, 1918 campaign by the grandiosely named Ottoman Army of Islam (led by Enver Pasha)[75] that pushed deep into the Caucasus, through the Georgian territories and into Azerbaijan, all the way to Baku. Other than that, though, Georgia's connection to the Ottoman state was severed decades before the conflagration of World

---

[74]   Abkhazia is one of Georgia's troublesome breakaway states, having declared independence from Georgia with the support of Russia. Its independence is not recognized internationally, however (as is also true for Transnistria). Batumi and the surrounding province of Adjara were also of a separatist bent in the early days of Georgian independence; this area happens to be where the Muslim minority of Georgia is concentrated—which is not surprising, as it was a full *sancak* of the Ottoman Empire. After Abkhazia was taken, most of the Muslim Abkhaz were forcibly expelled by the Russians, who became known as *muhajirs* (emigrants); they mostly ended up in the Ottoman Empire.

[75]   This campaign was one of the last major military actions of the Ottoman Empire during World War I; however, it was not simply fueled by a desire to push back the Russians in the Caucasus. It also, under the vision of Enver Pasha, was intended to set the stage for the creation of Pan-Turkic Empire. Truthfully, he was a little delusional. The campaign, while initially making good progress into the Caucasus, ended with Ottoman defeat; the Armistice of Mudros, which concluded the conflict, stated that the Ottoman Empire had to retreat to its pre-World War I borders—which meant that it relinquished claims to all the territories making up "Georgia."

War I. Moreover, much like what happened with the Russian conquest of the northern Black Sea Coast (what is now southern Ukraine and Crimea), most reminders of Ottoman (and Safavid) influence were erased in Georgian territory.

***

Due to my comings and goings in Georgia, the remainder of this chapter, moreso than of the previous ones, is really more a series of discrete reflections regarding various observations that I made on Georgian culture and history than it is a unified whole.

***

The climb from Kazbegi took almost two hours; the trail lead first across the Tergi River to the village of Gergeti and then gradually got steeper as it ascended into the hills and forests outside of town. The giant snow-covered pyramid of Mount Kazbek, a long-extinct volcano near the Russian border, dominated the horizon. I passed a few other hikers, but for the most part I had the trail to myself, which allowed me to enjoy the peaceful silence.

At one point, the foot trail merged with the deeply rutted road used by the lazier sorts who chose to drive; it was still banked with snow. Shortly after the road switchbacked, turning away from Mount Kazbek, we crested the hill and saw what we had come to see: Tsminda Sameba, one of the most stunningly situated churches in the world.

I may not be an Orthodox Christian, but just the sight of Tsminda Sameba (or Holy Trinity Church), standing small yet fiercely proud against the towering Caucasus Mountains stirred something mystical or spiritual within me. It was certainly appropriate that my new friends and I were visiting during the Easter season (or *ahdgoma*, as it is called by the Georgians).

Tsminda Sameba

Inside the church, we discovered that there was a service in progress. The priest's face was framed by a wild, black beard. Candles flickered, casting a faint glow in the dark interior. A small crowd of worshippers huddled in the center, enacting the rituals I couldn't comprehend. I thought: this is what Easter should be.

***

In my first week in Georgia, I inadvertently found myself in more church services than I probably had attended in the previous decade. Almost every day I wandered into a church, just to look, only to find that I'd stumbled into a service in progress. I don't know how much of this simply was timing or whether there was an increase in ceremonies in preparation for the big event, Easter Sunday. Whatever the case, I was privileged to see Georgian Orthodoxy in action in some of its holiest places.

For instance, in Tbilisi I visited the thirteenth-century Sioni Cathedral, which was only a short walk from my guesthouse, and the twenty-first-century Tsminda Sameba Cathedral (the same name as the church in Kazbegi, but much, much bigger—and much, much newer). But I was just getting warmed up.

On Passion Thursday, I made the short journey from Tbilisi to Mtskheta, considered the spiritual heart of the Georgian Orthodox Church; it was here, during its heyday as the capital of the Kartli Kingdom, that the Georgians first adopted Christianity, becoming only the second kingdom to do so (after Armenia). Although the town itself is rather sleepy and now a tad over-restored, the churches in Mtskheta exude a truly ancient sense of spirituality. When I stepped into the soaring interior of Svetitskhoveli Cathedral, a Last Supper ceremony was underway, complete with the eerily beautiful polyphonic singing for which Georgia is famous.

When I wandered up the road to Samtavro Church, the former palace church of King Mirian and Queen Nana, the rulers who Christianized the kingdom, I found myself in a swirl of black clad nuns and more colorfully dressed laywomen.

Then later, high above Mtskheta and the valley in which it rests, I stood in the shadow of the Jvari Church, considered the holiest of holies in Georgian Christianity, as it marks the spot where King Mirian first erected a cross.

On Good Friday, I took a cramped *marshrutka* (mini-bus) to Kazbegi, which followed the Georgian Military Highway through increasingly dramatic Caucasus scenery—including passage through a 7805-foot-high pass before descending into the Tergi Valley where Kazbegi is situated.

I was awed by the church and its view, and happy that I was able to witness a service in action within its dark sanctuary.

***

In Georgian Orthodox tradition, the main event begins around midnight on Saturday, just as Easter day arrives. The service can go on all night—a serious commemoration of Christ emergence from the grave.

Curious to get at least a taste of what a Georgian Easter service was like, I joined a Ukrainian couple who had hired a "taxi" to drive the extremely rough road up to Tsminda Sameba (I hiked it once, so I can't be called lazy!). In the moonless night, the path through the woods—illuminated as it was by the headlights of the ancient, Russian-built car—looked like something out of the *Blair Witch Project*. When we pulled up to the base of Holy Trinity, all we could see were the dark silhouettes of the bell tower and church against a sky that was dense with stars. A bitter wind blew off the snow-covered mountain slopes behind us. The lights of the town of Kazbegi twinkled below.

However, a crowd had already begun to gather inside, warming themselves by the wood-burning stoves near the entrance. The same black-bearded priest who had conducted the Good Friday service was standing in the far corner, near the iconostasis, listening to confessions. At the conclusion of each hearing, he would cover the congregant in his golden-embroidered vestments and make the sign of the cross over them. Others milled about the small space, talking softly with neighbors or praying quietly in front of icons.

After the last confession had been heard, an altar boy slipped into the cold night and began ringing the church bell. Suddenly, the restless crowd grew attentive; those who had been sitting stood. The voice of the priest—now hidden behind the mystery of the iconostasis[76]—began to rumble, reciting in inscrutable Georgian the story of Easter. At signals known only to them, the devotees crossed themselves and bowed, somehow without upsetting the candles they clutched in the darkness.

***

The next morning as I breakfasted, Piqria, the cheerful proprietress of my guesthouse in Kazbegi, pulled out two hard-boiled eggs that had been dyed deep red, and we cracked the ends together. My egg stayed intact. She laughed: "You win!"

Actually, I had won as soon as I stepped out of the marshrutka and caught my breath at the sight of Tsminda Sameba framed against Mount Kazbek. This might just have been the most beautiful Easter I had ever experienced.

***

---

[76] An iconostasis is a screen or wall covered in icons that depict saints and other Christian figures; it separates the nave from the sanctuary in a church. Part of the liturgical service in an Orthodox church is conducted behind the wall, out of sight of the congregation.

Occupation:

    a: the act or process of taking possession of a place or area : seizure

    b: the holding and control of an area by a foreign military force

    c: the military force occupying a country or the policies carried out by it.[77]

"Occupation" is an interesting word. Or rather, I find it interesting how it is used in political and historical discourse.

As some of you may have gathered, I tend to be just as fascinated by how history is portrayed and used in the present as I am by the original historical events. In fact, sometimes more so.

Indeed, one the driving forces behind my decision to take a sabbatical in 2012 and 2013 was the desire to explore how the Ottoman period is perceived currently and how the Ottoman past shapes modern national narratives. In those narratives, the word "occupation" appears frequently. How often did I hear about two, three, five hundred years of occupation by the "Turks"? And yet I wonder: can a political situation that lasted centuries, one that changed considerably over time and space, really be called an "occupation"? (For example, see the chapter on Hungary.)

Of course, the term is not only used in former Ottoman territories for their time under Ottoman rule. I have noticed how often "occupation" has been used for more recent history, particularly in reference to the communist or Soviet era. In Tbilisi, a part of the newly renovated Museum of Georgia is designated the "Museum of Soviet Occupation," which covered a good chunk of the twentieth century. Again, one could quibble about the length of time that can constitute an occupation, but what got me more about this exhibit was how difficult it was to justify the word in Georgia's case—after all, the word certainly implies a distinct "us" versus "them," the occupied and the occupier. Yet so many of the "occupiers" in the Georgian case were of Georgian origin, not the least of whom was Joseph Stalin, who was born in Gori, Georgia with the very Georgian name Ioseb Dzhugashvili.

***

---

[77]   Definition found at http://www.merriam-webster.com/dictionary/occupation.

I made the trip out to Gori one rainy Sunday morning, curious to see how the museum would portray the town's native son.

It wasn't hard to spot the museum—a large, vaguely Italianate building set at the end of a large plaza and public garden. In front, protected by a large open pavilion, was a much more modest two-room house; this was where Stalin, the son of a poor cobbler and a housekeeper, was born, and where he lived his first four years, before his family moved to Tbilisi (or Tiflis, as it was still known). Quite a humble beginning for a man who would become one of the key figures of twentieth-century history and who inflicted great devastation upon the U.S.S.R., the vast country he led from 1922 to 1952.

Interestingly, the museum makes no mention of Stalin's dark legacies. There's nothing about the infamous political purges, the many deportations, the engineered famines. It simply chronicles his childhood in Gori and Tbilisi, his short stint in seminary, and his early revolutionary activity, followed by a broad overview of his years as supreme leader of the Soviet Union. There is a room with gifts from foreign dignitaries and a creepy chamber devoted to his death mask. Outside, I was able to wander through the bulletproof train carriage that carried him to Yalta and other important meetings. The gift shop sells mugs with his face on them (I bought one, I must admit!) and a wine brand named "Stalin."

It was both amusingly kitschy and more than a little frightening. Whereas I saw little love for Enver Hoxha, the ultra-paranoid Albanian dictator, in his hometown of Gjirokastra in southern Albania, I got the sense in Gori that there was still a bit of local pride in the fact that a figure such as Joseph Stalin had been born in the town—even if he was responsible for the deaths of millions.[78] Perhaps the logic was that bad press is better than no press?

Whatever the case, the Stalin Museum provides the best example of the complicated history Georgia had as part of the Soviet Union. Georgian

---

[78] The exact number of people who died in the U.S.S.R. due to Stalin's policies is unknown, but estimates range from a minimum of twenty million to as many as sixty million (though this is likely a stretch). However, even if the lower estimate is more accurate, Stalin outstrips his contemporary, Adolf Hitler, in the killing department, which makes him perhaps the most murderous dictator of the twentieth century.

Bolsheviks were key in bringing the country, which had experienced a brief three years of independence from 1918 to the invasion of the Red Army in 1921, into the Soviet sphere. And Georgians played major roles in the Soviet government up until the collapse of the U.S.S.R. Stalin, of course, is the most obvious example. However, I can also point to Lavrentiy Beria, who headed the secret police under Stalin, and more recent figures such as Eduard Shevardnadze, who served as president of independent Georgia from 1995-2003 and who once had been the Soviet Minster of Foreign Affairs in the final years of the Cold War.

So can Georgia really claim to have been occupied by the Soviets? What if the occupied are also the occupiers?

In Georgia, the use of the term is clearly a recent phenomenon—and one with a very twenty-first-century objective. In the Museum of Soviet Occupation, there was an obvious attempt to equate "Soviet" with "Russian" in the telling of Georgia's recent history, presumably in order to connect the Soviet "occupation" with Georgia's more recent confrontation with Russia in 2008 and Russia's current military support for—or occupation of—Abkhazia and South Ossetia, regions that Georgia adamantly insists belong to its national territory.[79]

Perhaps if tensions with their enormous, powerful neighbor decrease, Georgia's politicians and nationalist-leaning historians won't feel the need to recast the Soviet era for current political gain. Unfortunately, though, I think the idea of "occupation" is going to stick around for a long while.

***

For my last major Georgian excursion before I had to catch my train to Baku, I had originally contemplated making a dash to the seaside city of Batumi and its semi-tropical hinterlands in Adjara. However, at the last minute I decided that the coast was too much of a haul for a short trip and

---

[79] When I was in Kazbegi, I was within spitting distance of South Ossetia (and Russia for that matter). However, due to current tensions, it is all but impossible to visit the breakaway republic unless you do so from Russia—but Georgia considers such border crossings illegal. Apparently, Abkhazia is a little easier to visit, but you still have to get an Abkhazian "visa" in advance and then deal with the heavy military presence in the restive non-recognized republic. I was tempted, but ran out of time.

so instead I elected to go somewhere closer to Tbilisi. I settled on the region of Kakheti, famous as the premier wine-growing region in a country that is well known for its wine. Beyond that, I didn't really know much more about the area, other than that it had once been a separate kingdom, a fact in which some Kakhetis take a certain pride.

I chose Sighnaghi as my base, a town almost on the furthest edge of Kakheti, tucked into a tongue of Georgia that is surrounded on three sides by Azerbaijan. This is where I would truly come to understand Georgian hospitality.

"*Chacha*? Wine? Here, have some more cheese! Eat, eat!"

I had just returned from a long walk around the hilltop town, during which I marveled at its postcard-perfect panorama of the snowy Caucasus Mountains to the north and the incredibly flat valley below, which were vibrantly green with vineyards and small farms. I had also ventured out of town to pay homage to the grave and monastery of St. Nino, the woman credited with bringing Christianity to the Georgians. My plan had been to take a well-deserved nap.

However, when I returned to the guesthouse, I found what seemed to be the early stages of a spontaneous Georgian party. A lanky French guy, who had arrived around the same time that I had, was already several glasses of chacha (a very strong local spirit) into a series of playfully solemn toasts that were being called for by our host, Nato, and her husband, Lado. A small table was spread with warm, freshly baked bread, white sheep's cheese, and slices of tomato and cucumber. Simple fare, but amazingly tasty for its freshness. Somehow, almost immediately, a small glass of the amber liquid found its way into my hand, and I was pulled into the next toast.

Nato called for her young daughters, who were eight and ten, to sing Georgian songs for us. Not shy in the least, the duo performed one classic song after another in surprisingly strong, deep voices. The French guy pulled out a large, round hand drum that he had purchased in Turkey and began to accompany the girls. When a group of Polish women arrived, the music shifted to festive dance fare. All of us, Georgian and otherwise, weaved to the music and drank to friends, health, love, and whatever else seemed appropriate in the festive mood. The late afternoon sun cast a happy glow on the gathering.

***

"Look out for caves where the monkeys live!" my driver admonished. What? Monkeys? I knew there were poisonous vipers, but monkeys? "The churches where the monkeys pray!"
Ah! He means the *monks...*

I had a hard time believing that Davit Gareja, a lonely complex of cave churches and monasteries, was only a two-hour drive from Signhaghi. Sighnaghi exists in the more familiar Georgia of lush woods and verdant agricultural lands, lands seemingly ready to yield fruit as soon as it is planted, all framed by dramatic mountains. Davit Gareja, however, rests on a stony escarpment in a hot, treeless zone that in the summer, I am sure, is more brutal desert than the green pasture that it was when I visited, briefly alive in the Georgian spring.

Named for one of a group of Syrian ascetics who came to spread Christianity in the sixth century, the region is as remote as any that I had seen in Georgia. As soon as the driver from Sighnaghi turned off the main road to Tbilisi, the landscape began to change, growing increasingly desolate. Settlements became scarce. The last village before the monasteries was at least fifteen miles away, where it stood resolutely alone on the barren plain. The only traffic on the road consisted of sheep and cows that were being herded towards spring pastures by shepherds on horseback.

Although a bus of French pensioners arrived just before us, destroying the sense of splendid isolation, I was quickly able to pass them on the steep trail up to Udanbo, a string of abandoned churches and monk cells that were carved into a cliff that looks into the desert of Azerbaijan, the border of which was only a few feet away. Bored Georgian and Azeri soldiers, often standing within touching distance of each other, guarded a few points along the path. For the most part, though, no one was around to watch me clamber over the rocks to inspect the caves and their bright, disintegrating frescos. The sense of isolation returned.

Back down the hill, near the car park, I stepped into the only working monastery in Davit Gareja, the Lavra. Though large sections were off limits, as the monks lived and worked within the grounds, the main church was open. In the corner, under a gilded cover, stood the grave of the complex's namesake, Davit Gareja himself.

One of the soldiers I had seen on the hill had followed me in. He crossed himself, lit a prayer candle, and snapped a photo. Even the soldiers, it seems, are tourists in this otherworldly part of Georgia.

LAND OF ROCKS AND STONES: ARMENIA

When God was handing out land to all the peoples, the Armenians, of course, were late. By the time they arrived, God had given out all the lands.

"Please, God, we need somewhere to live! We will take any place that's left!"

"I'm sorry, but you are late. There's nowhere else available."

"Just give us some corner, anywhere!"

"Ok, ok... there is this place which is nothing but mountains and rocks. It's all that remains."

"We will take it! Thank you, thank you!"

So that is how Armenians ended up in Armenia.[80]

***

Almost as soon as the shared taxi from Tbilisi crossed the border and started heading south towards Yerevan, I was struck by just how different Armenia appeared from Georgia, despite the two being next-door neighbors. Even when we were still in the mountains, things had changed: gone were the soaring, jagged peaks of the Greater Caucasus and the dense forests that filled the deep valleys. Here the landscape, even while enveloped in spring greenery, seemed older, more worn. The

---

[80] The extension of the joke is: "The Georgians were even later than the Armenians. When they came before God, He said: 'But I have just given the Armenians the last place! You are very, very late!'

The Georgians though, being a stubborn people, kept insisting and insisting: 'Please, we will take *anything*, just let us have our own land!'

After a while, God couldn't take it anymore. 'OK, OK! I had been saving a piece of paradise on Earth for myself. But take it, take it!'

And that is how Georgians ended up with the mountains, the sea, and the wide valleys of Georgia... while Armenians only got rocks and stones."

mist-enshrouded mountains—still streaked with snow—were smoother, and gradually gave way to rolling, treeless plains that were scattered with rocks and boulders. Somehow, oddly, I was reminded of some Icelandic landscapes. It was beautiful, but still quite distinct from Georgia's dramatic vistas.

Similarly, when the taxi arrived in Yerevan, I discovered that it was quite another animal than Tbilisi. Central Yerevan is a neat grid of wide, leafy avenues, nestled into a bowl-shaped valley. The overall architectural scheme is rather restrained, mostly simple façades of dark pink stone, either tuff or basalt. Admittedly, though, Yerevan lacks the visual panache of Tbilisi or its rival's sense of great age. Due in large part to its location in a very seismic region, Yerevan's current form is quite new, with only a few rare buildings dating earlier than the mid-twentieth century—even though the city traces its history back to the founding of the Erebuni Fortress in 782 B.C.E.

Yet Yerevan, and Armenia as a whole, quickly began to seduce me with their subtler charms.

***

As the mini-bus from my hostel—shuttling a small clutch of guests on a day-trip tour called, appropriately, "Essential Armenia"—slipped past the Soviet-era suburbs that surround Yerevan and began the ascent into the surrounding highlands, I mentioned to our guide, Arpenik, how much the landscape—at least in its wetter springtime mode (since I am told much of the rest of the year Armenia tends to be, in a word, brown)—reminded me of Iceland. She said I wasn't the first to make that comparison, and then told the aforementioned joke about how Armenians ended up with rocky, volcanic Armenia.

Our first stop was on the high-altitude shore of Lake Sevan, the only lake of any size in this landlocked country; in the summer, it serves as the Armenian "seaside" escape for those seeking respite from the ferocious heat. However, I was not here for a dip; I was here to begin my immersion course in Armenian culture, of which the Armenian Church is a major component.

On a peninsula that once was an island[81], there stands a clutch of churches that were built in the stark style of the iconoclastic Armenian Apostolic tradition. As is the case for much of the traditional "history" of the Caucasus, legends intermingle liberally with hard facts. These churches—collectively known as Sevanavank, or Sevan Monastery—were supposedly built because Mesrop Mashtots, the inventor of the Armenian alphabet, had a vision of the twelve apostles walking across the lake and showing him the spot on which to found the first church. When Queen Mariam heard of Mashtots's vision in 874 C.E., she ordered the churches built. Further down the shore, at the edge of a village called Noratus, we stopped at what became my favorite of the Lake Sevan sights (and probably my favorite sight of all during this visit to Armenia): an ancient cemetery filled with Armenia's largest collection of *khatchkars*—literally, crosses of stone. Although the interior of Armenian churches tend to be extremely plain, these funeral markers are quite elaborate, a highlight of Armenian religious art. On a cool, misty day, with a view of snow-covered mountain slopes in the distance, the lichen-covered khatchkars made for a ghostly spectacle. Somehow, again, I was reminded of ancient Scandinavia, or perhaps the Celtic lands. Arpenik pointed out how each cross was unique, and mentioned how the lower portion represented earth and the upper portion heaven. Other stones showed in simple sculptural relief the stories of the deceased, both their lives and deaths. One particularly memorable gravestone portrayed an entire wedding party being killed by what appeared to be a rampaging Mongol.

In the afternoon, we drove to what might be the single biggest tourist attraction in Armenia, the Gerghard Monastery. The monastery is actually a set of cave churches that were carved into the walls of a scenic canyon; they

---

[81] The reason the peninsula is now a peninsula is that, during the Soviet period, Stalin ordered that a hydroelectric plant be built on the lake's outlet; the plan was to drain the lake to one-sixth its original size (one is reminded of the devastation wrought by similar planning around the much larger Aral Sea in Central Asia). However, the plan was not fully implemented—this was partly due to Stalin's death in 1953 and partly due to a trick played on Khrushchev by the head of the Armenian communists, who got him drunk on Armenian brandy and managed to get him to sign a document that ordered the construction of a tunnel to redirect waters back to the lake.

are named for the spear that pierced Christ's side during the crucifixion.[82] Of the many Armenian churches I entered, those at Gerghard evinced the greatest sense of spirituality and mysticism. When the pale sunlight filtered through the small windows that were cut into the rock face, penetrating the dark gloom of the sanctuaries, a sense of deep tranquility flooded through me. I could see why monks had chosen to worship here.

***

Of course, I continued my explorations of that important cornerstone of Armenian identity: religion. And so it was that one Sunday I headed to Echmiadzin, the "Vatican" of the Armenian Apostolic Church. The long service was already in full swing when I entered the cathedral of Mayr Tachar (Mother Church). The interior was the most ornate I've seen in Armenia: it included bright frescos that were most unlike the plain, stone walls of monastic churches such as Lake Sevan and Gerghard. A bishop in elaborate gold vestments stood before the altar, surrounded by a mixture of black-hooded priests—who looked to me like characters from a *Star Wars* movie—and red-robed altar boys, who chanted as the liturgy unfolded. A women's choir sang ethereally from the right arm of the cruciform sanctuary. Incense wafted through the air. Candles flickered. And I felt transported.

It occurred to me that my Protestant upbringing had been bereft of such wonderful mystery.

While I wandered through the holy town, I reflected on how deeply the Armenian identity is rooted to Echmiadzin and the very rocks of this desolately beautiful corner of the world—a corner that, according to Arpenik's joke, was given to the Armenians by God. Echmiadzin was the capital of ancient Armenia when it became the first "nation" to adopt Christianity as a state religion in 301 C.E. It was where the first Mayr Tachar (i.e., the first Armenian church) was erected. It is where the seat of the church remains.

---

[82] The spear—or at least what the Armenians believe to be the spear—used to be housed in Gerghard, but is now held at the Cathedral in Echmiadzin.

I started to understand why Armenians hold so tenaciously to their sense of difference...and to the very ground upon which their churches are built.

***

When I first entered the Mother Church in Echmiadzin, merging with the milling crowd listening to the Sunday liturgy, I had noticed a young man—he couldn't have been much older than twenty—lighting a prayer candle. He wore a black T-shirt that was emblazoned with the phrase: *1915, Never Forget the Truth.*

In Armenia, a country where history weighs heavily upon the hearts of all its residents, the shirt needed no further elaboration. 1915, in this case, could refer to only one thing: the event that most Armenians, and increasingly others, refer to as the Armenian Genocide.

***

As a history teacher, I often have to examine the darkest moments of the human experience with my students, from individual acts of violence, to wars, to genocides. Many of these topics, while disturbing, are generally not controversial—at least in the sense that they are accepted as having occurred and as having been appropriately labeled. For example, except for a few fringe loonies, no one denies that the Nazi regime instituted a systematic program to exterminate the Jews. However, frequently, many tragic historical events are wrapped in political discord with present-day ramifications.

Other than the better-known Arab-Israeli conflict, one of the most contentious topics I address in my world history and Middle East courses is the Ottoman deportations of the Armenians in 1915—during which a staggering number of Armenians perished. Like the Arab-Israeli conflict, it is extremely difficult to examine the events of 1915 dispassionately, as the story now plays a large part in modern nationalist narratives—especially in that of the Armenians and, less centrally, of the Turks. Any discussion of what happened and how it should be viewed frequently leads to vitriolic argument.

Much about this matter comes down to semantics. Armenians generally insist that the forced marches that were ordered by the waning Ottoman government during World War I—a government that was controlled by a triumvirate of Young Turk officers who had wrested power from the sultan, which left the Ottoman ruler essentially a political puppet—were intended to wipe out the Armenians, not "simply" to move them from the volatile border regions (where the Russians and Ottomans were fighting) to the more secure, interior Syrian lands. Armenians believe an official, not-so-secret order was given to eliminate as many of them as possible along the way; they also assert that at least 1.5 million were killed or died due to starvation and other deprivations. If this were the case, then the deaths could—and should—be considered genocide according to all official definitions.

However, the Turkish government estimates the death toll at a much lower 300,000, claiming that the losses were not the result of a premeditated order, but rather that they were an unfortunate consequence of the chaos of war. Thus, many Turks reject the term genocide. They also see little reason to apologize for actions conducted by the Ottoman state, as Turkey is, in this view, just one of many post-Ottoman states to emerge after the empire's dismemberment following World War I.

While I think this last point is a valid one—why should a political entity that did not exist in 1915 be held responsible for atrocities that were committed by its predecessor, whether a genocide or not?[83]—I also think that the official Turkish response undermines any moral high ground the government might otherwise have claim to. While many Turks are now ready to discuss the events of 1915 (and later) with more open-mindedness, the current government continues with its attempts to silence anyone who disagrees with the official position. Even the Noble Prize-winning author Orhan Pamuk was put on trial in 2005 for referring to the Armenian deaths as genocide during an interview. It is a highly misguided policy

---

[83] There are many who say the genocide didn't really end with the marches in 1915, but continued through the foundation of the Republic of Turkey in 1923. According to this perspective, actions during the Turkish War of Independence included attempts to eliminate the remaining Armenians in the territory that became Turkey.

that is aimed at protecting Turkish "honor" rather than dealing with the issue in an honest, constructive manner.

Obviously, 1915 plays a particularly significant role in Armenian historical narratives and has become central to the Armenian national identity. Unfortunately, this means that nationalist rhetoric often trumps a more nuanced portrayal of what happened and prevents more evenhanded discussions on how to negotiate present-day geopolitics. According to the Armenian perspective, for one, there can be no discussion without the use of the word genocide.

Moreover, the deaths in 1915 are now intimately connected with that potent Armenian sense of rootedness that I mentioned earlier. Thus, the genocide is not only a heartrending loss of life, but also a major loss of vital Armenian territory: after all, much of historical western Armenia was depopulated of Armenians during the deportations and now constitutes the far eastern side of the Republic of Turkey.

Not long before I finished up my two-year stint in Turkey in the late nineties, I drove through eastern Turkey; as I did, I saw some of the ghostly sights that remain of the once-vibrant Armenian presence in the region. I stood reverently in the empty chambers of the Akdamar Church, which sits proud and lonely on an island in the middle of Lake Van. I wandered the ruins of the ancient Armenian city of Ani with a Turkish soldier, where I gazed across the river that serves as the Turkish-Armenian border (which, incidentally, is still closed despite the recent attempts to thaw relations). I also met the last Armenian resident of Diyarbakir in the ruins of an Armenian cathedral. As I visited such places, I was easily able to understand the nostalgia for "Greater Armenia," which in its political heyday reached from the Caspian Sea to the Mediterranean. Modern Armenia occupies just a fraction of this former territory.

Yet there is an aspect of this nostalgia for lost Armenian lands that I find troubling. As is so often the case with modern nationalisms, nationalists will assert the equation land+people=nation. The Armenians have an unusually strong case, in some respects, compared to other nationalist claims, considering that that they have had a distinct state church since 301 C.E., a distinct alphabet since about 405 C.E., and a political history that predates even these events. However, at no time during this long history was "Armenia" a mono-ethnic territory. Indeed, it had always existed at one of the major crossroads of empire.

Armenia, and the southern Caucasus region in general, had been sandwiched between various pre-Islamic Persian empires (Achaemenid, Parthian, and Sassanid) and the Greco-Roman-Byzantine world, and then later between the great Islamic rivals of the Ottoman and Safavid empires. Moreover, the region was conquered, plundered, and often settled by various waves of Mongols and Turks who swept in from Central Asia. Finally, Russia came onto the scene in the late-eighteenth century.

Sometimes Armenia was a powerful rival to these competing states, but increasingly it served as a vassal to one or more of the imperial powers, and was often divided between two or more of them; in time, "Armenia" was simply absorbed into these states. Indeed, the last truly independent Armenian kingdom was that of Cilicia, which collapsed in the fourteenth century. Then, in the late-eighteenth century, the region became a three-way battleground between the Ottomans, Qajars (successors to the Safavids), and Russians.

It is not surprising, then, that the areas that once constituted "Greater Armenia" were always a rich mélange of ethnic, linguistic, and religious groups, of which the Armenians were one (albeit important) component. Even during the Soviet era—when the current borders of Georgia, Azerbaijan, and Armenia were established—the South Caucasus region remained extremely mixed. Cities, especially, reflected the great diversity of the region: Tbilisi, the capital of Georgia, had more Armenians than Georgians, while Yerevan, the capital of Armenia, was less than fifty percent Armenian.

However, since the collapse of the Soviet Union and the virulent resurgence of nationalism, Georgia, Azerbaijan, and especially Armenia have become essentially mono-ethnic states. Several times, I've heard the statistic that Armenia's population is now 98 percent Armenian.[84]

---

[84] Obviously, post-Ottoman Turkey has suffered the same loss of diversity due to ethnic nationalism. While Istanbul had once been a truly cosmopolitan city—with vibrant populations of Armenians, Greeks, Balkan Slavs, Jews, Arabs, Kurds, various Caucasian peoples, and others—it is now overwhelmingly Muslim and Turkish-speaking. The last major non-Turkish ethnic group in

So what "Armenia" do Armenian nationalists hope to revive? Although 1915 obviously marked a major rupture in the Armenian world, even at that time there was no independent Armenia. The Armenians were divided between the Ottoman and Russian empires, and had been for about a century (and between the Ottomans and the Qajars long before that). In both "Armenias" there were many non-Armenians. Can there be a place post-1915 in the land+people=nation equation for both the Armenians who live outside of independent Armenia and for non-Armenians who live inside it? If recent, tentative diplomatic efforts between Turkey and Armenian prove successful, then perhaps, just maybe, there can be.

***

The day was appropriately gray, the clouds low and threatening rain. The monument, too, was gray, a cone of twelve concrete slabs[85] with spaces between them that allow for glimpses of the eternal flame that burns in its sunken interior.

Nearby, a dark, jagged spire thrust towards the sky. A few mourners laid flowers by the flame.

I had climbed the hill to Tsitsernakaberd, the Armenian Genocide Memorial, to continue my own education on the Armenian perspective on 1915. The sense of loss—for the dead, for the land—was palpable. The monument serves as a more permanent, more visible version of the admonition I had read on the young man's T-shirt at the beginning of my Armenian trip: never forget the truth.

Turkey is the Kurds. There has been much struggle over how, and whether, to incorporate them into the Turkish "nation."

[85] Representing the twelve "lost" provinces that have become part of what is now Turkey.

The Armenian Genocide Memorial

Yet "truth" remains an elusive, contentious target. For the sake of the Armenians and the Turks, I hope that, between their differing senses of "truth" regarding the dark days of 1915, they can find a degree of concord and—eventually—peace.

LAND OF FIRE: AZERBAIJAN

Of the three southern Caucasus countries, the one about which I had the most pre-knowledge was enigmatic Azerbaijan, oil-rich and suspicious of the outside world.

Actually, my relationship to and interest in the country stretches back at least as far back as my sophomore year at Cornell, when I wrote a paper on the short-lived Azerbaijan Republic in Iran (1945-46) and its relationship to what was then Soviet Azerbaijan. That research project proved to be the foundation of my B.A. honors thesis two years later: "The Dual Historical Construction of Azeri Identity."

Even when I started my Ph.D. at Chicago, I remained intrigued by the Azeris, a Turkic-speaking, mostly Shi'a Muslim group who lived at the three-way fault line between the Turkic, Iranian, and Russian worlds. In large part, it was my earlier study of the Azeris that led me to focus on Shi'ism in the Ottoman Empire during my graduate studies.

Having read and written so much about the Azeris and Azerbaijan, I of course had to go. I even managed to secure a visa to Azerbaijan while I was living in Istanbul in the late nineties, but unforeseen events[86] prevented me from being able to go—which left me with the only unused visa I have in my passport. The closest I got after that first failed attempt was when I transitioned through Baku International Airport on my way to and from Turkmenistan in 2008—but I wasn't even allowed off the plane.

So after all these years, I finally managed to make it to the Caucasus, the final component of my sabbatical year. Azerbaijan was finally within easy reach!

---

[86]   I had befriended an Azeri guy who was staying in Istanbul for a few months. When he went back to Baku, he kindly went through the process of submitting an invitation so I could get a visa. As my friend still lived with his family, I was supposed to stay with a friend of his; unfortunately, his friend died in a major accident just a week before I was to fly to Azerbaijan. This sort of derailed the whole trip.

Unfortunately, however, there were still a few more obstacles along my path to the Land of Fire.

***

Nowadays, Georgia and Armenia are extremely easy countries to visit. Georgia has thrown open its doors, allowing many nationalities to enter visa-free (and often for great lengths of time). As a U.S. citizen, I can stay for a whopping 360 days without having to apply for a visa! Armenia, while still requiring a visa for Americans[87], also makes things easy: you can simply show up at the border, fill out a basic form, pay eight dollars, and be on your way. Moreover, both countries have well-developed tourist infrastructures, despite the fact that they are a bit off the radar for many travelers.

And then there is Azerbaijan.

Despite its status as the richest of the three Caucasian states, due to its oil and gas resources, and an extraordinarily cosmopolitan capital city (due, again, to the said oil and gas industry), Azerbaijan's government has moved in the opposite direction from its neighbors, making it increasingly difficult and expensive—not to mention frustrating!—to visit the country.

Back on my first full day in Tbilisi (and thus my first full day in the southern Caucasus), I had gone to a travel agency that specialized in helping people navigate the labyrinthine—one might even say Byzantine—mess that is the Azerbaijan visa application process. They got me an invitation letter from a travel agency in Baku, created a fake hotel reservation, and got the bank notice from the only bank (which happens to be on the opposite side of Tbilisi) that the embassy accepts as place of payment for the visa. I handed over the materials to the appropriate authority, and I was told that I would know the results in five or six business days.

However, the very next day I got a call from the agency saying that the embassy had informed them that they now wanted a letter from the Ministry of Foreign Affairs approving the letter of invitation—which would cost an extra $90 on top of the $160 I had already paid! I would

---

[87] Shortly after my visit to Armenia, the visa requirement for U.S. citizens, and all Europeans, was lifted. As I had suspected, Armenia seems to be following Georgia's example in making visiting increasingly easier.

have to resubmit the application and wait even longer, since this new development meant that I would now be applying during a holiday week.

I was almost shocked when—at last!—I was handed my passport with a shiny, new—partly handwritten!—Azeri visa. But I also half-expected that I would be turned away at the border, visa or no visa, when the border guards saw that I had visited Armenia. Thankfully, this was not the case! They didn't even notice the Armenian visa.

***

When I stepped off the train in Baku, I sighed with relief. I had made it, finally. I was in Azerbaijan! The worst was over.

Or so I thought.

I discovered on the day of my arrival that the Azeri government had recently put into law a requirement that all foreign visitors register within three days of entering Azerbaijan. In and of itself, this is not such a big deal: I have traveled in many countries that have similar regulations. However, the difference here was the lack of clarity regarding how to go about registering.

An American woman who I met at my Azeri host's birthday dinner told me that she had received a notification from the U.S. Embassy that announced the Azerbaijani government's stern warning that failure to comply with the new rules could result in a fine of up to four-hundred dollars, due upon one's attempt to leave the country, *and* the possibility of being denied exit until the State Migration Service had issued a letter of permission…which, of course, wouldn't be issued until after the fine had been paid. As my flight back to the U.S. was from Tbilisi, I couldn't risk being detained too much longer in Azerbaijan (and I couldn't really afford such a hefty fine, either).

I tracked down the Migration Service's webpage, but most of the pertinent information was buried several pages in, and the crucial form was only in Azeri. I could figure out the main points, since I am able to read Turkish (Azeri is quite close), but most visitors would have no clue where or how to begin. The rationale seemed to be that the form had to be submitted by whoever was hosting the visitor—whether a hotel or private individual. However, this required that the host know about the rule, but even many of the hotels didn't seem to know about the change. When I tried to see if I could pay one of the hotels to process the form for me, the staff looked at me like I was speaking Martian.

In the end, my very patient host[88] took me to an internet café where we could print out the form, scan my passport bio page and Azeri visa, and then submit everything to the specified email address (another odd thing to me—the requirement that I just send everything as informal email attachments). We even had a day to spare.

At last, I was legal! At least, I hoped so...

I should note that, despite the Azerbaijan government's clear efforts to discourage tourism, the Azeris—like everyone else in the Caucasus region—are some of the most hospitable people I have ever met. What a shame that such a wonderful place with such wonderful people should be so difficult to enter!

(By the way, in case you were curious, I was allowed to leave—so I guess my registration was in order.)

***

Azerbaijan, according to some etymologies, can be translated as "Land of Fire"—an appellation that seemed more than apt when I saw, from my train window, all the donkey-head oil pumps nodding up and down along the Caspian shore and the oil rigs jutting out of the sea itself. Oil and gas pipelines, refineries, and other oil-related heavy industry also scar the dusty landscape surrounding Baku. However, nowhere does the name seem truer to form than on the Abşeron Peninsula, which stretches just north and east of Baku.

In places like Abşeron, there have been times when the oil that has made Azerbaijan rich simply oozed from the ground, leaving black, viscous puddles. Natural gas also leaked into the air, sometimes set alight and sure to burn for eternity—or so it seemed to the mesmerized early inhabitants of this strange region. A land of fire, indeed.

Not surprisingly, the perpetual flames drew local fire-worshippers and Zoroastrians from Iran, who viewed fire as one of the sacred, purifying

---

88   While I don't suspect anything I write here would get him in trouble, I have decided to be a little extra cautious and not name my Azeri host or any of the other Azeris who helped me during my stay in Azerbaijan. Just in case.

elements. Others from further afield, too, were drawn to the flames. In the eighteenth century, in what is now the town of Suraxani on Abşeron, a group of Indian Shiva devotees established a temple around one the natural gas vents that had formerly been the site of a Zoroastrian temple. Although the Ateşgah has been heavily restored as a tourist attraction, it is still evocative of the earlier pre-industrial era of Azerbaijan's history... even if the temple's central flame is currently supplied by the Baku gas supply system. After all, the natural vent was depleted when the supply was tapped by industrial natural gas production!

The oil and gas in and around Baku began to draw a different, more worldly kind of attention in the nineteenth century as the industrial revolution created a demand for petroleum products. Baku transformed into a major boomtown in the late-nineteenth and early-twentieth centuries as the newly born oil industry kicked off; by 1905, it was supplying about half of the world's oil. Even the Nobel brothers got in on the act.[89]

***

In 2013, Baku still felt like something of a boomtown. Now that there is a pipeline that connects Azerbaijan to the Mediterranean via Georgia

---

[89] *Ali and Nino* is a novel set during that fast-changing time of Baku's history. It is a Romeo and Juliet-esque story about the ill-fated love of a Muslim Azeri boy and a Georgian girl that is told against the backdrop of Baku's wheeling and dealing oil barons and the looming Russian revolution. The novel, originally published in the 1930s, was almost forgotten until it was resurrected in the 1990s, shortly after Azerbaijan gained its independence from the U.S.S.R. and became embroiled in war with Armenia, thereby coming to the world's attention for the first time in decades. The novel, even in its most syrupy romantic passages, does a wonderful job of capturing the complexity of the Caucasus in general and of Baku specifically. The renewed popularity of the book has even spawned a mini-Ali and Nino industry: there's both an Ali and Nino Café and an Ali and Nino Bookstore in Baku. There's also an Ali and Nino monument in Batumi, though I didn't get a chance to see it.

Ali and Nino was first published with the author's name listed as Kurban Said. It was discovered later that this pseudonym belonged to Lev Nussimbaum, aka Essad Bey, a man whose life sounds more fictional than the fiction he (possibly) wrote. Check out *The Orientalist* by Tom Reiss for Nussimbaum's strange story.

and Turkey, the country is able to profit once more from its resources—though clearly, as with many other oil-rich countries, the wealth is not distributed evenly. Baku, as the capital, has experienced a dizzyingly fast development in the past decade or so; there are grand architectural projects going up seemingly overnight. One acquaintance told me that he left the country for a few weeks only to return to find an entire neighborhood had disappeared and been replaced with a large park!

Perhaps the most iconic of the new structures are the flame towers, a clutch of three sensuous, undulating skyscrapers that dominate the skyline above the old town. At night, they are lit by a flame-themed light show.

Everything is related to fire, of course, in the Land of Fire.[90]

Flame Towers and Ottoman Style Mosque: The New Baku

***

---

[90] Strangely, despite the Azerbaijani government's apparent disinterest in—well, active discouragement of—tourism, there is a tourist ad campaign promoting Azerbaijan as the Land of Fire. A notable example of this is the country's sponsorship of the Spanish soccer team, Atlético Madrid: all the players now wear jerseys emblazoned with the logo "Azerbaijan—Land of Fire".

Azerbaijan's experience of Ottoman rule, perhaps even more than that of other parts of the Caucasus region, was fragmentary at best. Although on the surface the Azeris, as Muslims and speaking a Turkic dialect quite close to Turkey-Turkish, would seem "natural" allies to the Ottomans, their history was even more entangled with the various "Persian," predominantly Shi'a, dynasties that ruled in Iran. Still, in the centuries long struggle between the Ottomans and the Safavids (and their successors), the territory that corresponds to modern Azerbaijan was occasionally conquered and absorbed into the Ottoman state. Ottoman forces took Baku and its surroundings from the Safavids in the 1580s, who then recaptured the territory in the early 1600s. A century later, in the early 1700s, much of Azerbaijan had once again come under Ottoman control—but only for a decade, after which it devolved into a patchwork of independent khanates. The last dance with the Ottoman Empire came during World War I, when the Ottoman Army of Islam (described briefly in the Georgia chapter), fueled by dreams of establishing a pan-Turkic empire, swept through the Caucasus and briefly occupied Baku. But, as is true for dreams, the final Ottoman hurrah in the Caucasus was to be short-lived. Indeed, the Ottoman Empire itself was soon to cease to exist.

I suppose I wasn't too surprised that I had a hard time getting a sense of the past—Ottoman or otherwise—in Baku, considering the massive "modernization" program that is transforming the cityscape. Even the historic center has been renovated to within an inch of its life; it is so polished up it appears to be a movie set. I also should not have been surprised that I had to leave Baku to find what I was looking for.

***

The first words that sprang to mind when I approached the building were: jewel box. The miniature palace for which Shaki (Şəki) is rightfully famous, despite being only two-stories high and—perhaps most surprisingly—only one room deep, is a confection of mosaics, mirror-work, bright frescos, stained glass, and interlacing wood. It was a lavish display, especially for a building that would be dwarfed by most homes in the American suburbs. Yet, I had to remember this was actually only the *summer* residence of the khans who once ruled this lovely corner of

Azerbaijan. The other buildings of the complex, including the winter palace, are barely a memory.

Shaki provides as good an example as any of the complexity of political and cultural allegiance in Azerbaijan, and really the Caucasus as a whole. The city claims a history that stretches back at least to the Bronze Age, if not earlier, but it first came to prominence under the now-confusingly named Albanian state that occupied a good chunk of what is modern Azerbaijan (and to which nationalists look for justification of their presence in the region). However, after the rise of Islam and the establishment of the Arab-Islamic Empire, Shaki was brought into the Muslim world. In the centuries that followed, it was sometimes ruled by Christian Georgian kingdoms, sometimes by Muslims of Turkic origin, sometimes by Muslims of Iranian origin. At times, such as after the collapse of the Mongol Empire, it was an independent state. However, with the rise of the Safavids and Ottomans, Shaki, just like the rest of the Caucasus, got caught in the middle of the imperial struggle, and fluctuated between Safavid and Ottoman rule for two centuries. Then, as Safavid power waned, the khans of Shaki managed once more to establish an independent state in 1743.

During the period of the Shaki Khanate, the city prospered; it became a major producer of silk and served as an important nodal point in the Silk Road trade that passed from Persia to the Ottoman Empire. Even today, one of the large caravansarays has been transformed into a modern hotel, so travelers can get an updated experience of staying the night in a traders' room.

But as with so many political configurations in the Caucasus, the Shaki Khanate was soon to become the target of yet another imperial power, Russia, which absorbed the state in 1813 under the terms of the Treaty of Gulistan.[91] The last khan was forced off the throne in 1819. Other than the brief occupation by the Ottoman Army of Islam in 1918, Shaki was firmly within the Russian (and then the Soviet) sphere of influence

---

[91] This was the conclusion of the first Russo-Persian war (1804-1814), fought between the expansionist Russian Empire and the relatively newly established Qajar state in Iran. The Treaty of Gulistan was one of the first official documents to grant large swaths of the Caucasus to Russia, making the region the nexus of a three-way struggle between the Ottomans, Qajars, and Russians all the way through World War I.

until Azerbaijan gained its independence in 1991 after the collapse of the U.S.S.R.

Although now eclipsed by the too-rapidly developing capital of Baku, present-day Shaki is a quiet, medium-sized town that takes great pride in its past. Many of the khanate era structures, like the palace and caravansaray, have been restored and repurposed. Parks have been cleaned up, which gives a green feel to the city—and in the parks, children play, young couples stroll, and grandmotherly and grandfatherly types gossip. Sweets shops proliferate along the main shopping streets, selling colorful treats and candies to passersby. It is perhaps the loveliest, most relaxed city in Azerbaijan; one that embraces rather than rejects its history. It was the perfect spot to end my journey in this country that had first captured my imagination as a young undergrad and that has haunted me ever since.

But there was an even more befuddling corner of the Caucasus to experience, one that also played a role in my undergraduate honors thesis—an unrecognized breakaway state that has caused a great deal of heartache and distrust between Azerbaijan and Armenia: Nagorno-Karabakh.

MOUNTAINOUS BLACK GARDEN: NAGORNO-KARABAKH

What struck me most was the emptiness.

For much of the way from the tiny, unrecognized capital of this tiny, unrecognized country, I and the other passengers on the mini-bus had the road all but to ourselves. The empty stretch led through an empty but gorgeous landscape of bare mountains and shadowed valleys. Then, around a bend, I saw the first building: an empty shell of a house. And then another.

As I began to register what I was seeing, I realized that this was just the edge of an entire city that was utterly… empty.

Welcome to Agdam, the "Hiroshima of the Caucasus."

Hiroshima of the Caucasus

Agdam is a city on the very frontline of the Azerbaijan-Armenia conflict over Nagorno-Karabakh; it was devastated by the war that erupted in the early nineties and left nothing but a ghost town, an eerie testament to the not-so-peaceful ceasefire. Although largely ineffective, the ceasefire was the only reason that we were able to slip past the city and a military training exercise (complete with ten bona fide tanks) that was occurring further down the road on our way to the excavation site of an ancient Armenian city.

I couldn't think of a more potent symbol of the Azeri-Armenian conflict than empty Agdam.

***

It's a strange name: Nagorno-Karabakh. Nagorno is the Russian word for "mountainous," while Karabakh is a Turco-Persian construction that means "black garden." Mountainous Black Garden. To confuse things even more, in Armenian, it is often called Artsakh (supposedly referring to "woods").

I first became familiar with this odd Soviet-era creation when I began to research the history of Azeri nationalism for my B.A. honors thesis.[92] As if designed to fuel future conflict, the political engineers of the U.S.S.R. created a veritable jigsaw puzzle out of the southern Caucasus (or, from the Russian and later Soviet perspective, Transcaucasia), thereby establishing the three main republics of Georgia, Azerbaijan, and Armenia. However, their efforts didn't end there: they also carved out a network of enclaves, exclaves, and autonomous republics/regions. When the Soviet Union collapsed, some of these areas sought independence from the "mother" republics, which often led to bloody conflict. In little Georgia, as we have seen, there is not one but two major separatist movements: in Abkhazia and South Ossetia. A third potential breakaway region, Adjara, has largely been reabsorbed, but operated all but independently until the early 2000s. However, the first major regional conflict—one that would prove perhaps the bloodiest of all—erupted between Armenia and Azerbaijan over

---

[92] *The Dual Historical Construction of Azeri Identity: Towards Nation-Statism in Northern Azerbaijan and Regional-Particularism in Southern Azerbaijan.* Could I have been more pretentious? But I did earn summa cum laude for my efforts!

Nagorno-Karabakh in 1989, two years before either country achieved independence.

Both Armenians and Azeris claim Nagorno-Karabakh as an important center for their respective nations. Armenians point to the region's long history with Armenian Christianity and its role in various Armenian states (as the province of Artsakh). Azeris, as a distinct Turkic-speaking Muslim community in the Caucasus, claim Karabakh (or Qarabaq) as their cultural homeland; they emphasize the important role that the city of Shushi (or Şuşa), the former capital of the Karabakh Khanate, played in the early development of a distinct Azeri language and literature. There are also Azeri nationalist claims—which seem like more of a stretch—that the local Christians were not Armenian *per se*, but Christianized "Albanians"; as previously mentioned, this was the confusing name given to a mysterious group who lived in the area (with no connection to Balkan Albanians). In this theory, some of the Caucasian Albanians converted to Islam and were absorbed into the Azeri "nation," while the others adopted Armenian Christianity and the Armenian language—and so, this argument goes, they can't really be considered Armenian!

Karabakh Armenians, of course, tend to disagree.

Whatever the case, by the early eighteenth century the area that is now Nagorno-Karabakh possessed a heterogeneous population of Turkic-speaking Muslims and Armenian-speaking Christians, but it is impossible to tell in what proportions. When Russia began to compete with Qajar Iran and the Ottoman Empire for influence and control of the Caucasus, important demographic shifts began to occur that laid the foundation for the more recent conflicts.

In 1805, the Russian Empire annexed the Muslim-ruled Karabakh Khanate. Many local Muslims migrated south into Persian controlled territories; meanwhile, many Christians—especially Armenians—moved into the former khanate. Thus, at least by the mid-nineteenth century, Karabakh had become a predominantly Armenian region, but a significant Muslim minority remained.

In the political shufflings of the early-twentieth century, after the Russian Empire had given way to the grand experiment that was the U.S.S.R., Nagorno-Karabakh was made a part of Muslim majority Azerbaijan, but declared an autonomous oblast. To add to the crazy patchwork, a region called Naxçıvan was declared a full part of Azerbaijan, but was separated from the main territory by a large swath of Armenia. It is perhaps not too surprising, then, that even before Azerbaijan and Armenia declared formal independence in 1991 they were at war over territory—and particularly Nagorno-Karabakh.

***

In 1994, a ceasefire of sorts was established, although there are still regular skirmishes near the contested borders. In general, though, throughout much of Nagorno-Karabakh one would never know that a war was still going on.

On the surface, Nagorno-Karabakh operates very much as an independent country. When I was preparing to visit, I had to get a visa and travel permit from the Nagorno-Karabakh Embassy in Yerevan. They did, however, honor my request to not affix it to my passport; I didn't want the Nagorno-Karabahkian visa to interfere with my plans to visit Azerbaijan. After I passed through the corridor that Armenia established to connect itself to the territory, taking the only usable road in and out, I arrived at a checkpoint that flew both the Armenian and quite similar Nagorno-Karabakh flags. Once there, my documentation was checked by uniformed Karabakh officers who were, thankfully, a lot more welcoming than those I met crossing into the Trans-Dniestr Republic.

The biggest surprise for me, however, was Stepanakert, the capital. I am not sure what I was expecting exactly, but I was taken aback by how tidy and prosperous the little city turned out to be. It was obvious that a fair amount of money—much of it from Diaspora Armenians—had been poured into the revitalization of the once war-ravaged town. The main street was lined with new buildings, including swank new hotels and shops. In the main roundabout, there was a small park with a dancing fountain; watching the high-pressure jets of water weave and wave was almost hypnotic. The scene was made complete in the evenings, when the fountain was the setting for musical performances and light shows. Nearby, new government buildings towered over a large pedestrianized square. It was a bit surreal, given the stark emptiness that I travelled through to get to this lavish location and the ongoing hostilities along the area's borders.

A short distance away, perched on a strategic hill overlooking Stepanakert, the ancient town of Shushi (Şuşa) showed more indication that a war had occurred (and was still simmering). This had once been the capital of the Karabakh Khanate, and so was of particularly strong importance to the Azeris who controlled it in the early stages of the war; plus, it provided a perfect vantage from which to shell the Armenians who were entrenched down the hill. But the tide turned in the Armenian forces' favor when they were able to capture Shushi, an important symbolic event in the conflict. The first tank to breach the Azeri resistance is now situated outside of town, where it serves as a monument to Armenian victory.

In town, although there has been some reconstruction, there are many buildings that show bullet holes and evidence of shellings. Many are completely destroyed. Some of the more haunting monuments of the conflict are the now-empty, derelict mosques—some of the last that remain within Nagorno-Karabakh territory. However, my local guide—an earnest young woman in her twenties, too young to remember the original conflict—tried to emphasize that the mosques were being restored and protected, as they were considered part of the Karabakh "national" heritage; she contrasted the beneficent Armenian efforts with the destruction Azeris wrought on Armenian structures in places like Naxçıvan. I bit my tongue; I didn't tell her that I had heard all this before—but from the Azeri perspective.[93]

***

When I reflect on my weeks spent crisscrossing the southern Caucasus republics, I marvel at the tremendous diversity I observed in, and especially between, the three countries, even though all of them are smaller than many U.S. states. Each has charted a unique path out of its recent Soviet past: Azerbaijan has become a wealthy, oil-producing state, led by a highly autocratic "president" and a government that puts tight controls on who can enter the country. Resource-poor Armenia relies heavily on support from the Armenian Diaspora, especially from Armenians who live in the

---

[93] Several times I was told of how Azeris destroyed all the khatchkars in Naxçıvan, which once possessed the greatest number of the Armenian cross-stones. Interestingly, in Azerbaijan, I heard almost the same story—how Armenians destroyed mosques and other Muslim sites, while Azeris of course never harmed any churches. Just swap the names.

U.S., but is slowly trying to build up a tourist industry and open its doors to the outside world. However, this small country remains isolated, due to its difficult relationships with both Turkey to the west and Azerbaijan to the east. And then there is Georgia, which—despite its troubled relations with Russia, its multiple secessionist movements, and the occasional coup—has developed rapidly and become a major tourist attraction, warm and welcoming to visitors.

Yet each country has become, sadly, more homogeneous than at any other point in the convoluted history of the Caucasus: this is largely due to their historical experiences of the past two-hundred-plus years at the crashing point between the Ottoman, Qajar, and Russian (and then later the Turkish, Pahlavi[94], and Soviet) worlds and due to the machinations of nationalists in each. Georgians live in Georgia, Armenians in Armenia (and Nargorno-Karabakh), and Azeris in Azerbaijan. The days of an Ali and Nino-style love affair in Baku are pretty much dead.

And yet, when I looked hard enough, especially in the isolated valleys of the Caucasus ranges, I was able to find hints of the mishmash of languages, religions, and ethnicities that once characterized the whole swath of territory between the Caspian and Black Seas. There are pockets of Iranian-language speakers in the mountains of Azerbaijan; there are still Muslims in Georgia. But I had to listen carefully to the echoes of the imperial past of the Caucasus to hear the former cacophony of voices speaking in Georgian, Armenian, Azeri, and so many other languages, voices that once used to sing out, side-by-side, in relative harmony.

---

[94] The dynasty of two—Reza Shah and Muhammad Reza Shah—that ruled Iran from 1925 up to the Islamic Revolution in 1979.

PART IV

Ottoman Central - Turkey

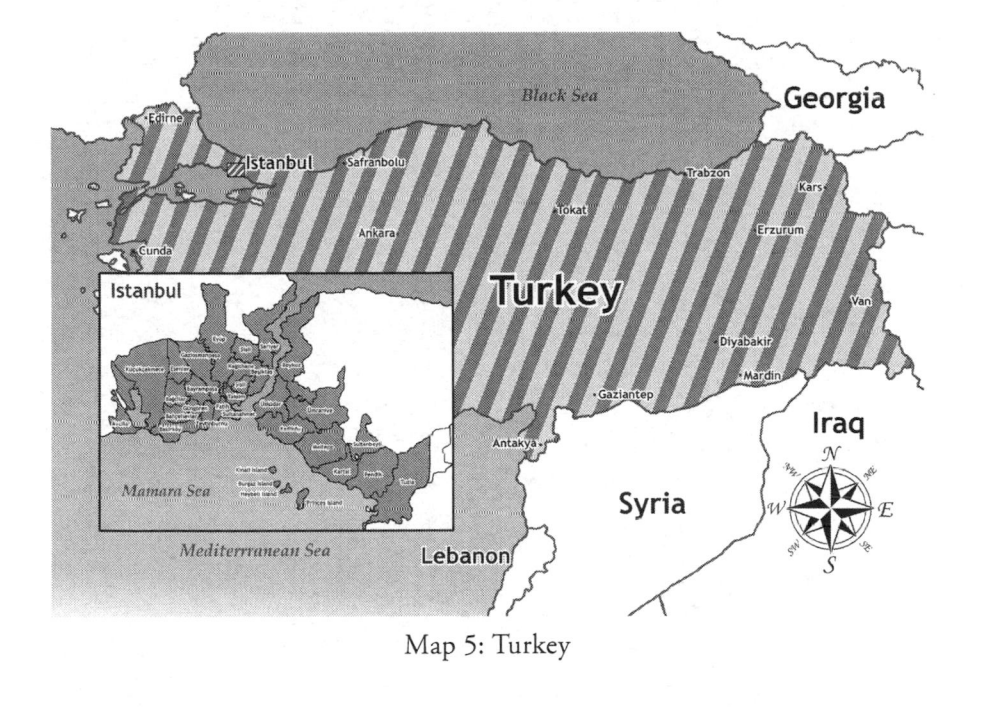

Map 5: Turkey

After that Dr. Zhivago-esque moment, securing my visa somewhere on the Greek-Turkish border in the middle of the night (see Part I), I laid down, ready to get some fitful shut-eye, wrapped in almost all my clothes against the bitter cold of the unheated train compartment. I couldn't have been asleep for a more than a few hours, though, when a beam of sallow, morning light hit my face. Across from me, the only other passenger in the compartment—an Argentine boy who was similarly bundled up—started to stir. Groggily, I pulled myself up and looked out the window, and there it was: Istanbul.

We were rounding the southern edge of the Old City, passing the crumbling remains of the former defense walls that lined the Marmara shore. Between the breaks in the wall I caught glimpses of sagging Ottoman wooden houses and the occasional bland, concrete structure. Further up the hill, I saw flashes of minarets and domes. There were more than I could count. The sky was dark gray, low; there was a threat of snow.

Before we pulled into Sirkeci Station, the terminus of the European portion of the former Oriental Express, I already knew I had fallen in love. I often say that is the moment when I truly became an Ottomanist.

Of course, I had an intellectual interest in the Turco-Islamic world well before I ever set foot in Turkey, but it was largely confined to books. However, my arrival in Istanbul—when I stumbled off that rickety, cold train that had transported me through the night and across two countries—produced a visceral response. Even Cairo, which I had also taken to quickly, had not elicited such a strong gut reaction. Somehow, even without having yet explored the city, I felt immediately at home. My intellectual pursuits were now combined with a palpable passion.

My first visit was relatively short. I was on my winter break trip between semesters at the American University in Cairo, trying to make my way by land between Athens, Greece, and Cairo, Egypt in around two-and-a-half weeks. Before the trip, I think my main aim was to see if I could travel solo successfully; this ability was confirmed by that trip. Actually, I look back at that early, multi-country journey—Egypt, Greece, Turkey, Syria, Jordan—with some pride. For a boy from Indiana who had never traveled further than Canada before his study-abroad year, I was able, on my own, to navigate through five countries and three linguistic zones by my own wiles. Towards the end of that summer journey, somewhere in my crossing between Syria and Jordan, I turned twenty-one—an event I celebrated with friends who I had made in Amman during my stint there. They bought me a cake and took me to see, of all things, Jim Carrey's *The Mask*.

But it was the trip that made me feel "grown up," not my age.

There was something else that occurred on that journey, however, that was even more important. By choosing to go the slow way—by train, by bus, by shared taxi—most of the time, I had the privilege of seeing how little borders really mattered.

Yes, there were differences. Obviously, in Greece, most people spoke Greek; in Turkey, Turkish; and in Syria and Jordan, Arabic.

Yes, there were official border crossings, at mysterious spots in the woods and at more formal junctures. When I arrived at the Syrian border, I was the only non-Syrian or non-Turk: I patiently answered the official's questions about whether I had been to Israel or whether I planned to go (a story I will relate in the chapter on Syria).

Yet, for all the linguistic and political barriers, I noticed far more in common in that arch of countries than I did differences. I saw a cultural and historical blend that seeped across their borders, taking on local flavors while still retaining a common essence. I knew even then, as a beginning student of Islamic history, that all these places had been under Ottoman rule. But I don't know if I was consciously seeing—yet—the Ottoman-ness of it all. That would develop further as I continued to live, work, and explore within the former Ottoman world.

*** *** ***

I have waited until now to discuss Turkey, rather than putting it at the front of the book (as might be expected) for several reasons. One reason, as I mentioned in the introduction, is that I wanted to de-emphasize the idea that Turkey equals the Ottoman Empire—and, conversely, to bring to the fore the other Ottoman territories.

As I also mentioned, modern Turkey—or, more accurately, the Anatolian peninsula that it occupies—does constitute the original core of the empire. So by placing it at the (roughly) center of the text, I am symbolically showing the country's geographic location and its political and cultural centrality to the Ottoman World, especially when, at its peak, Istanbul was one of—if not the—most important cities in the world. If one imagines the empire as a wheel, albeit a very unevenly shaped wheel, Anatolia is the axis around which the circle turns.

Lastly, I saved Turkey for now because it is the place I have visited the most.

Unlike my chapters on the Balkans, Black Sea, and Caucasus states, for which most of the materials were drawn from my sabbatical travels in 2012-2013, I have a particularly intimate experience of Turkey, and especially of Istanbul, that has been built over twenty years. From that first, brief visit during a cold January in the mid-nineties, through my more extended periods as a graduate student—first studying modern Turkish at Boğaziçi University in an intensive summer program and then as a pre-dissertation fellow, rummaging through the Başbakanlık (Prime Ministry) Archives, followed by a year of teaching English as a Second Language to keep me in the country for another year—to the periodic visits since (my last trip to Turkey, before the publication of this book, was in spring 2014), I have come to know the country in all its confounding complexity.

More than any place in the Ottoman world, Turkey has been a home for me—and I knew that was going to be the case from the first moment I spied Istanbul from my train in January 1995.

The early twenty-first century is a particularly interesting juncture at which to discuss Turkey and the Ottoman past, both in terms of Turkey's relationship to Ottoman history and its legacy as the imperial center among the Ottoman successor states. Over the last two decades, Turkey has emerged from its status as a relatively poor and insular state—much hated by some of the nationalists in neighboring countries for its association with "Ottoman oppression"—into a regional, if not world, power. When Recep Tayyip Erdoğan and his Justice and Development Party (known by the Turkish acronym A.K.P.), a moderate Islamist party, performed well in the 2002 elections and formed the first majority government in more than a decade, many secular Turks were extremely nervous, worried that the A.K.P. would lead the country down a path similar to that of neighboring Iran. At least initially, they were proven wrong.

Under the A.K.P., Turkey experienced an economic boom and an expansion of its influence within the Middle East and the Balkans (former Ottoman lands) and even beyond. This was particularly true in areas like Central Asia that shared both a Turkic and Islamic heritage, even if they had not been part of the Ottoman Empire. Even in countries where anti-Turk sentiment had been quite high, there was an influx of Turkish companies, often appearing on the heels of new Turkish Air flights. I was surprised to see that reach extend as far as Sudan, one of the furthest-flung corners of the Ottoman world, when I started working there in 2010. Turkish construction companies had built a number of the new structures in Khartoum, and Turkish entrepreneurs had set up shop all over town (strangely, they seemed to have cornered the curtain and barbershop markets).

Beyond its rapid economic growth, Turkey also became a more active leader in regional politics, often serving as an alternative—or more immediate—mediator in regional conflict, rather than the more expected U.S. and European actors. For example, Turkey began to take a greater role in issues involving Israel and Palestine. As Turkey's influence grew, many political and economic observers began talking of a growing neo-Ottomanism.

However, perhaps even more than the booming business and expanding political reach, nothing illustrates as well the growing influence of Turkey in the former Ottoman world—and the complex relationship all the former Ottoman territories (including Turkey) have with the Ottoman past—than the phenomenon that is *Muhteşem Yüzyıl*, or *The Magnificent Century*, a soap opera based on the life and times of Sultan Süleyman and his wife Hürrem Sultan (generally known as Roxelana to the "West").

After its initial airing in 2011, *The Magnificent Century* was soon broadcast throughout much of the Arab world and the Balkans[95], quickly becoming one of the most popular series in many countries—even in ones like Serbia that, as we have seen, had built its national identity in large part on a narrative of Ottoman oppression. Although (as is to be expected from a soap opera) the acting is terrible and the story is only loosely historically accurate, the fact that an Ottoman-themed show, set in the period when the Ottoman empire was at its most aggressively expansionist and at its peak geographic size, should become so popular with a modern generation

---

[95]   Apparently, the soap opera's appeal has gone truly global, gaining audiences in Latin America, too.

speaks volumes about how closely felt the Ottoman past remains. In some places, the streets would empty when the show aired.[96]

Interestingly, although in part produced because of the cultural climate that Erdoğan and the A.K.P. had fostered—one that embraced rather than rejected the Turkish Republic's connection to the Ottoman Empire—Erdoğan himself is not a fan of the show: he seems to see it as showing Süleyman in a bad light. Perhaps, in his not-so-subtle attempts to draw connections to Ottoman leadership, he sees himself as a modern Süleyman, building his empire.

Fluttering Politics

---

[96] Even the New Yorker noticed the phenomenon. See the article by Elif Batuman: http://www.newyorker.com/magazine/2014/02/17/ottomania

One could write an entire book on the growing megalomania of Recep Tayyip Erdoğan, but that is really not the focus of this book. Still, I think it is worth spending a little time looking at the tension that has risen in the country, especially since he won a third term as prime minister in 2011 and then, of course, managed to get himself elected president in 2014 in the first public elections for that office. In his early years as prime minister, he and the rest of the A.K.P. establishment seemed to buck most of the dire predictions that more secular Turks had made. Although many were uncomfortable with the growing visibility of women in headscarves, for example, the country seemed far from heading towards an Iranian-style theocracy. Instead, the A.K.P. government was actually extremely pro-European Union, fighting to get Turkey into the "club" despite the odds. It was also very pro-business, as evident by the Turkish economic "miracle" that resulted in the nation becoming one of the leading economies in the world—and even weathering the major global financial crisis in 2008.

Istanbul—while always beautiful, even in its melancholy[97]—began to be spruced up over the past decade or so. For instance, its transportation system was expanded and integrated. I was astonished when I visited in both 2013 and 2014 at how easy it had become to zip around this sprawling city by a combination of metro, tram, ferry, bus, etc., all while using a common transport card. On a social level, even with the general conservatism of the ruling elites, I noticed an increased visibility of minority groups—even L.G.B.T. communities. Although there were gay bars and clubs when I lived in Istanbul in the late nineties, people can now go to a café just off of İstiklal Caddesi and drink a beer, in the open and under a fluttering rainbow flag. So, from an outsider's perspective, the overall direction Turkey was taking seemed positive. It was becoming a different kind of successor to the Ottoman Empire.

Then came Erdoğan's third term. It was as if the prime minister saw the vote as a mandate to become an all-powerful sultan, free to act as he wished, regardless of the consequences. The building projects that had marked his period in office thus far began to become increasingly grandiose

---

[97] Orhan Pamuk, in his *Istanbul: Memories and the City*, beautifully capture's the city's melancholic nature, employing the evocative Turkish word *hüzün* (from the Arabic *huzn*). Hüzün is difficult to translate, but plumbs the spiritual depths of melancholia.

and thoughtless. Historic buildings, and even whole neighborhoods, were demolished and replaced with mall after mall. A third Bosphorus bridge was planned, and then begun, under much protest.[98] Construction began on a third international airport, designed to be the largest in Europe (rather than expanding the two already quite functional ones). Even more bizarrely, there was even a proposal to construct a second Bosphorus, an impossibly large manmade waterway that, like the natural Bosphorus, would connect the Black Sea and the Mediterranean—and which, if built, would prove an unmitigated natural disaster. It's so crazy, it is known simply as "the Crazy Project."

All this was bad enough, and discontent over the increasingly authoritarian measures was growing by the day, but the worst was yet to come. When I was in Istanbul in March 2013, at the beginning of my Black Sea leg of the Ottoman "tour," many of my Turkish friends were pessimistic about the future. They were troubled by the new laws that were creeping into place that seemed to be harbingers of a more Islamist ethos: new strictures on the sale of alcohol, censorship of certain websites, and the like. Still, I couldn't have predicted then what was to erupt just a couple months later in Gezi Park.

When I lived in Istanbul, Taksim Square was the mad heart of modern Istanbul. It was hardly beautiful, especially in contrast to the Old City and Pera, but it was an important transportation and social hub. In the urban sprawl of Istanbul, Taksim was where most paths crossed. It was thronged with buses, taxis, and *dolmuşlar* (shared taxis). Cheap fast food restaurants lined the roads. Major hotels, like the Marmara, loomed over the chaos. Even the Atatürk Cultural Center, a dismal modernist monstrosity, had its part in the scene. Almost lost in the midst of the hubbub was a bit of greenery right in the center of the square, Gezi Park. Admittedly, it was a scruffy place and, at night, a little dodgy to wander through. But it was the only green spot in this part of the city.

Not surprisingly, in the attempts to clean up and modernize the city, Taksim became a focal point of the A.K.P.'s redevelopment plans. Some of the earlier projects, such as the creation of a metro line stretching from Taksim up to some of the newer business districts and a funicular train

---

[98] At the moment, construction on the third bridge seems to have been halted— possibly due to its having been mislocated!

heading down to the Bosphorus shore, were improvements. The square became a little less chaotic, more pedestrian friendly. Then the space was going to be expanded, connected to the once down-and-out neighborhood of Tarlabaşı, which would make most of the square fully pedestrian. But the plan to rip up the park itself and build a replica of an Ottoman barracks— likely to house a mall, no less—in its place proved to be a step too far.

Although they ostensibly started as an environmental movement that was concerned with the increased bulldozing of the city at the whim of the government and its business cronies, the Gezi Park protests were to become something much bigger when the government, using very strong-arm tactics, came in with water cannons and tear gas to dispel the protestors. For those who were already anti-Erdoğan and anti-A.K.P., the true colors of the regime were revealed. The first protestors were now joined with a newly galvanized political opposition that saw the demolition of Gezi Park as merely a symptom of a wider, more dangerous, problem: unchecked political authority. I watched the news in astonishment while I was traveling in the Caucasus. How could *that* be the same city that I had just visited a few months previously? I had even stayed in the Gümüşsuyu neighborhood, just down the hill from Taksim; it had been so peaceful then!

The unrest continued for a number of months, spreading to other cities, but overall staying largely contained in a few key spots, such as Taksim. The A.K.P. supporters seemed to dig in their heels, believing the stories that Erdoğan and others told the protestors—that they were being guided by mysterious foreign interlopers or members of a "State within a State".[99] But by the time I revisited in March 2014, a year after the protests had started, Erdoğan was still in power—and Taksim Square was essentially one big slab of characterless pavement. It was a depressing, if

---

[99] In practice, this refers to the indeed rather shadowy followers of Fethullah Gülen, a mysterious religious leader of a modernist, vaguely Sufi, Islamic sect who now lives in Pennsylvania. Although it would take another chapter—or rather a whole book!—to really get at the Gülenist movement, suffice it to say that the Gülenists and A.K.P. worked closely together in the early years of Erdoğan's rise to power. Many Gülen supporters ended up in high-level positions in the Turkish judiciary, among other areas. However, something soured the relations between Erdoğan and Gülen in the past couple years, and the former allies have become bitter enemies. It is widely believed, for example, that the current news leaks on corruption in the A.K.P. have come from loyalists to the Gülen movement.

appropriate, symbol of the political impasse. I found myself nostalgic for the grittier, bustling Taksim that I knew in the nineties.

There were, of course, continuing attempts by the opposition to fight for political change. Even while I was there, there were preparations for local elections: ones that normally would not have been deemed too important, but that in the current political climate were viewed as a means to gauge the political winds. Most of my friends were shocked to see the A.K.P. do surprisingly well in these elections. This surprise was particularly sharp given the fact that, shortly before I arrived, there had been a resurgence of Gezi Park-style protests when a teenage boy, Berkin Elvan, died after being in a coma for a year—a coma that had been induced when he was hit in the head with a tear gas canister when he was on the way to buy bread during the original protests. He became a martyr of sorts for the anti-A.K.P. movement, and tensions rose once more; however, Erdoğan supporters remained loyal and large in number.

I suppose, in a way, that I shouldn't have been surprised. For many of these people, life had gotten much better under Prime Minister Erdoğan. They were earning more, had greater access to the outside world, and didn't feel as discriminated against for their religious views. Nevertheless, it was hard for me to understand how they couldn't see the disturbing draconian trend in his leadership.

Perhaps it took something like the Soma mine disaster to finally get the message across that Erdoğan was not just megalomaniacal, but perhaps genuinely unhinged. In May 2014, Turkey experienced its worst mining accident to date. By any measure it was a tragedy, the sort that calls for a national acknowledgment and official condolences from a country's leader. However, when Erdoğan went to Soma, he gave a bizarre speech in which he cited nineteenth-century mining accidents in places like Britain, apparently as a means to show that such things happen in mines. Obviously, the grieving family members and friends of those who died were not comforted. What made this egregious political gaffe all the more egregious was the fact that Soma and similar spots, which had seen an increase in production—and thus jobs—due to the frenzied building programs of A.K.P.-era Turkey, were actually bastions of A.K.P. support. However, Erdoğan's callousness led to a furious response by the locals. At one point, he had to be hustled into a shop to avoid an angry mob. For perhaps the first time, his core supporters got to see the prime minister at his worst. Only time will tell what his political future holds, though. As this book is printed, Erdoğan is still serving in his new role as president.

***

But what does all this have to do with Turkey's relationship to its Ottoman past? Since the founding of modern Turkey by Mustafa Kemal Atatürk, the Turks have had, to say the least, an ambivalent relationship to their Ottoman heritage.

Atatürk, himself, very much a product of the late Ottoman Empire— he was a tall, blue-eyed military figure who was born and raised in Salonica (now Thessaloniki, Greece) and who went to high school in Monastir (now Bitola, Macedonia) before joining the military academy in Istanbul. During World War I, he distinguished himself during the Gallipoli Campaign against the forces of the Australian and New Zealand Army Corps (A.N.Z.A.C.). Following the collapse of the empire after the war, he led the Turkish resistance against the Allied Powers' attempts to dismantle the Ottoman world, managing against great odds to carve out the territory that is now Turkey. It is likely that, without his leadership, Turkey would have become the rump state envisioned by the Allies, a swoop of territory in central Anatolia with a bit of Black Sea coast, surrounded by states under the neocolonial control of France, Britain, Italy, and even Greece. For that act alone, Atatürk was—and is—revered.

However, simply establishing a national state for the Turks was not enough for Atatürk. He wanted to make the new country a thoroughly modern "European" state on par with those that had defeated the Ottomans. With breathtaking speed, he set forth a series of westernizing reforms that continue to have a major impact on Turkish society. Perhaps the most profound changes were the language reforms[100], during which not only was Ottoman Turkish stripped of many of its Arabic and Persian loan words

---

[100] Other reforms included laws against certain styles of dress. Men, unless they were religious scholars and clerics, were even banned from wearing the "fez," the conical red hat that was a fashion among Ottoman subjects throughout the empire. Instead, they had to wear European brimmed hats. The veil for women was also outlawed, which is one of the main reasons it remains a highly contentious issue between Kemalists and A.K.P. supporters.

and grammatical structures in an attempt to "purify" the language, but the script was also changed from Arabic letters to a newly formulated Latin alphabet. In conjunction with a vigorous literacy campaign, Ottoman Turkish gave way, in a matter of a couple generations, to the language that it is now "modern" Turkish.

As a non-Turk who studied Ottoman Turkish, I always found it both amusing and a little sad—even melancholic—to wander the streets of Istanbul and other former Ottoman towns and be able to decipher the Ottoman inscriptions on older buildings: inscriptions that most Turks can't read. For them, just as for most Western tourists, they are not much more than decorative flourishes. One poignant example is the archway to Istanbul University, which overlooks busy Beyazit Square. Across the top of the arch, in gleaming gold letters, the name of the university is proudly displayed in Latin characters: İstanbul Üniversitesi. Below it, in Arabic script is: *daire-i umur-u askeriye.* Or, to translate: The Ministry of War. The main campus of the university once served as the headquarters of this ministry, but few would make that connection now that most Turks don't have access to either the script or the language of a period that ended fewer than a hundred years ago.

In the rush to become "European," the immediate Ottoman past was rejected as being too decadent and backward. Had not the empire lost against the more "advanced" European powers? Westerners must have been doing something right, right? Of course, the earlier periods when the Ottomans were ascendant might not be viewed so negatively, but in general there was almost a sense that a door was being shut on the past and that the country was beginning anew. It was a grand, national experiment, one that by any measure was remarkably transformative—though not without its problems.

The Ottoman era couldn't be physically wiped away, evident as it was in so many monuments and structures from the many centuries of Ottoman rule. There are the imposing, imperial mosques, such as the repurposed Haghia Sophia (Aya Sofya) or the purpose-built Süleymaniye and Sultanahmet (better known as "Blue") mosques. There are the many palaces: most prominently, Topkapı and Dolmabahçe. There are the many hamams and bazaars. There are tombs and cemeteries. There are even the numerous ornate fountains that once distributed water to the public. These have always been important tourist attractions, especially in Istanbul;

however, these structures were maintained, it sometimes feels, more out of necessity than real appreciation.

When I first visited Istanbul, I wandered the steep, cobbled streets that led down the slopes from behind the Byzantine hippodrome, the tourist area with the big hit attractions such as the Aya Sofya, the Blue Mosque, and Topkapı. There, within the shadows of these grandiose buildings, I found poor neighborhoods of dilapidated wooden houses from the nineteenth century and earlier, many of which were on the verge of collapse but still occupied. Across the Golden Horn, in the old European quarter of Pera, I climbed towards Galata Tower through rough streets that were lined with begrimed, but still stately, French and Italian inspired architecture. Closer to shore, I stumbled into the even rougher neighborhood of Karaköy, infamous for its brothels and known as a place to avoid after dark. Given the gloomy January weather, complete with gray clouds and rain, these scenes were very much steeped in the melancholic nostalgia described by the novelist Orhan Pamuk in his memoir (see the earlier footnote).

Here, Ottoman ghosts wandered freely. There were no tourists in these places.

Istanbul Melancholy

Two decades later, many of these downtrodden neighborhoods—the lower reaches of Sultanahmet, Galata, Karaköy—have been transformed, their streets now lined with boutique hotels and restaurants, many of which play up the Ottoman theme. On my most recent visit, I stayed in a small hotel in Karaköy; I barely recognized the neighborhood, which had gentrified into one of the hippest in the city (although, as happens with all gentrification, many of its previous inhabitants had been priced out). The number of international tourists has increased dramatically, too, over these years, many of whom want to see the fabled glory of Istanbul for themselves.

To some degree, this speaks to a growing appreciation of pre-Republican Turkish and Ottoman history, although much of the change has been driven by the A.K.P.-led government's economic policies—and, more pointedly, its attempts to appropriate the glories of the Ottoman past for its very contemporary political agenda. Yet, as the controversy over the soap opera *The Magnificent Century* reveals, even those who promote a greater appreciation of Turkey's Ottoman heritage often are in conflict regarding how to interpret and present the historical narrative. I am very curious to see what the next decade or so holds for the discourse of history in Turkey.

But let us return to my own history with Turkey and the study of the Ottoman past...

***

I began to learn Turkish informally at Cornell, where I took part in a study group that was led by a graduate student. Unfortunately, she was tapped to be our teacher based on her knowledge of the language rather than on her ability to actually teach it; as a result, it wasn't until I spent a summer in Turkey, right before beginning my Ph.D. program, that I started to really acquire the language. I had signed up for an intensive language program at Boğaziçi University, formerly an American missionary school called Robert College.[101] I also decided to arrive a few weeks early, both to explore the country and to prep myself for the course.

---

[101] When the Turkish government nationalized the university in 1971, renaming the institution Boğaziçi University, the Arnavutköy campus became a private

Today, one can travel quickly across Turkey in one of the many budget airlines that have proliferated in recent years. However, in the late nineties my main option was the bus. There were—and still are—innumerable companies plying the road, providing transportation service to almost ever corner of the country, no matter how remote. I was able to show up at a busy bus terminal and, with very few exceptions, find a ride to the town of my choice within minutes, without worrying about pre-booking.

During my first bus journey in Turkey, when I made an epic haul from Istanbul to Antalya (which took nearly twenty-four hours), I fell in love with the rituals of the ride. Every couple hours, we would pull into a rest stop for a tea and bathroom break. The toilets were generally immaculately kept, unlike those I had been to in the U.S. Sometimes, there were even attendants who handed out towels. Then, back on the bus, a young "conductor" would make the rounds, splashing lemon cologne into outreached hands, which provided a refreshing zing when rubbed into my face and neck. We would also periodically be served drinks and small snacks. It was all supremely comfortable. Over time, I saw a wide-swath of central Anatolia by bus.

However, there were times during that first summer that I spent exploring Turkey when my lack of planning backfired slightly. For some reason, when I arrived in the town of Tokat—famous, strangely, for supplying many of the burly masseurs, known as *tellak*s, to hamams—I was not impressed. I had planned on spending a couple days, but decided one was enough. I vaguely knew that I wanted to make my way to a small town called Safranbolu, one that I had heard possessed some of the best preserved Ottoman homes in the country but that was relatively far from Tokat. Still, I made my way to Tokat's bus station and hopped on a bus that was heading up to the Black Sea town of Samsun. I figured, surely, there would be some way to get to Safranbolu from Samsun, a bigger hub.

In Samsun, I was shuffled onto a bus that was heading to Istanbul, but was told that it would make a stop in Safranbolu; however, I failed to ask when it would reach there. I settled in next to a young Turkish soldier who was heading home after serving his mandatory term in the military. As night fell, we played cards, and he invited me to come visit him in his hometown, a small Black Sea village, the name of which I no longer

high school, retaining the name Robert College.

remember. He suggested we could even go find some "natashas"—slang for the post-Soviet prostitutes that had begun to ply their trade after the then recent collapse of the U.S.S.R. and the opening of the borders with Turkey. I politely declined the kind offer. At some point, we both nodded off.

I felt a gentle nudge on my shoulder. The teenage conductor indicated that we had arrived in Safranbolu. I looked out the window; it was completely dark. Rain beat against the glass. I glanced at my watch: 2:30 a.m. Groggily, I stumbled off the bus; I was one of the only passengers to disembark, and I watched the bus pull away into the darkness. Standing in the rain, in the middle of the night, surrounded by shuttered homes and shops with no one to ask directions, I was clueless as to what to do. It was not an auspicious start.

After I found a bit of shelter, I pulled out my guidebook and read that Safranbolu consisted of two distinct parts, old and new, that were separated by several kilometers. I guessed that the bus had dropped me off in the new quarter... but in what direction was the old? I made an educated guess, aiming for what seemed to be a major street heading into the valley. An hour later, soaked and shivering, I found myself in old Safranbolu, but it was still, obviously, too early (or late?) for anything to be open. So I located the *pansiyon* at which I hoped to stay and huddled in the doorway, preparing to wait until the owner materialized and opened up the guesthouse in the morning.

Around 7:00 a.m., as the sky brightened and the rain dissipated, a young man strolled by and, noticing the bedraggled foreigner sitting on the guesthouse doorstep, invited me into his small shop just down the road. He told me I could warm up and dry out there while I waited. He even gave me tea and some bread. That gesture endeared me immediately to Safranbolu and its people, despite the rough start. Although the old town, full of fantastic traditional half-timbered Ottoman houses, could easily be traversed in a day, I ended up staying for a week, just enjoying being in the town and practicing my nascent Turkish.

I look back at my time in Safranbolu as the point when I really started to "get" the language. I had to use it, and the Safranbolulus—who spoke little or no English—were immensely patient with my attempts at Turkish. By the time I pulled myself away from the town and headed back to Istanbul for my formal Turkish program, I felt more confident in my ability to learn and use the language. I revisited Safranbolu several times over the years, and still have a soft spot for this little town—even though it has now become more of a tourist attraction.

I returned to Turkey the following summer, this time as a full-fledged graduate student who had by then begun the process of learning Ottoman Turkish. I joined a group of about fifteen other graduate students from some of the top Middle East Studies departments in the U.S. to study in an Ottoman summer school in the unusual location of Alibey (better known as Cunda), a small island in the Aegean that is situated between the coastal town of Ayvalik and the well-known Greek island of Lesbos. Run by the eccentric Harvard professor Şinasi Tekin[102], with his mad-scientist mane of white hair, the program was designed to immerse us in the study of Ottoman Turkish and to provide some training in modern Turkish and Persian (so that we could better understand the many Persian words and grammatical structures used in Ottoman).

While the program succeeded on this front, I must admit that I was more fascinated by our location than our studies.

One of the first things one sees when approaching Cunda by ferry is the large shell of a Greek Orthodox church that looms above the main village of the island. When I landed, I heard refrains of Greek music wafting from the little restaurants lining the shore, a reminder that this island, which is now Turkish territory, was once the home of a Greek Orthodox community during the Ottoman period. However, in a reflection of the often-blurred lines of identity from that period, these Orthodox Christians had been Turkish-speaking.

In the 1920s, as the national borders between Greece and newly born Turkey were formed, a series of unfortunate population transfers were conducted in an attempt to more clearly demarcate nationality (as it was then defined). But who was Greek? Who was a Turk? As the population on Cunda was to illustrate, there were some who didn't easily fit into these neat categories. Perhaps as a holdover from the Ottoman notion of *millet*, a system of classification that defined Ottoman subjects by religious affiliation rather than by ethnicity or "nationality", the residents of Cunda were classified as Greek due to their adherence to the Greek Orthodox

---

[102] Şinasi Tekin, or Şinasi Bey, as his students affectionately called him, sadly passed away in 2004. It was a major loss to the Ottoman studies world.

creed. As a result, they were moved to an island that now belonged to Greece. The inhabitants of that Greek island, because they were Muslim, were shipped to Cunda—even though they were Greek-speaking: they were "Turks" because they were Muslim.

By the time I studied in the Cunda program in 1998, around seventy-five years had passed since the population transfers. Nevertheless, there were still some older members of the community who spoke Greek, and there were some families who tried to use the language at home. However, most of the younger generations had been educated in Turkish schools, and therefore only spoke Turkish. I suspect that, by now, Greek is all but lost on Cunda. I sensed the palpable nostalgia for the island from which they had been displaced, even if most had never been there. The descendents of their counterparts in the population swap also feel a sense of loss, it would appear, often returning to make a pilgrimage of sorts to the now empty church.

During my days that I spent deciphering Ottoman texts while sitting at one of the seaside cafés, I found that more often than not my thoughts drifted to the story of the transfer and the arbitrary means by which national identity is determined. While no political system is perfect, the idea of the nation-state that had riven the Ottoman Empire into so many pieces could be viewed as a particularly awful one. Had it not caused more damage than good? And, of course, that legacy was, at that time, still unfolding in other parts of the former Ottoman world. Actually, while I was on Cunda, conflict had erupted in Kosovo—that tinderbox of the Balkans—between the Albanian Kosavars and the Serbs. One of the Cunda students, an American of partially Albanian descent, left before the end of the program in order to go help the Kosavars set up a new government. Or so he said. (We suspected he was simply avoiding taking the final exam.)

From that experience on Cunda, I became increasingly fascinated with the ways post-Ottoman identities in the successor states of the Ottoman Empire were and continue to be formed. As you will have already noticed in previous chapters, I am especially fascinated by people and places that don't fit neatly into defined boxes and which challenge the very existence of the categories. I gravitate to the fluidity of borderlands—or better, the "between-lands"—and the people who occupy them.

***

After my summer spent studying in Cunda, I moved back to Istanbul, where I secured an apartment in Ortaköy, one of the coastal Bosphorus villages (*köy* = village; *orta* = middle) that had been absorbed into the ever-expanding city.

Although Ortaköy was already a popular place to come to sip tea by the shore, indulge in a *kumpir* (the baked potato phenomenon on which pretty much anything and everything can be served—including potato salad!), or perhaps shop in the weekend street market, the interior of Ortaköy, which stretches along Dereboyu Avenue, was more workaday. I loved the reminders of the neighborhood's once extremely diverse past—for example, its famous Baroque Mosque situated picturesquely over the waters of the Bosphorus, the arch of the Bosphorus Bridge high above (this image is one of the more popular promotional images of Istanbul), and both a Greek Orthodox church and a synagogue almost next door. Closer to my apartment on Dereboyu, there were even the remains of an Armenian church.[103]

I quickly learned that as the only *yabancı* (foreigner) living in the neighborhood, everyone at least knew of me, even if I didn't know them. Once, a new friend who remembered that I lived in Ortaköy, but who did not know my specific address, arrived and just started asking around for the *Amerikalı*. After just a few inquiries, he found his way not only to my building, but to my doorway. Yet, despite my fishbowl experience, I quickly grew attached to my life in Ortaköy, especially to the relationships I developed with the local grocers, barbers, and *börekçiler* (sellers of *börek*). It was, true to its name, like living in a village.

Nevertheless, all I needed to do to return to big city life was to walk a few minutes to the shore road and catch a bus heading to Taksim. It was also a perfect midway point between Boğaziçi University, my sponsoring

---

[103] During my more recent visits, I have found that the gentrification of Ortaköy has extended almost the entire way up my old street, nearly to the top of the hill, where a major mall project is under construction (yes, yet another mall).

institution during my pre-dissertation fellowship year where I still took an occasional class, and the archives in Sultanahmet.

One of the courses I took during my affiliation with Boğaziçi was an unusual social history study of an Ottoman cemetery that was just outside of Ortaköy, tucked away on a hill above the coastal road down to the Beşiktaş neighborhood. It was connected to a former Sufi tekke (lodge), so most of those who were buried in the cemetery had been affiliated with the *tarikat* (Sufi order). The professor hoped that—by recording all the tombstones and their engravings and mapping their location in the cemetery in relation to the burial sites of the Sufi leaders—we might learn something about the social situations of the deceased. As many of the tombstones were long neglected and half buried by time, the project took on elements of archaeology. We were often on our hands and knees, clearing away dirt and rubble in order to read the lower portions of the stones. Once, I brushed against fragments of bone. I shuddered.

I learned to "read" the stones themselves, not simply what was inscribed on them—which was often formulaic and dependent on the social status of the one buried (the richer or more important the deceased had been, the longer and more flowery the text became). The form of the headstone immediately told you whether the deceased was male or female and, if male, what profession he had had, as indicated by the shape and style of the hat carved at the top of the stone.

But I wasn't satisfied with solely studying dead Sufis. I wanted to experience the real deal, live and in person. However, this is not an easy endeavor in Turkey; in the wake of Atatürk's modernization program, the Sufi orders were officially banned.

Most people are familiar with the so-called Whirling Dervishes—or, more properly, the Mevlevis—the picturesque figures in swirling white skirts who twirl with heads tilted and arms outstretched. Tourists are able to watch a "performance" of the Mevlevis at the museum of Sufi music, which is situated near the end of İstiklal Caddesi. It is just that, though: a performance, presented as an example of cultural heritage rather than as a truly religious experience.

After some discreet asking around, I discovered that there was a working tekke in the Old City neighborhood of Karagümrük, not far from the old Byzantine walls. It operated out of a building with a plaque that stated that it was a Museum of Sufi Music: a ruse to keep the officials happy. But once I entered, it was more than evident to me that this was a genuinely religious establishment. The Sufis who gathered here belonged to the eclectic order of the Cerrahi-Helvetis, a *tarikat* that emerged in the Ottoman period and which incorporated styles of *zikir* (Arabic: *dhikr*) from a variety of orders—including the famous spinning of the Mevlevis. I went several nights to quietly observe the proceedings, listening to the musicians and chanters as they began to build their hypnotic rhythms and sway in increasing frenzy. The men and boys who whirled, while not as finely orchestrated as the ones I saw at the museum in Galata, were clearly losing themselves in the experience, their eyes rolled to the back of their heads, transported somewhere with God.

Sufism played an enormously important role in the Ottoman Empire, which is perhaps why Atatürk and his supporters distrusted it so much. The Ottoman Sultans often provided financial support to the orders, even commissioning the building of tekkes throughout the empire. Furthermore, the Janissary corps, the most elite military force in the empire, was historically affiliated with the Bektashi Order, a *tarikat* that traces its origin to the religious leader Hacı Bektaş. The order spread throughout the Ottoman Empire, gaining a particularly strong following in the Balkans. Even today, although the order is all but extinct in Turkey, there are a number of adherents in Bosnia and Albania.[104] And, as we have seen, the Gül Baba Tomb in Budapest is still a site of Bektashi pilgrimage.

***

---

[104] As my research for my doctoral dissertation—which was never to be completed—focused on another religious group, the Alevis, whose beliefs often overlapped significantly with the Bektashis, I visited Hacı Bektaş' tomb on several occasions. While generally not considered Sufis, the Alevis still revere Hacı Bektaş, and there is a large pilgrimage to his tomb in the town that bears his name. Unlike the Bektashis, however, who were so prominent in the empire, Alevis were severely persecuted and viewed as traitorous due to their historical roots in the conflict between the Ottoman and Safavid Empire.

The Alevis were in part descended from warrior-mystics that had supported Shah Ismail, the founder of Safavid Iran—and a major promulgator of Twelver Shi'ism. This conflict cast the Ottomans as the champions of Sunni Islam (versus the Safavids as the protectors of Shi'a Islam). When the border between the two

If there was one overarching theme of my time living and studying in Turkey as a graduate student, it was my constant search for the echoes of the Ottoman Empire's ethnic, linguistic, and religious diversity in the Turkish present. My fascination with these echoes is why I ruminated on the fate of Turkish-speaking Greek Orthodox Christians on Cunda and sought out underground Sufi orders in Karagümrük. Yet sometimes those echoes reached me even without my deliberately listening for them, as illustrated by the following anecdote:

If I were pressed to choose a favorite mosque, I wouldn't hesitate: the Selimiye in Edirne. Considered the masterpiece of the famous Ottoman architect, Sinan—who is so famous that he is one of the few to be known by name—this mosque was built for Sultan Selim II (the son of Sultan Süleyman and his wife Hürrem—so, yes, he is a character in the television series *The Magnificent Century*). One of the great innovations of the mosque is that the interior is almost completely open: the supports for the soaring dome are pushed to the outer edges, which allows the *mihrab*, which marks the direction of prayer, to be visible from any point in the prayer hall. Large banks of windows allow natural light to flood the beautiful openness of the space. Sinan, moreover, achieved astounding symmetry in this mosque, creating a perfect cascade of a dome and several half domes in a simple octagonal form that somehow is both delicate and imposing.

The Selimiye was empty when I visited, so I found a quiet corner and sat on the rug, letting the space envelop me. The vast dome, supported by eight delicate arches, seemed to hover, ready to float into the heavens; the improbably expansive candelabrum, composed of four concentric circles of flickering light, also seemed suspended in midair. The only sound was the ticking of an ancient clock in some distant corner. It was nearly a religious experience, transportative in intensity.

---

empires was essentially fixed and Shah Ismail no longer needed the services of the nascent Alevis, many found themselves on the wrong side of the dermarcation. Many of the Alevis hid their religious practices for fear of persecution by the Sunni Ottoman establishment, and over time developed a belief system quite distinct from both mainstream Sunnism and Shi'ism. The Alevis are believed to comprise as much as twenty percent of the Turkey's population, but it has only been in recent decades that they have felt confident enough to "come out" and openly declare their Alevi status.

While I sat in the magnificent silence of the Selimiye, I thought about an encounter I had experienced earlier that day. I had been tucking into a *pide* or *lahmacun* at a small *lokanta* in downtown Edirne. As it was a slow day, the waiter lingered and struck up a conversation (this seems to happen to me a lot). At first the chit-chat started with the simple questions, "Where are you from?" "What do you do?" and "Are you married?" that I had learned to expect in my travels in the Middle East. However, once he heard I was a graduate student of Islamic history, he somehow decided that it was safe to divulge to me that he was, surprisingly, a Baha'i.

I had never met a Turkish Baha'i. My interest was piqued.

He informed me that Edirne had actually been one of the main stopping points on the prophet Baha'ullah's exile from Iran. He had resided in the city from 1863 to 1868 before he made his way to Accra in what was then Palestine and is now Israel—where eventually the Baha'i faith would establish its world headquarters. Conspiratorially, the young man leaned over and told me he would take me to the ruins of Baha'ullah's residence in Edirne, a place that was gradually being restored through the efforts of the local Baha'i community.

The young waiter took leave of work—"There is no business today, anyway!"—and led me to a quiet neighborhood and a wooded lot with the ruins of a house. His interest in showing me the site was clearly of a missionary bent, made evident when he pressed a pamphlet on Baha'ism (in Turkish) into my hand. Still, I appreciated having my eyes opened to this tidbit of history about which I had known so little. The religious leader of what was to be the newest world religion had fled his native Iran to find refuge in the Ottoman Empire, where he died in 1892. Although Accra became part of the British Mandate after the dissolution of the empire post-World War I, Baha'ullah's legacy in Turkey continues with a handful of followers who live discretely on what is now the border between modern Turkey and Greece.

As I sat in a warm lozenge of sunlight in the Selimiye's prayer hall, thinking over this odd brush with Baha'ism and its history in Edirne, I couldn't help but also marvel at my great fortune as a student of Ottoman history. In my travels in Turkey, I didn't even have to seek out the empire's innumerable, fascinating stories—many stories came to me, basically falling into my lap. Each one added new characters and new plots to the ever more complex narrative. Now, I could imagine Baha'ullah, trying to find a place in the Ottoman realm that had given him refuge, walking through Edirne and admiring Sinan's greatest achievement, perhaps even finding inspiration in the mosque's near perfection. How could he not have?

***

As we drove into the chaotic town, cars zoomed past us, weaving in and out of traffic. I clutched the wheel nervously and tried to proceed at a steady pace. I tried to ignore the chaos that reigned around me and just hoped we could make it to our hotel in one piece. Then I glanced in the rear view mirror and saw flashing lights. A policeman was pulling *our* car over!

I pulled to the side and rolled down the window. "Yes, officer?"

Looking smug, the policeman leaned down and said: "You were going too slow."

Before I left Turkey in 2000, I undertook a major road trip through eastern Turkey; this trip was originally planned with a fellow Ottomanist friend, Kay, but by then also included my partner of the time, Öner, and his mother. We flew into Alanya, near the point in the Turkish Mediterranean coast where the shore begins to curve southward to form the odd dip of territory known as Hatay, and rented a car. We had mapped out a sweeping arch that would roughly follow the border along Syria, Iraq, Iran, Azerbaijan, Armenia, and Georgia before ending in the Black Sea city of Trabzon, from where we would fly back to Istanbul.

Much of this was, at the time, uncharted territory for tourists (and indeed for many Turks from western Turkey, for whom civilization basically ended at Ankara).

Beyond: the wild, wild east.

The southeast, especially, had been largely off-limits due to the long-running internal conflict with Kurdish separatists; however, with the capture of Abdullah Öcalan, the leader of the Kurdistan Workers' Party (P.K.K.), in 1999, the situation had eased enough for us to consider a trip through the region. We were, still, to encounter the occasional roadblock and tank puttering down the highway, but we were free to roam as we pleased.

We were to find that the east was a quirky, quirky place.

On my first trip through Turkey, when I had made my way back to Cairo by land, I had made a whistle-stop in the outpost of Antakya while on my way to Syria. Antakya—better known to the West by its ancient name, Antioch—was once a city of immense importance during the Greek and Roman eras. During that first visit, all I had time to see was the small but excellent mosaic museum that housed startlingly large and vibrant Roman floor mosaics from the sites of the ancient Roman villas that had been found in the area. I was not to see such impressive mosaics again until I moved to Tunisia and visited the El Jem and Bardo museums.

But on this trip, we had more time to linger.

Antakya, by that point, had become a place of particular interest to me. The city is nestled in the province of Hatay, the borders of which were established between Turkey and Syria following the signing of the Treaty of Lausanne in 1923. This thumb of land was granted to Atatürk's new Turkish Republic, much to the gall of the Syrians, who still don't officially recognize the border.[105] As always happens, this political division cut through the indistinct linguistic and religious lines that crisscrossed the area and resulted in a significant number of Arabic speakers who had now officially become "Turks." Moreover, many of these Arabic-speaking Turks belonged to a religious sect that, while a minority in Syria, were to become politically powerful there: the Nusayris, or, as they are more generally known, the Alawiyya (or Alawites). This group, although distinct from the Alevis who I was studying for my doctoral dissertation, were very similar in their origin and their beliefs, as both place a particular emphasis on the role of Muhammad's cousin and son-in-law, Ali.[106]

---

[105] It used to be that Syrian maps showed the Syrian border running straight to the Mediterranean. I am not sure if that is still the case; I suspect Syrians are more concerned with the ongoing bloody civil war that erupted in 2011 than a dispute over border demarcations.

[106] Ali was the fourth Caliph, or leader of the Islamic community, following the death of Muhammad in 632 C.E. Shi'a Muslims believe he was designated to be the first caliph, however, and subsequently they only acknowledged direct descendents of Ali as legitimate leaders, or imams, of the community. The Alawites and Alevis (these are derived from the same Arabic word, but in Turkish it is pronounced "Alevi") take this a step further and usually claim that Ali was to some degree divine, a manifestation of God on earth, not unlike Jesus in

One of my dearest friends back in Istanbul, Süheyla, was a Nusayri who had been born and raised in a village not far from Antakya. She was part of a large Arabic-speaking family; her mother still only spoke halting Turkish and her grandfather was a *dedebaba*, or spiritual guide, to their community. She had secured placement to Boğaziçi University after performing well in high school. This set her on a life path that would eventually lead to her acquiring a Ph.D. in clinical psychology in the U.S. and setting up practice in New York City—a long way from her roots in Hatay! Back when we first met in Istanbul, however, I would sit at her kitchen table, drinking tea and tucking into the delicious food she prepared using recipes from her remote corner of Turkey (I especially loved her *dolmas* made with the small, pale eggplants that I never saw anywhere else in Turkey).

During my second visit to Hatay, we weren't able to penetrate too deeply into the Nusayri world, but I was more attuned this time to the differences I noticed on the street and in the sounds of the Arabic conversations that I heard in the cafés. It was an excellent start to a journey that would ultimately challenge the whole idea of Turkish ethnic and cultural homogeneity that some nationalists tried to perpetuate—an idea that at its most extreme had tried to label the Kurds "Mountain Turks." The official statistics often tried to downplay the real diversity of the country, and even lumped the Alevis and Nusayris into the broad category "Muslim" on national I.D. cards so that Turkey can claim that 99 percent of its population is Muslim.

Still, it should be obvious to even casual observers that during the centuries of Ottoman rule there was a kaleidoscope of peoples who intermingled throughout the empire. The Ottoman family itself, after many, many generations, could hardly be called "Turkish," despite its origin in the Central Asian Turkic migrations that swept into Anatolia as the Byzantine Empire's power waned.

In order to preserve their power, the Ottomans created a fascinating—and still controversial in Balkan historiography—system called the *devşirme* (literally, "collection"). When the Ottomans would conquer a new territory, they would "collect" the most promising young men and boys and send

---

Christianity. This belief made both groups anathema to other "mainstream" Muslims, Sunni and Shi'a.

them to the capital, where they were given the best education in the empire. They would be made to convert to Islam and be given new names, and although they were officially slaves they would then take positions in the bureaucracy or in the Janissary corps. In essence, the system created a slave aristocracy in which slaves who owed allegiance to the Ottoman family occupied most positions of political importance. Even many of the grand viziers, the second-in-command, were often devşirme. These men were frequently of Balkan origin—Slavs, Albanians, Greek, etc.—or sometimes from the Caucasus—Georgian and Circassian, especially. But they were not ethnically "Turks."

Moreover, within the Ottoman family there was generally a policy to not produce heirs with official wives, as the marriages were used to cement political alliances with other important leaders. Rather, the sultans would father children with their concubines—also slaves from outside the empire or from newly conquered territory. Generally, the mothers of the sultans' children were rarely Turks, as this might provide a political toehold for one of the other Turkish families with which the Ottomans had vied for dominance in the early days of the Ottoman state. Many of the women in the harem were of European descent: Italian, French, or even Scandinavian. The most famous of these concubines—made all the more famous by the soap opera, *The Magnificent Century*, which I have already mentioned—was Hürrem, or Roxelana. Possibly of Russian origin, this slave was sold into the harem of Sultan Süleyman. Unusually, she became such a favorite that the sultan married her.

Really, the only thing very "Turkish" about the Ottoman Empire at its peak was the use of Ottoman Turkish as the main language of administration and culture.[107] At the end of the empire, with group after group peeling away on nationalist lines, it was almost by default that the notion of a distinct Turkish nationalism emerged. But the Turkish "nation"

---

[107] Unlike the other Turkic Muslim dynasties that were formed in the sixteenth century—the Safavids and the Mughals, who used Persian as the courtly language—the Ottomans promoted Turkish as a literary language; there is much wonderful poetry and other works of literature in Ottoman Turkish. But even this language is hardly "pure"—it not only included a substantial number of Arabic and Persian words, but it often incorporated grammatical forms from both.

was nearly impossible to define on ethnic lines (which didn't mean they didn't try).

From Antakya we drove northward to the ancient cities of Gaziantep (or simply Antep) and Şanlıurfa (or just Urfa). As I travelled through this region, I quickly realized the incredible depth of human history in this corner of the world. Many of the modern towns of Turkey are built upon the sites of settlements that date at least to the ancient Mesopotamian empires, and many made appearances in Biblical stories. In Urfa, for example, we were able to visit a famous set of fish ponds that were occupied by carp flecked with unusual black markings. These are claimed to be "burn" marks from the story of Nimrod throwing Abraham into a raging fire, who was saved when God turned the fire into water and the coals into fish. The site is now an important place of pilgrimage, even for Muslims. Antep, today most famous for its pistachios, ranks among the longest continuously inhabited spots on earth. It was also the place I got pulled over for going too slowly![108]

We then drove into the equally ancient town of Mardin, which is not far from Antep and perched defiantly on top of a tall hill, seeming to grow right from the rock; it overlooks the dry, forbidding landscape spread before it. While Mardin is now easily reached by air and has become a major tourist destination, when we visited at the turn of the millennium there were few visitors.

At a café near the top of the town, complete with a panoramic view over the surrounding valleys, it wasn't hard to see why the founders of Mardin had chosen this spot—easy to defend and easy to spot an enemy coming from a great distance. As business was slow, our waiter struck up a conversation, and even sat down to join us as we sipped our tea. It didn't take long for him to confess: "I am *Süryani*, a Syriac Christian." (Waiters always seem to make confessions to me!)

Today, there are very few Turkish citizens who are Christian— remember the 99 percent Muslim statistic?—but for much of the Ottoman era Christians of various stripes made up to fifty percent of the empire's population. Prior to World War I, even Istanbul was less than

---

[108]   All my passengers agreed there was something a bit odd about Antep in general— although I never said this to my undergraduate advisor, Leslie Pierce, who began her life as an Ottomanist when she was posted as a Peace Corps volunteer in Antep.

half Muslim. The best known of the Christian groups, of course, were the Greek Orthodox—even today the patriarch of the church resides in Istanbul—and the Armenians. But there were other important, and often more ancient, Christian communities deep in the Ottoman interior, including ones that called themselves Assyrian and Chaldean[109], names that originated even before the emergence of Christianity. These churches, while differing in theology, shared a common liturgical language, Syriac—a form of Aramaic, the language that Jesus is believed to have spoken. There are still a few villages in Syria where people use the language as a living language, but for most Syriac Christians it is used only in church services.

During the seventh to eleventh centuries (the Umayyad and Abbasid caliphates), Mardin was situated within the contested zone between the Byzantine Empire and the rapidly expanding Arab-Islamic state. It had also become an early and major center of Syriac Christianity, particularly of the Chaldean creed. This continued to be the case throughout the period of Ottoman rule (which, for Mardin, began in 1517). However, during the final years of the empire—and at the same time as the Armenian deportations of 1915—most of the Chaldeans and other local Christians were forced out or fled; many eventually immigrated to North America and Australia. Today, only a few Syriac Christians remain in Turkey.

Our waiter told us where to find the church in Mardin, which of course we tracked down.

This was to become something of a theme on our journey: meeting the remnants of once-vibrant communities who were clinging to a precarious existence in remote corners of Turkey. It made me, as always, wish I could have known this world before the advent of nationalism and nation-states.

In Diyarbakır, a city constructed largely of black basalt stone (and something of an unofficial capital for the Kurds), we found ourselves even further from the myth of Turkish homogeneity. Here, as we walked the famous city walls and poked around its many mosques, medreses, and grand homes built of alternating basalt and white limestone (a style

---

[109] Kay and I also discovered the Syriac Catholic Church, which was headquartered near her flat in Gümüşsuyu in Istanbul. This was a church that acknowledged the religious authority of the Pope in Rome, but which maintained its liturgy in Syriac. We even attended Easter Service there one year, to the bemusement of the congregants.

that predates the Ottomans, having emerged at least during the time of the Seljuks), we heard more people speaking Kurdish than Turkish. We also stumbled into the ruins of a once-grand Armenian cathedral, Saint Giragos, where out of nowhere an elderly man appeared and led us to a small building that was next to the shell of the church.[110] He unlocked the door and revealed a room full of church treasures that had been saved during the deportations. During our conversation, he told us he was one of the last Armenians still living in Diyarbakır.

We continued ever eastward, until we were within spitting distance of the Iranian border. Although I have tried on numerous occasions to get a visa to Iran, I have not yet succeeded; however, on that trip to eastern Turkey, we managed to go right up to the official demarcation and look over the fence. This border is not too different from the one established between Shah Ismail and Sultan Selim the "Grim" (really, *yavuz* = stern) after the Battle of Chaldiran in 1514, which became the fault line between the Safavid and Ottoman realms.[111]

Peeking over into Iran was not the focus of that day's adventure, though; our main goal here was to see Van.

Lake Van was extremely still, and the horizon filled with snowcapped mountains. A little island with a conical-shaped building thrusting from its center seemed to float on the waters.

Hardly a soul was in sight.

We boarded a small ferry that shuttled us out to the island; as we drew closer, the structure came into greater focus and it became easier to discern what it was: an Armenian church of great antiquity, standing alone in the middle of Lake Van. The Akdamar Church or Surb Khach (Holy Cross).

Although we had met the last Armenian of Diyarbakir, somehow it wasn't until we visited Surb Khach that the immensity of the Armenian

---

[110] I was pleased to hear that the church was renovated and reopened in 2011, making it the largest functioning Armenian church in the Middle East. This will prove to be a positive step in the right direction towards Turkish-Armenian reconciliation, I hope.

[111] Due to Sultan Selim's active persecution of the Alevis—he sees them as heretics and supporters of Shah Ismail—the current Alevi community protested vigorously against Erdoğan's proposal to name the third Bosphorus bridge the Yavuz Sultan Selim Bridge. Although construction of the bridge began in 2013, at the moment work has been halted, as has already been noted.

loss hit me. We were now in the territory that Armenians, scattered in Diaspora across the globe, consider to be their homeland; it is also the site of a number of old Armenian kingdoms, of which the church is a poignant reminder. A palatine church, Surb Khach was built in the early 900s C.E. and possesses remarkable stone reliefs of Biblical stories. When we visited, it was clearly in need of restoration, but due to the unfortunate political wrangling between Turkey and Armenia it was being neglected.[112]

Modern Van, not so far away from the lonely church on Akdamar, is a bustling Turkish city, seemingly far removed from the violence that swept through the region in the early twentieth century. We discreetly got directions to the remains of Old Van, which was further down the shore of the lake. When we climbed the hills, we could look down at the outlines of homes and streets and at the only extant structure, a lone mosque. Except for the mosque, we might have imagined that these were ancient ruins, much like others that litter the expanse of Turkey. However, this had been a living town until World War I, when in the struggle between Russia and the Ottoman Empire, Van found itself on the front lines. In a little-discussed story, the heavily Armenian town was leveled and its population deported to Syria; multitudes died along the way. After some political back-and-forth post-World War I, when the fate of the area was uncertain—contested as it was between the newly established Armenia and the young Turkish Republic (which ultimately "won" it)—the town was rebuilt several kilometers away, perhaps in an attempt to disassociate the destruction of the original with the construction of the new.

All of this indicated a deliberate attempt to forget the past, to wipe it clean. As if there had never been a large Armenian population here.

Yet I found it impossible to forget.

***

The conversation with the desk clerk at the hotel in Van was confusing, to say the least. When I asked him in Turkish for directions, he turned to Öner and exclaimed: "But I don't speak English!" Öner, of course, bemusedly replied, "He asked you in Turkish." After the surreal

---

[112]   However, Surb Khach/Akdamar was restored and officially re-opened in 2008—
        but, controversially, as a museum rather than as a functioning church.

conversation came to an end and we got the directions that we needed, we drove northwards, once again skirting the Iranian border and the Azeri exclave of Nakhchivan (Naxçıvan); we were heading towards Kars.

I suspect that, at the time we traveled, Kars was little known outside of Turkey. By now, however, due to the international success of Orhan Pamuk's *Snow*, the city is "on the map." Still, despite once having been a very important frontier city, it had the feeling of a forgotten place, sidelined by history. I immediately noticed the difference in architecture in the core of the city, which was more Russian than Ottoman in appearance. Indeed, it had been administered by the Russian Empire from 1878 to 1915; quite a long stretch. Our main reason for coming to Kars, however, was to secure permits to visit the archaeological site of Ani, on the border with modern Armenia.

At the time, this was a convoluted process that started with a visit to the Museum of Kars to sign a form, which we then had to take across town to get authorized by local security; we then returned to the museum to pick up the official permit. Lastly, once at Ani, we were required to have a Turkish soldier with us as we wandered the site.

Ani, once a major city in an ancient Armenian kingdom, is now a ghostly place situated on a bend in the Akhurian River, a branch of the Araks that now marks the official border between Turkey and Armenia— and although the city is of Armenian origin, it now rests on the Turkish side. Although tensions between the countries have eased ever so slightly, allowing for easier access to the site, such was not the case in 2000. As I looked across the small river, I noticed the dark guard towers strung along the border, each apparently holding an Armenian soldier or two. Our soldier-escort, sounding bored, waved his hand in their direction and told us not to take photographs of Armenia. "It is forbidden."

I also noticed a handful of people squatting on the riverbank, looking with great longing at Ani. Apparently, they were Armenians coming to pay homage to their past—unable to make the small leap across the river, as the border was and remains a closed one.

Although Ani is currently a collection of ruins scattered across a wide, grassy field, it was once a thriving city, rich from the trade that crossed through the region. At its peak from 961 to 1045 C.E., it was the capital of the Bagratuni Dynasty and a rival to cities such as Constantinople and

Baghdad. But its location in the center of such a sought-after region came with a price; it was, over the centuries, buffeted by the rapid shifts in power that occurred in this frontier zone. Ani was besieged and occupied by the Byzantines, the Seljuks, the Shaddadids (a Kurdish dynasty), the Georgians, the Mongols, and the Karakoyunlu (Black Sheep) Confederation; after all that, it then got caught in the tug-of-war between the Ottomans and the Safavids in the sixteenth century. By this point, the poor city had had more than it could take. It became a ghost town, unoccupied for centuries, all but forgotten.

As I described in the section on Armenia, the bitter feud over how to talk about the events of 1915 has been, to say the least, counterproductive. The loneliness of Ani, located as it is right on the border, and other spots such as Surb Khach, neglected on its island in Lake Van, are potent symbols of how the relics of the past can become political tools in the present. Although both historical sites predated the Ottoman Empire by centuries, they had not been seen as a "threat" during most of the Ottoman era. Actually, it is often forgotten how relatively integrated the Armenian community was until the late nineteenth century.

It was only in the years of the reign of Sultan Abdülhamid II, during which many of the Balkan Christian communities were fighting for or already had achieved independence, that the iron-fisted ruler grew deeply suspicious of non-Muslim groups under his authority. The Armenians became a particular target, less because of their ethnicity or nationality and more due to their supposed connections to and support from outside political powers (Russia in particular). In a bloody attempt to undercut the growth of Armenian nationalism, there were some horrendous attempts at purges in the 1890s that mostly focused on the intellectuals of the community. Then, under the militaristic, triumvirate government administered by Enver, Cemal, and Talat Pashas during World War I, the idea emerged that the whole Armenian community was a "third column" ready to aid Russia on the Caucasus frontline—hence the infamous deportations and massacres in 1915.

Only a generation earlier, the Ottoman sultans had been relying on Armenian architects, such as the Balyan family, to build many of the grand structures that line the Bosphorus today—including Dolmabahçe Palace and the mosque in Ortaköy. It is a stark reminder of how important it is to look at the circumstances of the time. Even if some nationalists talk about mutual hatred since the "dawn of time," we need to contextualize events based on time and place. The back story narrative is almost always more complicated than the present re-interpretation of past events.

***

About halfway up the mountain, our engine began to spew ominous white smoke. I pulled over, as much as was possible on the narrow road—avoiding the precipitous drop, unprotected by guardrail, on the left side—and took a look. The engine had overheated. Looking about, I saw nothing but mountains and forests, and we were quite a distance from Erzurum. We hadn't passed another car for some time. What were we going to do if the car needed attention? Trying not to panic, I just let the car cool down, and then proceeded. We had come this far. We couldn't turn back now.

After twisting up the side of the mountain for what seemed like hours, trying to think about what I would need to do if another vehicle came in the other direction, we finally reached the top, where a small village was nestled amidst some fresh-smelling pines. In front of us, rising like a small spaceship, was our main target: the remains of a beautiful Georgian monastic church. This was Öşk Vank (Oshki).

As we walked towards the church, a dapper village man who was dressed in a well-pressed suit and tie emerged from the church's shadow to come greet us: "Welcome! The tickets cost…"

I could only smile. How long between tourists must this poor guy have waited for customers? We gladly paid and then gawked at the delightful conical dome and Georgian inscriptions.

The modern states of Georgia and Armenia correspond only in part to the shifting boundaries of their earlier—and often fractious—incarnations. There was a point when what is now northeastern Turkey consisted of a patchwork of small kingdoms—some Christian, some Muslim—including a number of Georgian statelets. Although less prominent than the remains of the Armenian Christian past, a number of Georgian churches, perched in impossible locations high in the mountains and built more as retreats for monks and priests than as working chapels for lay people, are peppered throughout the region. Without your own transportation (or transportation without enough *umph*), it can be hard to visit them. But we had tracked down directions to one of the better preserved ones, Oshki, and made our way from Erzurum. Although we hadn't begun our journey in eastern Turkey with the intent to catalog all the Christian communities of the area, we seemed to have fallen into that pattern.

Back in Erzurum, in celebration of our success in locating the Oshki, we had dinner at a charming restaurant that seemed as if it was a holdover from at least a century earlier, from the period just before the collapse of the Ottoman Empire. Erzurum, yet another of the many eastern cities with deep, ancient, pre-Ottoman roots, has a contemporary reputation as one of the more conservative urban centers in Turkey—even now, it provides key support to the A.K.P. government. While there, we saw more fully-covered women and bearded men than we had seen anywhere else in our journey; nevertheless, at this surprising restaurant we were served Turkish coffee with mint liquor by waiters in white jackets and black bow ties. It was jarringly nostalgic.

In many respects, that sense of displacement in time characterized much of our experience during our trip through the wild east of Turkey. More often than not we asked the question: *When* (not *where*) were we?

***

The arch of our trip concluded in Trabzon, better known to some by its historical name, Trebizond; it is a bustling city situated on the eastern end of Turkey's Black Sea coast, a short distance from the border with Georgia.

The Black Sea region of Turkey has always been something of a world apart from the rest of Anatolia. It is backed by a ridge of mountains to the south that cut it off from the dry, interior plateau; because it is also fronted by the sea, it actually possesses its own microclimate. This region generally stays lushly green all year, even during winter, when elsewhere in Turkey it is cold and even snowy. The differences between this region and the rest of Turkey don't just lie in the climate and geography, however: the mountains and valleys helped the peoples of the Black Sea remain fairly independent of the political machinations of the empires that vied for control of the sea and its trade. Their villages became impregnable fortresses against the constant change on the coast.

For this reason, the Black Sea region exhibits more linguistic and ethnic diversity than almost any other part of Turkey, where a more thorough

"Turkification" had occurred. The best known of the Black Sea ethnicities are the Laz, a group that speaks a complicated language closely related to Georgian, and—for reasons that remain a mystery to me—that is often the butt of jokes in Turkey (as with the Polish jokes of old). This area was also where some of the last Greek-speakers of Turkey resided, although many of them immigrated to Greece in the first half of the twentieth century (however, in Greece their archaic Pontic Greek was barely understood).

Trabzon itself was an important Byzantine outpost, as it was one of the last Byzantine holdings to succumb to the Ottomans in 1461 (nearly a decade after the capture of Constantinople!). It has, through the centuries, been one of the major Black Sea ports on the Anatolian coast, serving as an important economic hub. In 2000, though, it exuded a bit of a lawless frontier spirit. Even at the small airport, from which we returned home to Istanbul, there was a place to leave your gun as you went through security screening. I am sure this is no longer the case!

Just outside of Trabzon, we visited our last historical site of the trip, the famous monastic complex of Sümela, carved high in a cliff. Sümela is a Greek Orthodox monastery, dating from the Byzantine era and in continued use throughout the centuries of Ottoman control; however, it closed in 1923 following the forced population transfers between Greece and Turkey that I have already mentioned. While it has been a major tourist attraction for decades, only since 2010 has the monastery been used for religious purposes again: the Divine Liturgy now is allowed to be recited on the Feast of the Assumption (August 15).

On the day we went, it was cool and rainy, which made for a slippery climb up the hundreds of steps. But at the top, amid Sümela's glittering frescos, we were rewarded with a view out to the steely Black Sea. A lonely cargo ship slipped across the horizon, headed to unknown ports.

Buffeted by the winds blowing off the sea, I remember thinking: "Somewhere over there is Crimea. I will get there someday." It took more than a decade but I did.

At that moment, I somehow knew that—despite all that I had seen and experienced on this road trip and all of my previous travels in Turkey and its neighboring countries—my Ottoman journey was really only just beginning.

***

As I've said many times, one of the reasons I was drawn to the study of Ottoman history was the empire's great diversity. It obviously was not the first empire to encompass a broad spectrum of linguistic, religious, and ethnic groups—just look at its illustrious predecessors in the region: Rome, Byzantium, the Umayyad and Abbasid caliphates, the Seljuk Empire, and the Mongols. However, the Ottoman Empire's longevity—with its roots stretching back as far as 1300 and lasting until the 1920s—and its many permutations give it a special appeal. Also, while the earlier empires are discussed, even celebrated (as are the Phoenician and Roman eras in Tunisia), they seem to rarely appear in the discussions of current politics, and they generally take little part in the construction of national narratives. The Ottoman era, however, is a more recent memory, and that memory continues to echo through many of the empire's former territories.

Late Ottoman Echoes

As it turns out, this is just as true for the "periphery" of the empire as it is for Turkey itself, the most direct political successor to the Ottoman state—as we shall see as we turn our attention southwards, towards the Middle Eastern and African worlds.

PART V

The Middle East and Africa

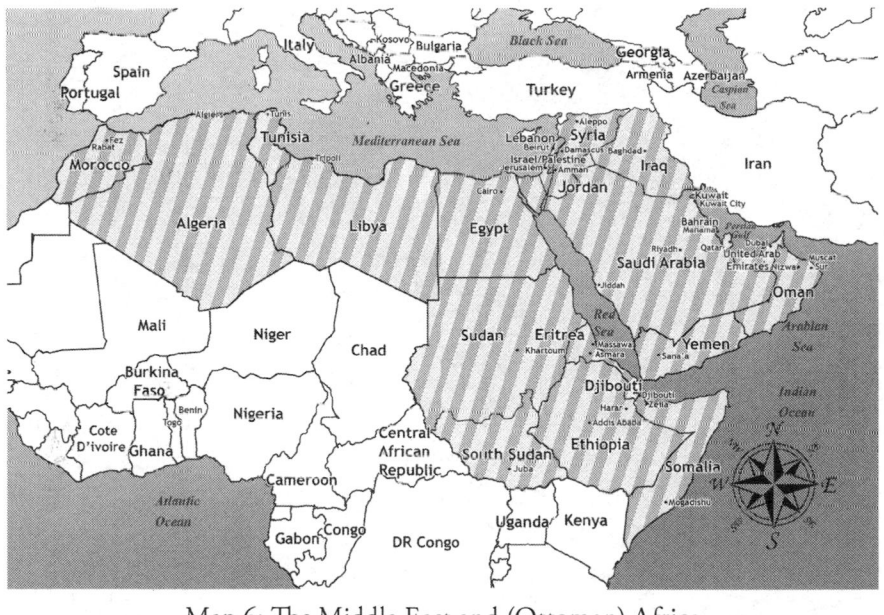

Map 6: The Middle East and (Ottoman) Africa

The Middle East doesn't exist.

At least, that is what I tell my history students. The phrase is actually of quite recent coinage; it only came into common use around the World War II era when it displaced the older—and arguably more reasonable—Near East (depending, of course, on your point of geographic reference). But whether one uses Near East or Middle East, the designation is a slippery fish: what does it actually refer to? When I pose the question to my students, they will often first aim for geography or culture, but as I press them with counterexamples they realize just how artificial and imprecise the label actually is.

First of all, the Middle East is not really defined in geographic terms, especially if one is referencing continents (also a very imprecise category). The region falls mostly in the southwestern corner of Asia, but most interpretations generally include bits of Africa (but to what degree depends on perspective, as we will see), and even a small chunk of Europe (again, how much depends on who you ask). The outer boundaries are not usually defined by natural features, either, but instead by national borders.

What about language and culture? My students might first offer: "It's all the Muslim countries!" But when I ask them about Indonesia, the most populous Muslim country in the world, they will admit that it isn't part of the Middle East. What about Arabic-speaking countries? But that would exclude Turkey, Iran, and (more ambiguously) Israel, which are pretty consistently included in the Middle East roster. And what about Arabic-speaking countries like Sudan? It usually is not included. So language and religion aren't really defining features, either.

Essentially, the Middle East is what one thinks it is. The core, though, is pretty widely held to include Turkey, Iran, Syria, Lebanon, Iraq, Israel/Palestine, Jordan, Kuwait, Bahrain, Qatar, the U.A.E., Oman, Yemen, Saudi Arabia, and Egypt. Sometimes the other North African states—Morocco, Algeria, Tunisia, and Libya—are included, and sometimes the phrase is expanded to: the Middle East *and* North Africa (M.E.N.A.). In rare cases, the phrase is used to encompass a "greater" Middle East, including the Caucasus and Central Asia, due to their historical links to the Islamic heartland.

In some ways, I have it easy in this project, as I don't really have to wrestle with whether to use "Middle East" or not, given that my focus is on any land or people who used to be ruled by the Ottomans. With this broader net, I can include territories that are deeper into Africa and that stretch along the Red Sea coast to the Horn of Africa, such as Sudan, Ethiopia, and Djibouti. I can also exclude Morocco, as it was largely not under the purview of the Ottomans (with the brief exception of Fez).

The "Middle East" was the portion of the former Ottoman Empire where I first experienced Ottoman architectural, historical, and cultural "echoes"—actually, it was the first area that I explored outside of the U.S. other than Canada. I spent my junior year of university in Jordan and Egypt, and traveled to Israel/Palestine, Greece, Turkey, and Syria while I was there. Little did I know then that I would return to the region to work as an international school teacher, first in Khartoum, Sudan and then in Tunis, Tunisia. This, in turn, would offer me the opportunity to expand my travels in the southern Ottoman lands and even to revisit some old haunts—such as Cairo, which I returned to just a few months after its Arab Spring Revolution in early 2011.

So, as with the section on Turkey, the chapters that follow are a mix of reminiscence about experiences from twenty years ago and my experience in the present, as well as some key moments in between. It is, due to the political circumstances and difficulties that plague many of the countries here, spottier in its representation. For example, despite many attempts to acquire a visa to hermit-like Eritrea, I was never successful. The same is true for Iran. I also have avoided Iraq and Somalia, for obvious safety reasons (although I still hope to make it to self-declared independent Somaliland, especially in order to see the crumbling remains of the once-important Ottoman port of Zeila[113]). I had planned on visiting Iraqi Kurdistan in 2014, but the startling emergence of I.S.I.S.[114] put that plan on hold.

Still, I have managed to visit a number of former Ottoman countries that few tourists get to see—such as Saudi Arabia and Libya, as very different examples. In order to follow a similar pattern as the "European" section of the book, the entries here basically follow an arch, beginning in

---

[113] One of the major Red Sea towns that fell under the purview of the Eyalet of Habesh, which I will discuss in the chapter on Djibouti.

[114] "The Islamic State of Iraq and al-Sham (Syria)", or now simply "The Islamic State", is an insurgent group that has taken control of large swaths of Iraq and Syria since 2013.

Syria and wrapping up in Tunisia; this does not reflect the order in which I visited the countries mentioned.

Since I have been living in Sudan and Tunisia for the past few years, these countries are somewhat disproportionately represented, but I hope I have managed to use them as platforms to discuss the broader legacy of the Ottomans in Africa.

GREATER SYRIA

The following chapter is based on my travels in Syria in the mid-nineties, long before the current civil war that has devastated the country. Much of what I describe is, I know, now severely damaged or even utterly destroyed. For the sake of the Syrians, some of the warmest, most hospitable people I have encountered, I hope that the conflict comes to an end very soon, so that they can begin the painful process of rebuilding their beautiful country.

***

At the border, I was shuffled to the counter for those with foreign passports. Apparently, I was the only one at the moment, as the rest of my fellow bus passengers crowded around the other counters on the other side of the building. The officer, looking slightly surprised by my U.S. documents, started drilling me about my itinerary: *Where have you been? Why are you coming here? Where are you going next? Have you been to Israel? Will you be going to Israel?*

For these last two questions, I smiled and replied "no" and "no." The first answer was a white lie (technically, I had never been stamped out of Jordan and never stamped into Israel, so there was no evidence that I had been to the country) and the second, at least for that trip, was the truth. Welcome to Syria!

Even when I applied for the Syrian visa in Cairo, I swear the first question on the application—even before it asked for my full name—was: "Have you ever been to Israel?" No, of course not. *Ahem.* At the actual Syrian border with Turkey, the official was still fixated on this.

Although the border official seemed skeptical of my lack of Israel travel plans, he stamped my visa and waved me in. I had finally entered Syria.

***

There are places that you know instantly that you are going to love, even before you have really explored them. Such had been my heart-swelling response to Istanbul as I woke on the final stretch of my train ride and looked at the cityscape just before I pulled into Sirkeci Station. I had a similar, in-the-gut, feeling about Aleppo as soon as I stumbled off the bus.

Just as it was back in Istanbul, the weather in Syria was wintery—cold, gray, and damp. Everyone was bundled in black jackets, their heads pulled to their shoulders in a futile effort to find a bit more warmth. Still, I was taken immediately with the place, especially its aura of faded grandeur.

Aleppo (*Halab* in Arabic) was once an extremely important city, right at the crossroads of trade and empire. An imposing citadel, a relic of those tumultuous years, when it needed to be defended from all the powers that coveted its riches, sits on a looming hill right in the heart of the city. Graceful mosques and palaces and souqs dot the neighborhoods that radiate out from the citadel. The Baron Hotel, a somewhat more recent structure that was built in the nineteenth century, sits close to the train station—once the terminus for the fabled Orient Express. Yet, due in large part to the political trajectory of the country since the dissolution of the Ottoman Empire, Aleppo had been sidelined, fading into a regional rather than an international hub.

During the Ottoman Empire, "Syria" was not really a political label, but rather a loose term that referred to much of the region the English and French called the Levant (or *bilad al-sham* in Arabic).[115] This was the territory sandwiched between the Anatolian Peninsula to the north and the Arabian Peninsula to the south, fronting the Mediterranean to the west and, more fuzzily, stretching somewhere into the desert shared by that other loosely defined region of "Iraq." This region, predominantly Arabic-speaking, with a significant urban population (centered in Damascus and Aleppo,

---

[115] In the early years of Ottoman rule, there were three main *eyalets*: Damascus, Aleppo, and Tripoli (not to be confused with the Tripoli in Libya). Later, the Eyalet of Adana would be split from Aleppo and the Eyalet of Safed (later Sidon) would be added to the mix. Due to the Tanzimat reforms, "Syria" was reorganized in 1864 into a group of *vilayets*, another term for province (but one more integrated into the centralized vision of the Tanzimat). The three vilayets were called Syria (centered in Damascus), Aleppo, and Beirut. A decade later, both the area of Lebanon and the city of Jerusalem would be granted a "special" administrative status as *mutasarrifiyyas*, due to European pressures.

most prominently) that includes a variety of religious communities—Muslim, Christian, and Jewish—was one of the first to develop what might be seen as a proto-Arab nationalist movement. After World War I, a delegation of "Syrians" went to the Paris Peace Talks in 1919 to advocate for the establishment of a Greater Syria, a state that would have included what is now Syria, Lebanon, Jordan, and Israel/Palestine. They referred to President Wilson's Fourteen Points, especially his promotion of the right to self-determination. Like many other non-"European" groups seeking such recognition, the Syrians were bitterly disappointed to find their cause all but ignored.

Great Britain and France had determined, even in the early days of the war with the semi-secret Sykes-Picot Agreement of 1916, that much of the Ottoman Empire would be divided into British and French spheres of influence. Although the resulting configuration was not exactly what had been mapped out in the original Sykes-Picot document, the two powers carved up much of the Middle East into new states over which they were to become mandatory powers—essentially, they were colonial rulers in all but name. Britain got Iraq and Transjordan (which were both founded as kingdoms or emirates, headed by the sons of Sharif Husayn of Mecca: Faisal and Abdullah), as well as the more contentious Mandate of Palestine. France acquired influence over a much truncated Syria, made even smaller when they managed to push for the establishment of a separate Lebanon (this is one of the main reasons Syria has never really acknowledged Lebanon as a separate country, considering it to be rightfully a part of its territory). The French would remain in the country until 1946, when they finally bowed to nationalist protests against colonial rule and granted the country full independence. A few years later, there was a coup d'état, the first in a series of military takeovers that would eventually lead to the rise of a certain Hafez al-Assad.

As I wandered the streets of Aleppo's Old City, I noticed that many of the buildings were festooned with bands of black flags. Walls were covered in posters that showed a handsome young man in sunglasses staring into the distance, looking regally important. On the grainy state television channel and crackly state radio station, elegiac music was played in a constant feed loop. I had inadvertently arrived for the first anniversary of Bassel Assad's death. The older, rather dashing, playboy son of President

Hafez al-Assad had been groomed to be his father's successor, but was killed in a car accident in January 1994 at the age of 31. Although not officially acknowledged, he was likely drunk at the time. His death was commemorated as if it were the loss of a demi-god. His brother, Basher, had been called back from London, where he had been studying to become an ophthalmologist, to begin his apprenticeship for the Syrian "presidency." He came to power after his father's death in 2000, and he remains president in the midst of his country's tragic civil war.

In the souq, I put on my game face and steeled myself against the hard sell that I had come to expect during my months spent navigating markets like the famous Khan el-Khalili in Cairo. However, I realized almost immediately that I didn't need to be so concerned in Aleppo. Despite being the only foreigner or tourist in sight during those cold January days, no one tried to sell me anything. Rather, more often than not, I was asked where I came from and why I was in Syria—questions similar to those I had been asked at the border, but here they were asked with a tone of friendly bemusement. Several times I was invited into a shop to have a tea, but rather than being shown the owner's wares, I was "interrogated" about my studies and family life. They were simply curious to know: Who was this young American guy strolling the market?

As the days unfolded, I learned to let my Egypt-forged guard down. I was invited for countless teas, and even on one occasion to dinner in a family's home in the city's former Armenian quarter. Kids would come up to me and shyly ask my name, then run back to play ball with their friends. No requests for *baksheesh*. It was all very refreshing.

This is not to say I wasn't cautious during my stay in Syria. I knew that I was in what amounted to a police state, and that I therefore needed to be careful about what I said when referencing President al-Assad, if asked (a friend who had tried to prep me for the trip told me to reply with the non-committal reply, "He's a clever man"). Once, in the town of Hama, south of Aleppo, two young men approached me, ostensibly to practice their English, but they were clearly undercover police trying to keep tabs on the strange foreigner who was poking around town. Overall, though, I found the Syrians I met to be remarkably open and ready to give of what little they had. They were genuine in their welcome of and interest in visitors. Especially in Aleppo.

In Hama, I noticed more tension than I had in Aleppo, and not just because it was here that I had been approached by the secret police. This was a city that had been the target of a Syrian military attack against anti-Assad oppositions groups in 1982, during which tens of thousands were killed—a massacre ordered by a president of his own people, in his own country. For obvious reasons, the residents of Hama were extra cautious about outsiders. The town, famous for its creaking *nurias*—the giant wooden waterwheels that line the Orontes River—was beautiful. But shortly after I tracked down the site of the Grand Mosque, which had been flattened in an airstrike and which was quietly being rebuilt by the government—no one would tell me where it was; I had to stumble onto the site, still largely a pile of rubble, a forlorn minaret looming above the scene—I decided it was best to move on quickly. After Aleppo, it was hard to take the sadness that pervaded Hama.

When I reached Damascus, a bigger and more hectic city, my spirits returned. Damascus is one of the great cities of the Middle East, one of impossible antiquity and historical depth—older even than Cairo. During the Byzantine Empire, it was one of the world's most important cities, at times only second to the capital of Constantinople. Not surprisingly, as the Arab Islamic state emerged in the Arabian Peninsula, Damascus would become a coveted target, and was eventually captured in 634 C.E. It would later, in 661, become the capital of the Umayyad Caliphate, marking the beginning of what might be considered the urbanization of Islam.

Islamic architecture, for one, would blossom in Damascus. The shining example of this new Islamic architecture was the enormous Umayyad Mosque, constructed, interestingly, with the guidance of Coptic and Byzantine artisans (not to mention Persian and Indian ones) who left their mark in the gorgeous, unusual mosaic work that covers the inner courtyard. Even after the fall of the Umayyads and the rise of the Abbasids, who moved the caliphal capital to Baghdad in 750, Damascus remained an important center in the Levant for learning and trade. The Ottomans, who conquered the region from the Mamluks in the early sixteenth century, maintained Damascus as an important link to their holdings in the predominantly Arab portion of the empire (even if Istanbul and Cairo eclipsed the Levantine city in political importance). Due to this long, illustrious history, many Arab nationalists who longed for either a

Greater Syria or an even more expansive Arab kingdom (as in the vision of Sharif Husayn[116]) looked to Damascus as their future capital.

While wandering through the Old City, I stumbled upon a large crowd of men who sported heavy beards and women who were covered completely in black chadors, something I had not seen much of in Syria. They were streaming into a mosque complex, which I hadn't noticed before and the significance of which I did not know. I inserted myself into the flow, wondering if anyone would call me out as an obvious interloper and tell me to leave, that I was not wanted here. But no one even glanced at me.

I was swept into a mausoleum unlike any I had ever visited, the cenotaph resting under a dome that was made of glittering crystal and mirror, reflecting bright shards of color over the blue tiled walls. If it had not been a gravesite, I would have almost felt like I was in a disco. But even more remarkable was the spectacle unfolding around me. The black clad women and the bearded men clung to the cenotaph or rocked in the corners, wailing and shedding real tears. I sat in the back, trying to be as unobtrusive as possible as a 6'2" tall American could be in such a setting. Still, no one acknowledged my presence as I watched this intimate scene.

In the moment, I had no idea where I was or what I was witnessing. I dared not ask any of the participants—who I had by this point figured out were Persian-speaking Iranians—for fear of disturbing their sorrow. However, I figured out later that I had inadvertently joined a group of pilgrims at the tomb of Sayyidah Ruqayya (or Sukayna), the infant daughter of Imam Husayn (the third Shi'a Imam, son of the Caliph Ali). It was a startling shrine for a four-year-old.[117]

Later, when I followed the remains of Damascus' old city walls, I discovered a small shrine to the Christian Saint George built into the wall. The elderly Syrian nun who sat by the door motioned me inside and

---

[116] Sharif Husayn was the Ottoman governor of Mecca and the Hijaz, who envisioned establishing a large Arab Kingdom. He called upon the British, then ensconced in Egypt, for support in what became known as the Arab Uprising against the Ottoman Empire during World War I. This, of course, was the conflict that brought the infamous T.E. Lawrence or Lawrence of Arabia to world attention. We will discuss this more in the chapter on Saudi Arabia.

[117] An even more important Shi'a shrine sits just outside of Damascus proper, the mosque-mausoleum of Sayyidah Zaynab bint Ali, the daughter of Caliph/Imam Ali and granddaughter of the Prophet Muhammad.

showed me the icon of the saint, lit only by flickering candlelight. I noticed that there was a cot set up in the corner of the dark, cramped space: the nun lived here, keeping watch over the shrine. She told me that the shrine was built to honor a miracle attributed to Saint George—the bells of the nearby Syrian Orthodox church had begun to ring of their own accord, which drew the attention of the neighbors, who discovered that the church was on fire. They were able to put out the fire before too much damage had been done. I left a small donation on the plate next to the icon.

A few days after my visit to the shrines of Saint Sukayna and Saint George, I crammed into a crowded bus that was heading to Jordan. Somewhere along the way to Amman, I turned twenty-one—a little older, but feeling more ignorant than ever about the complex world through which I was navigating.

CONFESSIONAL LINES: LEBANON

Lebanon, one of the smallest Middle Eastern countries—smaller than the state of Connecticut—is one of those crazy creations that emerged out of the dismemberment of the Ottoman Empire post-World War I; its borders are a result of the wrangling of the British and French over the territory between Anatolia in the north and the Arabian Peninsula to the south. One look at a map will show just what an odd jigsaw puzzle this region is. That weird wedge wedged into Jordan? Well, let's just say that's a story we'll deal with later.

Lebanon, at least from a geographical perspective, is also an odd gouge out of the coast, a bite into Syria. Why was this tiny place separated from its larger neighbors? What distinguished it from the rest of the French and British mandates? To better understand the geopolitics, one needs to go back to the mid- and late-nineteenth century, when the whole area was firmly a part of the Ottoman Empire, but was becoming of increasing interest to the imperial powers of Europe.

But first things first.

***

I initially tried to go to Beirut when I was studying in Cairo, back in the mid-nineties. At that time it was technically illegal for Americans to travel to Lebanon, as the long civil war (1975-1990) had only ended a few years earlier. The "Paris of the Mediterranean" might not have been burning, but it was still smoldering. Admittedly, the fact that it was off-limits made me want to go all the more, but in the end I let "common sense" prevail and didn't attempt it. I wouldn't, as a poor undergrad, have been able to afford the $10,000 or so fine had I been caught.

Still, the desire to cross into Lebanon never went away.

Oddly, perhaps, considering all my years of studying and traveling in the Middle East—including Jordan, Israel, and Syria, Lebanon's closest neighbors—I didn't reach Beirut until 2011. I was finally able to fill this major gap in my regional explorations while I was working in Sudan (Lebanon is an easy three-hour direct flight from Khartoum).

It didn't take me long to see that Beirut is a unique place. Even as I left the airport to head to my hotel downtown, I could see that the city is a patchwork of war-ravaged buildings—some are still shells ridden with bullet holes—and ultra-modern new construction. Mercedes jostle with army vehicles (and even the occasional tank) in the narrow roads. While some areas have been rebuilt, like the old downtown, it seems as though the Beirutis are fine with leaving reminders of the civil war in the midst of even their poshest neighborhoods. It's as though they have shrugged their collective shoulders and said: "Eh, why be concerned with the past? Let's enjoy the present!"

Reminders of War

Actually, what struck me most about Beirut was just how positive a place it is. Given its location in a country with such a troubled past—and troubled present—Beirut pulses with life. The city was bursting with restaurants, cafés, and shops; the streets, even during Ramadan, were packed with people. Families strolled along the corniche in the evening (often *late* into the evening), enjoying the breezes off the sea and drinking the strong, strong coffee offered from the vendors who dotted the way. Sometimes they stopped to smoke a *shisha* while gazing out at the Mediterranean.

Besides just soaking in the atmosphere, I played the tourist, visiting attractions such as the beautiful American University of Beirut and the National Museum. When I stepped into the leafy quiet of A.U.B.'s campus, perched on a hill overlooking the expanse of the sea, I could almost forget that I was at a university in the Middle East; it feels more like a college somewhere in New England. It would have been all too easy to forget that this famous institution, one of the most important universities in the region and one that played a major role in the history of the Arab world (after all, it is located in the intellectual birthplace of Arab nationalism), did not escape the ugliness of the Lebanese war. Dr. Malcolm Kerr, the ninth president of the university, was assassinated in 1984 right in front of his office. Other faculty and staff were kidnapped and murdered. Now, all that seems like ancient history.

The current state of the National Museum also belies its wartime experience. When I walked into the central hall, a bright, airy space, I found neatly presented artifacts from the Levant's astoundingly long history, each labeled in Arabic, English, and French (most Beirutis seem to be at least trilingual, easily able to converse in all three of these languages). It's a world-class institution that details the archaeological finds from the Neolithic era, through each of the many states and empires that ended up ruling what is now Lebanon and Syria—the Phoenicians, the Egyptians, the Achaemenid Persians, the Hellenistic Seleucids, the Romans, the Byzantines, the Arabs, the European Crusaders, the Mamluks, and the Ottomans, among many. But when I watched the museum's film on how the artifacts were saved during the civil war, I realized just what a miracle it is that the museum exists at all. The famous sarcophagi from Byblos were encased in concrete; smaller objects—pots, jewelry, miniature statues, etc.—were hidden in the basement. The building itself suffered extensive damage; its front columns are pitted from repeated gunfire and the interior was left exposed to the elements. However, the museum has been lovingly restored. You'd never know it had weathered a storm of war.

The end of my trip happened to coincide with *Eid al-Fitr*, the festival at the end of Ramadan. Hamra Street, one of the main shopping and eating districts in central Beirut, was cordoned off for a street fair, complete with craft and food stands. I wandered through the festivities, stopping to join the crowd that was gathering at a stage set up at the end of the street. A Lebanese singer named Aziza took the stage, and the audience joyfully began to clap, dance, and sing. Even when a power outage plunged the neighborhood into darkness, Aziza powered on and her fans continued to revel in the music.

Somehow, that experience sums up the appeal of Beirut: life must go on.

***

But let's get back to my favorite subject: Ottoman history. From its past as part of the Ottoman Empire, how did present-day Lebanon come to be?

The area that is now the independent state of Lebanon was under Ottoman rule from the early sixteenth century until 1918: basically, four hundred years. Due to its unique demographics, it was an unusual corner of the empire right from the start. Mount Lebanon, the mountain range that stretches about one hundred miles along the Mediterranean coast, harbored populations of fiercely independent Maronite Christians and Druze, among others. The Ottoman sultans often ruled through local feudal families (including the Maans, who were Druze, and the Shihabs, who were Sunni Muslim), figuring they were best suited to deal with the fractious community. In general, though, Lebanon was not a distinct territory from what came to be known as "Greater Syria," an area that, as I mentioned previously, would include present-day Syria, Lebanon, Jordan, and Israel/Palestine.

During the nineteenth century, a new player came onto the scene in the eastern Mediterranean: France. This European power would begin to intercede in the affairs of the Christian communities in the area, and focused particularly on aiding the Maronites. The first of these interventions, which proved successful, was in 1842; its aim was to get the Ottoman sultan to divide Mount Lebanon into two districts—one Druze, one Christian—after bitter clashes occurred between the two communities. Not surprisingly, this division simply fueled animosities between the Druze (who were supported by the British, by the way) and the Christians. As conflict grew increasingly common over the next two decades, a new system—again proposed by France and other European states—was put into place in 1861: the *mutasarrifiyya*. This was a semi-autonomous territory to be administrated by a non-"Lebanese" (i.e., not of the area) Christian governor on the behalf of the Ottomans. In many ways the mutasarrifiyya was the precursor to modern Lebanon, as it marked the formation of a distinct political unit based around Mount Lebanon.

When the Ottomans found themselves on the losing side of World War I, they lost their holdings in the Arab world. France and Britain carved up the region, almost at whimsy. A multitude of states that had no historical precedent, even as Ottoman provinces, came into existence. Lebanon, oddly, was one of the few that corresponded in some fashion to an earlier unit (albeit a quite recent one).

France insisted on Lebanon's independence from Syria (also a French mandate) in order that there be one state in the region with a Christian majority. However, as was always the case, there was still a crazy patchwork of religious communities in this tiny, mountainous region. Then, when France managed to expand the political boundaries of Lebanon at the expense of the Syrian mandate, they inadvertently "diluted" the Christian majority by bringing more Muslims under Lebanon's political umbrella.

When Lebanon gained independence from France in 1943, an unfortunate decision was made to organize the government along communal lines in an attempt to be "fair" to each of the religious communities. Parliament was divided by a 6:5 Christian to Muslim ratio, and each of the major political offices were designated for a particular group: the President had to be a Maronite Christian; the Speaker of Parliament, a Shi'a Muslim; and the Prime Minister, a Sunni Muslim. Others—the Greek Orthodox, the Druze, etc.—had little place in the system. Is it any wonder that resentments grew? Or that a bloody civil war erupted in 1975? Although the war ended in 1990, Lebanon has a long way to go before it achieves real stability.

While the Ottoman period in Lebanon should not be overly romanticized, as there were clearly tensions between the various communities that called Mount Lebanon and its environs home prior to independence, at least it was a time when politics were not defined so rigidly by confessional terms. Perhaps there is a lesson in that for contemporary

Lebanon. At least I saw glimmers of hope in the *joie de vivre* of the Beirutis, who were willing to celebrate regardless of the conflicts that were fracturing their little country.

Hope

LOOPHOLES: JORDAN, ISRAEL, AND PALESTINE

I remember pressing my nose against the airplane window as I stared down at the dry expanse of desert that seemed to stretch forever in all directions. I remember feeling giddy with excitement, and also with dread. This was the final leg of a series of flights that had taken me from Fort Wayne, Indiana to Newark, New Jersey to Paris, France and now to Amman, Jordan, where I was to begin twelve months of studies in the Middle East.

Other than family trips to Canada, I had never before been outside of the U.S.

I also remember how much I had left to chance then. A Jordanian friend of a friend was supposed to meet me at the airport, and then I was going to look for a cheap hotel near the university for a few nights—and then, somehow, find a place to stay more fixedly. What could go wrong?

In the end, despite my youth and inexperience, things pretty much worked out that way. After spending about a week in a slightly dodgy hotel that was within walking distance of the University of Jordan's campus, I joined a couple of British guys and a random Tunisian diplomat's son in renting a cramped flat in the basement of an apartment building near the university. As one of the Brits was in a wheelchair and needed more space for his medical equipment, he took one of the two bedrooms; the three of us who remained shared the other. The rest of the flat consisted of a narrow front room that served as a combined living room/dining room/ small kitchen. A tiny bathroom completed the picture.

My main aim for that summer was to work on my Arabic, so I had enrolled in the university's intensive Arabic summer school with the plan to continue with my studies at the university during the regular academic year. However, almost from the first day, I knew that I probably didn't want to stay the whole year in this particular program. When we sat for the placement exam, we were handed an extremely difficult test which we sweated over for nearly two hours—at which point one of the instructors appeared and informed us that there had been a mistake: they had given us the wrong test. We were to start over with the "proper" test, despite being exhausted and stressed by the first. This snafu, coupled with average class sizes of nearly forty students, convinced me to look for a transfer to the American University in Cairo for the academic year.[118]

However, despite my disappointments with the Arabic course, I made the most of my location in Amman by beginning my discovery of the Middle East region—the start of the journey that led me to write about my travels and reflections on history.

Within Jordan, I stood on top of Mount Nebu and looked out across a vista of mountains and desert from the spot where Moses supposedly stood. I crouched within the amphitheater of the Roman city of Jerash, where I watched a British theater troupe perform "Twelfth Night." I floated upright in the salty, salty Dead Sea. I hiked in soaring 120°F temperatures to gape at the wonders of Petra. I bobbed in a boat in the Red Sea where Egypt, Israel, Jordan, and Saudi Arabia were all within sight. I clambered around and through lonely Crusader castles in the desert. And I made the crossing into the West Bank, which was at that point still considered by Jordan to be a part of Jordanian territory.

I was completely, utterly hooked on this place that many had considered a "backwater" of the Ottoman Empire, but which had served as a stage for so much historical drama.

***

Jordan is a strange entity. No such country (or even lesser political unit of that name) existed prior to 1920s, when this stretch of the Ottoman Empire was dismantled and divided between the colonial interests of France and Great Britain. The newly formed Syria and Lebanon came under French control, while Britain was granted influence over the band of territory that began with the volatile Mandate of Palestine on the

---

[118]   I already had been accepted by A.U.C. when I was applying to study-abroad programs, so in the end it wasn't too difficult to make the switch. However, it did entail dealing with the limited technology of the time—locating a fax machine, for instance, and making several calls from call centers.

Mediterranean and stretched through the new Kingdom of Iraq, which was set at the top of the Persian Gulf and rich in oil. In between, and serving as an obvious land bridge between these two important territories, was the newly established, sparsely populated, and resource-poor Emirate of Transjordan. Even its name seemed an afterthought: it refers only to its geography, which straddles the banks of the Jordan River. The strange, wedge-shaped eastern corner of the country which thrusts towards Iraq, is often called "Winston's Hiccup" due to a possibly apocryphal story: supposedly, when the Great Powers were carving up the spoils of World War I, Winston Churchill had been sketching a map of the region on a napkin over dinner when he, enjoying his meal a bit too much, hiccupped. Hence, Jordan's weird shape.

Despite its not so auspicious beginning, Jordan (as it became known in 1946, when it was formally recognized as the Kingdom of Jordan) would eventually become a much more important player in regional politics than might have been initially anticipated. It also has been one of the more stable states since the end of the Ottoman Empire.

The first emir/king, Abdullah, a son of Sharif Husayn (or Hussein) and brother to the better-known Prince Faisal[119] (who later became King Faisal of Iraq), was immediately embroiled in the Palestinian struggle during the British Mandate era; at times, he served as the principal Arab leader in support of the Palestine cause. Although King Abdullah was assassinated in 1951 outside the al-Aqsa Mosque in Jerusalem by a young Palestinian man[120], his son, Hussein, would go on to reign in Jordan for more than four decades; during this time, Jordan often served as a buffer between the bigger powers of Egypt and Iraq, or even as a counterbalance to Syria to its north. King Hussein would even inform Israel of Egyptian and Syrian plans to attack in what became known as the October or Yom Kippur War in 1973.

---

[119] I will discuss these two important characters later, in the section on Saudi Arabia. But suffice it to say at the moment that they were connected to the story of T.E. Lawrence, a.k.a. Lawrence of Arabia, and the Arab Revolt against Ottoman rule during World War I.

[120] The assassination seems to have been motivated by fears that King Abdullah was going to establish a separate peace with Israel.

King Hussein's son, Abdullah II, has reigned since his father's death in 1999. Although his reign has not been without controversy, he has held onto power even as the Arab Spring swept other leaders out of office and wars have erupted all around him, flooding the country with refugees from Iraq and Syria. Jordan thus is the only state formed after the Paris Peace Talks that has maintained its original form of government and that seems likely to maintain it into the foreseeable future.

Of course, the major exception to Jordan's territorial "integrity" was the loss of the West Bank to Israeli occupation in 1967. That loss was not recognized officially during the first half of my stay in Jordan in 1994, which (as I mentioned) allowed me to take advantage of a strange political loophole to visit Israel without leaving Jordan.

***

The gates were locked by the time we returned. We would have to enter through a narrow door and climb the steep twenty-five steps up to the Austrian Hospice. Easier said than done, considering my companion was in a wheelchair.

Jerusalem, at least its historic core, is not exactly the most wheelchair-accessible city in the world; it dates back more millennia than can be counted and is chockablock with narrow, often steep—stepped even—streets. I had crossed from Jordan to Israel with Richard, who was one of my roommates in the Arabic program and who happened to be paralyzed from the waist down due to a horrendous car accident in Yemen several years earlier. We had learned to negotiate Amman, which was also not so wheelchair friendly, with its many hills and strangely high curbs—but Jerusalem was proving to be a particular challenge.

Richard had selected the Austrian Hospice, set right in the Old City, as our base precisely because of its rare sloping road to the main building. Since he was also able to secure a ground level room, this meant that most of the time he would be able to wheel up to the building with ease. However, there was one snag: there was a curfew, a point when the main gate was locked. And we missed it one night.

After I found a couple willing helpers, we were able to pop the wheels of his wheelchair off so we could slide Richard through the side door and then carry him up the twenty or so steps to the hospice.

All in a day (or night) in Old Jerusalem!

We had arrived in Israel at an interesting, if somewhat tense, time. With the official cold shoulder that Jordan was giving to its neighbor, news about the goings-on in Israel was tough to come by, especially as Internet access was not yet a ubiquitous thing (actually, it was non-existent for the public[121]). We traveled essentially blindly, first gathering the necessary permit from the Jordanian Ministry of Interior to visit the West Bank, a territory that, as mentioned, Jordan had not yet officially recognized as being under Israeli control. Although we could see Jerusalem from Amman on a clear day (they are that close), it took nearly a full day for Richard and I to get from one to the other, as we had to navigate a strange sequence of transport—taxi, shared taxi, shuttle bus, another shared taxi—in order to cross the tense border.

When we finally disembarked near the imposing walls of Old Jerusalem, we noticed a heavy military and police presence that was milling about. Little did we know we had picked the weekend when Yasser Arafat, longtime head of the P.L.O., was returning to the Occupied Territories (much to the anger of Israeli settlers).

The security, already tight in this corner of the Middle East, had been ramped up considerably. The air was tense; everyone seemed suspicious of everyone else. In all my travels in the Middle East then and since, I don't think I've experienced such a palpable sense of menace. This was to come to a head on our final night... but I'm getting ahead of myself.

As we wandered the streets, we were both struck by the immense weight of the history that surrounded us. The names and places were right out of my Sunday school classes and Vacation Bible School (before I became a heathen). Mount Zion, Gethsemane, the Lion's Gate... It became almost commonplace to see strange bouts of religious fervor in this epicenter of holiness for all three monotheistic faiths. One day, I had

---

[121]   It was not until I started my studies at the American University in Cairo in the fall (1994) that I had access to the Internet. A.U.C., at that point, was the only institution in Egypt with regular web service—and that came via a cable that ran through France. If something happened to the cable, there was no Internet in Egypt. Period. How quickly things have changed in the past two decades, considering the role that smart phones and services like Facebook and Twitter played during the revolutions in countries such as Egypt.

to press against an ancient wall on the Via Dolorosa, the Way of Grief, to make way for a group of garishly dressed American pilgrims carrying a cross—a *cross*—down the path that Jesus supposedly followed on his way to his crucifixion. I swear there was even a rainbow arching over them. I snapped a photo for proof.

Nowhere, though, represented the bizarreness of Jerusalem to me as much as the Church of the Holy Sepulchre, which is supposedly built on Cavalry (Golgotha). Calvary, of course, is the hill on which Jesus was crucified and where his tomb is located (and, therefore, where he supposedly rose from the dead). The holy of holies, this was prime territory for a religious struggle for influence—a struggle that plays out on a daily basis in the very layout of the church.

Many of the major branches of the Christian church—the Catholic, the Greek Orthodox, the Armenian, the Coptic, even the Ethiopian (but interestingly none of the Protestant denominations)—hold parts of the building, fief-style. But as the various churches are deeply suspicious of one another[122], they can't agree collectively on how to maintain the structure; as a result, the church is in disrepair. Also, one family has been in possession of the key to the front door for centuries—and a Muslim family at that. Since, of course, a Christian would likely be biased toward one group or another.

At the Western Wall, often called Wailing, we watched Hasidic Jews pray and insert slips of paper into the cracks. Above, in a zone that was at that time off-limits to all non-Muslims, we could see the glittering Dome of the Rock and the homelier but holier Al-Aqsa. The closest we—or rather I, as the only one of us who could climb the narrow staircase—could get to this Islamic holy site was the rooftop of a nearby café. It killed me to be so close, and yet be forbidden to visit. I told myself I would return one day. Sadly, due to all the current political turmoil, this seems less and less likely, at least for the near future.

On our final night in Jerusalem, we were to have dinner with one of Richard's graduate school friends at an Italian restaurant in the new city. On our way, we passed a few random groups of protestors who were shouting about Arafat and dangling what appeared to be effigies of the

---

[122] For example, there was even a story of the Ethiopians getting shunted to a rooftop position due to political machinations among the other sects.

Palestinian leader. After dinner, we made our way back to Zion Square, which we had to cross in order to get back to the Austrian Hospice. However, now (rather than just a few protestors milling about) the entire square was packed with settlers. Very, very angry settlers. With guns.

It was the end of Shabbat, so the settlers took the opportunity to gather in order to loudly denounce the return of the man they considered a terrorist, but who many Palestinians considered to be a freedom fighter.

We had to go through them, and Richard was in a wheelchair. This was going to be interesting.

As we pressed through the crowd, trying to ignore the bristling of weapons and the shouting, I was separated from Richard and his friend (who was wheeling him). I could only hope that we would somehow end up exiting the crush in roughly the same spot on the opposite of the square. As I pressed forward, I tried to concentrate on that objective—not the angry mob in which I was immersed. I ignored the sprays of spittle landing on my cheek, the feel of cold metal when I brushed against guns. I just needed to get to the other side. Thankfully, with much relief, our little group reconnected a long fifteen minutes later.

Shaken, we said little as we passed into the dark shadows of the Old City, which now seemed more ominous than they had before. The streets were eerily empty; only random alley cats skitted about. We hurried home.

The next morning, we began the trip back to Amman, trying to process what we had seen and experienced. It seemed as though little was amiss as we went across the border, but we were to find out later that the border had been closed for several days just an hour after we passed. We had narrowly missed being "trapped" in Jerusalem for up to another week. We had witnessed firsthand the birthing pains of what Palestinians hoped would become a more independent Palestine, a project that still seems a long way off.

Although I am not one to look at the past through rose-colored glasses, I couldn't help but wonder, even in that early experience of Israel, whether there had been a time when things were less tense in Jerusalem. Many years later, when I was starting to teach Middle East history at the high school level, I came across the story of Wasif Jawhariyyeh and his extraordinary memoirs, which covered six decades[123]—and found my answer.

Wasif Jawhariyyeh, a famous *'oud* (lute) player, composer, and chronicler, was born in the late nineteenth century into an Orthodox Christian family in Jerusalem. The family spoke Arabic, Ottoman Turkish, Greek, and French. They socialized with Christians, Jews, and Muslims, and took part in the blossoming cultural and intellectual life of the city as the Ottoman state made a belated attempt to modernize this religiously important (but politically neglected) corner of the empire.

Through Jawhariyyeh's words and firsthand experience, we get a snapshot of what late Ottoman, pre-British Mandate, Jerusalem and Palestine were like. While not devoid of tension, there was obviously a greater fluidity of identity and a greater appreciation of the many cultures and religions found in the area. Jawhariyyeh's father, for example, insisted that his son study the Qur'an as a part of a common Arab literary legacy, even though they were Christian. This musician's story is a good example of how careful we have to be with nationalist propaganda that tries to cast communal enmities as "age-old." The traumas of the Israeli-Arab conflicts in the twentieth century are recent developments; in Jawhariyyeh's world, prior to dismemberment of the Ottoman Empire, Muslims, Jews, and Christians intermingled much more freely.

***

A few weeks after Richard and I made our foray to Jerusalem, Jordan and Israel announced a formal peace agreement that officially opened the border between the two countries. We had been among the last to travel under the loophole that allowed us to be in two countries at once: never stamped out of Jordan, stamped on a separate piece of paper into Israel. I have no evidence—other than this story—to say that I was in Israel.

---

[123] Jawhariyyeh's diaries are an invaluable source for both the history of pre-World War I Jerusalem and the transformations that came under the British Mandate through the establishment of the state of Israel. He wrote all the way through 1968. An accessible translation of a part of his memoirs can be found in Salim Tamari's *The Storyteller of Jerusalem: The Life and Times of Wasif Jawhariyyeh, 1904-1948*.

SAUDI ARABIA DOES NOT EQUAL "MIDDLE EAST"

You know, warm, frothy camel milk straight from the source ain't so bad. I bet it would even go well with coffee. A Saudi Starbucks original!

Our group of social studies teachers and librarians had originally met in Houston before our flight to Saudi Arabia. Back in Houston, we had been teased with the prospect of a visit to Shaybah, a major oil drilling development in the Rub' al-Khali (or Empty Quarter), an area of dramatic, towering red sand dunes. A desert's desert. But, alas: a tease was all it was. Thankfully, though, our ARAMCO guide sensed our disappointment and organized a venture into the desert just outside of Dhahran, where we got to meet a camel herder. While perhaps not as spectacular, this visit was the first time on the trip that I truly thought: *Yes, I am in Saudi.* It was also the moment I began to see just what a muddle of tradition and modernity the country really is.

To get to the herder's base of operations, we had to abandon our bus near a ramshackle village (a clutch of corrugated metal huts that must be oven-like in the summer) just off the twentieth-century highway. We piled into S.U.V.s that could tackle the sand and roared into nothingness, back to the pre-industrial age. Soon we were greeted with the bellows of dark camels and the hearty hospitality of our host.

Meeting the Camels

While my colleagues took turns riding (or better attempting to ride!) one of the camels, I escaped to the far side of one of the nearby dunes. It was utterly silent there. No sounds of cars or trucks. Not even of camels. I had a hard time imagining the American world of Dhahran just over the horizon, or the sprawling cities of Jeddah and Riyadh that were next on our itinerary. I was alone in a Saudi desert for the first and last time of the journey.

***

For many people, I think, Saudi Arabia equals the Middle East. On a map, it certainly does take up a large chunk of the Arabic-speaking world (although, let's be honest, much of that great expanse is desert). It also is home to the two holiest cities of Islam, Mecca and Medina, the latter of which is the birthplace of a world religion that at last count has more than 1.5 billion adherents who are found in almost every country on the planet (Middle East=Islam).

It is, in more contemporary terms, identified as one of the major producers of petroleum (Middle East=Oil) and as the original home of Osama bin Laden (Middle East=Terrorists).

Of course, these simplifications belie the great diversity of the region that gets labeled "Middle East"—not everyone in the Middle East is Muslim; not every Middle Eastern country is a rich, oil-producing state; not everyone in the Middle East is a terrorist (nor, for that matter, are most Muslims terrorists!). But Saudi Arabia does tend to hog a lot of the limelight when the Middle East is discussed. It also tends to be a little tough to visit.

As my years living, studying, and traveling in the former Ottoman world continued, I kept circling and flying over this important country. I kept looking for a way to get in, although as a non-Muslim and non-business type, the options were severely limited. Then, a great opportunity arose in 2008: an ARAMCO-sponsored study trip for U.S. social studies teachers. Although the funding source gave me pause, I also knew this would be my only way to finally see the Kingdom.

Not surprisingly, the study tour began in Dhahran and Dammam, seat of the ARAMCO oil empire. However, the second part of our journey—to Jeddah and the Hijaz—was an opportunity for me to walk the walk of the Arabian Peninsula's Ottoman past. And with the end of the Hajj just a few days before our arrival, I got to experience the aftershocks of the most important of Islam's communal rites. It was an Ottomanist's dream come true.

***

When our group landed in Jeddah's airport, I realized right away that we were in a very different Saudi compared to what we'd experienced in Dhahran, even considering the foray into the desert. From its earliest days (which stretch back well over a thousand years), Jeddah has long been a cosmopolitan entrepôt and the staging point for the pilgrimage to Mecca. The hustle and bustle of people coming and going, wheeling and dealing, give the city a wonderful energy. And, while still extremely conservative by "Western" standards, there is a definite sense of openness that might surprise the casual observer of Saudi culture and politics. Every Hijazi we met expressed a certain pride in their difference from the rest of the country and kept warning us how conservative Riyadh and the rest of the interior were. Not surprisingly, Jeddah is where many of the major advocates of social and political change live and work.

Unfortunately, for fear of drawing undue attention to the Saudis that we met in Jeddah, I cannot use names. However, I do want to describe some of the inspiring individuals we had the privilege of meeting.

First, there was the charismatic woman in charge of an organization of Saudi businesswomen who was working within the Wahhabi-Islamic framework to get the government to overturn the laws that limit the role of women in commerce. It was fascinating to see how she used Islam to show the inconsistencies in the Wahhabi clerics' interpretations of Islamic law. Pointedly, her organization was named for the first wife of Muhammad, Khadijah, who was herself a merchant and Muhammad's employer.

There was the young woman who, right out of college, had started the first design magazine in Saudi Arabia. In addition to providing a platform for Saudi designers, she was pushing boundaries with provocative social awareness campaigns (such as ads about censorship and the mistreatment of foreign drivers).

Then there was the Sufi-leaning architect/dissident trying to protect the cultural heritage of Mecca and Medina from the relentless pace of condo development. He has made it his mission to save what few historic buildings remain in these important holy cities.

And I cannot forget the benefactors of the first center for kids with special needs who deliberately refuse government sponsorship so that they can operate free of the laws requiring gender segregation of employees. They are working hard to make the plight of these kids known and to help the children be more accepted in Saudi society.

The list of such Jeddah-ites was long and impressive.

On our last day, we visited the atmospheric souq of Old Jeddah; while there, I escaped from our group to explore on my own. I wandered the narrow streets, admiring the fading coral block buildings with their wooden lattice window boxes, many of them askew and seemingly ready to collapse on the heads of the pedestrians walking below. Although neglected, these buildings were a reminder to me of what pre-Saudi Jeddah was like[124]—a time when most visitors to the city arrived by boat, not plane. In the old town's market, lost in a dizzying array of colorful *hajji*s who were shopping for post-Hajj gifts to take back to their home countries, I made a promise to make every effort possible to return to this city that is so grounded in history and yet also racing towards an uncertain future.

Old Jeddah

***

---

[124]   Also, little did I know then, but they were extant examples of what the buildings of Suakin, on the other shore of the Red Sea, once looked like (see the chapter on Sudan).

Although the movie is usually too long to show in its entirety to students, I will sometimes show clips of *Lawrence of Arabia* in order to illustrate aspects of the Middle East front during World War I, and specifically the Arab Uprising. One of the scenes I usually play has the white robed, blue-eyed, and blindingly blond Peter O'Toole—who bore an uncanny resemblance to T.E. Lawrence—peering over a sand dune down towards a steam engine train that is chugging along a track that stretches across the barren desert. At his signal, one of his Arab irregulars detonates a bomb on the track, overturning the train in a grinding mess of steel and iron. With a loud whoop, the rest of the Arab irregulars descend on the wreck, battling with the handful of Ottoman soldiers who can still stand and looting the rich furnishings of the train.

My students don't usually get why this is a significant scene until I provide a little more context. For one, most of them can't remember a time when trains played a major role in the transport of people or goods. We live in an age of easy flights to almost anywhere we could want to go. But in the nineteenth and early twentieth centuries, the expanding network of railways represented the height of the industrial and technological advances of the time, changing the economic balance of the global economy. In the Ottoman Empire, the first tracks were laid in the 1870s, although major construction didn't start until a decade later when, with financial backing from German banks, the *Société du Chemin de fer Ottoman d'Antolie* was formed.[125]

The Hijaz Railway was completed in 1908 and stretched from Damascus to Medina, tying the central Ottoman lands with the Hijaz, the region fronting the Red Sea, and the Arabian Peninsula more generally. When the war broke out in 1914, it became an important conduit for the transport of troops, weapons, and munitions.

So, of course, it also became a lucrative target.

T.E. Lawrence, better known to the world as Lawrence of Arabia, was an eccentric British officer who was "loaned" to the services of the Arab

---

[125] When I was first learning Ottoman Turkish, I was given an article from a nineteenth-century newspaper. Early in the article, I came across a phrase I couldn't figure out for a long time—was it Turkish? Arabic? Persian? Finally, it dawned on me as I read it aloud: it was the French phrase *chemin de fer* (railway), but in Ottoman-Arabic script!

Uprising, which was officially led by the elderly Sharif Husayn of Mecca but spearheaded more by his sons, especially Prince Faisal (future king of Iraq). Lawrence guided Prince Faisal's men against the Ottoman forces, which had, initially, the advantage of more advanced technology and the backing of the German military. Due to their technical disadvantages, Faisal's forces generally employed guerilla tactics. One of the most effective of these strategies was to occasionally blow up the Hijaz Railway.

Lawrence of Arabia certainly shows the importance of the Hijaz to the Ottoman Empire in its final days—by the time World War I began, the once sprawling, multiethnic, multi-confessional empire had effectively become a predominantly Turkish and Arabic-speaking, Muslim majority state—both for its commercial importance in the Red Sea-Mediterranean trade routes (which were made all the more important due to the opening of the Suez Canal in 1869) and as the site of the important Muslim pilgrimage (which allowed the Ottomans to claim preeminence in the Islamic world at large). In addition, *Lawrence of Arabia* also provides a good example of how difficult it was to define who an "Arab" was and what Arab nationalism was or should be. The bedouin who united under the leadership of Prince Faisal, in the name of Sharif Husayn, generally saw themselves first and foremost as members of specific tribes or clans. They were working together only because they were, by the early twentieth century, convinced that the "Turks" were oppressing the Arab world in some fashion. They had seen pretty much all of the empire's holdings in Europe breakaway on "national" lines, and they had seen the British, the French, and the Italians colonize most of Ottoman North Africa and gain significant influence in the Levant and the Persian Gulf. They saw the Ottoman world shrinking and wanted to carve out an "Arab" space. However, there were major divisions between urban Arabic-speakers and the nomadic groups (who the city dwellers often viewed at best as country bumpkins and at worst as barbaric holdovers—even if they romanticized their desert living ways as the "real" Arab life). And, as I have said, there were major divisions by tribe or family, as well as loyalties that were geographically defined (e.g. Hijazi versus Najdi; see below).

To some extent this conflict between local and pan-Arab sentiments remains, a century after T.E. Lawrence assisted in the overthrow of Ottoman authority in the Arab lands.

***

"On your left, you see a popular mall. On your right, there's another one people like to visit... also, there's a mall attached to your hotel. It has a great sushi place."

In the twenty-minute ride from the airport, I counted no fewer than eight megamalls in Riyadh. In a place where there's no public cinema and few cultural event venues, where restaurants are divided into men's and "family" sections, where few people walk outside (especially in the summer, when temperatures can soar over 140°F), what is a young Saudi to do? Go to the mall! Hey, they are air-conditioned and allow for flirtatious glances at passing members of the opposite sex (even if the women are often covered from head to foot).

In our progression through Saudi Arabia, Riyadh (the capital) was fittingly our last major stop. It is a sprawling city set deep in the arid heart of the Najd, the desolate region that gave rise to the Saudi family. The Najd was largely ignored by the imperial powers that came and went in the Middle East (including the Ottomans), as it only supported a few oasis towns and a handful of tough bedouins. Now Riyadh is a glittering Las Vegas—sans alcohol and gambling (and most other public vices!)—with a population that is approaching five million. Desalinated water from the coasts flows hundreds of miles through pipes that follow the oil lines to keep the thirsty city hydrated. Iconic buildings like the Fasialiah (where we teachers got pampered with five-star service) and the Kingdom Tower thrust into the sky; meanwhile, the sounds of new construction echo throughout the city, promising new, over-the-top showcase structures. And more malls, of course.

Everyone we met in Jeddah had kept warning us about how much more conservative Riyadh was in comparison to the rest of the country. My time spent poking into the malls seemed to verify this, at least in terms of outward form. When I stood on the top level of the Fasialiah Mall and looked down through the cross-section provided by one of its atriums, I could watch the shoppers coming and going, stopping at windows, sipping their Starbucks lattes. Typical mall sights, right? Well, except for the fact that the women admiring the Victoria's Secret lingerie were more often than not enshrouded in black, without even their faces showing. The men checking out Adidas footwear were decked out in *thobe*s and *ghutra*s and frequently sported large, bushy beards. Any ad with a human figure and any mannequin posed in a shop window had its face blurred or pixilated. That muddle of modernity and tradition I mentioned when I was frolicking with the camels? It was in full glaring view in Riyadh's malls: it was equal parts disconcerting and fascinating.

Of course, as the capital, Riyadh is more than just malls and fancy buildings. It's not only the present center of government—including the seat of the *Majlis al-Shura,* a consultative body of appointed members from all over the kingdom—but also an important symbol in the Saudi nation-building project. Riyadh, a historic home of the Saudis, was (re) taken in a nighttime raid by Abdulaziz ibn Saud, who would become the founding king of Saudi Arabia. In the reconstructed fort of al-Musmak, which Abdulaziz stormed in 1902, exhibits tell the story of this event with nationalist gusto. According to this narrative, a relatively minor skirmish has been transformed into the birth of a nation. Similar themes are expounded at the state-of-the-art National Museum, which traces the history of the Arabian Peninsula from the moment of creation to the present.

Surprisingly, the Kingdom of Saudi Arabia is actually one of the youngest states in the "Middle East": it was not officially formed until 1933, when King Abdulaziz merged various territories he had conquered. Despite promises that had been made to Sharif Husayn of Mecca by Sir Henry McMahon, the British High Commissioner in Egypt, a unified Arab kingdom that encompassed the whole Arabian Peninsula and stretched north through Syria obviously never materialized post-World War I. Rather, due to conflicting agreements with other parties (especially the French), much of this former Ottoman territory was divided into "mandatory" states such as Syria, Lebanon, Iraq, Jordan, and Palestine, which were placed under either British or French guidance. Even before World War I, many of the current Gulf states—such as Kuwait and the United Arab Emirates (once called the Trucial Sheikdoms), among others—had become British "protectorates" by the end of the nineteenth century.

So what about the rest, the area that is today's Saudi Arabia?

To put it simply: no one knew what to do with it. The Red Sea coast, the Hijaz, was the most developed due to its long history as a trade route between the Mediterranean and Indian Oceans and for its location at the center of the Hajj. Although the Ottomans had controlled both the Persian Gulf and Red Sea coasts of the Arabian Peninsula, most of the attention had been put on the more cosmopolitan Hijaz, which was the stronghold of Sharif Husayn and his family. However, in the wild, desolate interior—the vast desert lands that make up most of this jut of land—there were some nascent political formations that gave only a nominal nod to Ottoman (and later British) suzerainty.

One of the most important challenges to Ottoman authority in the interior of the Arabian Peninsula was the early Saudi dynasty. There was actually an earlier "Saudi Arabia" than the one we know today, a small state centered in the desert that emerged when the Saudi family joined forces with Muhammad ibn Abd al-Wahhab in the mid-eighteenth century. Al-Wahhab was a religious leader who preached an austere form of Sunni Islam, one that is now familiar to the world as "Wahhabism." This first Saudi state did briefly gain enough power to threaten the Ottoman hold on Mecca and Medina, but the Ottoman viceroy of Egypt, Muhammad Ali (whose story we will revisit in the chapter about Egypt), put the Saudis in their place in 1818, thereby regaining control over most of Arabia. For most of the rest of the nineteenth century, the Al Saud family simply competed for local authority with another clan, the Al Rashid, without asserting themselves beyond the Najd—and thus not risking an Ottoman backlash.

However, the dawn of the twentieth century[126]—especially the upheaval caused by World War I and the subsequent dissolution of the Ottoman Empire—opened new possibilities for the Al Saud. Sharif Husayn, who had been promised rule of most of the Arab world, was acknowledged only

---

[126] Abdulaziz began consolidating his holdings even before World War I. First, he defeated a rival family-confederation, the Al Rashid, in 1906, thus gaining control of the whole Najd. Then, right before the war broke out, he managed to wrest al-Hasa, a territory on the Persian Gulf, from the Ottomans (despite the fact that he was technically still an Ottoman client!). His conquests were accomplished with the help of the now-infamous band of bedouin fighters called the Ikhwan ("Brothers"), who followed the Wahhabi doctrine.

as the king of the Hijaz. The British, who were playing multiple sides, also gave their political support to Abdulaziz—essentially pitting the rivals against one another. Emboldened, Abdulaziz and his forces invaded the Hijaz and deposed Husayn, annexing the territory to his ever-growing realm (while the British turned a blind eye). By 1927, Abdulaziz ibn Saud was acknowledged to be the King of the Hijaz and the Najd, which were still considered separate kingdoms: they weren't merged officially as the Kingdom of Saudi Arabia until 1933.[127] Not surprisingly, there are still distinct Hijazi and Najdi identities in Saudi Arabia, the source of some significant regional rivalry.

As I have already pointed out, the Saudis who I met in Jeddah—which is in the Hijaz—seemed proud of their more "liberal" ways compared to those in Riyadh—which is in the Najd. Considering that Jeddah, which has always been a major port of trade on the Red Sea and a major conduit for pilgrims coming and going from Mecca (just over forty miles away), it's probably not so surprising that the locals were more "worldly." It is also probably not so surprising that many there resent the dominance that the more conservative center has on the Hijaz, as the Najd is still seen as the "homeland" of the Al Saud and the birthplace of the kingdom. The political heart of the country is still there, too, in Riyadh.

But I still think Riyadh is best understood through its malls, not its museums and *majlises*. They are where the social and political contradictions of the Kingdom collide most visibly. Most importantly, they are where the young people hang out. Considering that more than sixty percent of the population is under the age of twenty-five, these mall walkers will be a force to be reckoned with in the not-so-distant future.

***

As it turned out, Saudi Arabia was just the starting point for my explorations of the Arabian Peninsula and Persian Gulf. During the years

---

[127] The Ikhwan who had helped Abdulaziz gain power in Arabia hoped to continue their conquest northward in order to absorb Transjordan and Syria. However, the king was not dumb; he knew this would anger the British, who had given their tacit support to his conquest of the Hijaz. When the Ikhwan rebelled, Abdulaziz fought them in 1930 at the Battle of Sabilla and had the brotherhood's leadership massacred.

when I worked in Sudan, I managed to visit all the remaining member states of the G.C.C., or the Gulf Cooperation Council: Bahrain, Kuwait, Oman, Qatar, and the United Arab Emirates. I detail some of my adventures in these countries in the upcoming chapters.[128] As you will probably notice, the Ottoman references are often more fleeting in these chapters; this is in part due to the lighter touch of Ottoman rule in the Persian Gulf. It also doesn't help that in some of these countries there has been a rapid rush to "modernize"; much of the history of the region, Ottoman or otherwise, has literally been bulldozed.

---

[128] The only state on the Arabian Peninsula I have not had the opportunity to visit is Yemen—one of the major lacunas in my Ottoman travels. Sadly, with the current political unrest in Yemen, it may be a number of years before I finally get to see the remarkable mud brick "skyscrapers" of its capital, Sana'a.

SOUQS AND MALLS: DUBAI

I admit it: I am a hypocrite.

I have often told people that I have little interest in visiting Las Vegas. I have often explained how much I dislike Florida. The main justification I usually give for these bits of travel snobbery revolves around how fake everything seems to me. Everything seems like a movie-set façade; look behind that façade and you'll find little of substance.

Yet, oddly—even before I moved to Sudan and it became much easier to reach—I had long been intrigued by that weird little emirate on the sultry Persian (or Arab) Gulf: Dubai.

Why would I ever want to go to a place that appears to be one big air-conditioned temple of capitalism run amok, a mirage of over-the-top architecture and grandiose projects built on the backs of near slave labor?

Well, perhaps precisely for those very reasons. I was curious to see with my own eyes if these were accurate images, and perhaps to also compare it with my experiences of Saudi Arabia. I wanted to see how this strip of sandy coastline developed from a tiny pearling village and trading post into one of the most iconic cities in the world, all in a matter of decades.

When I lived in Sudan, I had easy access to Dubai—there are daily direct flights on the low-cost airline, flydubai—and a practical reason to go: to shop. Dubai sort of serves as a stocking-up station for those who live and work in Khartoum, since they can find almost anything they could possibly want in its souqs and malls, and usually for prices much lower than are found in Sudan. I ended up getting a number of odds and ends, such as towels, a decent skillet, and a number of grocery items that are hard to come by in Khartoum and/or that were beyond my budget.

But the main reason for my visit was not to shop. It was, as I have said, to investigate the myths and realities of Dubai.

Of Souqs and Malls

***

My friends and I arrived on the last day of Ramadan, the day before *Eid al-Fitr*. This, of course, added a unique flavor to our visit. Our plane landed bright and early at 6 a.m.; as we disembarked, the humidity slapped us in the face (the fogging of my glasses every time I left a building would become a recurring theme of our stay in Dubai). Groggy from the overnight flight, all we could think about was getting settled into our hotel and finding a place to eat and quench our thirst.

However, we soon discovered that this was not going to be an easy task, even in the most "Western" seeming of areas. After we dropped our bags off at the hotel, we ventured over to the nearby Mall of the Emirates (the first of many on this trip) hoping that maybe, just maybe, even with Ramadan still in force, we could rustle up a coffee. We wandered the empty halls, passing shuttered store after shuttered store. Coffee shops abounded, but all were closed. Perhaps it was just too early? Perhaps we just needed to be patient? We noticed a crowd starting to gather by the entrance of Carrefour, the French "hypermarket" that would become one of our favorite shopping destinations; perhaps we could find something there to take-away. As soon as the gates were opened, we rushed in and swept up some delicious looking breads and pastries and some bottles of juice. One of my colleagues, as soon as he paid, tried to open his milk, but a security guard came rushing at him—"No drinking! No eating!"

Thus began a day of covert meals. Some cafés and restaurants, like old-time speakeasies, pulled their curtains and put up temporary screens to shield views of their food and drink from fasting Muslims passing by; others simply stayed closed till *iftar*. I knew to expect this, but others in our group who were less familiar with life in a Muslim country (and who were able to eat and drink fairly openly at our school) found the restrictions more challenging.

But the next day was Eid—freedom! *Eid Mubarak!*

But, wait—now the souqs were closed! It was a holiday, after all.

My friends and I were not going to let this stop us, however. First, we fortified ourselves with coffee and pastries at Paul (a French café in the mall), and then we made our way down to Dubai Creek, the center of "old" Dubai and perhaps the most "Middle Eastern" part of the city.

The Bastakia Quarter, a warren of recently restored wind tower homes that were originally occupied by Persian merchants, sits on the bank of the waterway; souqs of all sorts (for textiles, spices, gold) cluster on both shores. Despite the ferocious heat, we explored the area, and even hopped on a couple of *abras* (little wooden boat-taxis) to crisscross the Creek. When we needed some respite, we ducked into a wonderful oasis in the Bastakia, a café built into the courtyard of one of the historic homes. The fresh juices, enormous salads, and homemade ice cream we indulged in proved to be some of the best food we had had since moving to this part of the world; this set the stage for a day of gluttonous enjoyment of all the food options available in the city. Our next stop in the area was the Dubai Museum, which is built into Al-Fahidi Fort, the oldest structure in town (dating from 1787), which provided a fascinating window into the astoundingly rapid growth of the city.

In the late afternoon, we journeyed on the brand new metro, a sleek system that would not look out of place in a Star Trek movie, in order to return to the "new" Dubai: this time, our destination was the base of the Burj Khalifa, the tallest building in the world, and then onwards to the overwhelming Dubai Mall. The Burj, for all its issues, is impressive.[129] Even though it is right next to it, the tower seemed unreal, as if it had been Photoshopped into the background. I went a little snap-happy with the camera.

The Dubai Mall, which is next door to the Burj, was a wonder of a different sort. We had been overwhelmed by the size of the Mall of the Emirates, but this place… well, we worried we were never going to find our way out. Every high-end brand is represented in the labyrinth of stores. A self-contained gold souq meanders through the center of the building. There is a full-size ice rink (an attempt to draw the ski crowd from the enclosed Ski Dubai at the Mall of the Emirates?), a huge cinema, and restaurants galore (we just *had* to stop for some sushi). As this was Eid, the place was packed with Emiratis and expats, as well as a large contingent of other Gulf Arabs who came to throw around their money. If all this wasn't surreal enough, there were stations throughout the mall where local "culture" was being exhibited: for example, there was traditional dancing (on a disco-lit floor), Bedouin weaving, and falconry (with live falcons). These scenes could not have been more incongruous.

---

[129] Dubai couldn't afford to finish the tower when the global economic crash occurred in 2008, so it had to borrow money from Abu Dhabi (hence the name change from Burj Dubai to Burj Khalifa). The building also is nearly empty, as it is harder to entice tenants in these tighter economic times. Oh, and apparently Burj Khalifa is plagued with water and electrical issues due to its extreme height.

Dubai Disco

Once we figured out how to escape the mall, we emerged into the humid night to find a fireworks-like display of dancing water that shot from the enormous artificial lagoon that wrapped around one side of the complex. The Burj, soaring above us, was a riot of flashing lights. It might have been my imagination, but I swear I heard the sound of energy being sucked from across the Arabian Peninsula to fuel this display.

To round out the long day, we slingshotted back to Dubai Creek, where we found a local cafe on Al-Shindagha Promenade. As I smoked my apple shisha and my friends tucked into delicious kebabs (yes, more food), we watched the dhows slip by and the less ostentatious lights of this neighborhood play across the dark water. It seemed as if it were another planet from the Dubai we had just seen. But was it really?

***

You can't escape the dark realities of modern Dubai. The drive to be the biggest, best, and flashiest has come with a big price tag—not just financially, but also socially and culturally. The buildings go up so rapidly because the labor is cheap—they are built by people who are essentially indentured servants, brought from South and Southeast Asia and, increasingly, Africa. The financing for most of the early expansion was built on shifting sand, which was revealed when the global economic crisis hit the emirate. Thousands of Westerners who had come to get rich fast in the overheated Dubai economy were suddenly faced with lost jobs and large debts; many simply absconded, leaving behind everything— including their cars (you can still find these dust-covered corpses in some places in the city). Many buildings are nearly empty. Many of the big artificial islands that were being constructed in the Gulf are now nothing more than sandbars.

Still, the government does a good job of keeping up appearances, despite being broke. Everything gleams and glitters. The metro runs smoothly and efficiently. The city is perhaps the world's most impressive smokescreen.

Still, I couldn't help but be fascinated by this bizarre place. In some ways, despite the dramatic physical changes and population explosion, the new Dubai builds on the trading heritage of the old Dubai, when it was contested territory between the Ottomans and Portuguese, and then the Ottomans and the British. The old-fashioned souqs of central Dubai might be seen as precursors to the megamalls. Merchants from around the Indian Ocean used to come here to wheel and deal; Arab sailors set forth from this port to return the favor (even now, wooden dhows ply Iranian ports). Today, the wheeling and dealing is just done on a much grander scale; the merchants and consumers come by plane rather than by ship.

I wouldn't want to live in Dubai. But I am glad I embraced the possibility of becoming a hypocrite and made the journey anyway.

AL-JAZIRA: QATAR

By now, most people have heard of the news sensation that is Al-Jazeera. In the U.S., many still view it with deep suspicion due to a misguided perception that it is, somehow, anti-American, but generally it has developed a reputation as one of the better international news services in the world. Fewer know that it is based in Doha, Qatar, and even fewer know what its name means. In Arabic, *al-jazira* translates as the "the island" or, more aptly in this case, "the peninsula." Qatar is a spit of a peninsula that juts off the enormous peninsula of Arabia. You get the picture.

Although I was only in Qatar for a short weekend, and am therefore in no real position to make any sweeping analytical assertions about Qatari society, I was struck by the differences I noticed between it and all the other Gulf states that I have visited. That said, though, I have been struck by the differences I have seen between all of them. Each, in their own way, is a grand societal and economic experiment, some more successful than others.

What gets me about Qatar is that while the Al-Thani royal family and most native Qataris share close ties with the Saudis—both "tribally" (the two royal families are both from the Najd in central Arabia) and religiously (both adhere to the austere Wahhabi strain of Sunni Islam)—Qatar has taken a very different approach in its dealings with both domestic policies and international relations.

In Saudi Arabia, all citizens and non-Saudis are forced, when in public, to adhere to pretty strict social norms for fear of religious corruption; in Qatar there is a much more relaxed attitude. This difference is made especially clear in the case of local women. In Saudi, women still are not allowed to drive and there are severe limitations on where they can work. Qatari women cannot only drive, but they are also remarkably integrated into the workforce (for instance, I noticed that most of the guards at the Islamic Art Museum were women, as were many of the customs officials at the airport). As for the large expat community (which is, in Qatar's case, nearly seventy-five percent of the population), people are for the most part allowed to live their lives as they see fit (within "reason"), rather than trying to make them conform to much of the Wahhabi strictures. I was almost shocked to see men running in shorts... And there were even bars where alcohol was freely available!

But these "lax" attitudes go well beyond being able to get a drink. Rather than trying to control the flow of information, as is the case in Saudi, Qatar is one of the few countries in the region with a basically free press—Al-Jazeera being the most famous case in point (which is why it is not very popular with many of the governments in the Middle East). Al-Jazeera even broadcasts items that are critical of the Al-Thani family.

The Qatari royals also made an early push to make Qatar the intellectual and educational hub in the Gulf, most obviously with the establishment of the Education City—even my alma mater Cornell maintains a branch of its medical school in this complex that is just outside of Doha. The development of Education City preceded the rapid expansion of the foreign universities that are being set up in the U.A.E. and elsewhere in the Gulf. And, from what I can tell, this endeavor has been successful due to the thoughtfulness of Qatar's approach—rather than simply throwing money at the buildings and facilities, Qatar allows the partner schools full intellectual freedom to develop their programs.

All of this political and cultural experimentation made me interested in Qatar before I arrived. But I must admit that I was convinced that I would find Doha a little soulless, perhaps a bit like Dubai. However, once again my preconceptions were proven wrong. Doha actually felt more "real" to me than Dubai, more solid, more livable.

***

Since I had limited time, I concentrated on the grand sweep of Doha's corniche and the attractions around it.

First and foremost, I made a beeline to the brand new Museum of Islamic Art, an I.M. Pei-designed stack of postmodern cubes that rises out of the bay on its own artificial island. It is an obvious example of Doha's attempt to invent itself as a cultural center. The exhibits are beautifully displayed: thematically on one floor, chronologically and regionally on another. Fortuitously, considering my Ottomanist inclinations, there was also a temporary exhibit regarding European perceptions of the Ottomans that took up much of the ground floor. Perhaps not surprisingly, considering the light hold that the Ottomans had on this stretch of Persian Gulf territory, the exhibit was one of the only indications I saw in Qatar of its Ottoman past.

Souq Waqif, a nearby site that was just a bit inland from the museum, confounded my expectations (as had the city as a whole). I had read in my guidebook that, while there had been a market at the spot since at least the nineteenth century, the area had turned into a warren of ugly concrete structures by the 1980s. Some Qatari entrepreneurs, recognizing the potential tourist value of the souq, replaced the concrete with a re-imagined vision of a "traditional" mud-walled market. I fully expected it to feel very "Disney" and very touristy. But despite the fact that this was a fabricated "traditional" space, I was surprised by how real—and how Qatari—it all was. Most of the shops were not selling tourist trinkets, but rather spices, kitchenware, fishing gear, horse tack, clothing, etc. And while the food options included plenty of international chains (even Dunkin' Donuts), there were also many hole-in-the-wall restaurants and food stands that were advertised only in Arabic and that served local fare. I stopped for *haree*s, a porridge-like, wheat-based dish at a home-cooking spot run by a feisty bedouin woman named Umm Ahmad. There were also several *majlis*-style coffee houses where men were smoking shishas.

Much of my time in Doha, though, was spent simply walking the corniche. The waterfront walkway is quite long, stretching almost five miles from one end to the next, and has been developed into an inviting strip of parkland and paths. It is perhaps the best place to see the Old Doha and the New Doha, from the old wooden dhows that are lashed to the jetty next to the über-modern Islamic Art Museum, to the low-slung architecture of Souq Waqif and the bold line of futuristic skyscrapers on the northern edge of the bay.

Doha and the rest of the *jazira* definitely deserved more than a stopover. Next time, I will have time to look beyond the corniche; perhaps I will venture into the desert, which remains the heart of Qatar.

Qatar, Old and New

OF SEA AND SAND: OMAN

There are occasionally certain advantages to being delayed for nearly twelve hours, even when it means waiting out that time in a tiny, characterless terminal in Dubai with only a McDonald's and Baskin-Robbins to keep oneself occupied. In this case, the advantage was that my new flight left after dark. From my fortuitous window seat on the plane, I was able to see my destination come into view all aglitter in the night. There were the long ribbons of highways, as well as the bright curves of the bays and harbors that are the reason this city exists. I could also see the black gaps in those lights, mysterious to me from my aerial perspective—but once we landed I could see that those unlit spaces were craggy mountains, another shaper of the city.

I had arrived, at last, in Muscat.

***

I fell for the idea of Oman before I really knew much at all about the country; mostly, I just wanted to go because I couldn't.

When Oman first came onto my radar, which was perhaps back in my early college days, I was enticed by the fact that it was a relatively closed place with fairly restrictive visa requirements. I saw it as a challenge of sorts: my desire to see what is hidden is perhaps why I have sought out opportunities to travel to such "out there" destinations as Turkmenistan and Saudi Arabia, and why I scheme to get into places like North Korea (someday, I will make it!).

However, as I actually began to seek out information on the country and its history, my reasons for wanting to go to Oman multiplied and became more tangible. I was fascinated by the story of Sultan Qaboos overthrowing his father in 1970 and working gradually to modernize Oman without causing the Omanis to lose touch with their cultural heritage; indeed, part of the reason it was so difficult to get a visa for so long was that the sultan didn't want the country flooded with tourists and expats while the nation was finding this balance.

Given this longtime resistance to tourism, it's perhaps not too surprising then that the hotel I stayed at while I was in Muscat bills itself as the first hotel in Oman, even though it was only built sometime in the 1970s (and, from what I can tell, it has not really changed its décor since). There wasn't much of a need for hotels for a long time.

I was also fascinated to learn that the Omanis practiced a form of Islam that is different from both the Sunnis and the Shi'as, a kind called Ibadhi (Khariji). The Ibadhi school of Islam emerged from a fiercely egalitarian vision of who rightfully could serve as the spiritual-political leader of the Islamic community.[130] As the years went on, the subject of Oman kept popping up in my studies and teaching. Increasingly, I became entranced by its pivotal role in the Indian Ocean world, a position that many in the sixteenth century—including both the Portuguese and Ottomans—tried to control. Muscat, however, was only briefly under Ottoman control, as it yo-yoed between the Ottomans and the Portuguese during their struggle for dominance.[131] The Ottoman navy first captured the city in 1552 under the command of the famous Ottoman Admiral Piri Reis, who is perhaps better known to history as a cartographer.[132] Then, there was the vast Omani empire that emerged in the nineteenth century and that

---

[130] In general, in Sunni Islam there is the ideal of having a caliph, a leader who should guide the entire Muslim community ('*ummah*), and who should descend from the Quraysh tribe—though in practice there hasn't been a caliph with any real authority since the end of the Abbasid dynasty in 1258. For most Shi'ia Muslims there is the belief that the spiritual leader, or Imam, should be a descendent of Ali and Fatima, the prophet Muhammad's daughter. Ibadhis, however, maintain there is no need for a spiritual guide or leader for all Muslims, especially if there is no one appropriate to lead. And if there is, that leader need not be from any particular lineage; he must simply be the most pious individual.

[131] Giancarlo Casale details this fascinating era in his *The Ottoman Age of Exploration* (2010). While I had known of the Ottoman-Portuguese struggles around the Arabian Peninsula and East African coast, this book opened my eyes to the broader interest that the Ottoman Empire had in the Indian Ocean world. While an academic treatment of the subject, the text is accessible and engaging; I highly recommend it to those with an interest in sixteenth century and/or world history.

[132] Many of Piri Reis' maps and charts, some of the most accurate produced during the 1500s, were collected in the *Kitab-ı Bahriye* (Book of Navigation). He is

encompassed much of the east African (Swahili) coast, as well as parts of Iran and what is now Pakistan. I became curious to see how this cultural mishmash might reveal itself in today's Oman. My curiosity was especially heightened given that the country closed in on itself for a good chunk of the twentieth century, under the leadership of Sultan Said bin Taimur (Sultan Qaboos' father).

But other than a quick transit through the Muscat airport back in 1997 on my way to Sri Lanka, I didn't get a chance to make my pilgrimage to Oman until my time spent living in Sudan.

Of course, Oman is not a closed country anymore. As part of the Sultan's plan, it has gotten increasingly easy to get a visa. All I had to do, in 2010, was show up at the airport, pay the visa fee, and be on my way (it took me twenty minutes flat to get from landing to getting into a taxi—one of the easiest customs and immigration processes I have ever experienced). But all its historical and cultural allures drew me in, and I was not disappointed.

***

Since I had arrived in Muscat a day later than planned, I decided to make up for lost time. I woke up early and descended from Ruwi to Mutrah[133] and its souq and corniche. It was early enough that I nearly had the harbor front to myself. I made my way to the northern edge of the corniche to see the fish market in action, the vendors' wares literally still dripping from the sea as they were dragged from the fishing boats just a few feet away. A section of the market was devoted to "cleaning," so you could hand over your newly bought fish (swordfish, anyone?) and get it gutted right in front of you.

A short distance away, the Bayt al-Baranda (House of the Veranda) Museum was opening up, so I ventured in. The place, a lovingly restored traditional house, is now a museum of Muscat, where the displays attempt to trace the area's history all the way from the age of the dinosaurs (I am

---

particularly famous for his world map (1513), which shows the eastern coast of the "New World" and, some argue, Antarctica.

[133] Muscat is really composed of a collection of distinct towns. There is Muscat proper, as well as suburbs such as Mutrah and Ruwi, among others that together constitute greater Muscat.

not kidding) through the glories of the Al-Busaidi dynasty (that of the current leader, Sultan Qaboos). While a sophisticated museum, I found myself amused at the nationalism oozing from most of the exhibits—such as the description of the valiant Omani Arab efforts to rid the coasts of the brutal Portuguese. Interestingly, there was no mention, no echo, of the period when the Ottomans held the Omani coast at the expense of the Portuguese in the sixteenth century

From the museum, I retraced my steps back to the souq, which was now bustling with a wonderful mash of Omanis in national dress and inappropriately dressed Germans.[134] Omani men could win an award for best dressed in the Arab world: with their spotless *dishdasha*s, floor-length dress shirts (usually white, as in other parts of the Arabian peninsula, but here they were also sometimes in other colors) with a tassel hanging at their neck (apparently, the tassels are usually perfumed), not to mention their *kummah*s (flat-topped caps that are embroidered with beautiful patterns, no two alike) or *msarr*s (turban-like wraps of patterned cloth, like pashmina shawls), they are quite striking. I felt so underdressed.

But as much as I would have enjoyed staying in the souq all day, the sea beckoned. I returned to the corniche and, despite the growing humidity, began to follow the coastal path towards old Muscat, a two-mile jaunt that hugs the rugged shore. I passed under the shadows of the Mutrah Fort (there seemed to be a fort or watchtower on every hill) and the gigantic incense-burner monument (this is, after all, the land of Frankincense) and made my way to the gates of the old city of Muscat.

Old Muscat is a statelier place than the mercantile tumble that is Mutrah. This is the seat of government in Oman, the place where the Sultan lives in his sumptuous palace (it actually verges on gaudy, which is striking in this country of such refined, understated architectural tastes), and the part of Muscat where most ministries are housed. It also has a great museum, the Bayt al-Zubair; like the Bayt al-Baranda, this one housed in

---

[134] I traveled in Oman during what is perhaps the busiest travel week of the year, the Eid al-Adha holiday. Oman seems to be a major destination for expats from around the Gulf region who are seeking a more relaxed setting than the U.A.E. or Bahrain or Qatar and who, perhaps, are also hoping to soak in some "authentic" Arab culture. It doesn't hurt that the country is also gorgeous and full of outdoor activity possibilities.

a restored mansion. The Bayt al-Zubair focuses on Omani handicrafts and the household of the original inhabitants (who were, oddly, Anglo-Indian in taste!). And to round out the sites—you guessed it—forts, two of them: al-Jalali and al-Mirani, both of Portuguese origin.

As night fell, I found myself back in Mutrah, where I ate kebab at an outdoor restaurant near the entrance of the souq. A television flickered with a show in honor of the fortieth anniversary of Qaboos' reign. Omani and Indian families tucked into their food and fresh juices. I was exhausted but happy. I had made it to elusive Muscat.

***

The water in the Gulf of Oman is jewel colored. It shimmers with intense blues and greens that seem unnatural. I had noticed this that first morning as I walked along the corniche in Mutrah. Yet I was still awed by it as I walked along the beach in Sur, where I watched dhows bob in that sea of color. It was easy to imagine jumping on one of these wooden boats and setting sail into the Indian Ocean.

The sea defined most of my second day in Oman. Much of the fortune of the country was built by its seafaring coastal people; it is the coast that most people probably think of when they think of Oman.

All the same, though, to only know the coast is only to know half the story, as I will try to illustrate.

To make the most of my short stay in Oman, I had decided to rent a car. And since I planned to get off the beaten path a bit, I opted for a 4WD. However, I was a little stunned when an immense Toyota Landcruiser showed up at the hotel. I prayed I would not have to do much backing up!

Early that Sunday morning, I navigated out of Muscat's morning rush-hour traffic and onto the road that would lead me over the foothills of the Hajar Mountains and down to the coastal plain. With my own wheels, I had the freedom to go where I liked, when I liked. This allowed me to have some solitude, as well as to escape the occasional Italian tour group bespoiling a remote spot of beauty (see below).

My first stop was the village of Qurayat. After not encountering much traffic between Muscat and this coast, I was initially perplexed by the traffic jam that I found myself mired in upon entering town. Why would there be so many people here on a Sunday, particularly at this hour? Then I saw the reason: there was a sheep market in the main square in preparation for Eid al-Adha, the Feast of Sacrifice that marks the end of the Hajj. These little sheep were destined for a bloody end come mid-week.

I am told that the road from Qurayat to Sur was once mostly a bumpy, gravelly affair. However, a brand-new paved highway has been built along the same route. While I am sure it has increased the speed with which one can traverse the coast, I sort of regretted the disappearance of the rough gravel path. For one, the new road is so new that signage was iffy at best, which played havoc with my ability to find the places I wanted to see. But it was all part of the adventure.

My first post-Qurayat stop was Bayt al-Afreet, the House of Demons, otherwise known as the Bimmah Sinkhole. Despite the fact that it was all but unmarked and out in the middle of nowhere, this gorgeous pool of unknown depth, was, alas, brimming with Italian and Russian tourists. Apparently, they all got the memo on how to find this spot.

My greatest challenge, however, was figuring out how to enter Wadi Shab. Despite the sign (which someone had perhaps forgotten to remove) that pointed into the village of al-Shab, the remnant of the former gravel road ended abruptly where it had been destroyed—at the edge of a cliff! I had to get back on the highway, pass in front of the mouth of the *wadi*—it was so maddeningly close!—drive down to the next village, Tiwi, and then find my way through its tangle of narrow streets until I got to the entrance of the valley.

Just as I was starting to feel smug about discovering the "secret" trail to the wadi, I pulled up to the cleft's entrance only to find a clutch of other Landcruisers and similar 4WD vehicles. So much for having nature all to myself!

I guess I couldn't blame them; it was spectacular, a real Arabian oasis experience. It was a winding, narrow canyon with pockets of date palms and pools of clear, cold spring water. When it rained, the wadi would become a river; however, I was there in the dry season, and therefore only had to ford one stream. As I ventured deeper into the canyon, the sounds of civilization disappeared. All I could hear was the burbling of water and the rustle of palm leaves.

Sur marked the end of my day's journey. I hadn't really thought much about the town beyond I decided that it seemed a convenient point to stop for the night. But as is so often the case, I found great pleasure in the unexpected. While strolling along the town's corniche, I stumbled on the dhow building yards, having forgotten that the town was known for its shipbuilding. These wooden boats, right out of *1001 Nights*, still ply the Persian Gulf and the coast all the way to East Africa. Their prows curve upward, ready to tackle the currents of the Indian Ocean; their triangular white sails look like giant wings. These elegant boats were the vessels by which Oman built its empire, when it was an empire.

While I contemplated the dhows, the call to prayer began echoing across the town and off the surrounding hills. The picture was complete.

As much as I would have liked to linger on the coast, it was time to turn inland.

***

I smelled it before I saw it, the sharp scent of smoldering charcoal mixed with something I couldn't quite put my finger on—though it was familiar. I followed my nose down a narrow backstreet in Nizwa, where I found a crowd massed around an enormous, stone-lined pit. The men were heaving large, charred lumps out of the pit and into wheelbarrows that were waiting at ground level. On closer inspection, the lumps seemed to be blackened burlap sacks, but I was still mystified by what they contained. A number of men in this early morning huddle (it was barely 7 a.m.) noticed the gawking foreigner and waved me to the front for a better view. One flashed a big smile and asked in English: "You want meat?"

Suddenly it all made sense. And I could pin point the mysterious smell: barbecue! So this was what had become of all the slaughtered sheep from Eid—they had been slow cooked in an earthen oven, possibly for the last two days. Now, these Nizwais were disinterring the tender roasted lamb, preparing to distribute it among the community as part of the observance of the holy celebration.

I politely declined a portion and continued on my morning stroll. Nizwa was constantly throwing such lovely moments in my path.

The interior, defined in large part by the mountains, is in some ways literally the heart of Oman. At times it was the political center of the region, at times it was a rival to the coast. Indeed, not long after the Omani Empire was divided into two (Oman and Zanzibar went their separate ways under the leadership of rival brothers), Oman proper divided into coast (which was called Muscat) and interior (which was called Oman—confused yet?); at that point, Oman was ruled by a sultan and an imam respectively. Sultan Said attempted to reassert his authority over the mountainous regions by setting off the Jebel (Mountain) Wars of the 1950s; Oman wasn't formally reunited until 1959. So to know only the coast of Oman really is, as I noted, to know only half the story.

To understand the interior, then, you need to understand Nizwa, the "Pearl of Islam," the political and cultural heart of the heart. At some points, it was the power center of Oman in totality; when the country was divided into Muscat and Oman, between Sultanate and Imamate, it was the seat of the interior's imam. It remains an important second city to Muscat.

When I arrived in Nizwa after my explorations of the coast, I had planned on spending two nights, using it as a base from which to explore the region. I did that, but then I also decided it was good place to just be, from which to witness Eid al-Adha and the fortieth anniversary of Sultan Qaboos' reign.[135] As a result, I booked a third night in what might have been the last available hotel room in Nizwa (and possibly in all of Oman— the Eid holiday was in full swing, and the country's limited hotel offerings were booked to the max).

The day I arrived (November 16) was Eid itself. Nizwa was eerily quiet, as all of the Omanis seemed to be celebrating at home with their families. The only people in the streets were a few Indian men, lounging in the shade of the shuttered streets of the souq or under the trees that lined the town's dry riverbed. So, I went exploring through some of the other towns in the area, particularly focusing on the forts—some of which are quite impressive.

---

[135]   Celebrated on Oman's National Day (November 18).

Fort and Cannon

The forts and castles that seem to dot all of Oman[136] were even more impressive in al-Dakhiliyah (the apt name of the province, which means "The Interior"), where they almost grew out of the mountains. The Nizwa Fort was closed for the holiday, but I vowed to come back before I left.

---

[136] The number of forts scattered across the country is a good indication of the many struggles that the region has faced, both in terms of deflecting attacks by outside forces (such as the Portuguese and Ottomans) and for protection from internal competition (as various factions fought for control of the coast and interior of Oman).

Heading west out of Nizwa, I aimed for the town of Bahla. After I wound a bit through the new part of town, I crested a hill and saw the dramatic line of mud wall fortifications that snaked into the surrounding mountains and then, rising above the valley, a dramatically situated fort that has been in the process of being restored since the 1980s (which meant, of course, that it was closed to the public).[137] Perhaps due to the stormy sky as backdrop—this was the only time I thought it might rain while I was traveling in Oman—this fort really struck me. I decided it was my favorite, and it remained so even after I saw the one in nearby Jabrin, which is often noted as a prime example of the genre.

Perhaps getting a little fort-fatigue, I spent the rest of the afternoon exploring some of the villages in the foothills of the mountains—and one up in the mountains, Misfat. I discovered the hairpin road up to this precariously perched town in time to be able to catch the sunset over the mountains and plains. Like a biblical painting, the sun's rays seemed to beam from the puffy, white clouds, casting an orange glow on the whitewashed towns in the valley. The jagged mountains sank into darkness.

I watched the drama until the sky turned a velvety navy blue; I was reluctant to pull away from such beauty, but I needed to return to Nizwa before it got too dark.

***

The following day, I woke bright and early to head up into the mountains proper. I actually made my way up the highest mountain in Oman, Jebel Shams (Sun Mountain), which is the vantage point for the deepest canyon in the Arabian Peninsula, Wadi Ghul—one of the sights I had been most looking forward to on this trip.

With the Land Cruiser, the drive up was surprisingly easy (although I dreaded the long descent; I learned to drive on the flatlands of Indiana, and am not well-versed in the ups and downs of mountain driving). But as

---

137   In the end, I only got to see the inside of one fort, the one in Nizwa. It seemed that all of the Omani forts were either closed permanently (some still are used as security stations), being renovated and refurbished, or simply shut for the holidays. But at least I managed to see the interior of one! It would have been really weird to leave Oman without having done so—especially for a history buff.

I had encountered elsewhere, the way to the viewing point for the canyon was anything but obvious. At one point, I ended up taking a very rough track only to find myself smack-dab in the middle of a lonely village, with no one beside the local goats out and about to greet me. But with some perseverance, I found my way—and the view was worth the mis-turns.

Called the "Grand Canyon of Arabia," Wadi Ghul is a cleft of 3,250 feet or more into the mountains, its sides dropping sheerly to the distant bottom. It would be a long, long way to fall!

But I wasn't going to let the precipitous drops deter me from my hike. There is an amazing trail that starts in a tiny village at the rim of the canyon and then snakes along the canyon wall, without much between you and the void. The end of the trail, about a one-and-a-half hour's hike, was an abandoned village, ghostlike, crumbling on its narrow ledge. What a place to have lived! I imagined the previous villagers, their lives defined by a few terraces hundreds of meters in the sky, with only a narrow path to connect them to the rest of the world.

Except for a few other hearty hikers, I had the trail and the village to myself. As I sat and ate my lunch, staring deep into the wadi, a curious goat came to keep me company. He seemed to enjoy the bit of biscuit I shared with him; he also seemed to be the sole inhabitant of the village of Sap Bani Khamis.

When I returned to Nizwa, I found that it had come to joyous life. A "souq" for children was set up outside the city walls, a group of Omani men were singing and dancing with swords outside of the main gate (in the parking lot), and everyone was in a holiday mood.

It made me glad that I would be spending another day just in Nizwa, without plans to do anything "touristy" (other than going to the fort… but, hey, it was there!).

When Friday arrived, it was with some sadness that I packed the car and began the last leg of my Omani journey. There is much to draw me back to Oman's "heart"; I never got to see Jebel Akhdar, the "Breadbasket" of Oman, or to drive over the mountain pass to Rustaq and Nakhal.

There's never enough time.

***

Having made a grand circuit of sea, sand, and mountain in Oman—with a good balance of both urban and rural, coast and interior thrown into the mix—I was happy to return for one more day to Muscat. After having spent a week in more sparsely populated areas, Muscat seemed a veritable metropolis when I drove in on the Nizwa highway. But I suppose that could have been partly due to the fact that the city is quite long, strung along the coast for a good thirty miles, but not very wide.

Although I didn't have much specifically planned other than to enjoy my final moments in the country, I did make a point to stop at the Sultan Qaboos Grand Mosque, which I had only glimpsed on my way from the airport a week earlier. Unfortunately, since it was Friday, I couldn't actually enter the mosque, but I could wander the grounds. It is indeed an impressive piece of modern Islamic architecture, enormous but tastefully minimalist in form, with gorgeous accents from around the Muslim world (like the mihrabs set into the colonnade). Apparently, the interior is more overtly sumptuous, but I will have to wait till next time to check it out.

Back in Mutrah, the market was shuttered for the afternoon, but I followed a crowd of Indian men who were heading from post-noon prayers to a nondescript lunch spot near the souq entrance. I think they were bemused to see the clearly non-local joining them at the communal tables and ordering, like them, the chicken biryani. I tucked in with my fingers, too, and loved every bite.

Once the sun began to set, the souq came back to life, and I spent my remaining hours just wandering amid the crowds.

I wouldn't have spent my last day in Muscat any other way.

KOUT TO KUWAIT

It was another of those not-so-auspicious starts.

First, I had mistakenly paid for a set of visa stamps I didn't need as I stumbled through the very unclear visa process—head up to the departure lounge (really?), get a copy of your passport made, take a number, fill out this form, buy the visa stamps from a vending machine (oops, unless you are from the U.K. or U.S.), get an 8"-by-11" piece of paper that serves as your visa (don't lose it!), get your entry stamp, and *then* head downstairs to immigration.

Second, I couldn't get a taxi driver to take me into town, at least not at first. The first guy, a grizzled old Kuwaiti man in *gutra* who was puffing away on a cigarette, took one look at me and, before I could explain where I wanted to go, waved his hand dismissively: "*Mushkilah!*" ("Problem!") How was it a "mushkilah"? He didn't even know where I was trying to go.

Finally, I got a driver willing to take my fare, but then he had no clue how to get to my destination…

Welcome to Kuwait!

But any negativity I felt after these little arrival-related "adventures" soon vanished as I really began my explorations. As so often has been the case in my travels, first impressions proved erroneous.

***

Kuwait is not generally high on most people's travel lists, unlike some of its neighbors—notably Dubai, and increasingly Doha—which are major transit hubs and major tourist draws in and of themselves (if, for anything, their shopping opportunities). Kuwait, however, is generally a destination for business types. One rarely goes to Kuwait unless one has to go there. Thus, I raised a few eyebrows when I told people I was going just to go: "Isn't it just a bunch of glitzy malls?" they asked.

Yes, You Can.

But I've never been the type to follow the typical tourist routes. I had my reasons, of course, for wanting to spend a long weekend in the tiny country, which is essentially a city-state, at the northwestern end of the Persian Gulf. For one thing, it was formerly an Ottoman territory (albeit nominally so). Furthermore, I wanted to complete my Gulf Cooperation Council (G.C.C.) "tour." Without really having planned it, I had been checking off the list of G.C.C. member states: first Bahrain[138], followed

---

138   I have actually been to Bahrain twice, once on a stopover between Turkey and Sri Lanka in 1999 and more recently at the end of my study tour of Saudi Arabia in 2010. Both visits, however, were so brief that I decided not to include a separate chapter on this smallest of Arab states. I will relate this anecdote, though, to illustrate what an odd little place Bahrain can be: Our flight at the end of the ARAMCO-sponsored trip to Saudi Arabia was oddly out of Bahrain, rather than Saudi (something to do with connecting flights in Europe). We drove the long causeway between the two countries, the largest and smallest in the Gulf region, and found a place for dinner before we headed to the airport. The restaurant selected was ostensibly a Thai place, but was decked out as if it were an Old West American saloon, with Asian waitresses in mini cutoff jean shorts. As it was the holiday season, a Christmas tree was propped up in the corner. Several Saudi

by Saudi Arabia, the U.A.E., Oman, and Qatar. All that remained was Kuwait (I had once landed there on my way to Saudi in 2008, but since I hadn't even gotten off the plane, it doesn't count). Lastly, there's the simple challenge of discovering what it is that makes any destination, regardless of its tourist appeal, fascinating. If someone tells me a place isn't worth visiting, it doubles my interest in traveling there.

It didn't take long for me to discover that there was much more to see and experience than shopping at the latest mall development or stopping for a latte at Starbucks (though I did all that, too).

***

Once I had managed to get out of the airport and find a taxi driver who was willing to drive me, I made a beeline to the Tareq Rajab Museum. This gem of a museum is not easy to find, as it is tucked into Jabriya, a residential neighborhood far from the main sights of the city. Even once I was in Jabriya, no one seemed to have heard of the place; I basically had to stumble on it. But the search was more than worth the effort.

This museum is housed in the basement of the former home of the first Kuwaiti minister of antiquities; it showcases his private collection of mostly Islamic arts and crafts. Apparently, as he traveled the world, gathering items for the Kuwait National Museum, he would also make private purchases, eventually ending up with an astounding collection of textiles, ceramics, jewelry, and manuscripts from across the Islamic world. What makes this museum all the more important is that during the Iraqi invasion in 1990, when the National Museum was decimated, Tareq Rajab managed to hide his collection by building a false wall in his basement. The priceless artifacts survived the war unscathed. So, as the country tries to rebuild and refurbish the once-impressive National Museum, the Tareq Rajab Museum soldiers on.

---

men in national dress sat in the shadows, enjoying sinful rounds of beer and chatting up what appeared to be Russian and Ukrainian prostitutes. I felt like we had arrived at the end of the world.

As I was soon to discover, there were many other quirky sights hidden in surprising corners of Kuwait City.

***

Unbeknownst to me when I purchased my ticket to Kuwait, my time in the country was going to coincide with one of its biggest holiday weekends—the back-to-back National Day and Liberation Day. The city was awash in green, white, red, and black, the colors of the Kuwaiti flag; little girls were even wearing dresses in these national colors.

The festivities—which included boys armed with Super Soakers hosing down passing vehicles on Arab Gulf Road—provided a colorful backdrop to my visit, although they also proved to be something of a challenge. Some places were closed for the holiday, and some taxis would refuse to go anywhere near Gulf Road for the above-mentioned reason. I had to plan accordingly.

There were times when I simply stuck to the streets of Hawalli, the neighborhood where I was staying, and played the local—drinking tea and coffee, smoking a shisha or two, noshing on great Syrian and Lebanese food (the Levantine Arabs do corner the market on the best Arab cuisine, I must say)—especially when the craziness of the celebrations prevented me from going further afield.

But the dual holiday—National Day (February 25), which celebrates the country's independence from Britain in 1961[139], and Liberation Day (February 26), which marks the routing of the Iraqi forces during Operation Desert Storm in 1991—provided the perfect context for me to begin thinking about Kuwait's rather intriguing history.

***

The name Kuwait stems from the Arabic word for a small, seaside fort: *kout*. Honestly, it's a fitting name for the country. This flat, flat wedge of desert doesn't at first glance seem to offer much of a draw, especially for human settlement. Indeed, it wasn't permanently settled

---

[139] A little oddly, February 25 is not the day Kuwait gained independence from Britain—that was June 19, 1961; rather, it is the date when Sheikh Abdullah al-Salem al-Sabah, who negotiated for independence, came to the throne.

until approximately three hundred years ago. But the territory does have one major advantage: it possesses one of the best natural harbors in the Gulf region.

In the mid 1700s, the Bani Khalid tribe from the Najd (the central region of the Arabian peninsula, from which the Saudi ruling family also emerged) settled on the coast. They built the original kout to protect the cluster of bedouin tents that was the first Kuwaiti "city" and appointed Sabah (the First) bin Jaber to be their leader. From these humble beginnings, a distinct Kuwait would emerge—one that has been ruled by the al-Sabah family ever since (although sometimes with outside "guidance"). Under the al-Sabah, Kuwait grew from a cluster of tents surrounding a fort into a more permanent settlement that eventually played a key role in the lucrative trade—pearls, spices, dates—that passed through the region. The town grew into a local power in the Gulf, becoming a transit point between overland and sea trade.

While the Ottomans generally claimed sovereignty over the region, their control of Kuwait was never very tight, especially in comparison to the region that eventually became Iraq or even further down the Gulf coast in al-Hasa, in what is now Saudi Arabia. In an attempt to keep the Ottomans at bay, Emir Mubarak al-Sabah aligned himself with the British, first by signing a treaty in 1899 that gave Britain control of much of Kuwait's foreign policy and later, in 1913, by pushing for the Anglo-Ottoman Convention that got both Britain and the Ottoman Empire to formally accept Sabahi authority in Kuwait. This convention would prove short-lived, however; as soon as World War I was over, Britain declared Kuwait and the other Gulf states to be "autonomous" parts of the British Empire (i.e., protectorates).

During the first half of the twentieth century, Kuwait would remain a sleepy, pearl-producing corner of Britain's vast empire. However, the discovery of oil in 1938 set Kuwait on path that would change it (and the Gulf) forever. Kuwait City would grow from a small community of low-slung mud brick buildings that were surrounded by a mud brick wall into a sprawling city of multi-lane highways and towering, state-of-the art skyscrapers. It would go from being one of the poorest countries in the world to one of the wealthiest, and all in the matter of a couple generations.

Such rapid growth is never easy. Kuwait is now struggling to find its balance as it both recovers from the setback of the Persian Gulf War[140] and enters full steam into the twenty-first century.

***

Even though I tried not to listen to those who claimed that Kuwait was just a collection of malls, I really didn't expect to find many—if any—physical remains of the city's earlier history. But when I looked closely, the Kuwaiti past rubs shoulders—perhaps uneasily at times—with the Kuwaiti present and future.

On my last morning, I jumped into a taxi and headed to the last stretch of Gulf Road I had not yet explored. In the brisk morning (having come from Sudan, I was taken aback by how chilly the Kuwait winter was at times!), I strolled, almost alone, along the portion that had been the original town.

With a backdrop of futuristic skyscrapers on one side and the blue expanse of the Gulf on the other, I stumbled on one treasure after another. Dhows, those ancient pliers of trade around the Indian Ocean, bobbed in a harbor right next to the Sharq Souq Mall (yes, a mall); white-washed buildings with heavily carved wooden doors have been refurbished and reappointed as government offices; the not-so-lovely, boxy house of the last British governor holds its own in the middle of a large construction project; the elegant Sadu House, one of the last remaining pre-oil era houses, serves as a museum of traditional bedouin textiles/weavings; a short distance in from the coast, right in the downtown area, a lively, full-on souq in the old style sprawls with all the wares one could hope to find. This is a Kuwait that many overlook, I think.

And it's the Kuwait I will remember. And it, rather than the misanthropic taxi driver who I met upon my arrival, is the Kuwait I will remember most fondly and vividly.

---

[140] Although the Persian Gulf War, which began with Iraq's invasion of Kuwait in 1990, unfolded more than two decades ago, the aftermath of the conflict is still very present in Kuwait. Even the National Museum, which was nearly destroyed in the conflict, is not yet back in full working order.

MOTHER OF THE WORLD: EGYPT

"Welcome to Egypt! Hey, you look like Egyptian man!"

It had been twelve years since I last set foot in Egypt and sixteen since I lived in Cairo. Those years represented a significant chunk of my then thirty-seven years on this planet, yet somehow I felt immediately at home as soon as I stepped into the chaos of Cairo's streets. It was as if I had left only yesterday; all was familiar.

Admittedly, Cairo was not always the easiest of cities in which to live. It was—and is—a maddening place with its street-choking traffic jams, its noise (including the incessant honking horns of said traffic jams), and its often thickly polluted air. Not to mention the constant attention of hucksters who are trying to con a pound or two out of an unsuspecting *khawaga*.[141]

But Cairo is also a place that is easy to love. It gets deep under your skin.

I adore its elegant, but now crumbling, nineteenth-century buildings; its countless coffeehouses that spill into the street, packed with men smoking apple-flavored *shisha*, sipping mint tea, and playing backgammon; and its gregarious people, always ready to joke and chat. Its inconceivably long history seems to tumble all around me, each part of the story overlapping and blurring in fascinating ways. The Pharaonic, Greco-Macedonia, Roman, Arab, Mamluk, Ottoman, and British periods all intermingle with the twentieth and twenty-first centuries. All of Cairo's past is very much present and alive.

Cairo is a city made for nostalgic souls.

---

[141] This is the Egyptian pronunciation of a Persian word, *khawajah*, which technically means "lord"—but in the Egyptian context translates as "stupid tourist." In the Egyptian dialect, the Arabic letter ج ('jîm') is pronounced as a 'g,' rather than a 'j.' This meant that many Egyptians misspoke my name, James, as 'Games.' In the chapter on Sudan, you will see how the word khawajah is used somewhat differently in that country.

Being the nostalgic sort myself, I decided to stay at the Windsor Hotel during my most recent trip. While it is very much a part of that crumbling nineteenth-century world of downtown Cairo, with its peeling walls, iffy hot water supply, and doors that don't quite close, it was also the perfect home base for my triumphal return. I used to visit the Windsor's lounge when I was studying at the American University in Cairo (A.U.C.), where I enjoyed its ancient waiters in bowties, its faded yellow walls, and its antler chandeliers. Not surprisingly, the space had not changed a bit (I swear that even some of the waiters were the same!). A friend from my hometown in Indiana, Danni, who happened to be working in Amman at the time, became my partner in crime during this visit. We were fascinated by the hotel's hand-operated elevator—the last one still in use in Cairo—every time we went up to our room on the sixth floor.

Over the course of our four days in the city, I dragged Danni along my nostalgia tour. We made the grand circuit of Islamic Cairo on Day One, when we climbed to the rooftop and minaret of the venerable Al-Azhar Mosque, one of the most important centers of Sunni Islam in the world (although it was originally founded by the Shi'a Ismaili Fatimids).[142] We peered into the ghostly central yard of the Al-Hakim Mosque, which was rarely used for prayer as its benefactor was a tad crazy.[143] We stopped for tea at Al-Fishawi's, the oldest continually operating coffeehouse in Cairo, buried deep in the bustle of the Khan al-Khalili market. We wandered from Bab al-Futuh to Bab al-Zuweilah, through the Tent Makers Street, and down to the Sultan Hassan Medrese-Mosque, before eventually arriving at the *maidan* (square) in front of the Citadel. We finished things off by retreating into the calm, cool interior of the Ibn Tulun Mosque, perhaps my favorite mosque in this city of countless mosques. I find its austere but

---

[142] Actually, much of Islamic Cairo's urban fabric was woven by the Fatimids, but successive Islamic dynasties added their own textures.

[143] Al-Hakim was known for riding a donkey around Cairo at night while disguised as a pauper. During these excursions he tried to listen to what common folk had to say about him, often then punishing those who spoke ill of his rule. One night he never returned. Most historians believe he was assassinated on the order of his sister, in an attempt to put a saner male relative on the Fatimid throne. Others believed he went into "occultation"; these people would eventually form the group now known the Druze. See the chapter on Lebanon for more information on this fascinating religious movement.

refined courtyard an oasis of calm; it is a place where it is easy to forget the madness and noise of Cairo that lay just outside its towering walls.

On the following days, we got both an ancient Egypt fix by visiting the pyramids at Saqqara and Giza, as well as a very contemporary one; we also sought out signs of the recent revolution—which I will get to shortly—in and around its birthplace, Tahrir Square.

Yes, revisiting Cairo was like coming home, even with the changes wrought by the revolution. Somehow, I felt as comfortable as if I were returning to my birthplace in Indiana. Perhaps it had something to due with the fact that, in a fashion, Cairo was where I started to become an adult. Just as my childhood in Indiana contributed to making me the James I am today, my time in "The Mother of the World" shaped me profoundly.

***

As mentioned, I had the benefit of living in Cairo while I was in college. I was not originally supposed to spend my junior year in Cairo, however. My plan had been to try something "different" by heading to the University of Jordan in Amman instead, where I would first spend a summer in an intensive Arabic program and then, hopefully, start taking classes at the university proper starting in the fall. As my first Arabic instructor at Cornell was Palestinian and had taught us his Levantine dialect for speaking purposes,[144] Jordan seemed like a logical place to continue my language training. Why start with a new, quite different dialect? But, as I have described in the chapter on Jordan, the program in Amman had its issues, and I decided to transfer to the venerable American University in Cairo. It turned out to be a good decision.

---

[144] Munther Younes, my Arabic teacher, was ahead of his time in the design of his Arabic course. Rather than teach the formal Modern Standard Arabic (M.S.A.) for all language skills—reading, writing, and speaking—he developed a program that is much more in line with how Arabs learn Arabic: first by learning how to speak a local dialect, and only then gradually learning to read and write in M.S.A. Although M.S.A. is understood by educated elites throughout the Arab world, it is not used as day-to-day language by anyone. You sound like a very formal newscaster if you speak it!

After the relative calm of Amman, Cairo assailed the senses as soon as I landed at the airport. I remember vividly waiting in the long line to get my passport stamped and looking up to see a big, bold sign that listed the consequences for trying to smuggle anything illegal in or out of the country; let's just say the punishments were dire. The ride from the airport into the city further underlined what a different place Egypt was going to be. The air was tinted brown with smog, the traffic was a crush of slow-moving cars that were all honking at once, and the buildings were from a wild array of centuries. The crowds on the sidewalks mirrored the traffic jam on the roads. I was thrilled.

Things at A.U.C. couldn't have been more different than at the University of Jordan, also. Its very name—the American University—had at first dissuaded me from attending. Why attend an English-medium, American-style university while abroad?[145] I wanted full immersion. But as I settled into my new routines, I realized there were certain advantages to being at a school that had, for one thing, been around awhile (nearly a century) and which had some experience dealing with international students (and not simply study-abroad kids like me). I was able to put together a program that allowed me to study Arabic semi-intensively[146] while also taking a few other classes in history and politics: Islamic Institutions, Classical Sufism, and International Relations in the Modern Middle East, among others.

Being able to take classes outside of the Arabic Institute also allowed me to get to know more Egyptian students. Many, of course, were generally from affluent, influential families, as A.U.C. was the only private university in the country at the time. They often had known each other their entire lives, as they had grown up in the same rarified social circles. But there were others—such as my friends Lamia, who was Egyptian but who had grown up in the U.A.E, and Ghazi, who was Libyan but raised in London—who

---

[145] The American University in Cairo was founded in 1919 by an American missionary group that was sponsored by the United Presbyterian Church of North America.

[146] The semi-intensive program meant that half my schedule consisted of Arabic language courses, which freed me to take others in history and political science. The students who were studying in the intensive program only took classes on Arabic.

were just as much "outsiders" as the American and European students. Joining some extracurricular activities, such as the Egyptian Folk Dance group, also helped me to expand my Arab and Egyptian social network.

But I have to admit that most of what I learned in Cairo was not at A.U.C., but rather from the city itself. I had enjoyed Amman, which was rich in history too, but Cairo... well, it was wonderfully overwhelming. Any city that has the pyramids of Giza within its boundaries, those hulking structures from the earliest days of complex human society, is going to provide invaluable opportunities for a budding historian.

Sometimes, A.U.C. organized trips to various sites in and around the city for the year abroad students, for which I gladly signed up. These excursions often allowed us to gain access to places that we normally wouldn't get to see. We poked around the archaeological excavations of the remnants of Fustat, the original Arab settlement that would give rise to Cairo proper, in a portion that was generally off limits to tourists. We were able to enter crumbling Mamluk palaces that were closed to the public while sporadic bouts of restoration were underway. We entered tombs and shrines of various Sufi figures, many of which were well off the tourist path.

Sometimes, I went on the tours simply to get more information, such as the day I joined a guided walk through the City of the Dead, a vast cemetery that has become something of a living neighborhood as poor families moved into the mausoleums, some to be close to ancestors, others simply because they needed a roof over their heads.

However, as I got more and more familiar with the city and more comfortable in my own explorer's skin, I began to drift away from the formal tours and ventured solo (or occasionally with a friend) into the nooks and crannies of the city. The mosques, the Coptic churches, the palaces, the tombs, and the *madrasa*s became my historical playground.

Mosque and Armenian Church in Cairo

The many centuries—well, more accurately, the millennia—of Cairo's history often made it difficult for me to discern the specific era of a building or landmark. Often, an earlier structure had been appropriated by successive waves of rulers, each putting their unique stamp on the layout and décor while ultimately forming a whole that could simply be defined as "Cairene." The Al-Azhar Mosque and University complex, for example, while initially constructed around 970 C.E. by the Fatimids—an Isma'ili Shi'a dynasty who first emerged in Tunisia, my current home, but then conquered Cairo and created a rival Caliphate to the Sunni Abbasids—was then transformed into a center of Sunni learning by Salah al-Din (better known as Saladin in the "West"), the Kurdish hero of the Crusades. Each Muslim dynasty, up through the Ottomans, contributed to the maintenance and expansion of this venerable seat of learning; even in the twentieth century, in an attempt to rein in the independence of Al-Azhar's Muslim scholars, the secular Egyptian government under Gamal Abdul Nasser reorganized the institution and made it a national university. It is, with all its wild architectural accretions, a microcosm of the past thousand-plus years of history in the city.

One of my favorite things to do in Cairo was to climb the narrow, dusty staircases of one of the Al-Azhar minarets and then look out on the vast spread of the city; the sun was often glowing through a thick haze, casting obscuring shadows. For all the difficulties the city had and has, that view was dear to my heart, and is the view I seek whenever I return to Cairo. So, of course, I had to show it to my friend Danni on my most recent visit. I smiled as I watched her soak in the scene, snapping photographs of the city's unforgettable skyline. She seemed to find it just as magical.

***

When I was settling into my student life in Cairo, one of the big adjustments I had to make was adapting to the Cairene dialect of Arabic; it was so different from the Levantine version I had learned to speak while at Cornell and during my summer stint in Jordan. At the time, I didn't realize that many of the strange new words—*oda* instead of *ghorfa* for "room", for example—were not actually of Arabic origin. It wasn't until I later started studying modern and Ottoman Turkish that I had an "Aha!" moment—those odd words were Turkish. It made sense, as Cairo was second only to Istanbul in importance in the Ottoman Empire. There had been a more concentrated presence of Turkish-speaking elites in the city, so the imperial language influenced the local lingo more deeply than in other parts of the Arabic-speaking world. This realization was to prove an important step in my education about the long, important, and often strange Ottoman period of Egypt's history.

But the first step in my learning process was puzzling over the Mosque of Muhammad Ali (no, the name has nothing to do with the boxer!), a domed mosque that sits on a hill overlooking old Cairo; it has a slender minaret, and is so unlike the flat-roofed, courtyard Arab-style mosques that dominate the city.

I was soon to find out that it was an Ottoman-style mosque—and that Muhammad Ali was a particularly important character in the story of Ottoman Egypt.

Historically, Egypt has always been something of a special case. Due to the verdant band of the Nile River valley and its blossoming delta, it was one of the earliest centers in the development of what we now call "civilization" and "society" (the show-stopping pyramids are just the most obvious example of that growing complexity of the human experience). As empires and states rose and fell through the millennia, Egypt was a much-desired prize, the crown jewel of the Mediterranean world. Despite the long and impressive list of political forces who ruled Egypt after the height of the Egyptian pharaohs—the Achaemenids, Greco-Macedonians, Romans, Byzantines, Umayyads, Abbasids, Fatimids, Ayyubids, Mamluks, Ottomans, and even the British—and despite all the influences those various cultures left behind, somehow the identities of "Egypt" and "Egyptian"[147] remained pretty constant.

Egypt's long and convoluted history as part of the Ottoman Empire also illustrates its unique status and disproportionate role in the politics and economics of the Mediterranean and "Middle East." Egypt was initially wrested from the Mamluks[148] by the Ottoman forces in 1517, in the days of the empire's rapid expansion into the Islamic heartland; it was events like these that demonstrated the imperial ambition that would eventually lead to the extension of Ottoman authority across most of the Levant, the Arabian Peninsula, and North Africa.

Interestingly, the Mamluks didn't just go away. Rather, the Ottomans co-opted them into the Ottoman system, often using them to rule Egypt in their name. This remained the case until a certain European adventurer, Napoleon I—you might have heard of him—decided to invade Egypt in 1798. This, of course, did not make the Ottomans very happy, so they called upon an Ottoman military leader, a devşirme of Albanian origin named Muhammad Ali Pasha, to drive out the French forces. After this was accomplished in 1801, the Mamluks tried to reassert their original authority in Egypt in opposition to their Ottoman superiors; Muhammad Ali managed, rather shrewdly, to make himself popular on both sides of

---

[147] I am not saying these words—which are obviously the English forms derived from the Greek word, *Aegyptos*—were the words that were used. I am simply saying that the region and its people—no matter what they have been called—have long been recognized as distinct.

[148] The Mamluks were a fascinating group that ruled Egypt (and Syria) from 1250 to 1517. The word *mamluk* means "owned" or "property." The Mamluks, with a capital M, were originally slave-warriors, many of Turkic or Circassian descent, who became powerful enough to establish their own state and to fill their ranks with other slave-warriors.

the conflict, and by 1805 he had, with the support of the Mamluks, been appointed the Ottoman governor of Egypt.

Just as one cannot deny the prominence of the silver-domed, Ottoman-style Mosque of Muhammad Ali sitting high above the sprawl and congestion of Cairo, one cannot but see how influential its namesake, who came all the way from the opposite shore of the Mediterranean, was on the formation of modern Egypt. Although he ostensibly owed his position to the sultan in Istanbul, he would eventually establish himself as the *de facto* ruler of an all but independent Egypt, one that he hoped to modernize in a way similar to that of the French who had come so close to taking control of the land. His power and influence became so great that the sultan called on him to quell the Saudi rebellion in Arabia (which he finally achieved in 1818). He would later even challenge the Ottoman Sultanate itself by leading an expedition to conquer "Syria" (*bilad al-sham*) and which, if only briefly, threatened Istanbul itself (1831-1832). In the midst of all this, Muhammad Ali established a dynasty that would rule in Egypt and Sudan[149], a rule that technically lasted up until the start of World War I. His successors also ruled with the Persian title *khedive* ("lord" or, perhaps better here, "viceroy") starting in 1867 (a title that was, by the way, unique among Ottoman rulers and administrators).

By the time the British entered the Egyptian political context in 1882—you know, stepping in to settle some debts, that's all—the Khedivate of Egypt had become one of the stranger political units of the Ottoman Empire. It remained *de jure* Ottoman, paying lip service to the Ottoman sultans; yet, it had its own khedive, and was also a British colony in all but name. No wonder the Egyptians were a little confused by the time they reached the twentieth century.

One of the best places from which to contemplate the pre-World War I Egyptian confusion is not in Egypt, but is rather at a spot nearly eight-hundred miles away, across the Mediterranean: the Istanbul residence of the last Khedive of Egypt, Abbas II (r. 1892-1914).

---

[149] Not only did Muhammad Ali challenge Ottoman authority, he also charted an independent path of expansion for Egypt, thereby adding much of Sudan to his territory. His successor, Khedive Ismail, would envision an even bigger African empire for Egypt, but his efforts came into conflict with growing European interests in interior Africa during the mid- to late-nineteenth century.

This summer palace was built in a fascinating mélange of Italian Art Deco and Neo-Ottoman/Neo-Islamic styles. It's an unusual building; fitting, I suppose, for its unusual history during an unusual part of the late Ottoman era. It is located far off the main tourist tracks of Istanbul, situated in a leafy park in the neighborhood of Çubuklu on the Asian side of the Bosphorus. Unlike his predecessors, Abbas II had tried to warm up relations with the Ottoman center in order to possibly expel the British from Egypt (or at least diminish their influence). Under their neocolonial control, he had become nothing more than a figurehead; in that way, he was so unlike his powerful ancestor, Muhammad Ali. Now, the palace is a somewhat forlorn spot, once converted into a hotel-restaurant but now largely neglected. I find it a suitably melancholic symbol of the end of the hybrid state that Egypt was during the turn of the turn of the twentieth century, at the advent of the collapse of the Ottoman Empire.

The Khedive's summer palace is a good reminder, as well, of the ties that used to bind much of the Mediterranean basin—the memories of which I began to trace during my travels through the former Ottoman land; travels that started while I was living and studying in Egypt.

***

During my junior year, I left the relative tranquility of A.U.C.'s campus every day and confronted the quite definite chaos of Tahrir Square. I would turn left and begin my twenty or so minute walk home to Garden City (which is even known in Arabic as *garden siti)* along the wide stretch of Avenue 'Asr al-'Aini.

After the first week of this journey, I noticed that I was pretty much left alone. If I were to take any other route, I would immediately be assailed by people who tried to sell me every imaginable piece of Egyptian paraphernalia, especially papyrus (had I bought a piece of cheap papyrus every time it was pushed into my face, I could have easily wallpapered a house within a matter of days).

However, on 'Asr al-'Aini I became part of the scenery. "Ah, the young *khawaga*, he seems to live here…." As the months unfolded, I also found myself, unwittingly, becoming a regular at various shops and eateries along the way. There was my usual *khoushari* place, my falafel stand, and my shawarma joint. There were the shops where I bought my fruits and vegetables. There was the butcher where, when I was feeling brave, I pointed to a live chicken and soon had a warm carcass in a plastic bag to take home. Without fully realizing it, I had become a member of the neighborhood, taking part in its rhythms.

When I entered the decaying grandeur of Garden City, things became even homier. The incessant honking of the main road was now muffled by curving, leafy lanes. Though only a shadow of its nineteenth-century self, the Belle Époque apartment buildings lent a solemn air to the scene. When I entered my building, I nodded to the ancient *bowaab* (doorman) who slept on a cot that was tucked just inside the doorway. He was the gatekeeper of all that occurred in the building: nothing escaped his keen eye. He knew who came and went, and when. Who had visitors, who didn't. Who might be doing something inappropriate. As the only two foreigners in the apartment building, my American roommate—another year-abroad student—and I were watched with a heightened sense of suspicion. I think the bowaab wondered what we might do to sully the reputation of the building. He never was able to "catch" us, though, and for the rest of the neighborhood we were simply unusual parts of the local scenery.

My walks to and from Garden City, as well as my explorations of Cairo at large, only whetted my appetite for more Egyptian experiences. As I settled into my Cairene life, I began to venture further and further afield. I occasionally joined other students on outings, such as weekends up to Alexandria and its nearby beaches on the Mediterranean. But I discovered early on that I preferred to travel alone, or at most with a trusted friend or two, rather than in a group.

I can't begin to capture all my travel memories of Egypt, but what follows are a few highlights.

***

First, there was the time I was Czech.

In my early days as a student of Arabic, I often found myself frustrated when I would try to use the language only to have the person with whom I was talking respond in English—for the very legitimate reason that he or she wished to practice English. But I wanted to practice Arabic. In Cairo, particularly, I frequently found myself in strange bilingual conversations during which I would be speaking caveman-ish Arabic and my partner would be speaking to me in caveman-ish English, and both of us would be getting frustrated by the resultant miscommunication.

So when I took one of my first solo trip in Egypt, a long weekend to Luxor, I decided, naively, to adopt a new identity for a few days. Not wishing to be caught out with a more common language—French, German, or even Russian—as I found many Egyptians surprisingly multilingual, I aimed for something obscure but still plausible. I decided that I would be half Czech, half Egyptian, coming to Egypt to learn my mother's language but only knowing Czech as my first language. Surely, I reasoned, there would be few Egyptians who would know this Slavic tongue.

At first, my story held up well. During brief exchanges with ticket salesmen at the big attractions—Karnak, the Valley of the Kings, Hateshepsut's Temple, etc.—or with taxi drivers or shopkeepers, it worked nicely. I had a basic family history and could field most of the polite questions I got. Everyone welcomed the half-Czech, half-Egyptian man who was looking for his roots.

But then things got more complicated: I met Ahmed.

Ahmed was a *felucca* captain who operated one of the elegant single-sailed boats that ply the Nile (nowadays, usually for tourist fares rather than ferrying goods and people people to the riverine towns). I hired him one morning for a short excursion on the river; he seemed intrigued by my tale. For an hour or so, I was fine. My story unfolded as we drifted on the muddy expanse of the river. He didn't seem suspicious, just curious. At the end of my short cruise, I paid the seasoned sailor and assumed I would never see him again.

But Ahmed just kept appearing. Wherever I went into Luxor, he was there. And he kept wanting to spend time with me, over coffee or shisha. He even invited me back to his felucca one night to have tea—made, as I observed in silent horror, from water taken directly from the Nile and served in classes that had been "washed" with a quick rinse in the same river.[150] The more time we spent together, the more elaborate my story had to become. I began to panic, worrying that at some point my charade

---

[150] There is a well-known proverb that if you drink of the Nile, you are destined to return. I was more concerned, in the moment, of acquiring bilharzia (also known as schistosomiasis), caused by parasitic worms often found in standing

would be revealed and I would have to deal with the fallout caused by lost trust and a sense of betrayal. Ahmed even began to talk of coming up to Cairo to see me sometime.

Somehow, I managed to finish my long weekend in Luxor without giving away my lie, but I had learned my lesson. I would never, ever again in my travels pretend to be someone I was not. I haven't even passed myself off as Canadian. Not once, I swear.

But telling a lie about my nationality wasn't the only stupid mistake I made during that trip to Luxor.

The shower facilities at the fleabag hotel where I was staying—as I was remarkably cheap in my student days—were so horrendous that I decided it was best to avoid using them. Not surprisingly, after a few days of exploring Luxor *sans* a real bath or shower, I was not looking very "fresh." Perhaps to avoid too much human contact in that state, I decided to take a felucca (not Ahmed's!) across the Nile to visit some pharaonic ruins and the *faux*-Fatimid tomb of Agha Khan III, the spiritual leader of the Isma'ili Muslim community.[151] When I climbed to the top of the riverbank and up to the edge of the great desert that begins so abruptly in Egypt, I saw in the distance the remains of a Syriac monastery. I thought: *Why not? I am here, and it doesn't look so far.*

So I ventured into the desert, on my own.

Hours later, dusty and thirsty, I had managed to circle back to the Nile shore, but far from where I had disembarked from my felucca. Only by luck did I encounter an Egyptian family on an outing who were willing to take me back across the river. While I must have looked a bedraggled sight (and I'm sure that by this point I didn't smell too sweet, either), they happily bundled me into their boat. As we sailed across the river, back to Luxor, the family peppered me with questions and laughed at my exploit in the desert. The two older daughters offered me tea and, to my great surprise,

---

water. Thankfully, I did not get infected with the disease. I did, however, return to Egypt.

[151] Due to Egypt's history as a seat of the Isma'ili Fatimid Dynasty, the Isma'ili Imams, who now also possess the title of Agha Khan, have long maintained strong connections to the country. The current imam, Prince Karim Al Husseini, Agha Khan IV, has supported major restoration efforts of historical sites around Egypt, especially in Cairo.

even proposed marriage… Their parents just laughed. So I did, too. And avoided responding to the offer!

***

The wizened guard, having just unlocked the gate, nearly had a heart attack as I emerged from the depths of the Great Temple of Ramses II at Abu Simbel. For a moment, perhaps, he might have imagined I was a ghost straight out of ancient Egypt, coming forth from the shadows.

Instead, I was just a random American tourist who managed to get himself locked inside the temple during the noon prayer time.

Rather than join one of the many organized tours from Aswan, all of which descended on Abu Simbel at once (and left together, too), I chose to take the local bus. This meant I arrived at this strange clutch of temples—all of which were carved from their original sites and relocated to higher ground, so as not to be submerged by Lake Nasser, a byproduct of the construction of Aswan Dam—after all the other tourists were already safely back in town. I basically had the place to myself, except for a single Israeli couple.

Several Nubian children started trailing me from temple to temple, hoping to sell me a postcard or two. When I replied in Arabic that I didn't need a postcard, they giggled and called over all their friends: "Come meet the Arabic-speaking *khawaga!*" Soon, I felt like the Pied Piper, leading an ever-growing group of children around the ruins. They wanted their photo taken with me, too. One boy wrote out their village's address on the back of one of the postcards he had just been trying to sell me so that I could mail a copy of the picture to him.

Although they were adorable, I needed a break from my fan club, so ducked into the quiet recesses of the main temple—somehow doing so without the guard noticing. As I reached the back of the warren of chambers, I heard a clang; the door had been shut. I glanced at my watch and realized, oh, prayer time.

So I didn't panic, but just waited out my solitary confinement, reveling in being alone in an ancient Egyptian tomb complex, and that of Ramses II no less. It was eerie but beautiful. The minimal light from the electric lamps cast long shadows across the hieroglyphics-covered walls and played across the faces of the somber statues. I could almost hear the chants of ancient Egyptian priests echoing in the chamber.

And the look on the guard's face when I did finally walk out: priceless.

***

Getting to the oasis of Siwa in those days was far from straightforward. I had to take the train up to Alexandria, then catch a bus traveling nearly the full length of the Mediterranean coast until I arrived in the town of Marsa Matruh, where I crammed into yet another bus to go south, into the desert, to the oasis.

When Barb, a fellow year-abroad student, and I arrived at the Marsa Matruh bus station, we were nearly separated in the crush that was pushing into the Siwa-bound bus and jamming into every possible nook—including what should have been the baggage racks. I ended up stranded in the back stairwell, seatless and freezing (as the window was broken, which let in the cold night air of the desert). It was an uncomfortable five-hour long ride.

But Siwa was worth it. It was a world away from the madness of Cairo, a genuine oasis of bright green palm plantations and hundreds of springs, encircled by an endless desert.

Barb and I spent our days bicycling or walking through the date orchards; sometimes, we would stop to swim in one of the larger springs, evocatively called Cleopatra's Bath. We also stumbled upon various ruins that were tucked amid the greenery, including the remains of the temple where Alexander the Great supposedly had himself proclaimed pharaoh of Egypt during his campaign to conquer the world. The Siwans, most of whom were of Berber origin, looked at the pale Americans tooling about their oasis community with a certain degree of bemusement, but they showed us incredible hospitality.

On our last night, while we were having dinner at a small outdoor café that we had come to frequent for its simple but delicious fare, I informed our young waiter/cook of our imminent departure the next morning. He took off a ring, a simple silverish band, and tried to press it into my palm, a "gift" he said. Embarrassed, I tried to return the ring to the boy, knowing how little he probably had. But I didn't want to offend. He insisted, smiled, and walked back to his makeshift stove.

***

The last trip I made outside of Cairo before I returned to the States was also to an oasis; this one, Farafra, was slightly easier to reach, though still a long journey. While close to the famous White Desert, Farafra itself has few real sights. Jacob, yet another year-abroad student, and I just wanted to get away, to find a little peace. A retreat to make sense of all we had experienced in our wild year of studying in Cairo.

At the time, there was only one place to stay in Farafra, a small government-run guesthouse that was set just outside of the oasis proper. The rooms there were splotched with the evidence of the disconcertingly large spiders that previous guests had smashed with shoes and guidebooks. Jacob and I moved our beds away from the walls.

During the day, we wandered through the rows of date palms, and in the early evening we dipped into the hot springs with the local farmers. Back at the guesthouse, we slid past the group of German backpackers who played cards on the concrete terrace, a group who never seemed to leave the premises despite the proximity of the beautiful patch of green that was just a hundred meters away.

On our last morning in Farafra, we rose before dawn in order to take one more dip in the warm mineral waters of the springs. This time, we had the pool to ourselves. We didn't say much as we floated in our nakedness under the brightening sky; we just watched the sun rise, feeling the cool breeze on our faces. We were both quietly mourning the end of our time in Egypt.

***

From the moment I took the job in Khartoum in 2009, I knew I would be making a trip up to Cairo at some point. I had to go, not simply because it would be so close but because I had lived there in what by then seemed like the distant past (my junior year of college). I had not been back since I attended a graduate school conference in 1999. More than a decade! So it was a given that at some point during my stay in Sudan I would head northwards to my old home; I just didn't know when.

However, the events that began to unfold on January 25—coincidentally my birthday (or maybe not so coincidentally?)—would nudge me to plan a visit sooner rather than later. I was riveted by the scenes that were unfolding on Al-Jazeera of the growing protests in Tahrir Square, an area I had crossed nearly every day I lived in Cairo. Despite the potential for serious unrest—and for a serious military crackdown—all I could think was: *I need to be there.*

Although Hosni Mubarak was now out of the picture—at least in terms of his role as president—and the protests were drawing only a fraction of the crowd that had packed into Tahrir at the height of the revolution, I was curious to see what I could of revolutionary Egypt.

As I wandered through my old stomping grounds, I was a bit surprised that it felt like nothing momentous had happened. There were no immediate signs of the revolution or of the fact that Egypt was now under military rule. Shops and restaurants were open and bustling. Traffic was still as insane as I remembered. People seemed relaxed, as if they were just going about life as normal.

It was only gradually that I started to notice the occasional bit of revolutionary graffiti, such as the word "Optimism" (Arabic: *tafaa'ul*) spray-painted on a wall in Islamic Cairo.

And then Danni and I went down to the revolution's epicenter: Tahrir Square. There was much more graffiti here—"Enjoy the Revolution!", "Victory!", "25th of January!", etc.—and a few more police than usual. But the biggest sign of the recent changes was the charred government building that rose above the Egyptian Museum. This was the only evidence of how serious things had been—a building burned for its association with the Mubarak regime.

Will it be?

Yet despite the gloomy shadow across the museum and the bustle of Tahrir, everyone went about their business as if nothing unusual had occurred. I was a little surprised to see just how many tourists were flowing into the museum. They might not have been back to their pre-revolution numbers, but there were quite a few German, French, and Italian speakers milling about—as well as a few English speakers. Revolution, shmevolution.

On Friday, after the midday prayer, Danni and I returned to Tahrir to see what was going on with the post-revolution protests. The crowd wasn't huge at first, just a small cluster occupying a small corner of the "square" (which is really a circle) near the old campus of A.U.C. However, the atmosphere was an interesting mix of earnest political protest and festiveness. While fiery speakers screamed through bullhorns, vendors hawked revolutionary merchandise: bumper stickers, hats, T-shirts, flags. More than once, someone offered to paint the Egyptian flag on my arm or cheek (for a small fee, of course). And the crowd grew as the day progressed, which caused an even greater traffic snarl than was normal around Tahrir (although why anyone would want to drive through the area on a Friday afternoon is beyond me, protest or not).

No fighter jets buzzing overhead, no camels charging through the crowd, no riot police. Nothing Al-Jazeera worthy—which will probably make my family happy—but I am glad I got to see this small slice of history in the making.

Whither Egypt? Nobody really knows.[152]

***

When we decided to take a short break from the protests, we headed up Talaat Harb Street to Café Riche for a coffee or tea. However, despite appearances that indicated otherwise, the ten-year-old son of the proprietor told us: "We are closed for the revolution."

---

[152] Since my visit to Cairo in 2011, the "transitional" military government, run by the Supreme Council of the Armed Forces, remains in power.

TRANSITIONS IN BILAD AL-SUDAN

As the KLM flight descended, I pressed my face against the glass to get a better view of the fast-approaching landscape below.

It was very flat.

It was very brown.

Two muddy snakes of rivers merged into one and flowed in a slow, muddy ribbon out into a forbidding, brown desert. Clusters of brown buildings, many seeming to be unfinished, crowded the shores at the confluence of the rivers. A summer storm seemed to be building on the horizon. It, too, was brown.

This was going to be my new home for two years. This was Khartoum, Sudan.

When I studied in Cairo, I had a number of crazy travel ambitions. I looked around me and wanted to see and experience it all. I thought about sneaking into Lebanon, despite the potential fine from the U.S. government. I half-jokingly conspired with a Libyan student to figure out a way to smuggle myself into Libya. Although neither of those schemes materialized during my stay in Egypt—in part because Egypt contained more than enough to occupy me for the year that I was there, but also because they were ultimately too costly, too risky—I have been able, in the past few years, to undertake trips to both Lebanon (2011) and Libya (2014).

The other crazy trip I dreamed about when I was a study-abroad student was crossing into that vast country to Egypt's south, Sudan. I envisioned sailing down Lake Nasser to the northern Sudanese outpost of Wadi Halfa, then taking a long, slow, and likely dusty train ride all the way to the mysterious-sounding Khartoum.

As had been true for Lebanon and Libya, political tensions (in this case, those between Egypt itself and Sudan) put a damper on my plans. Not only was Egypt dealing with internal threats from Islamist groups who were attacking tourists—something that understandably made my family nervous about my year-abroad choice—but it was also embroiled in a dispute with Sudan regarding a contested part of their shared border. Although I was unaware of it at the time, the two countries had a long, intimate relationship that had only been severed in the 1950s—and parts of the newly defined border were still not agreed upon. In 1994, while I was in Cairo, Sudan accused Egypt of kidnapping a Sudanese officer; in retaliation, they impounded an Egyptian passenger ferry (like the one I had envisioned taking!). Egypt, tit for tat, then seized a Sudanese minister's plane while it was on a refueling stop. The borders clamped shut; no slow train to Khartoum for me.

The closest I got to Sudan that year was Abu Simbel, an ancient Egyptian temple complex that had been moved to save it from the creation of Lake Nasser after the building of the Aswan Dam (see the chapter on Egypt for a tale of that adventure). Shortly after the local bus started puttering back to Aswan itself, a policeman waved us to a stop and bundled four unhappy looking guys into the front: Sudanese camel herders who had been caught crossing the closed border.

Perhaps I should not have been so surprised that life would take me to Sudan eventually, although I would never have guessed when I was a young university student that I would not only visit this gigantic country, the largest in Africa (at the time), but that I would be living and working there for two years.

***

My Cairo-honed nerves kicked into gear as I weaved my way between the crush of mini-buses, moto-rickshaws, and cars that were jockeying for openings in the traffic that swirled around the large roundabout. The vehicles did their dance, horns honking, and I walked between them calmly, as if I did this every day.

I had spent much of the hot afternoon cooped up inside my apartment, plowing through a stack of grading and getting some lesson planning out of the way. But by 6 p.m. I was feeling antsy, ready for some fresh air. When I stepped out of my apartment building, I thought I would make a simple loop around Abdul Moneim "Square" (which is really a huge circle, its interior largely taken up by the so-called "Family Park"); however, I was greeted by pleasant, very walkable temperatures (ok, so this meant it was 97°F—which in turn meant I already had been in Sudan too long). Quickly, I decided that my walk was to become a real walk.

I made a quarter turn around the "square" and veered onto one of the dusty spoke roads, heading northwest. The late afternoon sun was beginning to sink, casting that orange glow I love so much; there was little traffic, and most shops were shuttered. A few men lounged in doorways, playing cards and sipping tea. It was all sleepily peaceful. Friday does tend to be a quiet day in Khartoum, which is not surprising considering that it is the Muslim holy day (and often the only day off for some people). This Friday was no exception.

When the spoke hit Al-Huria Street, I turned right and was soon walking over the bridge that leads into downtown. The moment I had decided to make this a longer walk, I had known that this was where I would head. I had driven through this area after I visited the National Museum and had been intrigued by the vibrancy I had seen, vowing to return on foot. But I was not certain I would see much, given that it was Friday. Perhaps, as in my neighborhood, everything would be closed up and people would be resting at home.

But as I reached the bridge's crest, I saw that I needed not have worried; as quiet as the walk had been up to that point, the other side of the bridge revealed a wonderfully boisterous world. Directly beneath me ran railway tracks that were littered with rusting train cars. Just a little further on, to the left, there was an enormous, bustling mini-bus terminal and, to the right, a large lot that served as a makeshift soccer field with many lanky boys running helter-skelter. Ahead: a large market. And everywhere: people, lots of people.

There are no tourists in Khartoum. However, there are plenty of foreigners—more than I had anticipated before I moved to Sudan to work at the Khartoum American School. These *khawaja*s tended to work for the large U.N. mission[153], for one of the many international N.G.O.s, for the diplomatic services, or for one of the large oil companies. They tended to live and play in the neighborhoods east of the airport, particularly in areas like Al-Riyad where most of the western-style shops and restaurants are

---

[153]   That is, until the U.N. moved most of its operations to South Sudan after the country split in two in 2011. See the following chapter for more about these changes.

clustered. When I was in such areas, I felt less conspicuously foreign, but I also felt like I was in a "bubble," a comfortable expat cocoon removed from the "real" Khartoum. (Of course, I worked in a bubble at the English-medium American school, too.)

But I did not come to Sudan to hang out only with other khawajas. Why be in Khartoum, then? I got far away from that bubble on my walk. Very far indeed.

As soon as I crossed the traffic snarl at the base of the Al-Huria Bridge and entered the market area, I was clearly the only non-Sudanese person as far as the eye could see. Yet as I merged into the crowd, no one batted an eye; it was as if I was invisible.

I intimated in the chapter on Egypt that *khawaja* (or in Egyptian Arabic, *khawaga*) often has a negative undertone. However, this wasn't the case in Sudan, where khawaja-ness rarely elicited overt interest, unlike so many other places I have visited where I didn't exactly blend. If I were to say it was like being invisible, I perhaps would be overstating the case: it's not like I was being looked through or ignored. It was more like I was simply accepted as part of the scenery without question. There were no stares, no calls of "my friend, my friend!", no hassles with touts. If I offered an *As-salaam alaykum* to someone I passed on the street or to a shopkeeper as I entered his store, I almost always got a warm *Wa alaykum as-salaam* and a big smile in return. There wasn't even a barrage of overly prying follow-up questions—"Where are you from? Why are you here? Are you married? How much money do you make?—as there might have been in Egypt.

It was no different in that Friday evening market on the edge of downtown. I ambled "invisibly" through the rows of vendors who were hawking everything from cheap Chinese-made clothing to mobile phone chargers and (oddly) megaphones, from piles of dates and fruits to pungent slabs of raw meat. No one tried to perform a hard sell on me; I could wander and look without pressure. I exchanged smiles with my fellow shoppers as I squeezed through the human surge. I soon forgot to be self-conscious about being the only khawaja around and enjoyed my invisibility.

In an enormous lot that was framed partly by the market and partly by the mini-bus terminal, I found dozens of makeshift tea cafés, each a simple circle of plastic stools or chairs presided over by a colorfully clad tea lady, and a similar number of stands serving *ful* and kebabs. Against a fence of aluminum siding, a long row of barbers were shaving their clients *al fresco*. Another corner served as an open-air mosque. It was a perfect people-watching area, less crowded than the market; all of life was turned out into the open. I lingered for a bit over a tea, soaking up the scene—a scene of which I was a part.

As the call for the *maghrib* (the evening/sunset) prayers began to belt from the surrounding mosques, I crossed the bridge once more, retracing my steps home as the sky turned a deep, dusky blue.

At home, I removed my sandals and laughed at how filthy my feet were. The hazards of a walk around Khartoum, I suppose. But it was more than worth it to have been able to enjoy the rhythms of a Friday evening in Khartoum outside the "bubble" taking refuge in the simple joys of a person who was trying to make the city his home.

***

I ducked through the unpretentious entrance. The interior was equally simple: essentially a tall, whitewashed space with a floor that was covered by a green, mosque-style carpet. But in the center was a wooden cenotaph, a large marker for the now-empty grave; a group of men dressed in crisp, white *jalaba*s and turban-esque head-wraps and a few women in floral-printed *thobe*s, circled the structure, praying while touching, occasionally even kissing, its surface. I have seen such devotion in other Sufi shrines, but this was not just any Sufi's tomb—this was the Mahdi's.

Tomb of the Mahdi

Other than a glimpse of its conical, silver dome when I was on the way to the Omdurman Souq, I had not yet visited the Mahdi's tomb; this was a major lacuna in my early explorations of Khartoum, especially as a historian. So, on a quiet Friday morning not long after my invisible stroll through downtown, I decided that I would finally cross the Nile to see this important site, perhaps the most important in Sudan.

Omdurman was the Mahdi's city, and nowhere is that as apparent as the area immediately surrounding his tomb, a complex that includes the house of the Mahdi's successor (the Khalifa), a religious school, and a mosque that is affiliated with the tomb. The Mahdist's distinctive red, black, and green flag, emblazoned with a trident, fluttered prominently from numerous flagpoles and rooftops. It was like entering a forgotten corner of the Mahdist state, held over since the 1890s.

So who was the Mahdi?

Muhammad Ahmad, born in the mid-nineteenth century in northern Sudan, apparently showed an early proclivity for religious study, but he felt that the Ottomans in Egypt—who controlled Sudan at this point[154]—were not proper Muslims. He refused to go to Cairo to study, choosing instead to remain in Sudan. Over time, he became respected as a leader of the Sufi order called the Samaniyyah. Then, in 1881, he proclaimed himself the Mahdi: the Awaited One, the Renewer of Islam who would herald the second coming of the Prophet 'Isa (Jesus). As part of his mission, he was going to cleanse Sudan of the "infidel" Ottoman Egyptians and their British supporters. Thus began what is sometimes seen as the first major anti-imperialist revolt in Africa—one that would ultimately prove dramatically successful, at least in the short term.

From the Egyptian and British perspective, the Mahdi was initially more of a shadowy nuisance than a real threat. But he gathered a considerable force, one emboldened by his claims of infallibility; he and his men also knew the treacherous terrain of Sudan in a way that their opponents never could or would. Despite the efforts of General Gordon, the Egyptian Khedive's British former Governor-General of Sudan[155], to hold onto Khartoum, the Mahdists took control of much of Sudan and eventually captured the city; Gordon was killed in the process (although the Mahdi had commanded his troops not to harm his British opponent).

---

[154] The period of Ottoman-Egyptian rule in Sudan is often called the *Turkiyyah*—the time of the Turks. However, as we have seen, "Turk" really doesn't capture the complexity underlying Ottoman identities. Remember: the founder of the khedival dynasty in Egypt, Muhammad Ali, was ethnically Albanian.

[155] Charles George Gordon, popularly known as Gordon of Khartoum, entered the service of Khedive Ismail in 1873 (with permission from the British government). He was soon appointed Governor-General of Sudan, a post he held until 1880. When the Mahdist uprising began, he was asked by Khedive Tawfiq, Ismail's successor, to return and help save Khartoum. That mission proved fatal.

While the Mahdi would die a short five months later (likely from typhus), and was therefore barely able to relish his victory, the symbolic power of a native African force defeating imperialist oppressors cannot be over emphasized, both for the Sudanese and for the many others who were struggling against the imperial ambitions of Europe in the last decades of the nineteenth century. Abdallahi ibn Muhammad, the Khalifa—literally, "successor"—had a tough act to follow, but he kept the *Mahdiyyah* (the Mahdi's state) going for nearly another decade.

The current tomb is not the original, as that was completely destroyed by the British shortly after the Battle of Omdurman as part of their revenge for the death of General Gordon in 1885. On September 2, 1898, approximately eight-thousand British and another seventeen-thousand Egyptian and Sudanese soldiers who were led by the soon-to-be-famous Horatio Herbert Kitchener gathered ten kilometers north of the Mahdiyyah's capital. Facing them were the Mahdist forces, or the Ansar, who were far greater in number at around fifty-thousand. One might think this put the Sudanese at an advantage, but Kitchener had something they did not: guns—powerful guns, such as the Maxim. In a matter of hours, the Ansar were decimated; the British were left essentially unscathed.

Not content with simply leveling the structure of the original mausoleum, General Kitchener, who led the assault, had the Mahdi's remains thrown into the Nile and contemplated turning his skull into an inkstand. Luckily, there was enough of an outcry over Kitchener's excess that the skull was, instead, buried somewhere in Wadi Halfa, in the far north of Sudan. The British seemed to hope that eliminating the tomb and scattering the bones of the Mahdi would help dissipate the veneration for this important religious and national figure, that their actions would emasculate a potent symbol of anti-imperialism. But they didn't understand that symbols are not so easily eliminated or forgotten; this act of desecration resulted in a deepening resentment of British rule during the era of the Anglo-Egyptian Condominium (1899-1956), which emerged after the Battle of Omdurman.[156]

An exact replica of the tomb was quietly erected in 1947, a half century after the original's destruction. Despite the fact that the Mahdi's body is no

---

[156] Sudan was officially ruled jointly by Egypt and Britain (hence the phrase "Anglo-Egyptian Condominium"), though in practice it was solely a British colony.

longer in the grave, the site remains a place of pilgrimage that seamlessly combines the spiritual and the political.

There are other remnants of the Mahdist era scattered near the Mahdi's tomb; for example, just down the road I found the Khalifa's house. From the outside, the house looked like a rather small and simple mud structure; however, I discovered that it was an extensive warren of rooms and courtyards, full of fascinating artifacts from the Khalifa's life and the British takeover after the Khalifa was killed in the latter part of 1899 (he had fled Omdurman after the British routed his army in September and evaded capture for another year). In particular, I was intrigued by the Khalifa's "cave," a dark room that he constructed as a retreat for prayer (in imitation of a real cave that the Mahdi supposedly used for similar purposes). The historian in me also got a thrill from seeing a bilingual Arabic-English newspaper that had been published in Khartoum in the early twentieth century.

A little further down the river shore, I came across one of the Mahdist forts that lined the Nile to fend off the British gunboats that puffed towards Khartoum. Although the fort is heavily eroded now—it's basically a misshapen lump of mud, perforated with holes once used for firing on said boats—it still gives a sense of the Khalifa's efforts to fend off the invaders. The rusting hulk of an iron-sided paddleboat has been positioned on the bank of the Nile, next to the fort. It's a telling contrast—mud (Sudanese defense) and iron (British offense).

Perhaps the strangest artifact of this strange time is Kitchener's own gunboat, *The Malik,* which is now stranded in the midst of the Blue Nile Sailing Club in downtown Khartoum. The name of the "club" is a little misleading, suggesting something greater than it is—though it was perhaps a posher affair during the Anglo-Egyptian Condominium era. It is now a run-down launch for small river craft and a campground for overlanders driving from Cairo to Cape Town. The boat is grounded and slowly falling apart. Its interior is used for storage. However, it once led a British flotilla during the Battle of Omdurman.

I suppose the Sudanese see *The Malik*'s restoration as a low priority, considering that it symbolizes the end of the Mahdiyyah.

***

"La illaha illallah, la illaha illahah, la illaha illallah... There is no god but God, there is no god but God, there is no god but God..."

I quickly lost count of how many times the phrase was repeated. A billow of incense passed over me. The men around me swayed. A dreadlocked shaykh beat a drum. It was all so joyful.

Dhikr is an Arabic word with the root meaning of "recollection" or "remembrance," which stems from the verb "to remember." However, dhikr is perhaps more famously is associated with Sufism, or Islamic mysticism, and is applied to any of the Sufi practices that invoke God and help the mystics feel closer to God's presence. In my years spent traveling and studying in the Ottoman world, I have had the opportunity on numerous occasions to witness the ecstatic dhikr ceremonies of various Sufi orders. Perhaps most intimately, I spent several late evenings at the tekke of the Halveti-Cerrahi Order in the backstreets of the Karagümrük neighborhood of Istanbul. The Cerrahis draw upon a variety of Sufi forms in their dhikr ceremony, from the typical repetitive chanting of God's "names" to the famous Mevlevi-style whirling (the Mevlevis are the so-called "whirling dervishes"). However, all these dhikrs were performed indoors, away from prying eyes.

Somehow, then, I wasn't quite prepared for the dhikr at the tomb of a local Sufi saint-missionary, Shaykh Hamad al-Nil, in Omdurman; a dhikr like I had never before experienced. First, there was the openness of it all, both physically and ceremonially. The tomb and mosque complex is set in the middle of a large, rough-and-tumble cemetery (which makes for a slightly depressing lead-in, as I had to walk through the jumbled, poorly marked graves—basically ill-defined piles of dirt—to get to the much better-kept tomb). Due to the cemetery's low profile, I was able to see the pointy dome of the tomb and the onion-top of the mosque from quite a distance; I could also easily see the growing crowd of Sufis and their admirers milling in the empty space in front of the tomb. The dhikr itself is performed in the open air, visible to anyone who cared to look and audible (I am sure!) to anyone in the surrounding area. There was no hiding this act of remembrance.

Given the importance of recollections and remembrance in the ceremony, it is no surprise that the rituals are influenced by the history that brought them into being. Hamad al-Nil was a nineteenth-century Sufi missionary of the Qadiri Order, part of a long tradition of Sufi involvement in the spread of Islam in Sudan and other parts of sub-Saharan Africa (pre-dating the rise of the Mahdi). These intrepid Sufis often incorporated local religious practices into their dhikrs in order to make them more accessible to the people to whom they were preaching. The approach was generally more about love and tolerance, stressing the universality of God, than it was about imposing a strict doctrine. The Qadiri dhikr in Omdurman thus draws upon the Qadiri dhikrs of its "Middle Eastern" roots, and yet is uniquely Sudanese, too.

As a result, the form of the dhikr, too, was new to me—and also spoke of its greater openness. I had been told beforehand that these Sufis "whirled" as part of the process, but this was nothing like the stately spinning of the Mevlevis.

About an hour before sunset—and after a little pre-dhikr chanting and dancing—the Sufis started the official ceremony by parading the green banner of the order to the tomb and back. They then gathered in a large circle to chant "There is no god but God" and the attributes of God over and over, increasing in speed and volume, breathing in sync and bobbing to and fro. In the center, Sufi "cheerleaders"—many garbed in wildly patched robes of green and red, and some laden with large wooden beads (some also, interestingly, sporting dreadlocks: Rasta-Sufis?)—led the chant and waved clouds of incense. Drummers pounded out a hypnotic beat. Clappers clapped. As the spirit led them, individuals entered the circle to dance or whirl wildly, like a child spinning to get dizzy on purpose.

As with any dhikr, the aim is to lose oneself in the presence of God, but that abandonment of the world was somehow more obvious in this case— this dhikr was more frenetic, more frenzied than any I had ever witnessed. Individuals, lost in the moment, were transported by the chanting, the clapping, the drumming, the wild spinning. There was little pattern, yet it was somehow still a collective act.

At first I felt like I was invading something intensely private, but I quickly came to realize that, just as the dhikr was being held in the open, these Sufis didn't mind others watching this ecstatic expression of their devotion to God. Actually, they genuinely seemed to want to share the experience with anyone who showed up, whether a Sufi, a traditional

Muslim, or even a khawaja like me. The original spirit of Hamad al-Nil's mission? I suspect so.

Alas, this broad acceptance of difference, this focus on love and joy as opposed to doctrine, is no longer the norm in Sudan (or much of the world, for that matter). Whereas Sufism used to define Islam in Sudan, the current regime has been bent on portraying itself as the torchbearer of "traditional" Islam, imposing a more rigid interpretation of the religion not only on Muslims but also on the many non-Muslims in the country. This is one—of many, I must stress—reasons for the rift between north and south; the south felt, quite rightly, that the north wanted an "Arab"-led Islamic state. President Bashir even said that he planned to tighten Islamic law in the north after the south seceded.

I wish the government officials and other decision makers would develop policy less out of their desire for more power, and instead take their lead from the Sufis in Omdurman—remembering (dhikring?) what is most important: loving acceptance. If they had managed to do this earlier, then perhaps Sudan would not have been split into two countries. There would have been no need.

***

I finally made it. In my efforts to play the tourist in my adopted home of Khartoum, I had been trying to see all of the museums and historical sights that the city had to offer. The last on my list of museums was the Republican Palace Museum.

Part of the difficulty in visiting this museum was that it is only open a few days during the week, and at odd hours, too (no surprise, I am sure, to old Khartoum hands). Of those few days, the only one that was possible for me was Friday, as it was part of our weekend. But it took me awhile to track down the opening hours—and when I finally did, I confused the opening hours with the long closing period midday. So when I first tried to go, early in my tenure in Khartoum, I arrived just as the museum was shuttering for a long afternoon siesta.

But once I was armed with the correct hours, I managed to actually visit this little gem of a museum shortly before I departed Sudan for good.

Its name is a tad misleading in that it is not in the Republican Palace, but rather in the Anglican Church that once was on the grounds of the palace—the site of General Gordon's death and former seat of the Anglo-Egyptian government. The church is now cut off from the palace (which is off limits to the public), but it serves as the museum space for the Republican Palace, detailing the history of government in Sudan. This is a tricky endeavor, as you might have guessed.

The chance to see the church itself is worth a visit to the museum. It is one of the best preserved remnants of the British era in Sudan, a lovely sandstone structure complete with pretty stained glass windows. All the Christian iconography and memorials for dead British officials and officers serve as a rather incongruous backdrop to the museum's exhibits.

These exhibits are, to put it mildly, eclectic. Before I even entered the church, I noticed a glass-sided pavilion to the left of the museum entrance—a pavilion that showcased the presidential cars (many of them bulletproof Rolls-Royces) that have been used in the past fifty years. Inside the church, the left side of the sanctuary was devoted to a collection of state gifts to President Omar Bashir—some from other heads of state, others from more local groups and individuals.

There seemed no real order to their presentation. "And here is basket from Kordofan... And here is a sword from one of the Emirs in the U.A.E..." The right side had a series of panels with images and bullet points about the history of Sudan from the Anglo-Egyptian Condominium through Independence, highlighting in particular all the anti-colonial rebellions that occurred during that time. In the center, there were pieces of furniture that were used by political figures such as Ismail al-Azhari, the first prime minister of independent Sudan, and, of course, Bashir. More bizarrely, there were also items used by John Garang—the main southern rebel leader who died under mysterious circumstances in 2005, during the time when a peace agreement between Khartoum and the Sudan People's Liberation Movement/Army (S.P.L.M./A.) was being hammered out—and Salva Kiir, the current president of South Sudan. In the back, in what had been the nave, there is dusty collection of Condominium-era portraits and busts, including several of Lord Kitchener who, as we have seen, had reestablished British control of Sudan in 1889 after defeating the Ansar forces decisively in the Battle of Omdurman.

What interested me more than the individual items or the displays, however, was the overall message of the museum.[157] Or, rather, the lack of one. It was glaringly obvious that the curators had struggled to decide just what to focus on.

What history to present? Whose history to present? How could they explain the political history of a country like Sudan that has experienced so many coups and counter-coups? Who gets to be the hero? Who gets to be the villain?

The display of gifts presented to Omar Bashir obviously emphasized his current status as the leader of Sudan, but the more informational half of the museum seemed to downplay the story of his rise to power in the late eighties. Rather than make any one figure—whether al-Azhari, the major independence movement leader from the waning days of British rule, or John Garang, who fought Khartoum long and hard before being appointed a vice-president just before his helicopter "accident"—stand out, the curators just mentioned everyone in cursory fashion. Rather than stirring the political pot, they tried to keep everyone happy. They couldn't seem to answer the question of whose history it isto tell.

The result is a museum whose structure tells more than its exhibits. There is no hiding that the building was a British church of the Anglican bent. Its solid, no-nonsense walls, studded with memorial plaques detailing the lives of British men who died while serving in the colonial service, offer a poignant contrast to the fragility of post-independence Sudanese politics.

A fragility that led to the dramatic division of Sudan into two countries.

***

As I learned during my time in Sudan, there is no such thing as a quick-and-easy getaway from Khartoum, and my journey to visit Suakin was a case in point. I had kept putting off the trip until I would have a substantive amount of time to explore, until the sultry coastal weather

---

[157] My interest in the museum as an object of study in and of itself stems from a fantastic seminar I took in London in the early days of my teaching career. The topic was the influence of colonialism on the shaping of English identity; the professor often used museums as examples of how knowledge and identity are shaped for a general audience.

would be more tolerable, until perhaps I could get others to join me to defray costs, until... I had figured there was plenty of time.

And then there wasn't.

So, as my contract in Khartoum began to draw to a close, I took the last of my personal days and acquired the necessary travel permits, and then set forth on my Suakin pilgrimage.

No one really knows what the name "Suakin" means. In Arabic, *sawakin* is a plural construction for "dwellers" and, more poetically, for "stillnesses." There's a possibility that the name has a pre-Islamic/pre-Arabic origin, as the site of the city has been occupied since ancient times (indeed, it may well have been the Port of Good Hope described by the polymath Ptolemy). But until I learn otherwise, I think I will go with "stillnesses"—as it more than aptly captures the city's current state of being (or not being, as it were).

***

Suakin as Suakin initially rose to prominence during the medieval era, when it entered the orbit of Fatimid and Ayyubid Egypt, although often as the center of independent sultanates. By 1517, the Ottomans had swept into the region, and the town became part of the ever-expanding Ottoman Empire, acquiring a truly cosmopolitan character at that point. The city also gained prominence for a period when it served as the residence for the pasha that oversaw the Habesh Eyalet, the empire's rather odd "African" province that consisted of a disjointed patchwork of coastal territories that dribbled along the shores of the Red Sea and out to the Indian Ocean. Habesh included parts of what are now Eritrea, Ethiopia, Djibouti, and Somalia, as well as Sudan.

Unfortunately for the Ottomans, they also had to contend with the rising presence of the Portuguese in the Indian Ocean at around the same time they were establishing their presence in the Red Sea—a contest that eventually tipped in the favor of the Portuguese. Suakin lost some of its import as a center of trade, as it was marginalized in the lucrative exchange network that crisscrossed the Indian Ocean world.

Yet throughout its many centuries under Ottoman control, Suakin remained an important trading center and a vital crossing point in the Red Sea region, especially as it served as a transfer point for pilgrims from Africa who were heading to Mecca. It also regained some of its earlier panache when the Ottoman sultan handed control of the city to Khedive Ismail of Egypt in 1865.[158] The Khedive poured money into the revitalization of the town's infrastructure and had several new buildings built—even a Coptic church.

It was only after the British established the Anglo-Egyptian Condominium of Sudan following the collapse of the Mahdist state—and began in 1909 to develop the new Port Sudan further up the coast—that Suakin's star truly started to wane.

Slowly, Suakin's coral infrastructure began to crumble.

***

The core of Suakin was built on an almost perfectly round island within a bay on the Red Sea, connected to the mainland by a short causeway. Almost all the buildings were built of coral, much like the wonderful old city of Jeddah on the opposite shore of the sea. It must have been beautiful.

But now… Well, the first thought I had as I walked through the city gate was that I must have entered Kabul, circa 1996.[159] I wanted to weep.

Almost the entire urban fabric of the island—its Ottoman and Ottoman-Khedival warp and weave—has been rent asunder. Were it not for the few stalwart walls rising from the rubble, I might not have known that I had entered a former city. All the coral bricks rested in shapeless heaps; only the odd door or window frame poking out reminded passersby that there had once been a house or business there.

It would, perhaps, not have been so gut-wrenching (at least for a historical softy like me) if the collapse were of a more ancient order; after all, every monument collapses at some point. Even the pyramids of Egypt are a little ragged around the edges compared to the days when they

---

[158] As I've described elsewhere (see the chapter on Egypt), nineteenth-century Egypt was a strange beast: an essentially independent state that was still technically within the Ottoman Empire. When it was made a British colony in all but name in the latter part of that century, it became even more anomalous as a political entity: Ottoman, Khedival, and British all at once.

[159] The year the Taliban captured Kabul, after several years of fighting with government forces.

were originally erected. And coral is admittedly a lot more fragile—it is especially susceptible to the high humidity and salty air of the Red Sea region—compared to the solid limestone and granite of the pyramids. But Suakin Island was inhabited, at least in part, into the 1960s. A half-century of neglect has since left it in utter ruins.

Of course, as I have already noted, the port had begun to decline well before the sixties, having lost its *raison d'être*. Although there is still a daily ferry between "new" Suakin (the town that emerged on shore opposite the island) and Jeddah in Saudi Arabia, almost all other sea traffic now goes through the bustling modern city of Port Sudan. It's understandable that as jobs vanished, so did the inhabitants. It's understandable that the buildings were left empty.

What is less understandable—at least for me—is why no one seemed to recognize that a historical treasure was in dire need of protection. It was simply left to collapse, to disappear.

There are some feeble attempts underway to restore a few of the structures. Most notably, two mosques are in the process of being resurrected with the help of the Turkish government—an attempt to salvage something of the disappearing Ottoman heritage of the empire's deep south, I suppose. There are a few other buildings—a bank, a former warehouse—that are not so far gone that they couldn't be saved. But I am afraid the damage is mostly permanent. Without a tourist industry to support the costs of preservation and conservation work (work that should have been started decades ago), there's little hope that the decay will be slowed, let alone reversed.

Suakin, Restoration

Suakin is a monument that should be a national treasure for Sudan, a UNESCO World Heritage site of international importance; however, it won't be much more than a memory in a generation or so.

It will truly be a site of "stillnesses."

***

It was 6 a.m. The streets of Khartoum were nearly empty and the temperature almost comfortable, even during this period, the brutally hot days of May. Men still dozed on string cots in front of their shops, their bare feet sticking out from under thin sheets. The only businesses open were the bakeries, which were already churning out fragrant rounds of *'aish*, the bread that is life for so many; stacks of this bread, wrapped gently in yellow plastic bags, awaited distribution to corner markets throughout the neighborhood. A horse-drawn ice cart—a ghost of an earlier century—clip-clopped along the pavement, urged on by a droopy-eyed teenage boy. The tea ladies were just emerging, setting kettles to boil and arranging low-slung stools for their first, sleepy customers. My feet kicked up small dust clouds and discarded bottle caps.

In anticipation of my departure from Sudan, I had sold my Miss Daisy, the little white KIA Vista that had shuttled me to and from work (and around the rest of Khartoum) for two years. While I knew it was going to make life a little more complicated—suddenly going grocery shopping required a little more forethought, since I couldn't just jump in the car and go—it was also rather freeing. I decided to take advantage of the lack of wheels to do something I had missed since my days teaching in Chicago: walk to work.

While the actual distance between my apartment in Taif and Khartoum American School wasn't so great (perhaps 2.5mi/4km), it was not the pleasantest of strolls throughout most of the day. In addition to the ferocious heat and the omnipresent dust, I had to contend with crossing three major intersections—and considering the nature of Sudanese driving, I might as well have just plopped myself on the frontline of the Sudan and South Sudan not-quite-war.

But mornings were different. I was able to safely cross even the widest of roads without fear of being flattened by a speeding bus or an over-anxious motor-rickshaw. I enjoyed the solitude and the gradual awakening of the city as I passed all the landmarks that had only flashed by while I was driving. The remains of the Bayt al-Shami restaurant; the Reem Bookstore with its comically spooky logo of a girl staring into space; the Beyoncé Beauty Center (and the nearby Oprah Salon); the incongruous, gleaming BMW dealership next to the Turkish baklava shop; the charred hulk of the Afra Mall; the Khartoum Breast Cancer Clinic; the countless shells of buildings that will likely never be completed...

I quickly came to treasure those forty-minute walks: they were my slow good morning greeting—and my slow, unfolding goodbye—to Khartoum.

While not always a walk in the park, life in Khartoum proved surprisingly easy—dare I say comfortable?—in its way. Even when there were State Department warnings of "surveillance incidents" and possible plots by "extremists" to kidnap foreigners (disrupting my morning walks!), the city remained perhaps the safest I've ever lived in, and it certainly had its charms.

If anything, Khartoum is too quiet. There are few typical outlets for entertainment (not helped when the city's only semblance of a mall burned down mysteriously—taking with it the city's only cinema and only bowling alley), so people have to make their own fun much of the time: dinners, movie nights, rooftop parties, Nile excursions... Actually, for those so inclined, Khartoum has a surprisingly active expat party scene, but I quickly tired of the frat party-esque nature of many of those affairs. I much preferred hanging out with small groups of close friends, smoking shisha and having the occasional illicit drink (both of which are illegal in Sudan—shame on us!). Or going out for a coffee or dinner. I still miss, especially, circling around a small table and tucking into fried fish at Saj as-Samak or roasted lamb at Al-Waha with said friends.

These are the gentle moments I will never forget, and the ones I will hold most dear.

My walks through the all-but-empty streets of the early hours are memories, too, that I want to hold onto. Not the headline-grabbing news of conflict in Darfur and the Nuba Mountains, of wars in South Sudan, of tanking economies. Rather, I want to conjure up the peace of a slumbering city, the smell of freshly baked bread, the morning cool on my face.

I will remember the gentle side of that crazy, crazy place called Sudan.

BIRTHING PAINS: SOUTH SUDAN

The word "referendum" defined my time in Sudan. Actually, it had defined my relationship with Sudan ever since I accepted the teaching gig at Khartoum American School in October of 2009. I knew I would be heading to a deeply troubled country, one that had established a fragile peace between north and south in 2005 with the signing of the Comprehensive Peace Agreement (C.P.A.) by the government in Khartoum and the Sudan People's Liberation Movement (S.P.L.M.)—although, of course, the horrible tragedy unfolding in Darfur at the time marred the occasion. One of the major cornerstones of the C.P.A. was the promise of a referendum on independence for southern Sudan to be held in early 2011.

So, I knew the referendum was looming even before I set foot in Khartoum. However, like everyone else, I had no idea what to expect. When would the vote actually take place? Would it even take place? How would it be accomplished? How would sticky issues (such as the need to define borders) be addressed? What would the reactions to the vote—or even the lead-up to the vote—be among northern Sudanese, southern Sudanese, government officials, etc.? Would violence, even a renewed civil war, erupt? I knew that I, like everyone else, would just have to wait and see.

Through the fall of 2010, I tried to gather what news I could (which wasn't always easy from within Sudan, as the local media is pretty tightly controlled by President Omar Bashir), largely by asking friends in the diplomatic and N.G.O. worlds for tidbits. As the days ticked away, it got clearer and clearer that some major foot-dragging was occurring regarding the important issues that needed to be addressed before the referendum took place (the border, the allocation of the oil profits, etc.). But it was also quite clear that the government in southern Sudan was going to hold the north to its promise, no matter what. The referendum would be held, even if the details had not yet been hammered out.

As January approached, I worried about possible pre-referendum violence. But there was little, if any; other than a few minor protests, life remained quite calm. The school, however, postponed the start of the semester in anticipation of difficulties around the referendum itself, and put contingency plans in place should we not be able to open even then. The uncertainty grew as January 9 drew nearer.

But then the day arrived; it was met with joyful celebrations in the south and an almost blasé, shrug-of-the-shoulders "oh well" attitude in the north. Even President Bashir publically announced that he would accept the results, no matter what they were. When I returned to Khartoum in the middle of the week-long vote, after having been away for a month, I was struck by how bizarrely normal everything seemed. I wouldn't have guessed the country was in the midst of a historic moment, one that might lead to the separation of north and south, the establishment of a new country. No one, including me, had expected it to go so peacefully.

Yet I remained cautious.

As voting concluded, exit polls showed an almost certain vote for separation (some early numbers put the vote for independence at 98 percent or higher in some places), and there began to be some whispers of troubles—or at least challenges—ahead. There was some violence in Abyei, a contested area that was to have a separate referendum once the main results were known (the original plan was that, if the south seceded, Abyei would vote on whether to join Juba or stick with Khartoum). Darfur, which had been relatively "quiet" in recent years, seemed to be heading toward renewed conflict. Indeed, some of my N.G.O. friends who worked in or with Darfur were called back to Khartoum, and many of them feared that their organizations were going to be kicked out of the region.[160] Bashir made pronouncements that he would tighten Islamic law—or at least his version of it—if the south went its separate way. The prices of food and other essentials were climbing; foreign exchange regulations were becoming

---

[160] Not an unreasonable concern, as not long before I moved to Sudan, the Sudanese government expelled thirteen international relief agencies after the International Criminal Court (I.C.C.) issued an arrest warrant for President Bashir in 2009. He claimed they were spying on Sudan. Interestingly, several of those organizations returned shortly after they were expelled, but under new names. It seemed to be more of a big P.R. stunt than anything else.

so difficult that some airlines threatened to pull their flights. Security tightened in places like the American Recreation Site and the U.S. Embassy.

Still, most of those issues only caused minor ripples in my day-to-day experience in Khartoum. But they did make me wonder what was coming next.

When the formal results were announced in mid-February, the message of the South Sudanese was clear: we want independence, and independence it would be. Almost immediately the U.N. mission and many N.G.O.s began to pack up and plan a move southward. More darkly, South Sudanese in Khartoum, many of whom had had lived and worked in the north for decades, migrated to the south for fear of recriminations.

As if things weren't crazy enough in Sudan with all the upheaval resulting from the referendum, the rest of the Arabic-speaking world had begun to convulse with the series of revolutions that would become known as the Arab Spring. Many of the khawajas who were living in Khartoum at the time began to wonder what would become of our adopted home (and of us) during this uncertain time.

***

As we descended through the thick clouds, we noticed the difference right away. When we had taken off from Khartoum, the brown upon brown of the northern desert was all that we could see—and that monochrome landscape remained a fixture for most of the two-hour flight. Then the clouds appeared, obscuring the earth below. Soon, the flight crew announced our descent; we pressed our faces eagerly to the window, waiting to see our destination emerge below. When we broke through the cloud line, we were greeted by another world, green and wet; it was nothing like the brittle, dry desert we had just left. Were we really still in the same country? Were we still in Sudan?

The answer was: both yes and no.

Technically, at that moment, our destination—Juba—was a city within Sudan, the largest country in Africa. It is almost 750 miles (more than 1,200 kilometers) due south of Khartoum, and a world away in both climate and culture. While I still find the observation problematic, I began, even before we disembarked from the plane, to understand why so many people call this part of Sudan the "real" Africa. Khartoum, and the rest of northern Sudan, is a transition zone between what is seen as "Middle Eastern" and "African." But Juba, even from the air, had no such sense of ambiguity. This was clearly sub-Saharan Africa. Yet it was, in May 2011, still part of greater Sudan.

In a short couple of months, however, Juba was set to become the capital of a brand new country, the Republic of South Sudan. The deep fissures between north and south (culturally and politically) were to be demarcated by an official border that would almost exactly follow the line between desert and lush green.

***

The trip was a spur-of-the-moment thing, starting with a conversation between some of my more adventurous friends at school. Once the seed of the idea was planted, we couldn't not try to make it a reality. Most of us would be leaving in early June, not to return to Sudan until August. By that point, the north-south split would have occurred, to unknown effect. Though the violence that was emerging around the contested province of Abyei, sandwiched between north and south, provided a strong indication that future for the young state might be grim.

Secession Politics

At the very least, we knew that travel between Khartoum and Juba would get much more complicated. In the period between the referendum in January and the formal declaration of independence in July of 2011, the south operated in a fascinating shadowland between federation with the north and independence. This meant that one didn't need a travel permit to visit the south; the Go.S.S. (Government of Southern Sudan) didn't require it (unlike the government of northern Sudan, which did).[161] As a result, it was more difficult to drive out of the city limits of Khartoum than it was to fly to Juba. However, after secession, a visa from the north would no longer be valid for travel in the south (and, obviously, the reverse would be true as well). The details of how visas for South Sudan would be handled were still very much unknown, as were most of the technical details of independence. So we figured: why not take this opportunity to travel now, while we still could, and see first-hand the soon-to-be-capital?

In short order, we secured seats on a Marsland Air flight and a place to crash with some embassy folk. And off we went!

I only had twenty-four hours to experience Juba, and can of course only share what I observed. As such, I will not jump to any great political conclusions based on that brief visit.

***

Our weekend getaway began with a not-so-welcoming visit to the U.S. consulate, where Rudy, one of our gang, had to drop off some materials; it was not so welcoming due to the fact that our driver had taken us into the compound before we got our visitors' badges, which upset the security guy. I guess life is a little tense in the diplomatic world of Juba! Soon, though, we were off to see the town.

As we drove around Juba, we got a taste of the city's weirdness. For one thing, other than a handful of paved roads, the "city" is crisscrossed by a tangled network of deeply rutted roads (some of the ruts are deep enough to swallow a small car) that turn into a muddy mess when it rains (which they were at the time, since it had rained heavily the day before). Indeed,

---

[161] The reverse was not always so easy. Apparently, some U.N. and N.G.O. workers in Juba had a special allowance by Go.S.S. to be in Juba and its environs, but had no visa from the Khartoum government. Thus, they couldn't travel to the north.

there was no real infrastructure of any sort. Electricity was, and I imagine still is, provided by generators. Water came from wells and tanks.

All the same, the town was expanding at an alarmingly fast rate (it was noted in a "travel guide" that Juba was supposedly the fastest growing city in the world at the time; whether you could really call it a city is up for debate, but it certainly was growing). As the day wore on, the contrast between the thatched huts of the more village-like portions of Juba and the new construction made possible by the money that poured into the almost-capital became all the starker.

For example, we were able to shop in the sprawling Konyo-Konyo Market, a traditional African market where we walked thorough narrow, muddy pathways between makeshift stalls. We could also duck into the Jit Supermarket and be greeted by a wall of liquor from all around the world (including rare, expensive bottles of Russian vodka) and rows of gourmet food—not to mention the collection of massage chairs and round mattresses that were available in the furniture section upstairs. Who was buying all this? I was not sure I wanted to know.

There were other signs of difference. For our little group, which had gotten used to the more conservative norms of Muslim-majority Khartoum, we marveled at the women who were walking bare-shouldered and the men who were strutting about in shorts, as well as at the advertisements for (and the drinking of) alcohol in public venues. Also, Christianity was clearly the norm, as was represented by the amazing array of churches; Muslims were present, but visibly a minority, and towering Dinka men strolled by with tribal scars on their forehead.

We definitely were not in Khartoum.

We stopped for lunch at Spices 'n Herbs, an Indian place that was recommended by many regulars to Juba. As we gobbled up *pakoras*, *samosas*, *naan*, and various curries—washing it all down with Tuskers and Heinekens, of course—we kept asking ourselves: where are we?

***

This "almost country" was always an odd appendage to the states that dominated the north, a region that was kept at arm's length but that was also vital for its resources and riches. Shortly after Muhammad Ali took power in Egypt, he had turned his attention to the south and eventually incorporated most of what is now northern Sudan into his state-within-a-state[162], using it as a base for his slave-trading endeavors and other revenue-generating ventures. Later, Khedive Ismail, swept up in a vision of creating an Ottoman-Egyptian empire in sub-Saharan Africa, extended Egypt's reach further down the branches of the Nile; by the onset of Britain's colonial ambitions in 1881, he had acquired most of what is now South Sudan. Where Juba now stands, then, was probably the southernmost outpost of the Ottoman Empire—albeit part of that strange political configuration that I described in the Egypt chapter: Ottoman and Khedival Egyptian and, soon, British, all at once. But even more than the northern Sudanese territories, the deep south of Sudan was viewed as a zone of exploitation rather than an integral part of Egypt or the greater Ottoman Empire.

That attitude toward the south would remain even when the British took more formal control of Sudan following the Battle of Omdurman. The south of the Anglo-Egyptian Condominium of Sudan was little developed and largely left to European missionaries. Arabic-speaking Muslim Sudanese from the north were forbidden to travel in the south, but were favored in the colonial political and economic structures in the north. This divide, which would lead to deep resentment among the diverse peoples of the south, haunted Sudan from the day it officially gained independent in 1956, and culminated in the secession of South Sudan in 2011.

Unfortunately, post-independence South Sudan has continued to struggle. It has recently been embroiled in inter-ethnic conflict and civil war that threatens to end its short-lived experiment in freedom.

***

In the evening of our first day in Juba, our hosts threw a house-warming party at their place—aptly called Jebel House, as it is in the shadow of a rocky *jebel* (mountain or hill) on the edge of town. That sense of strangeness, of dislocation, we had all felt throughout the course of our

---

[162] The goal of his initial campaign in Sudan was actually to chase down and eliminate a faction of the Mamluks who had fled south and established a short-lived state in Dunqulah (or Dongala)—the area from which the Mahdi would emerge later in the nineteenth century.

day simply intensified. A slushy machine was set up on the porch that churned out fruity, icy, vodka-based drinks; a few guys were grilling pork (pork!) on the barbecue; and someone had made hand-pressed tortillas, too. The enormous house had a beautiful garden, complete with banana trees—and a razor wire fence. Someone casually mentioned that they wanted to hike to the top of the jebel, but that they had to be careful, as there were still mines. An enormous beetle, perhaps four inches long, dropped into the middle of a group of expats who were shooting the breeze. It all seemed so normal. And yet so not.

The more I observed this out-of-kilter world, the more I wished I could have stayed longer. Still, I was happy to have had the opportunity to get a small taste of pre-independence Juba.

Although I hadn't known it then, after July 9, 2011—South Sudan's official day of independence—I would never get the chance to return.

PLANET OF THE APES
SANS APES: DJIBOUTI

While I hadn't expected my excursion to Djibouti to be a straightforward affair, it was ultimately so complicated that it almost didn't happen at all.

When I got up to the Ethiopian Airlines counter at Khartoum International Airport, the agent decided on the spot that she couldn't check me in because I didn't yet have a visa for Djibouti. I tried to explain that as a U.S. citizen I was allowed to get one upon my arrival in Djibouti, but to no avail. She claimed that the airport manager would be over in a "minute" to make the final decision; at least twenty minutes later, there was still no sign of the manager, and now the agent had turned back three others who were seeking to go to Tanzania. They were equally baffled—it is well known that Americans can get visas at the border in Tanzania. Ms. Counter Agent was being rather overly zealous in her duties!

Finally, after what seemed an interminable time, the manager appeared and gave us all the green light, and I was able to leave Sudan.

However, once I arrived in Addis Ababa, things continued to go a little strangely. When the flight to Djibouti appeared on the announcement board, passengers were told to proceed to gate 4. There was a rather large crowd there that was already milling about, not to mention a line at the entrance ramp, which surprised me: how many people were going to such an out of the way place? I asked one of the Ethiopian Airlines personnel who was zipping to and fro if I should queue up; they waved me towards the line. Only when I was about to board the plane and the flight attendant double-checked my boarding pass did someone finally exclaim: "No, this plane is going to Luanda, Angola!" A number of us had to shuffle back up the ramp to wait for our turn. Apparently, three different flights—one to Angola, another to Rwanda, and ours to Djibouti—were all using the same gate at about the same time. Confusion reigned.

But when all of that was behind me, I finally got on the proper plane and landed more or less on time in Djibouti. And I was indeed able to get my visa there, although it took a long while—one guy was processing everyone and was taking his own sweet time.

What's the rush, when you've arrived at the end of the world?

***

Djibouti is one of the places that had been on my travel "bucket list" for a while. I think it was its name first that grabbed my attention—it's also one of my students' favorites: "Shake, shake Djibouti!" But I also liked that it was a far-flung place, a strange little outpost on the Horn of Africa, right at the mouth of the Red Sea as it spills into the Gulf of Aden. A place best known as a home to French Legionnaires and for being the "hottest place on earth."[163] How could I not go? Especially since I was living in the "neighborhood"?

While driving from the miniscule airport in an ancient, battered taxi—the driver, a gregarious Djiboutian, speaking to me in a mash of French, Arabic, and English (which I was soon to realize would be the norm here)—my first impression of Djibouti City was that it looked a lot like Khartoum. The outer edges of the city had that same low-slung, incomplete, dusty look. However, once I got into city center, my impression changed.

The European Quarter, where I was staying, was much more what I had imagined; decaying colonial façades surrounded the main square. It was a Friday afternoon, when almost all the shops were closed and the streets mostly empty, which just added to the sense that I had landed in an all but forgotten colonial backwater, lost on the edge of space and time.

In other words, my kind of place.

---

[163] I arrived at perhaps the best time of year to visit; the temperature was actually pleasant and the humidity relatively low. But somehow when the sun was high, I got a sense that under normal circumstances the weather here would be hell on earth. Blazingly hot with high, high humidity. 150°F, anyone? I can't imagine summer…

Djibouti "Downtown"

But Djibouti is not really forgotten, and it was most definitely not empty. Once I checked into my hotel and freshened up a bit, I went out to explore. The main part of the city is quite compact. The European Quarter can be almost completely circled in minutes; the adjacent African Quarter, while bigger, is still manageable.

North of the center, the city is more industrial, as this is where the main port is—which in and of itself is a reminder that Djibouti is actually a quite strategic place, important for the shipping business that passes between the Red Sea and Indian Ocean and as a base from which to combat the Somali pirates that harass that business. For much the same reasons, the Ottomans extended their control along the coasts of what are now Sudan, Eritrea, Djibouti, and Somalia, thereby forming the Habesh Eyalet.[164]

***

---

[164] Someday I hope to visit Somaliland, the northern region of Somalia that declared independence in 1991—although that independence remains unrecognized by

Before I began planning my trip to Djibouti, I had heard horror stories of how expensive the country was, that it was maybe one of the most expensive in Africa. But even forewarned, I nearly had a heart attack when I was quoted the price for a two-day, one-night trip to Lac Abbé. However, with no public transport between most of the major sights and, in many cases, no real roads to get to them (which made driving on one's own a challenge), I had to decide whether it was worth the huge bite out of my budget (I won't embarrass myself and say how much it was). In the end, I took the plunge and signed on—how could I not see these surreal places when I was so close? When would I get the chance again?

After completing that circuit, I can definitely say it was worth every penny.

I had met my driver-guide, Muhammad—an affable Afar[165] guy—early Saturday morning, and off we went. Despite his smattering of English and his Afar- and French-inflected Arabic, not to mention my caveman-ish French, we somehow managed to communicate.[166] Indeed, we sort of developed this hybrid language, in which we sometimes mixed Arabic, English, and French in the same sentence. Too bad my Afar was really rusty!

As we left Djibouti City behind us, the first thing I noticed were the number of Ethiopian trucks plying the highway. Roadside shops and call centers all catered to these truckers, displaying signs in Amharic. Muhammad informed me that one of the goods being brought over the border was *chat* (or *qat*), a plant with mildly hallucinogenic properties that was chewed by a significant percentage of the population here and in the

---

the international community. The reason for my interest is that the port city of Zeila, the remains of which are now crumbling in modern Somaliland, was one of the key Ottoman strongholds in the Horn of Africa. Indeed, Zeila was even more important than Djibouti.

[165] The term Afar refers to an ethnic group that lives mostly in the Danakil Depression region, which straddles northern Djibouti and parts of Ethiopia.

[166] French and Arabic are the official languages in Djibouti, though there are many other languages spoken, particularly outside the capital—Afar and Somali are perhaps the most common. French is by far the dominant lingua franca (even the native Arabs seem more comfortable in it), but Arabic is widely understood—which was a big help to me.

rest of the region. Fresh vegetables? Or chat? You know, you have to have your priorities straight.

After we passed through the village of Oueah and its Foreign Legion outpost, signs of "civilization" diminished rapidly. Nevertheless, I soon found myself amazed, as we made our circuit through the hinterlands of Djibouti, at just how much human activity I witnessed in this desolately beautiful, yet harsh, country. I was standing in the middle of a sunbaked desert plain that may not have not seen rain in five years, without a living green thing in sight, and a goat-herder or camel-driver would, out of nowhere, wander by with his charges. What were these animals feeding on? When I visited it was winter and the temperatures were decent, but what about when it's 150°F? With no shade? All I can say is that Djiboutians sure are tough people. I felt so "soft" in comparison.

On our way to Lac Abbé, Muhammad drove me onto the Barra Depression, an expanse of ancient seabed, now a pancake flat desert of salty sand that was prone to dust devils and sand storms. We then stopped for lunch in Dikhil, an oasis town with a shocking bit of greenery. Later, we passed through a couple of hardscrabble Afar villages (collections of small, domed huts that were set among thorn trees). Then, finally, by late afternoon we reached the main attraction: the real *Planet of the Apes*.

When Muhammad crested the hills of black, volcanic rock, powering over them in his trusty 4WD, we got our first view of the area around Lac Abbé; I understood perfectly well, then, why someone might choose to come to this far-flung corner of the globe to shoot a scene for a movie that takes place on another world. While I will admit that I have never seen the movie, part of the original *Planet of the Apes* is often rumored to have been filmed in this otherworldly landscape on the remote edge of Djibouti, a country that is already quite remote.[167] A forest of fanciful stone "chimneys" juts out of the plain, some belching smoke. Boiling hot springs gurgle out of the salt-encrusted ground. It all looked like something out of a 1960s Sci-Fi vision of another planet—yes, like *Planet of the Apes*.

---

[167] This seems to be something of an urban myth. There's no evidence that this actually was the case.

Another World

After we strolled through the famous smoke-belching "chimneys," we went down to the shore of the lake itself, where flocks of flamingos waded in, and then flew across, the saline waters. The water looked inviting, but I remembered that it is useless to the Afar nomads who live near its shores; it is just a taunting expanse of undrinkable water.

The camp where we were staying for the night was perched in a perfect location on a hill overlooking Lac Abbé and the nearby lunar landscape of rock formations. I could sit in front of the main hut, sipping sweet, cinnamon-laden tea and see it all. And, as we were the only guests, we had the view to ourselves.

That night, I fell asleep under a sky full of more stars than I knew existed.

***

The next morning, after trekking out to the hot springs and eating a hearty breakfast of fried bread, we ventured to the bigger chimneys, which were to be my last view of the Lac Abbé region. A pair of jackals joined us on the adventure, loping alongside us but keeping a wary distance

But Muhammad had more treats in store for me. Before we returned to Djibouti City, he took me to the edge of a deep, desolate canyon that is part of the Rift Valley and to the other famous lake of Djibouti, Lac Assal (Lake of Salt), which was even more impressive than the canyon. The lowest point in Africa and the center of an ancient salt trade that was carried out by Afar tribesman who crossed the deserts into Ethiopia, it is a mirage of unreal blues fading to white. When I put my hand into the water, it dried with a coating of white. It made me beyond thirsty to think of so much salt surrounding me.

Again, I couldn't help but wonder: how does anyone live here?

***

The Ottoman forts and trading centers strung along the shores of the Horn of Africa, lonely outposts of empire, must have been have been tough places to live. I imagine forlorn Ottoman soldiers, sweating under an unrelenting sun, peering across blinding landscapes that were colored by volcanic activity and the vestiges of ancient ocean salts, dreaming of the more salubrious climes of the Mediterranean or Black Sea shorelines back home. But perhaps some of those soldiers in Djibouti saw—just as I had—a beauty in the unforgiving harshness.

THE NEW LIBYA

Just a couple months after my visit to Tripoli, Libya devolved into some of its most serious post-revolutionary violence yet. Tripoli's international airport, which I flew in and out of, was destroyed; the U.S. and British embassies evacuated by land (and under gunfire) across the border into Tunisia. The news continues to be bleak, as groups such as Islamic State gain a foothold in the fractured country.

***

Kids were eating dripping cones of soft-swirled ice cream and bright pink cotton candy. Others were riding fantastically colored amusement rides while their parents watched indulgently from slick cafés where they were served espresso drinks by smartly uniformed waiters. Shoppers were jostling amid the narrow rows of an open-air market that was spread just outside the old city's walls. A gentle breeze was blowing off the sea; a bright blue sky arched overhead.

I am not sure what I was expecting, but it wasn't this. The scene was joyful, relaxed, and completely, utterly… normal.

How could I be in Tripoli, capital of the deeply fractured post-revolutionary, post-Gaddafi Libya?

Festive Tripoli

I have done my fair share of travel in politically unstable countries, such as Lebanon and the D.R.C., among others. Heck, I lived in Sudan when it split in two! While I generally have found the reality on the ground to be quite different from the images that are shown on the news, I was still surprised to see how little evidence of upheaval and civil strife there was in Tripoli. In Beirut, for example, life might go on as usual, but I still saw the occasional tank, roadblock, or row of razor wire. In Tripoli, however, there was barely a police presence. People were out and about, shops were open and bustling; electricity, water, and the Internet were all functioning at full steam.

This is not to say that all was rosy. On my first night, I woke up in the wee hours, as I am sometimes wont to do, and was surprised to hear: nothing. Considering the apparently perpetual traffic jam on Omar al-Mukhtar Street, just a block from my hotel, this was a little unsettling. I looked out the window and saw: no one. Nothing was moving.

As I drifted back to sleep, though, I was pretty sure I heard distant echoes of gunfire.

The deep night is still an uneasy time in Tripoli. Then again, the sounds might just have been a wedding…

***

Due to my fascination with closed countries, it's probably not too surprising to hear that I've wanted to visit Libya for quite some time. Of course, during the long, idiosyncratic rule of Muammar Gaddafi (1969-2011)—a leader who went so far as to invent a new Arabic word to describe his country, *jamahiriyya* (basically, "state of the masses")—that was not going to be easy. For one thing, U.S.-Libyan relations were, at best, cool due to many issues; examples included the Lockerbie bombing and other incidents that caused the American government (and others) to classify Libya as a state-sponsor of terrorism. Even for other nationalities, tourism was tightly controlled during the Gaddafi years, with rules that changed at random. I remember hearing the story of a plane full of tourists that arrived from Europe, only to be sent back because none of them had their paperwork translated into Arabic—a new regulation instituted just before the tourists' arrival.

Then came the so-called Arab Spring and the overthrow and death of Gaddafi in early 2011. Unlike what happened in Tunisia, where revolution unfolded relatively peacefully, things turned bloody quickly in Libya. There was even foreign military intervention. Tourism, of course, was impossible during this time.

However, when I learned that I was moving to Tunisia, I began to hope that I would finally get my wish to peek inside the mysterious country. I was going to be right next door, just over an hour-long flight away. I had to go. So, shortly after I settled into my life in Tunis, I began to explore options for travelling to the "New" Libya, only to discover that the Libyan government wasn't issuing tourist visas at that time. One tour company was willing to sponsor me for a business visa—which would have cost a whopping $450—but I didn't think that entering Libya under false pretenses was the best idea. I would just have to wait and see how the political winds blew.

As it turned out, early in the new year, I got a message from one of the other travel agencies I had contacted in the fall: they were informing me that it was now possible to apply for a tourist visa. I was already largely booked for my spring holidays, but I had a few days at the end of my break—perhaps I could at least undertake a long weekend in Tripoli? Thus, the ball started rolling.

Mostly, I kept quiet about my plans, informing only a handful of friends of the deal. In part, I wasn't a hundred percent hopeful that I would secure the visa; perhaps the government would change its policy at the last minute, perhaps they would find an excuse to deny me. I wouldn't know until a week before my scheduled departure. So why get my hopes up?

The other reason for my partial secrecy was that I didn't want my family to worry. I have long maintained a policy of telling my family after the fact if I am traveling to a place that might make them nervous (a policy that began with my trip to Jerusalem in 1994). Although I had done my research, knew that I would be in a relatively safe zone, and was certain that I would have people looking out for me (tourists to Libya must apply for their visas through travel agencies and generally have to have a guide— at least when they are outside of the city), I also was more than aware that the news coming out of Libya is usually grim.[168]

In the end, though, I did get the visa. I would actually be setting foot in the New Libya.

***

---

[168] In the spring of 2013 (not long after I visited), the tenuous peace in Tripoli was shattered as rival political groups turned on each other. A flood of Libyan refugees poured over the border into Tunisia. Due to the current political instability, the school where I teach has taken in a number of Libyan students.

In addition to its inaccessibility, Libya had another pull for me: it was yet another Ottoman territory to explore. The Ottomans established the Eyalet of Tripolitania in 1551, around the time they were vying for Tunis, after wrestling with the pesky Barbary Coast pirates. Tripolitania (Libya) would remain in Ottoman control until 1911—it was the last territory the Ottomans lost in North Africa, actually. This province consisted mostly of the coastal region, as the vast desert of southern Libya was next to impossible to control—similar to how it is today. Later, the Ottomans would try to expand their influence deeper into Libyan territory by setting up the province of Fezzan. The original Tripolitania province actually brought together two distinct territories: the western region around Tripoli and the eastern region, which was centered on modern Benghazi in a territory once known as Cyrenaica. In the earlier stages of Ottoman rule, these areas had been maintained as separate political units. Interestingly, these geographic and political fault lines—Tripolitania, Cyrenaica, and Fezzan—seem to have reemerged in post-revolutionary Libya; some areas have even attempted, at times, to secede from greater Libya.

As with other regions on the outer edges of the Ottoman Empire, Tripolitania was largely administered by local elites. Most famously, this role was played by the Karamanli Dynasty from 1711 to 1835; the dynasty was founded by Ahmed Karamanli, an Ottoman cavalry officer who was the son of a Turkish military officer and a local Libyan woman. The beautiful Karamanli Mosque in Old Tripoli, one the city's major attractions, contains the graves of most of these Ottoman pashas.

The Ottomans would continue to control Libya, or at least its coast, until just before World War I. In 1911 and 1912, Italy and the Ottoman Empire fought a war over the province, a conflict from which the Italians emerged victorious. The Italians would maintain Libya as a colonial possession until their defeat in World War II, leaving a visual legacy in the Italianate architecture of new Tripoli (and a culinary one in good coffee!). But the Italian era, known for its brutality, is obviously not fondly remembered. Unlike Tunisia, where French persists as a major second language, Italian is virtually unknown in Libya (except among some elderly Libyans).

The long Ottoman period, however, seems to have a greater hold on the public imagination, and is more readily evident in the physical fabric of Tripoli's medina than is the case in Tunisia.[169] There are many Ottoman mosques and houses, defined as such, dotting the old city. The Ottoman architectural heritage is embraced, even celebrated.

***

In any other country, Leptis Magna would be a world-famous tourist destination like the Coliseum in Rome, swarmed by gawking thousands every day. But it's in Libya. And I was the first non-business, non-political delegation tourist to visit the site in weeks.

Leptis Magna was founded as a Berber-Phoenician town, even before the establishment of Carthage. After the Romans destroyed Carthage in 146 B.C.E. and all of North Africa came under Roman control, Leptis Magna was rebuilt on Roman lines and became one of the most important trading centers on the southern Mediterranean coast. It rose to further prominence when its native son, Septimius Severus, became the Roman emperor in 193 C.E. (he is often referred to as the African Emperor due to his Berber roots). Through his lavish patronage, the city experienced a building boom and expansion that made it rival Carthage and Alexandria in greatness. Unlike these rivals, however, much of Roman-era Leptis Magna was preserved almost intact, as after the fall of the Byzantines to the Arabs around 650 C.E. it was swallowed by coastal sands for nearly nine centuries.

The result is a spectacularly well-preserved Roman city (of which actually only about forty-percent has been excavated) that occupies a gorgeous stretch of Mediterranean coastline. And it is all but devoid of tourists.

---

[169] Connections to post-Ottoman Turkey abound, as well. I was pleasantly surprised by the large number of good Turkish restaurants scattered around Tripoli, often packed with Turkish customers (many of whom appeared to be employees of Turkish construction companies).

Leptis Magna

I had the great privilege of having a local guide, Nader, who was genuinely passionate about Leptis Magna. Since there are too few tourists to make a living as a full-time guide, he also works as a secondary school English teacher. He grew up just a few miles from the site; however, as he explained, he and most others from the area were never really taught the importance of these ruins right in their backyard. But after years of poking around the remains of the once-great city, enjoying its deep peace and solitude, his curiosity was awakened and he began to read whatever he could about Leptis Magna. He bemoaned the neglect of the site both during the Gaddafi years—he said that the dictator didn't embrace Leptis Magna or similar sites as really "Libyan," but rather saw them as products of invading peoples—and under the current government. He pointed out several spots where the Libyan Ministry of Antiquities had botched restoration attempts or tried to cover up acts of vandalism. He shook his head sadly at the local tourists we passed who ignored the impressive monuments surrounding them as they bee-lined to the coast to enjoy picnics on the beautiful spring day.

"They don't know the importance of this place. No one has ever taught them about it."

But Nader taught me much, and his enthusiasm was infectious. I might have enjoyed wandering the extensive ruins on my own, but under his guidance the ancient city came alive to me. He also pointed out little details that I might have missed (like the strange hybrid phallus-camel sign at the intersection of two roads, apparently a good luck symbol) and the best views (like the one from the top of the Byzantine basilica). I could imagine the bathers who had enjoyed the extensive Hadrian Baths and the spectators at the theater, amphitheater, and hippodrome. I could almost hear the babble of multiple languages at the marketplace—Latin, Greek, Punic, and Libyan-Berber. I could envision ships pulling in and out of the now silted-up harbor...

Shortly before we wrapped up the tour of Leptis Magna, a giggling group of girls approached to have their photo taken with the obvious foreigner. I realized I was just as much a tourist attraction to them as the surrounding Roman monuments were to me. From their perspective, these remains of a once-mighty empire were just rocks. But I found them to be a humbling reminder of what a magical place the past can be.

***

Although my time in vibrant—dare I say joyful?—Tripoli was much too brief, I feel honored to have been one of the rare visitors to have gotten a glimpse of its difficult transition and transformation during the early, heady days of post-revolutionary independence. It is a city with a fascinating past that reaches back at least to Roman times, and which has seen myriad empires come and go. Indeed, in just over a century it has seen Ottoman imperial and Italian colonial rule, has experienced a local monarchy, Gaddafi's "state of the masses," and now is witnessing a volatile attempt at democracy. Now, Tripoli and the rest of Libya face a daunting, uncertain future. I will be watching from Tunisia, hoping that Libyans achieve a degree of prosperity and gain a much-deserved sense of peace.

TUNISIA AND A NON-CONCLUSION

We had reached the area known as the Kasbah, on the far side of the medina, where our tour with Faouzi was coming to an end. He waved us into the shade of a simple tomb I had seen on my first wander of Tunis's old city, but of which I had taken little notice.

"Have you heard of the Laz?" Faouzi asked.

A little startled, I replied: "Yes, they are an ethnic group from the Black Sea region in Turkey."

I think our enthusiastic guide was just as startled by my answer. "Yes, yes! This is the Laz *tourbet*, from the days of the Janissary garrison." Faouzi gestured towards the wall, where a simple blue plaque proclaimed the Laz-ness of the site.

Faouzi went on to explain that, for whatever reason, Laz soldiers played a significant role in Tunisia during the Ottoman era, achieving a certain prominence in the politics of this far-flung corner of the empire. This historical tidbit about the prominence of Laz soldiers in Tunisia was particularly intriguing to me; after all, the Laz in Turkey are often the object of jokes, in which they are generally portrayed as stupid (although I don't know why—I mentioned this previously in the chapter on Turkey).

Although Faouzi's story was almost an afterthought, mentioned briefly as we wrapped up our exploration of the medina, it underscored just how much I had to learn about my new and fascinatingly complex home.

Who would have thought? The Laz were in Tunis?

***

One of the draws for me when I was considering the job in Tunisia—where I have worked for three years—was that I would be able to explore another former Ottoman territory, one utterly new to me. Although much of my first few months in the country were consumed with simply settling into my new life and getting a handle on my teaching responsibilities at the

American Cooperative School, I slowly tried to ferret out what I could of Tunis' Ottoman past—a surprisingly difficult task considering that it was only in 1881, not so long ago, that the Ottomans lost this sliver of North African territory to the colonial ambitions of the French.

Ottoman rule in Tunisia was actually relatively light, administered largely by *beys* (a Turkish title) who acknowledged the authority of the Ottoman sultans in distant Istanbul but who often were *de facto* independent rulers. The beys were supported by Ottoman troops who were sent from the capital—and, as shown from the example of the Laz, the soldiers were brought in from all corners of the empire. The last beylical dynasty was the Husaynid family, which actually retained the title "bey" through the French colonial era, although the beys of this period wielded little more than symbolic authority.

In part, the difficulty that I had in finding Ottoman references was due to the greater attention paid to the region's more distant past. Carthage, anyone? My neighborhood is literally littered with Punic and Roman ruins, and a little further afield I was able to find some of the world's best preserved examples of Roman architecture and engineering (e.g., the remarkable amphitheater in El Jem).

Still, the obsession with Tunisia's ancient history can't fully explain the seeming neglect of its more recent Ottoman history. Perhaps—similar to what happened in early Republican Turkey—the westernizing and secularizing policies of Habib Bourguiba, Tunisia's first president (for life) after the country's independence from France in 1957, contributed to this historical amnesia. Although it is entirely possible that I am just reading too much into things…

Whatever the case, little is made of Tunisia's more than three hundred years of Ottoman rule.

One weekend, I went up to the seaside suburb "resort" of La Marsa to track down one of the Ottoman bey's summer palaces. After I spent some time wandering aimlessly, attempting to follow the extremely vague directions that I had been given, I finally stumbled on it—unmarked and echoingly empty, save for a couple entrepreneurial booksellers who had set up a few rickety tables in the entranceway. Other than its size, I might have assumed it was just another villa. All indication of its royal past had been stripped clean.

Another weekend, I went down to La Goulette, a place more famous for its ferry port and many fish restaurants than as a historic destination, to take a look at the Ottoman fort—the Borj el-Kerrak—only to find its hulking stone edifice crumbling and occupied by some homeless men (and many, many cats).

Tunis' medina, of course, retains more from the Ottoman era. But here, too, much of it remains hidden from the untrained eye.

As a result, I was thankful to have the opportunity to join a tour of the medina with the famous Faouzi. He not only pointed out the Laz tomb, he also showed us the door to the Ottoman garrison, which is now all but obscured by a display of tourist knick-knacks. He explained that the city museum used to be the home of the famous Ottoman reformer, Hayrettin (or Khayr al-Din) Pasha, who happens to grace the Tunisian twenty-dinar note. He told the story behind the Aziza Uthmana Hospital, named for a beloved princess of Ottoman origins who endowed several medical establishments in the city. He noted the differences between the Ottoman style mosques and the more typical North African ones, as well as the accompanying differences in the surrounding commercial districts (for example, the Ottoman structures often have shops built right into the outer walls or base of the mosque-complex).

Oddly, despite all my Ottoman explorations of the greater metropolitan area of Tunis in first weeks in the country, it took me six months before I finally stepped foot into the most important Ottoman monument in the city: the Bardo Museum.

The Bardo is one of the first places to which package and cruise ship tourists are shuttled on their often lightening-quick visits of the Tunis metropolitan area[170] (the circuit usually includes twenty-minute stops at the Antonine Baths in Carthage and a twenty-minute stroll up and down Sidi Bou Said's main street—and then back to their bland seaside resorts or

---

[170] Tunisia experienced one of its worst cases of post-revolution violence on 18 March 2015, when three armed gunmen attacked the Bardo, killing more than twenty people and injuring at least fifty others, most of whom were tourists. It was, at that point, the deadliest terrorist attack in Tunisian history, the number of deaths exceeding that of the 2002 attack on the Ghriba Synagogue in Djerba. However, with the Tunisian resilience I have come to respect deeply, the Bardo Museum reopened for business just over a week later.

ships). It is one of the largest archaeological/historical museums in Africa, and houses perhaps the most extensive collection of Roman mosaics in the world. Moreover, the original heart of the museum is the former palace of the Ottoman beys, which of course made it a particular draw for the Ottomanist in me.

So why did it take so long? The short answer is that I really don't know.

In part, there was no rush, since I lived in the city. I knew I would get to it eventually. Even before I bought a car, there were several times I planned to go, but each time something—such as the day a sudden downpour flooded downtown—made the trip by public transport seem like a hassle.[171] But once I had my own wheels, there were no more excuses.

The Bardo, when it was the beylical palace, was actually outside of Tunis proper, set amid a leafy "suburb." However, modern Tunis has engulfed the location (about two-and-a-half miles away from the original medina). Indeed, Bardo Square has become the epicenter of the country, since the palace grounds include not only the museum but also the National Assembly building. Considering that the original palace on the site was built during the era of the Hafsid kingdom (1229-1574) before it was taken over and expanded by the Husaynid dynasty of Ottoman beys (1705-1957), the Bardo represents a remarkable sweep of Tunisia's political history. A recent expansion of the museum includes a very modern entrance hall with all white walls and glass, which admittedly obscures some of that history. However, once I entered the exhibition halls, the layers gradually peeled back.

Although the museum in El Jem perhaps ruined me for Roman mosaics ("oh, yes, another amazingly intricate image made with minute, colored tiles"), the sheer quantity of the Bardo's holdings—not to mention the size of some of the individual pieces!—is without a doubt impressive. Still, I found myself more often than not looking up: it was in that direction that the opulence of the Husaynid palace was most visible in the beautiful wooden ceilings and domes that were bedecked in bright colors and patterns, shielding the archeological treasures below.

---

[171] The reality is that it is not such a big deal. From Carthage, I can take the T.G.M. commuter train to downtown Tunis, and then at the Tunis Marine station transfer to the metro system, which then takes me directly to the Bardo. It was only about an hour each way.

I managed, too, to mostly avoid the packs of tour groups that disgorged from their buses for a quick run-through of the museum, all seeming to follow the same trajectory through the museum. I often had corners of the museum entirely to myself, including, for a minute or two, the lovely former harem with its stuccoed domes and blue tiled walls.

Ottoman Echoes in the Bardo

I also wandered into the emptier reaches of the new extension; there were several parts left bare, perhaps due to a drying up of funds following Tunisia's revolution in 2011. In that relative solitude, I found myself wondering: What's next for the Bardo? For Tunisia?

I also realized, as I stood in the quiet chambers of the Bardo, that I was in the midst of multiple beginnings: the beginning of a new life in a new Tunisia, at the beginning of new opportunities to learn and grow—especially in my understanding of the Ottoman past in a new context, both in terms of place and time.

***

So this chapter on Tunisia is not a conclusion. It really can't be.

For one thing, I have yet to see all the territories that were once encompassed by the expanse of the Ottoman Empire. I still need to make it to Algeria, to Yemen, and to a number of other places when—*inshallah*—it becomes possible to do so.

Secondly, the past will always be considered and reconsidered, shaped and reshaped for present—and continuously changing—purposes. Even if I return to a place, such as Istanbul, there will be new observations to be made, new interpretations to offer.

Nevertheless, I must provide some degree of closure, and how more fitting that I should end where I began: Tunisia.

Tunisia is not the furthest-flung corner of the Ottoman Empire, as it is relatively easily accessible to the center by means of that great conduit of people, goods, and ideas, the Mediterranean Sea. Although the connections between Tunis and Istanbul weakened with the decline of Ottoman naval power and the rise in the nineteenth century of modern European seafaring powers—England and France, in particular—one could still travel relatively easily between the Ottoman capital and the Beylik of Tunis, even when it became physically separated from the empire with the British occupation of Egypt in 1882 and the Italian takeover of Libya in 1912.[172] Today, it's a two-and-a-half hour direct flight on either Turkish Air or Tunisair.

But the Mediterranean Sea that provided a means to travel also provided something of a psychological barrier, I think. Unlike some of the territories that were more directly tied to the Ottoman core, especially the Balkans, there was a sense of separateness that was manifest even in the way Tunisia was ruled: as an all but independent beylik, with a hereditary line of beys. As long as they acknowledged the sultan as the supreme authority and paid the requisite tribute, the beys essentially did as they pleased much of the time.

Perhaps a little ironically, it was the growing threat to Ottoman suzerainty in North Africa from European colonial ambitions that actually spurred the Ottoman government to bring Tunisia, and other similar territories, into a more centralized administration during the

---

[172] Algeria went to the French in 1830, but this didn't cut Tunisia off from the Ottoman land route, obviously.

mid-nineteenth century. The *Tanzimat* (Reorganization) reformers, who hoped to bring the Ottoman state into line with political developments in Europe, also hoped to replicate their plans in the periphery of the empire. In Tunisia's case, the man most identified with this period is Khayr al-Din Pasha al-Tunsi—or, as the Ottomans called him, Tunuslu Hayrettin Paşa (Pasha).

"Tunisian" Hayrettin Pasha was, in many respects, a perfect example of the complex identity encompassed by the label "Ottoman," as he represents the empire's still great diversity in one neat package that brings together many of the themes and topics I have discussed in this book. Born in the 1820s in Abkhazia—the current breakaway region in modern Georgia—to a Circassian family, he was later orphaned when his father died while fighting against a Russian attack on the town of Sukhumi. As was still common practice in the early nineteenth-century Ottoman Empire, promising boys from the frontiers were often sold into slavery (a holdover from the devşirme system). Such was the case with young Hayrettin; however, as was the case for many devşirme "recruits," slavery ended up being a path to his prominent political career.

Throughout most of his youth, Hayrettin served as a companion to the son of a poet of Cypriot origin, Tahsin Bey, who lived near the Bosphorus. Although a slave, he was, like other devşirme boys, provided with the best education that was available at the time, including the study of Turkish and French. When he was about seventeen years old, Hayrettin was brought to the court of the Husynid Bey of Tunisia, Ahmad Bey (r. 1837-1855), which was centered at the Bardo Palace. There, he continued his studies, focusing now on military science and on acquiring Arabic.

Apparently, Hayrettin was a talented young man, and Ahmad Bey soon recognized his gifts. He rose quickly both in rank within the bey's new "Western"-style army and in political importance, and was even sent on several diplomatic missions back to Istanbul during the 1840s and 50s, when the Tanzimat reforms were being instituted in the center. He also accompanied Ahmad Bey on a state visit to France, the first time Hayrettin traveled outside of the Ottoman Empire; he later spent four years in Paris. His experience of both the Tanzimat in Istanbul and the advances being made in France seemed to have shaped his vision of what Tunisia should become in the "modern" world.

By 1873, Hayrettin Pasha had become the Grand Vizier of Tunisia, second in command to Sadiq Bey (who was the last Husaynid Bey before the French takeover). Among his many attempts to modernize and reform Tunisia[173], he founded the first secular school in Tunisia, Sadiki College, in 1875; it still operates as a prestigious high school. Despite Tunisia's distance from Istanbul, his service was recognized by the Ottoman court, which led to his being appointed Grand Vizier of the entire Ottoman Empire from 1878-79—a remarkable journey for a Circassian boy born in Abkhazia, on the Ottoman-Russian frontier.

But the reforms were almost too little, too late, and Tunisia would ultimately fall into the orbit of French colonialism in Africa, following its Ottoman neighbor Algeria. Hayrettin Pasha would end his days in Istanbul, cut off from his adopted home of Tunisia due to the establishment of the French Protectorate in 1881. He died in 1890, far from his adopted land.

For nearly a century more, the Husaynid beys would remain in the Bardo and their other palaces, but served only as figureheads who were no longer bound to the Ottoman sultanate; rather, they had to defer to the French Republic. And with independence in 1956, under the heavy-handed westernization/secularization of Tunisian society and government that was instituted by Habib Bourguiba (who was following the model of Mustafa Kemal Atatürk), the connection to the Ottoman past was all but severed.

Now, Tunisia's Ottoman period—a nearly five-hundred-year stretch—is rarely discussed, and its Ottoman monuments are rarely presented as worthy of tourism. Almost all attention goes to the region's more distant past—the Phoenician, the Roman, and even the Byzantine eras. The more recent French period, despite its being viewed as a period of oppression, is also more visible—in the obvious use of French as a second language in

---

[173] Hayrettin Pasha seemed to want to align Western political models with a "modernized" vision of Islam, similar to the efforts of other Ottoman reformers in the late nineteenth century. Interestingly, he advocated for closer ties between Tunis and the Ottoman imperial center, with the hope that this would help Tunisia resist European colonial encroachment. He wanted Tunisia to compete with Europe by modeling European "progress."

this polyglot society, in the cuisine, in its bureaucratic methods, and in much of its architectural fabric.

I had to really search in order to discern the Ottoman layer. In my neighborhood in Carthage, several structures from the beylik have been repurposed, one as the Museum of Oceanography and another as headquarters for the Tunisian Academy of Arts and Sciences. A casual observer would see that they are older, once-grand buildings, but only someone looking for hints of Ottoman-ness might connect the remains of the Bey's Standard above the entrances with the Ottoman period.

Further down the coast, Hayrettin's seaside villa near La Goulette rests empty and forlorn. Its significance is all but unknown to the locals. Even the most obvious point of Ottoman historical interest—the medina of Tunis, the tomb complex of the beys and their families—is, as I pointed out in the opening of this book, closed for restoration, lost in a neglected corner of the old city.

I could analyze this forgetfulness at length, but here's my short-and-ready explanation:

Today, most of the energy of the Tunisian powers-that-be is focused simply on finding a working path out of the Arab Spring that began in Tunisia in late 2010 with the self-immolation of Mohamed Bouazizi. There might not be a direct connection to the Arab Spring and the Ottoman era, but I do think there is relevance.

One of the things that is most remarkable about being "on the ground" in North Africa in the post-revolutionary era is to see, firsthand, just how varied the experiences and responses to the political upheaval have been. Although Algeria, Tunisia, Egypt, and Libya were all part of the Ottoman realm for centuries, they were ruled in different manners and with varying degrees of closeness to the center. They then fell under different European colonial authorities—Algeria and Tunisia to France in 1830 and 1881, respectively; Egypt to Britain in 1882; and the last island of Ottoman territory in the region, Libya, to Italy in 1912.

Even when they were under the same colonial authority, as was the case with Algeria and Tunisia, they were treated differently. Coastal Algeria was fully incorporated into France and divided into three *départements*, while Tunisia was treated as a protectorate, under the fiction maintained by the bey who sat on the throne. Thus, when nationalist movements in these two countries began to advocate for independence, France was ultimately more willing to part with Tunisia—but went into a protracted, bloody *civil* war in Algeria. The departure of Algeria was seen as though a part of France was being torn asunder.

With independence, the political and cultural—and, yes, historical—paths of the North African states continued to diverge. Egypt, while ostensibly independent as a kingdom since the 1920s, was still very much a puppet state of Britain. A military coup in 1952 brought a "republic" into being, at first under the charismatic and controversial leadership of Gamal Abdul Nasser. In general, Egypt was to be ruled by men of military background up until 2011, when long-"reigning" President Hosni Mubarak was ousted. Interestingly, in the mayhem that followed, the military once again took control.

Libya came under the quixotic rule of Muammar Gaddafi for forty-two years, a period that saw most contact with the outside world heavily restricted. His strategy to essentially rule by divide-and-conquer by delegating responsibilities of local administration to tribal and clan leaders eventually backfired; it ended up being a root cause of the current crises that have brought Libya to the point of being a failed state, one that is potentially ready to divide into several states (fascinatingly, along old Ottoman provincial lines).

Algeria remained largely untouched by the Arab Spring—but it went through its own dark period for most of the nineties. In 1991, an Islamist party was on the verge of being elected, and the Front de Libération Nationale (F.L.N.)—which had ruled Algeria since the war of independence in 1962—rejected the results. This set off a civil war that didn't officially end until 2002—a period that has become known as the "Black Decade." As a result, the government was quick to clamp down hard before much could happen in Algeria during the Arab Spring.

But what of Tunisia? Sitting as it does between the chaos of Libya and Egypt to the East, and the uneasy calm of Algeria to the west?

Tunisia, where the "Spring" sprung, seems to be charting a relatively positive, if still rocky, path.

Not surprisingly, the situation in Tunisia didn't improve overnight after President Zine el-Abidine Ben Ali fled the country, despite the hopes of many. There have been fits and starts—including the attack on the U.S.

embassy and the American Cooperative School in 2012 and some unusual (for Tunisia) political assassinations in 2013 (including the opposition leader, Mohamed Brahmi, who was killed just a week before I landed in Tunis). However, in early 2014, the unpopular Ennahda Party-led[174] government, which was moderately Islamist, stepped down peacefully and a caretaker prime minister, Mehdi Jomaa, was appointed without much resistance. The new constitution, after some delay, was approved shortly thereafter—one of the most "progressive" in the Arab world, as it enshrines equal rights for women.

Furthermore, in October of 2014 the new parliamentary elections occurred without incident, and in December a new president, Beji Caid Essebi, was elected. With a new, democratically elected government in place, the country is poised to finally get to work on much-needed political and economic reforms, ones that will hopefully address the concerns that gave rise to the Arab Spring in the first place. All in all, Tunisia seems to be the most likely to succeed at establishing something resembling the democratic ideals the revolution espoused.

Much of the rest of the former Ottoman world, however, is still in the midst of great upheaval—the continuing civil wars in Syria and Yemen, the takeover of large swaths of Syria and Iraq by Islamic State (I.S.I.S.), the implosion of Libya, the struggle between Russia and Ukraine, chaos in South Sudan, sword-rattling between Armenia and Azerbaijan over Nagorno-Karabakh, financial fragility in Greece, growing authoritarianism in Turkey... the list goes on. We shall see what unfolds in the years to come for these troubled spots.

Still, there is room for hope. In the Balkans, there is the growing integration of the former Yugoslav republics into Europe, some of which are already members of the E.U. (such as Slovenia and Croatia) and others of which are on their way (Serbia); relations between these states, bloody

---

[174] Ennahda, or "Renaissance," was one of the few organized resistance movements during the late Bourguiba era and through the period of Ben Ali. Its leader, Rached al-Ghannuchi, lived in exile from 1988 until the Arab Spring, when he returned to lead his party to victory in the first post-revolution election. Soon, however, Ennahda was accused of not delivering on their election promises and, more darkly, of supporting more radical Islamist actions (including the assassinations in 2013)—which the party denied vehemently.

enemies less than twenty years ago, also seem to be normalizing. In the Caucasus, Georgia is opening up to the world, becoming an important tourist destination and economic hub; Armenia might be following suit. And, as I mentioned above, there is Tunisia, which just might become a model for what is possible in North Africa and beyond.

So this is not an end. I am only just beginning my journey through the fascinating post-Ottoman landscape.

ACKNOWLEDGMENTS

Writing and preparing *Echoes of Empire: An Accidental Historian's Journey through the Post-Ottoman World* has been a fantastic journey. And, in fact, the book was in the making long before I knew I was going to write it. Due to a series of wonderful academic "accidents," I was put on a path more than two decades ago that led to my studies of Ottoman history and to my travels within the world the Ottomans created. I haven't looked back since.

The number of people who have inspired me and offered their knowledge, insights, and support over the years is vast, and I will be unable to name them all here. However, I would be remiss if I didn't acknowledge the following scholars who first sparked the flame: Dr. Ross Brann, whose fascinating course on Muslims, Christians, and Jews in Islamic Spain inspired me to study in the Near Eastern Studies Department at Cornell University in the first place; Dr. Leslie Peirce, who then introduced me to the full sweep of Ottoman history through her scintillating courses, her warm-hearted guidance as my major advisor, and her thoughtful, hard-hitting critiques of my B.A. honors thesis on the Azeri Turks; Dr. Robert Dankoff, from whom I began learning the intricacies of that beautiful linguistic beast known as Ottoman Turkish during my first year at the University of Chicago; Dr. Selim Kuru, who helped me deepen my love of and facility with the language; and Dr. Ronald Inden, who took on a wayward graduate student in Middle Eastern/Islamic history as an M.A. thesis advisor, despite the fact that his specialty is South Asian history.

As I began to live, study, travel, and then work in various parts of the Ottoman world, I met countless individuals who offered their firsthand experiences of life in their home countries, their interpretations of local history and culture, and their simple companionship. I also encountered other travelers and amateur historians, each trying to get a better understanding this complex planet. Among the friends and guides, formal and informal, who I would especially like to acknowledge are: Abigail Wilson, Adnan Gusić, Alberto Frisiero, Ali Resul-Zadeh, Arpenik, Artur

Hakhverdyan, Barb, Bata, Buğra Giritlioğlu, Dajana Zildzić Hudek, Denis Pesut, Dorsaf Kouki, Dusica Civokrg, Egbal Karrar, Elshad Yusif, F., Faouzi, Grzes (Gregory) Koronkiewicz, Ian Fitzmorris, Jacob Hathaway, Jelena Stojanović, Kay Ebel Agoston, Lamia, Matthias Weezer, Nader, Nato Sozashvili, Öner Ceylan, Richard, Robert Post, Sabina Nikšić, Samir Gusić, Samiye Zubaroğlu, Sara Hommel, Scott Maxwell, Shevkiye, Skender, Slavko, Süheyla Zubaroğlu, Vanessa Austen, and Velin Mitev. All of you made my travels richer, more meaningful, and more enjoyable!

Echoes of Empire would never have materialized without the generous support of family, friends, colleagues, former students, and even complete strangers who took a risk on this project by contributing to my spring 2014 Kickstarter campaign. I was deeply humbled by my backers' collective generosity, which enabled me to not only reach, but exceed, my original goal. I couldn't have put this book together without you! So thank you to: Omar Acosta, Raaid Alireza, Eric Anderson, Heidi Bohrer, Ellen Boomer, Julie Bredy, Elizabeth Buchanan, Tina Bui, Alexander Brandt, Tifin Calgani, Laura Callaway, Jen Cerny, Christopher Coe, Shawn Crawford, Susan Diamond, Zapryan Dumbaslski, Tomiko Evans, Karin Fisher, Vika Gardner, Sara Russell Gonzalez, Donald Hargraves, Katheryn Harrison, Lee James, Rebekah Joslin, Kyle Kessler, Niraj Kumar, Kevin MacNeil, Zoe Malcolm, Chris McGovern, Joe Parrino, Jon Pestana, Colin Pickell, Magnus Sand, Michael Schenkel, Phil Thomas, Soukeina Tharoo, Fadi Toonsi, Peter Vancoillie, and Mehboob Vellani. And a special thank you to those who pledged in the higher rungs: Ali Bhanji, Craig Campbell, Pam Connerly, Chris David, Mark Galpin, Vika Gardner, Denis Pesut, Robert Post, Troy Prinkey, Werner Rehm, Bryan Strawser, and Abigail Wilson. Stephen Gunn, a former Indiana Academy classmate, went even a step further: all I can say is that I am deeply humbled by his generous donation to the project!

I must give a huge *shukran jazilan* to Jen Cerny, a friend, a fellow teacher, and a fellow enthusiast of the Middle East. She has not only been one of my most devoted followers of, and insightful commentators on, my blogs, she graciously accepted the challenge of editing the rough draft of *Echoes of Empire*. Her skills as both an English teacher and a student of Middle Eastern history and culture made her the ideal editor; I owe her a million!

I also owe a great debt of gratitude to Lore McSpadden, my tireless line editor. Her meticulous eye and attention to detail made *Echoes of* Empire a better book.

Of course, any remaining errors are my own.

Lastly, none of this—either the book or the life that gave birth to the idea—would have been possible without the two most important people in my life: my parents, Steven and Shirley Kessler. Long before they knew they had an Ottoman historian with nomadic tendencies on their hands, they supported all my crazy endeavors with unwavering, unconditional love. As I began to venture beyond the relative safety of Indiana's borders, flying off to such far-flung corners of the world as Jordan, Egypt, Turkey, and, more recently, Sudan and Tunisia, I knew they worried; nevertheless, they were always my biggest cheerleaders, willing to listen to every story I had to tell. They were my biggest blog fans, too, sharing my writings with friends and family back home; they were thrust unwittingly into the role of impromptu geography teachers ("Where exactly is Transnistria?"). I would not be the man I am today—the traveler, the teacher, the writer—without their example. *Echoes of Empire* is for them, with deepest love.

FURTHER READING

As *Echoes of Empire* was not intended to be a scholarly tome, but rather a more personal meditation on my travels and experiences in the post-Ottoman world, I have decided to pare the bibliography down to a more manageable "Further Reading" section. What follows is by no means comprehensive, and does not encompass all the books, articles, and other sources that have informed my understanding of Ottoman history and current politics and culture—that bibliography might very well constitute an entire separate book. Rather, I have chosen materials that encompass the full range of the countries through which I have traveled that I think are generally accessible to a lay public (though some are intended for an academic audience) and that have been particularly important in shaping my ideas. Some materials are here simply because I enjoyed them, and I hope you will, too!

Fiction:

Andrić, Ivo. *The Bridge on the Drina*. Chicago: University of Chicago, 1977. Print.

Kadare, Ismail. *The Siege*. Translated by David Bellos. Edinburgh: Canongate/Grove, 2010. Print.

Kadare, Ismail, and David Bellos. *Chronicle in Stone: A Novel*. Translated by Arshi Pipa. With contributions by David Bellos. New York: Arcade, 2011. Print.

Kadare, Ismail. *Broken April*. New York: New Amsterdam, 1990. Print.

Said, Kurban. *Ali and Nino: A Love Story*. New York: The Overlook Press, 1999. Print.

Non-Fiction:

Al-Rasheed, Madawi. *A History of Saudi Arabia*. New York: Cambridge University Press, 2010. Print.

Barkey, Karen. *Empire of Difference: The Ottomans in Comparative Perspective.* New York: Cambridge University Press, 2008. Print.

Batuman, Elif. "Ottomania." *The New Yorker,* 17 Feb. 2014. Web. 10 Nov. 2014.

Casale, Giancarlo. *The Ottoman Age of Exploration.* Oxford: Oxford University Press, 2010. Print.

Çelebi, Evliya, Robert Dankoff, and Sooyong Kim. *An Ottoman Traveller: Selections from the Book of Travels of Evliya Çelebi.* London: Eland, 2010. Print.

Cleveland, William L., and Martin P. Bunton. *A History of the Modern Middle East.* Boulder: Westview, 2012. Print.

Collins, Robert O. *A History of Modern Sudan.* Cambridge, UK: Cambridge University Press, 2008. Print.

Derengil, Selim. *The Well-Protected Domains: Ideology and the Legitimation of Power in the Ottoman Empire, 1876-1909.* New York: I.B. Tauris, 1998. Print.

Fisher, Alan. *The Crimean Tatars.* Stanford, CA: Hoover Institution Press, 1978. Print.

Fromkin, David. *A Peace to End All Peace: The Fall of the Ottoman Empire and the Creation of the Modern Middle East.* New York: H. Holt, 2009. Print.

————. "The World; A World Still Haunted by Ottoman Ghosts." *The New York Times,* 08 Mar. 2003. Web. 14 Jan. 2015.

Gelvin, James L. *The Arab Uprisings: What Everyone Needs to Know.* New York: Oxford University Press, 2012. Print.

————. *The Modern Middle East: A History.* New York: Oxford University Press, 2011. Print.

Glenny, Misha. *The Balkans: Nationalism, War, and the Great Powers, 1804-2011.* New York: Penguin, 2012. Print.

Göçek, Fatma Müge. *Denial of Violence: Ottoman Past, Turkish Present, and Collective Violence against the Armenians, 1789-2009.* New York: Oxford University Press, 2014. Print.

Gratien, Chris. "State and Society in Ottoman Syria." *Ottoman History Podcast.* 28 Sept. 2011. Web. 11 Nov. 2012.

Hanioğlu, M. Şükrü. *A Brief History of the Late Ottoman Empire.* Woodstock: Princeton University Press, 2010. Print.

Judah, Tim. *Kosovo: War and Revenge*. New Haven, CT: Yale Nota Bene, 2002. Print.

_____. *The Serbs: History, Myth and the Destruction of Yugoslavia*. New Haven: Yale University Press, 2009. Print.

Kaplan, Robert D. *Balkan Ghosts: A Journey through History*. New York: Picador, 2005. Print.

King, Charles. *The Black Sea: A History*. Oxford: Oxford University Press, 2005. Print.

_____. *The Ghost of Freedom: A History of the Caucasus*. Oxford: Oxford UP, 2010. Print.

_____. *Odessa: Genius and Death in a City of Dreams*. New York: W.W. Norton, 2012. Print.

"Kosovo Row Mars Historic Visit." *BBC News*. Web. 11 Nov. 2014.

Malcolm, Noel. *Kosovo: A Short History*. New York: HarperPerennial, 1999. Print.

Mazower, Mark. *The Balkans: A Short History*. New York: Modern Library, 2002. Print.

Minawi, Mostafa and Chris Gratien. "The Ottoman Scramble for Africa." *Ottoman History Podcast*. 1 Feb. 2014. Web. 5 Feb. 2014.

Miran, Jonathan. *Red Sea Citizens: Cosmopolitan Society and Cultural Change in Massawa*. Bloomington, IN: Indiana University Press, 2009. Print.

Nouheihed, Lin and Alex Warren. *The Battle for the Arab Spring: Revolution, Counter-Revolution and the Making of a New Era*. New Haven: Yale University Press, 2012. Print.

Peirce, Leslie. *The Imperial Harem: Women and Sovereignty in the Ottoman Empire*. New York: Oxford UP, 2010. Print.

_____. *Morality Tales: Law and Gender in the Ottoman Court of Aintab*. Berkeley, CA: University of California Press, 2006. Print.

Perkins, Kenneth J. *A History of Modern Tunisia*. New York: Cambridge University Press, 2008. Print.

Reiss, Tom. *The Orientalist: Solving the Mystery of a Strange and a Dangerous Life*. New York: Random House, 2005. Print.

Schneer, Jonathan. *The Balfour Declaration: The Origins of the Arab-Israeli Conflict*. New York: Random House Trade Paperbacks, 2012. Print.

Segev, Tom. *One Palestine, Complete: Jews and Arabs under the Mandate.* New York: Metropolitan, 2000. Print.

Sheldon, Chad. "The Palace and the Poet." *Saudi Aramco World.* March 2012. Web. 18 April 2015.

Smith, Robert. "After 450 Years, Archaeologists Still Hunting for Magnificent Sultan's Heart." *National Geographic.* 20 June 2014. Web. *National Geographic News.* 12 August 2014.

Tamari, Salim. *The Storyteller of Jerusalem: The Life and Times of Wasif Jawhariyyeh, 1904-1948.* Northampton, MA: Clockroot Books, 2014.

Wigen, Einar, Chris Gratien, and Timur Hammond. "Empire in Question: Did the Ottomans Consider Themselves an Empire?" *Ottoman History Podcast,* 5 Nov. 2012. Web. 10 Nov. 2012.

INDEX

N

Nader Shah 124
Nagorno-Karabakh 125, 161
Nagy, Imre 15
Najd 237, 239, 268
Nakhchivan. *See* Naxçıvan
Nana, Queen 133
Napoleon I 277
Nasser, Gamal Abdul 275, 342
National Day, Kuwait 267
National Museum, Beirut 218
Naxçıvan 164
Nazarbayev, Nursultan 110
neo-Ottomanism 171
Ni' 25
Nizwa 258, 259, 262
Novi Pazar 27
Nusayris 191, 192

O

Öcalan, Abdullah 190
Occupation, meaning of 14, 135
Odessa 113
Ohrid 73
Omar Bashir, President 301, 302, 309, 310
Omdurman 298
Omdurman, Battle of 296, 301, 315
Oranto 6
Orheiul Vechi 102
Ortaköy 185, 186
Öşk Vank 200, 201
Osman Bey 11
Ottoman Army of Islam 157, 158
Ottoman Turkish 177, 178, 183, 193, 235, 276

P

Pahlavi Dynasty 165
Palestine Mandate 211
Pamuk, Orhan 146, 173, 198
Peace of Amasya 129
People's House 99

Persian Gulf War 269
Petar II Petrović-Njegoš 54
Peter the Great xvi
Philip of Macedon 90
Piri Reis 253
P.K.K. 190
Plovdiv 90, 91, 93, 94, 97
Počitelj 40
Poltava, Battle of xvii
Potočari 48, 49
Princip, Gavrilo 29
Pristina 85
Pushkin, Alexander 114

Q

Qaboos, Sultan 252, 259
Qadiri Order 299
Qırım Giray 118

R

Ragusa, Republic of 53
Ramadan 243
Republika Srpska 33, 36, 48, 49
Riyadh 237, 238, 240
Rub' al-Khali 230
Ruschuk. *See* Ruse
Ruse 97
Russo-Ottoman War, 1787 129
Russo-Ottoman War, 1792 112
Russo-Turkish War, 1877-78 56

S

Sabah I bin Jaber 268
Sabilla, Battle of 240
Sadiki College 340
Sadiq Bey 340
Safavid Dynasty 124
Safavid Iran 187
Safranbolu 181, 182
Saint Giragos Cathedral 196
Saint Nino 138
Saladin. *See* Salah al-Din
Salah al-Din 275
Salonica 12, 177